The Quest for Change

in Latin America

The Quest for Change in Latin America

SOURCES FOR A TWENTIETH-CENTURY ANALYSIS

EDITED BY *W. Raymond Duncan*

STATE UNIVERSITY OF NEW YORK AT BROCKPORT

AND *James Nelson Goodsell*

THE CHRISTIAN SCIENCE MONITOR

NEW YORK

Oxford University Press

TORONTO 1970 LONDON

Printed in the United States of America
Library of Congress Catalogue Card Number: 79-82994

We Dedicate this Book

to the People of Latin America

Preface

This volume furnishes some major sources for an analysis of reform policies, both violent and peaceful, in twentieth-century Latin America. The editors focus on the quest for social and economic change because it very much characterizes the course of recent history in Latin America. Although the selections here do not encompass all that has occurred since the turn of the century, they offer a point of departure for interpreting the political, economic, and social systems south of the Rio Grande.

Since the opening of the century, there has been a growing acceptance by Latin American leaders of the idea that man makes and is, at least in part, responsible for his own society. That idea is the common denominator of the sources brought together in this book. The acceptance of the idea brought about a willingness to change that could well be compared to the radical nature of the Copernican Revolution, for it led to a dramatic reversal of Latin America's approach to society. Once the disposition to change took hold, many revolutionary ideas appeared. They in turn nurtured a host of government-sponsored political, economic, and social reforms.

All of this took place against the backdrop of traditional, conservative Hispano-Catholic culture but by no means eclipsed this culture; indeed, there was a significant interaction of the old and new. While economic and social change occurred in virtually every Latin American land, there was one other important result: the Latin American people were gradually becoming involved in national goals.

It is characteristic of Latin Americans to argue and discuss issues at length, and they often become intensely preoccupied with the world of ideas. It is not surprising then that a confusion of proposals for change arose during this period in much of Latin America. Some of these proposals were based directly on Western European ideas such as anarcho-syndicalism, Communism, and Christian Democracy. Others were clearly indigenous, such as Víctor Raúl Haya de la Torre's *Aprismo* in Peru, Juan Domingo Perón's *Justicialismo* in Argentina, and Gétulio Vargas's *Estado Novo* in Brazil. Still others were inspired less by ideologies at the outset than by the magnetism of one leader or by general discontent with poverty. The Mexican Revolution of 1910 and the Cuban Revolution of 1959 illustrate this point. Yet neither was an isolated development and each was a part of the social ferment evident in almost every corner of the hemisphere since 1900. This ferment included growing discontent with Latin America's conservative economic and social structures. Moreover, society was becoming more industrialized and urbanized. And increasing commerce and a steady flow of new immigrants brought the area into closer contact with other parts of the world. The traditional rich-poor class structure was showing signs of change as a result of the rise of middle classes and new labor groups. The new classes became sources of political power, used by the area's leaders to challenge ruling elites. This was particularly true as the growth of mass communications created opportunities for establishing a national audience.

Other forces for change were at work. The Great Depression of 1929-32 introduced liberal economic practices to Latin America, notably in Colombia, Venezuela, and in Mexico. The rights of labor were extended to match innovations in development banking, economic regulations, land tenure, social security, and education. Between the two World Wars the appearance of international Communism added a catalytic agent to the pattern of growing unrest, while participation of many Latin American nations in World War II provided a new sense of national awareness. Both increased the push toward social reform. Finally, the dominating position of the "Colossus of the North," the United States, in the economic and political affairs of Latin America frequently fomented a backlash of nationalism.

Latin American leaders by no means agree over methods of reform, as may be seen in the strong contrast between Fidel Castro of Cuba and Eduardo Frei Montalva of Chile. While Castro advocated and followed a policy of violent action, particularly after he came to power in 1959, Frei spoke for moderation and reform within the established order as he headed the "Revolution in Liberty" after 1964. A good portion of this book is devoted to pointing out similar disagreement. Moreover, no single approach on how best to achieve a better material and moral life and an increased sense of *dignidad* (dignity) for Latin America's 290 million people has yet found general favor.

Many individuals have helped the editors indirectly in the preparation of these materials, but the two of us share responsibility for these pages. Probably no one knows better than our wives the amount of effort that went into the preparation of these pages, and so we wish to express our gratitude to Ute Duncan and Alice Goodsell. Raymond Duncan worked primarily on Parts II, V, and VI; James Goodsell on Parts I, III, and IV, and both prepared Part VII. Mr. Goodsell did the translations. Each of the book's seven parts begins with an introductory essay and includes brief headnotes on the readings.

The editors are conscious of the many traps into which writers on Latin America frequently fall, including oversimplification, generalization, and a host of other errors. We may well have fallen into some of these, but we hope that the effort of presenting these sources, many of them for the first time in English, and all of them for the first time in a single volume, will override whatever shortcomings the book may contain.

W.R.D.
J.N.G.

February 1970

Note to the Reader

The term "JPRS" is used in parts of the text and in several footnotes. It refers to the United States Joint Publications Research Service. This service was founded in 1957 to serve the research translations needs of the Federal Government with translations of unclassified foreign documents, scholarly works, research reports, and other selected source materials not available in English. Its data are now available to the academic community.

Contents

The Quest for Change

in Latin America

1 *The Century Begins: Nationalism and Reform*

Latin America in 1900 was a study in sharp contrasts. Ruling elites were generally satisfied with conditions; the 1890s had brought some industrialization and mounting prosperity for the more privileged classes. But for the masses, life was hard and not very pleasant. Among the socially conscious intellectuals, politicians, socialists, and others, there was developing a concern over the plight of the masses. And there were rumblings for reform and change, although only faintly heard.

The thin veneer of prosperity throughout Latin America could not mask the underdeveloped nature of things and the way in which economic and social pressures were beginning to be felt. A restlessness was evident in many countries. In part, it resulted from the influx of new ideas from Western Europe and the United States. It stemmed also from the arrival of hundreds of thousands of immigrants from Western Europe. And it resulted still more from a feeling among intellectuals and others that stability and outward prosperity were not enough and that more stress had to be placed on the condition of the masses. There were many able spokesmen for these ideas at the turn of the century and they were effectively setting the stage for many of the big social movements which were to follow. Their writings helped to set the climate for such movements as the Mexican Revolution. Moreover, they embodied a new sense of nationalism and evinced clear calls for reform.

Latin American nationalism dates to the nineteenth century's independence period, but the hemisphere's present day nationalism is more the result of events and trends toward the turn of the century. By 1900, the hemisphere had long since passed from being a colonial preserve and had begun to occupy a place of some prominence in world commerce. Mounting foreign investment began to worry some Latin Americans. For example, Argentine socialists were sharply critical of foreign capital, even before the turn of the century. A reaction against the apparent increase of United States influence was evident in 1900. However, it was left for later generations of Latin Americans to argue against the pervasive economic influence of the United States on Latin America and to take steps to sharply limit foreign investment.

What worried Latin Americans in the early twentieth century more than foreign investment was the effect of foreign influence upon the culture and political structures of the hemisphere. Even people who were genuinely sympathetic toward the United States, like José Martí (1853–95), the Cuban patriot who lost his life in his island's struggle for independence from Spain, were worried about North American expansionism. In many of his articles written for Latin American newspapers, Martí expressed this concern in dramatic and lucid terms. His now famous two-part letter to the Buenos Aires newspaper *La Nación,* dealing with the United States-sponsored first Pan American Conference in 1889, is a good example (Reading One).

Martí was not alone. Still widely read throughout Latin America is the essay *Ariel* (Reading Two) by the Uruguayan José Enrique Rodó (1872–1917), which is perhaps the most eloquent opposition to the United States and its society. Rodó saw the Latin American as the heir to Mediterranean culture and the personification of Ariel, the spirit of culture, poetry, and joy, as opposed to the North American, the heir to the Anglo-Saxon culture of Northern Europe and the personification of Caliban, the spirit of materialism, utilitarianism, and science. Rodó did not reject all that is embodied in North American culture, but he questioned its fitness for Latin America. Were he writing today, he might well fit into a new generation of writers, particularly in Western Europe, who repeatedly lament the way in which Western European life is being "Americanized."

Not all the criticism stemming from Latin American nationalism was directed at the United States. Luis María Drago (1859–1921), the Argentine minister of foreign relations at the turn of the century, wrote a lengthy letter to his government's minister in Washington concerning the naval action taken by Britain, Germany, and Italy off the Venezuelan coast that resulted from the failure of Venezuelan debtors to pay bills due their European creditors. His famous Drago Doctrine (Reading Three), adopted in part by the Hague convention of 1907, declared that, just as the Monroe Doctrine is a principle enforced by the United States for the preservation of the territorial status quo throughout the American continent against European encroachment, there should also be a principle protecting the Latin American republics against the collection of pecuniary claims of citizens of any country by armed force, as the European powers were attempting against Venezuela.

Other forces of nationalism were also evident during this period. Andrés Molina Enríquez (1868–1940), a Mexican author and anthropologist, argued for a nationalism that was clearly Mexican in character, emphasizing the virtues of the mestizo (mixed Indian and white) middle class and calling for an end to the Díaz dictatorship. In his book, *Los grandes problemas nacionales,* published in 1908, he outlined a program for Mexico based in part on agrarian reform. Molina Enríquez believed that Mexico would progress through the action of the mestizo, and thus develop a nationality (Reading Four). In fact, he went so far as to say that the mestizos were the foundation of nationhood. Throughout his life Molina Enríquez called for a return to the Indian pattern of communal land ownership based on the *ejido* system of alloting land to peasants to farm. He is today considered the father of Mexican agrarian reform and was largely responsible for the wording of Article 27, dealing with such reform, in Mexico's 1917 Constitution (see Part II, Reading Nine).

Even earlier than Molina Enríquez, there were clear calls for social reform. Juan B. Justo (1865–1928), the founder of the

Socialist Party in Argentina, wrote long pleas for better working conditions and more pay for Argentine workers. His writings and activities made the Argentine party the most serious socialist experiment in the Americas of his day. There were rival reformers in Argentina, including Hipólito Irigoyan (1850–1933) on the political front and the anarchists in the labor movement. And separatism repeatedly divided the party. But Justo labored on in a determined struggle to spread socialism in Argentina (Reading Five).

Karl Marx had paid scant attention to Latin America. But Justo and others had paid close attention to his writings which were fairly well known in intellectual circles in the hemisphere. The reaction of José Martí, the Cuban independence leader quoted previously, was in some ways typical of the reaction of many informed Latin Americans. Apparently he did not approve of Marx's support of violence, although he seemed sympathetic to Marx's ideas for change (Reading Six). After 1959, Fidel Castro in Cuba began using many of Martí's ideas to support aspects of the Cuban Revolution. Martí's writings were put out in new editions in an effort to show the independence leader's sympathy with Marx and socialist theories, as well as to give historical depth to the Castro revolution.

In Uruguay, José Batlle y Ordóñez (1856–1929) was building another sort of social movement. He not only reorganized the structure of Uruguayan government, he brought about a social reform that became the most advanced in the hemisphere. Much of his philosophy came out in signed columns in the Montevideo newspaper *El Día,* published in the last fifteen years of the nineteenth century and the first twenty years of the twentieth.

Although the appeal for social reform was strongest in the far South of the hemisphere, the call for educational reform was much more evident in the more industrialized nations in the far North. Instead of rejecting the value of scientific education, like Rodó, Mexican thinkers, influenced more by European educators and philosophers than by their neighbors in the United States, were revamping the whole structure of Mexican educational theory. Under the general term "positivism," they developed an educational theory which was to have far-reaching consequences not so much throughout the hemisphere, but right at home. The philosophical doctrine of positivism—adopted from the works of the French philosopher Auguste Comte (1798–1857)—became the central doctrine of the Mexican school system in the 1870s and a key approach to reform and national development under the guidance of Gabino Barreda (1820–81), who had studied with Comte earlier. Positivism became particularly popular in Brazilian military elites once Benjamin Constant (1838–91), a professor in the military school at Rio de Janeiro, began to emphasize its relevance to Brazilian development. In Argentina, the ideas of positivism were linked to the social democratic writings of Estebán Echeverría (1805–51) in the 1880s and later to Justo and to José Ingenieros (1877–1925). Positivism also spread through Venezuela, Uruguay, the Dominican Republic, and Chile, where schools, specialized reviews, and cultural associations became the vehicles of transmission. One of the best studies of positivism in Latin America, with special reference to Mexico—where positivist ideology was most consistently applied—is a 1949 essay written by the Mexican social critic Leopoldo Zea (1912–) (Reading Seven).

A brief examination of positivism in Mexico suggests the nature of its underlying appeal in Latin America. By 1867, when many Mexican liberals began to adopt positivism as a philosophy of national development, Mexico had experienced years of political chaos, little economic development, and wounded national dignity. Mexican independence had not led to rapid social, economic, or political development as some revolutionaries had hoped, but rather to several decades of civil disorder, vast social cleavages, and—on top of all this—foreign intrusions. Much of Mexico's territory was lost in the Texas incident of the 1840s, followed by the humiliating French invasion of 1861. Thus, by 1867, when Benito Juárez (1806–72), candidate of the Liberal Party, returned to power, many leading Mexicans were indeed ready for a philosophy of Order and Progress—the hope held out by positivism as introduced by Barreda (Reading Eight).

The objective of positivist teaching was to transform Mexican culture in order to inject order and development into the political, economic, and social structure of the nation, contrasting with the other-worldliness of Hispano-Catholic traditions. Positivism promised educational reform that would create an action-oriented and logical approach to life's problems, thus laying the groundwork for political stability and technological advancement. Mexico would thus be enabled to develop sufficient strength to resist the threat of the northern colossus and take its place among the developed nations of the world.

READING 1 *José Martí on the United States and the Pan-American Conference*

Introductory Note

Although much of his short life was spent in active participation in Cuba's drive for independence, José Martí (1853–95) was a prolific writer as well. On subjects ranging from politics and economics to culture and poetry, Martí became widely known not only in his island, but also throughout Latin America. A compilation of his works often tends to suggest conflicting views on various subjects such as the United States and its role in the Western Hemisphere. This selection shows his suspicions of United States intentions in calling the Pan-American Conference of 1889 in Washington, but does by no means represent the whole core or focus of his work.

There never was in America from her independence to this day, a matter requiring greater good sense, nor forcing a greater vigilance, nor demanding clearer and more detailed study than this invitation which the powerful United States—replete with unsaleable products and determined to increase its rule over America—extends to the less powerful American nations—linked by free and useful trade to the European peoples—to agree upon

Translated from two letters by José Martí published in *La Nación* of Buenos Aires, December 19 and 20, 1889.

an alliance against Europe, and to close all relations with the rest of the world. Spanish America succeeded in overcoming the tyranny of Spain; and now, after examining the background, causes, and factors of the invitation with a judicial eye, it is urgent to say—for it is the truth—that the hour has come for Spanish America to declare her second independence. . . .

From the cradle did the people of the North dream of this domination, with Jefferson's "Nothing would be more convenient"; with Adams's "thirteen destined governments"; with Clay's "prophetic vision"; with Webster's "great Northern light"; with Sewall's verse going from mouth to mouth "Yours is the entire continent, and without limits"; with Everett's "continental unification"; with Douglas's "commercial union"; with Ingall's "inevitable result" and "to the isthmus and the pole"; with Blaine's "need of extirpating from Cuba the focus of yellow fever". When a thoroughly rapacious people, nourished in the hope and certainty of the possession of the continent, come to be so spurred on by Europe's jealousy and by their own ambition to be a universal people, as the indispensable guarantee of their future power and the sole and obligatory market for a false production which they find necessary to maintain and increase so that their influence and ostentation will not diminish, it is urgent to place in their way as many restraining obstacles as can be forged with the decorousness of ideas, the swift and skillful increase of opposite interests, the honest and ready adjustment of all those who have the same reason to fear, and the declaration of the truth. Sympathy toward free peoples lasts until they betray freedom or endanger that of our country. . . .

There can be no Cains in our America. Our America is one!

READING 2 Ariel *and the North American Threat*

Introductory Note

Probably more than any other figure of his era, José Enrique Rodó (1872–1917) embodied the hopes and ideals of the turn of the century. Rubén Darío called him the Hispanic American thinker of his times, a Latin American Emerson. He wrote of the isolation of the Latin American nations, a theme which came forth in his work, Ariel, *which called for a new sense of idealism in Latin America. First published in 1900,* Ariel *was a lesson in democratic idealism and in cultural unity.*

Ariel *pictured the United States as dominated by materialism. Rodó saw the North American colossus as devoid of a real culture, whereas Latin America was pictured as having a far greater appreciation for cultural values, a view that is still prevalent throughout much of Latin America.*

The utilitarian conception as the idea of human destiny, and equality at the mediocre as the norm of social proportion, make up the formula which in Europe they call the spirit of Americanism. It is impossible to think on either of these as inspirations for human conduct or society, while contrasting them with those which are opposed to them, without at once conjuring up by association a vision of that formidable and fruitful democracy

José Enrique Rodó, *Ariel,* translated by F. J. Stimson (Boston: Houghton Mifflin Company, 1922), pp. 89–95, 111–23 passim.

there in the North, with its manifestations of prosperity and power, as a dazzling example in favour of the efficacy of democratic institutions and the correct aim of its ideas. If one could say of utilitarianism that it is the word of the English spirit, the United States may be considered the incarnation of that word. Its Evangel is spread on every side to teach the material miracles of its triumph. And Spanish America is not wholly to be entitled, in its relation to the United States, as a nation of Gentiles. The mighty confederation is realizing over us a sort of moral conquest. Admiration for its greatness, its strength, is a sentiment that is growing rapidly in the minds of our governing classes, and even more, perhaps, among the multitude, easily impressed with victory or success. And from admiring it is easy to pass to imitating. Admiration and belief are already for the psychologist but the passive mood of imitation. . . . We imitate him in whose superiority and prestige we believe. So it happens that the vision of a voluntarily delatinized America, without compulsion or conquest, and regenerate in the manner of its Northern archetype, floats already through the dreams of many who are sincerely interested in our future, satisfies them with suggestive parallels they find at every step, and appears in constant movements for reform or innovation. We have our mania for the North. It is necessary to oppose to it those bounds which both sentiment and reason indicate.

Not that I would make of those limits an absolute negation. I well understand that enlightenment, inspiration, great lessons lie in the example of the strong; nor do I fail to realize that intelligent attention to the claims of the material and the study of the useful, directed abroad, is of especially useful result in the case of people in the formative stage, whose nationality is still in the mould. I understand how one must try by persevering education to rectify such traits of a society as need to be made to fit in with new demands of civilization and new opportunities in life, thus by wise innovation counteracting the forces of heredity or custom. But I see no good in denaturalizing the character of a people—its personal genius—to impose on it identity with a foreign model to which they will sacrifice the originality of their genius, that, once lost, can never be replaced; nor in the ingenuous fancy that this result may ever be obtained artificially or by process of imitation. That thoughtless attempt to transplant what is natural and spontaneous in one society into the soil of another where it has no roots, historically or naturally, seemed to Michelet like the attempt to incorporate by mere transference a dead organism in a living body.

In societies, as in art or literature, blind imitation gives but an inferior copy of the model. And in the vain attempt there is also something ignoble; a kind of political snobbery, carefully to copy the ways and acts of the great; as, in Thackeray's satire, those without rank or fortune ineffectually imitate only the foibles of the mighty. Care for one's own independence, personality, judgment, is a chief form of self-respect. A much-commented passage of Cicero teaches how it is our duty sedulously to preserve our original character; that which differentiates and determines, so far as may wisely be, the primal natural impulses, as they derive from a various distribution of natural gifts and so make up the concert and the order of the world. And even more would this seem to be true as applied to human collectivities. But perhaps you will say that there is no seal, no peculiar and definite thing to mark the quality for whose permanence and integrity we should do battle in the actual organization of our people. Perhaps there lacks in our South American character the definite contour of a personality. But even so, we Latin-Americans have an inheritance of Race, a great ethnic tradition to maintain, a sacred bond which unites us to immortal pages of history and puts us on our honour to preserve this for the future. That cosmopolitanism which we have to respect as the irresistible tendency of our development need not exclude that sentiment of fidelity to the past, nor that moulding and directing force of which the genius of our race must avail itself in the fusing of the elements that shall constitute the American of the future.

It has more than once been pointed out that the great epochs of history, its most fertile periods, are always the result of distinct but coexisting forces which by their very agreement to oppose maintain the interest and stimulus of life, which in the quietism of a universal accord might tend to disappear. So the two extremes of Athens and Sparta revolve on an axle around which circles the race of greatest genius man has known. So America needs at this time to maintain its original duality, which has converted from classic myth to actual history the story of the two eagles, loosed at the same moment from either pole, to arrive at the same moment at each one's limit of dominion. This difference in genius does not exclude honourable emulation, nor discourage in very many relations agreement or even solidarity. And if one can dimly foresee even a higher concord in the future, that will be due not to a one-sided imitation of one race by the other, but to a reciprocity of influences and a skilful harmonizing of those attributes which make the peculiar glory of either race. . . .

And now I come to the very theme of my discourse, and the relation to it of this spirit of imitation. Any severe judgment formed upon our neighbours of the North should begin, like the courteous fencer, by lowering a rapier in salute to them. Easy is this for me. Failure to recognize their faults does not seem to me so insensate as to deny their qualities. Born—to employ Beaudelaire's paradox—with the innate experience of liberty, they have kept themselves faithful to the law of their birth; and have developed, with the precision and certainty of a mathematical progression, the fundamental principles of their organization. This gives to their history a unity which, even if it has excluded the acquirement of different aptitudes or merits, has at least the intellectual beauty of being logical. The traces of its progress will never be expunged from the annals of human right, because they have been the first to evoke our modern ideal of liberty and to convert it from the uncertainty of experiment and the visions of Utopia into imperishable bronze and living reality. For they have shown by their example the possibility of extending the immovable authority of a republic over an immense national commonwealth, and, with their federal organization, have revealed—as de Tocqueville felicitously put it—the manner in which the brilliancy and power of great states may be combined with the felicity and peace of little ones. . . .

They have a sleepless and insatiable instinct of curiosity, an impatient eagerness for the light; and, carrying a fondness for public education almost to the point of monomania, have made the common school the surest prop of their prosperity, believing that the mind of the child should be the most cherished of their precious things. Their culture, while far from being spiritual or refined, has an admirable efficiency so far as it is directed to practical ends and their immediate realization. . . .

But in the ambience of America's democracy there are no heights so lofty as to escape the climbing of the flood of vulgarity, and it spreads and extends itself freely as over a level plain.

Sensibility, intelligence, manners—each is marked in that enormous people by a radical unaptness for selection; and this, with the mechanical ordering of their material activities, makes a chaos of all that pertains to the realm of the ideal. It were easy to follow this unaptness from its most obvious manifestations to the more intimate and essential ones. Prodigal of riches—for meanness is not his fault—the North American has learned only to acquire by them the satisfaction of his vanity and material luxury, but not the chosen note of good taste. . . .

The ideal of beauty does not appeal to the descendants of the austere Puritan, nor even a passionate worship of the truth; they care little for any thinking that has no immediate practical object—it seems to them idle and fruitless; even to science they bring no selfless interest for discovery, nor do they seem capable of loving its truths only because they are true; investigation is merely the necessary antecedent of practical application. Their praiseworthy efforts to extend the benefits of popular education are inspired with the noble motive of communicating the rudiments of knowledge to the masses; but it does not appear that they also concern themselves over-much with that higher education which shall rise above the general mediocrity. And so the outcome is that of all their struggle with ignorance the only gain has been a sort of universal semiculture and a profound indifference to the higher. . . . As fast as the general ignorance decreases, so in the air of that giant democracy, decreases the higher learning and vanishes genius itself. This is why the story of their intellectual activity is of a retrogression in brilliance and originality. For while at the era of their Independence and Constitution many famous names illustrate their history in thought as well as in action, a half-century later de Tocqueville could say of them, the Gods are disappearing. And, when he wrote his master work, there still radiated from Boston, the Puritan home, the city of learning and tradition, a glorious pleiad which holds in the intellectual story of our century a universal fame. Who since has picked up the heritage of Emerson, Channing, Poe? The levelling by the middle classes tends ever, pressing with its desolating task, to plane down what little remains of intelligentsia: the flowers are mown by the machine when the weeds remain.

Long since their books have ceased to soar on wings beyond the common vision. To-day the most actual example of what Americans like best in literature must be sought in the gray pages of magazines or periodicals which seldom remind one that that mode of publication was employed in the immortal "Federalist."

In the domain of moral sentiment, the mechanical impulse for the utilitarian has, indeed, encountered a certain balance-wheel in a strong religious tradition; but one may not conclude that even this has given to the direction of conduct a real, disinterested principle. . . . American religiosity, derived from the English and exaggerated, is merely an auxiliary force for the penal law, and would disappear on the day it was found possible without it to give to utilitarian morality that religious sanction which Mill desired for it. The very culmination of that morality is only that of Franklin; a philosophy of conduct which has for its goal a commonplace sagacity, a prudent usefulness, in whose bosom will never rise the emotions of holiness or heroism; and which, fit only to give to one's conscience in the common affairs of life a certain moral support—like the apple-tree cane with which Franklin ever walked—is but a fragile staff with which to surmount great heights. And yet his was its supreme height: it is in the valleys where one must seek for its actuality. Even if the moral critique were not to descend below the probity and moderation of Franklin's standard, its necessary termination, as de Tocqueville wisely said of a society educated narrowly with similar notions of duty, would surely not be in that superb and noble decadence which gives us to measure a Satanic beauty of tragedy in the downfall of empires, but rather a kind of pallid materialism, drab culture, and finally the sleep of an enervation without brilliancy in the silent decay of all the mainsprings of the moral life. In that society whose precept tends to put outside of what is obligatory the higher manifestations of abnegations and of virtue, practical considerations will always make the limits of obligation recede indefinitely. And the school of material prosperity, always a rude teacher of republican austerity, has carried even further that simplicity of the conception of a rational conduct which now obsesses the mind. To Franklin's code have succeeded others franker still in their expression of the national wisdom. A book by one Swett Marden was recently published in Boston, "Pushing to the Front," which announced, apparently with much popular approval, as a new moral law, that success is the final end of life; this book was praised even in church circles, and compared to the "Imitation" of a Kempis! . . .

And public life does not escape the consequences of the growth of this germ of disorganization in society generally. Any casual observer of their political customs will tell you how the obsession of material interest tends steadily to enervate and eradicate the sentiment of law or right; the civic virtue of a Hamilton is as an old and rusty sword, every day the more forgotten, lost in the cobwebs of tradition; venality, beginning at the polls, spreads through the working of all their institutions; the government by a mediocrity renders vain that emulation which exalts the character and the intelligence, and imposes itself even on the imagination as an unavoidable future. A democracy not subject to a superior instruction, not trained in liberal schools to the understanding of true human excellence, tends always to that abominable brutality of the majority which despises the greater moral benefits of liberty and annuls in public opinion all respect for the dignity of the individual. And to-day a new and formidable power arises to accentuate this absolutism of numbers: the political influence of a plutocracy represented only by the agents of the trusts, monopolies of production, and lords of the economic life, one of the most noteworthy and significant features of the United States of to-day. Their advent has caused almost everybody to recall to mind the coming of that proud and over-rich class which at the end of the Roman Republic preceded the tyranny of the Caesars and the ruin of liberty. And the exclusive preoccupation with material aggrandizement, the deity of such a civilization, has its logical result on the State as on the individual, putting the struggle-for-life principle also at the head of national policy, and making its representative the supreme personification of the national energy—the postulant of Emerson, the ruling personage of Taine.

To the impulse which drives the spiritual life toward that deorientation of the ideal to the selfishly useful corresponds physically that other principle which in the astounding increase of that people impels both the multitude and the initiative ever in the direction of that boundless West which in the times of their first independence was all mystery, veiled behind the forests of the Mississippi. In fact that improvised West—which grows so formidable to the older Atlantic States and already claims hegemony in the near future—is where the most faithful representation of American life is to be found at this moment of its evolution. It is there where the definite results, the logical and natural fruits of the spirit that has guided the great democracy from its origin, are brought into relief for the observer so that he can picture to himself the aspect of its immediate future. To the Virginian, the Yankee, has succeeded the master of the yesterday empty prairies, of whom Michel Chevalier predicted, half a century since, "The last shall one day be the first." Utilitarianism, empty of all ideal content, a certain cosmopolitan levity of spirit, and the levelling of a falsely conceived democracy, will in him reach their ultimate victory. Every noble element of that civilization, all which binds it to the generous traditions and lofty origin of its historic dignity—the arrival of the men of the Mayflower, the memory of the Patricians of Virginia and the warriors of New England, the spirit of the people and law-makers of the Emancipation—will remain only in the older States, where a Boston or a Philadelphia still maintain "the palladium of the Washingtonian tradition." Chicago will arise to reign. And its overweening superiority over the original States of the Atlantic shore is based on its belief that they are reactionary, too European, too subject to tradition. History confers no claims on any, where popular election confers the purple.

As fast as the utilitarian genius of that nation takes on a more defined character, franker, narrower yet, with the intoxication of material prosperity, so increases the impatience of its sons to spread it abroad by propaganda, and think it predestined for all humanity. To-day they openly aspire to the primacy of the world's civilization, the direction of its ideas, and think themselves the forerunners of all culture that is to prevail. The colloquial phrase, ironically quoted by Laboulaye, "America can beat the world," is taken seriously by almost any virile Westerner. At the bottom of their open rivalry with Europe lies a contempt for it that is almost naïve, and the profound conviction that within a brief period they are destined to eclipse its glory and do away with its spiritual superiority; thus once more fulfilling, in the progress of civilization, the hard law of the ancient mysteries, whereby the initiated shall put to death the initiator. It were useless to seek to convince them that, although their services to inventions and material advance have been doubtless great, even rising to the measure of a universal human obligation, they do not of themselves suffice to alter the axis of the earth. It were useless to seek to convince them that the fires lit upon European altars, the work done by peoples living these three thousand years gone by about the shores of the Mediterranean, though rising to glorious genius when bound with the olive and the palm off Athens, a work still being carried on and in whose traditions and teachings we South Americans live, makes a sum which cannot be equalled by any equation of Washington plus Edison. Would they even revise the Book of Genesis, to put themselves upon the front page?

But, aside from the insufficiency of the part that is given

them to play in the education of humanity, their own character itself precludes all possibility of their hegemony. Nature has not granted them the genius for propaganda, the vocation of the apostle. They lack that great gift of amiability—likeableness, in lofty sense; that extraordinary power of sympathy with which those races endowed by Providence for the task of education know how to make of their culture a beauty, as did Greece, loveable, eternal, and yet always with something of their own.

North American civilization may abound—it does abound—in fertile suggestions, profitable examples; it may inspire admiration, astonishment, respect; but it is rare for the foreigner to feel his heart come to his mouth with strong emotion when first he sees that Bartholdi statue holding high its torch of Liberty over New York Harbour; that thrill profound with which the ancient traveller saw the rosy light of the marble and the sheen of Athena's spear over the early dawn on the Acropolis.

READING 3 Drago and the European Threat

Introductory Note

Luis María Drago (1859–1921), author of the noted doctrine bearing his name, was an Argentine statesman and writer, and at the time he penned the famous document, was Argentina's minister of foreign affairs. The Drago Doctrine is a clear example of the eloquence of Latin American jurisprudence and the contribution of Argentina to the body of world law. It did not win general acceptance, although a portion of it was included in the Hague convention of 1907.

. . . Among the fundamental principles of public international law which humanity has consecrated, one of the most precious is that which decrees that all states, whatever be the force at their disposal, are entities in law, perfectly equal one to another, and mutually entitled by virtue thereof to the same consideration and respect.

The acknowledgement of the debt, the payment of it in its entirety, can and must be made by the nation without diminution of its inherent rights as a sovereign entity, but the summary and immediate collection at a given moment, by means of force, would occasion nothing less than the ruin of the weakest nation,

Foreign Relations of the United States, 1903. This extract represents about one-third of the original letter written by Mr. Drago to Mr. Merou, the Argentine minister to the United States, December 29, 1902.

and the absorption of their governments, together with all the functions inherent in them, by the mighty on the earth. The principles proclaimed on this continent of America are otherwise. "Contracts between a nation and private individuals are obligatory according to the conscience of the sovereign, and may not be the object of compelling force," said the illustrious Hamilton. "They confer no right of action contrary to the sovereign will."

The United States has gone very far in this direction. The eleventh amendment to its Constitution provided in effect, with the unanimous assent of the people, that the juridical power of the nation should not be extended to any suit in law or equity prosecuted against one of the United States by citizens of another State, or by citizens or subjects of any foreign State. The Argentine Government has made its provinces indictable, and has even adopted the principle that the nation itself may be brought to trial before the supreme court on contracts which it enters into with individuals.

What has not been established, what could in no wise be admitted, is that, once the amount for which it may be indebted has been determined by legal judgment, it should be deprived of the right to choose the manner and the time of payment, in which it has as much interest as the creditor himself, or more, since its credit and its national honor are involved therein.

This is in no wise a defense for bad faith, disorder, and deliberate and voluntary insolvency. It is intended merely to preserve the dignity of the public international entity which may not thus be dragged into war with detriment to those high ends which determine the existence and liberty of nations.

The fact that collection can not be accomplished by means of violence does not, on the other hand, render valueless the acknowledgement of the public debt, the definite obligation of paying it.

The State continues to exist in its capacity as such, and sooner or later the gloomy situations are cleared up, resources increase, common aspirations of equity and justice prevail, and the most neglected promises are kept. . . .

As these are the sentiments of justice, loyalty, and honor which animate the Argentine people and have always inspired its policy, your excellency will understand that it has felt alarmed at the knowledge that the failure of Venezuela to meet the payments of its public debt is given as one of the determining causes of the capture of its fleet, the bombardment of one of its ports, and the establishment of a rigorous blockade along its shores. If such proceedings were to be definitely adopted they would establish a precedent dangerous to the security and the peace of the nations of this part of America.

The collection of loans by military means implies territorial occupation to make them effective, and territorial occupation signifies the suppression or subordination of the governments of the countries on which it is imposed.

Such a situation seems obviously at variance with the principles many times proclaimed by the nations of America, and particularly with the Monroe doctrine, sustained and defended with so much zeal on all occasions by the United States, a doctrine to which the Argentine Republic has heretofore solemnly adhered. . . .

The only principle which the Argentine Republic maintains and which it would, with great satisfaction, see adopted, in view of the events in Venezuela, by a nation that enjoys such great authority and prestige as does the United States, is the principle, already accepted, that there can be no territorial expansion in America on the part of Europe, nor any oppression of the peoples of this continent, because an unfortunate financial situation may compel some one of them to postpone the fulfillment of its promises. In a word, the principle which she would like to see recognized is: that the public debt can not occasion armed intervention nor even the actual occupation of the territory of American nations by a European power. . . .

READING 4 *Andrés Molina Enríquez and Mexican Nationality*

Introductory Note

As one of the leading social critics in early twentieth-century Mexico, Andrés Molina Enríquez (1868–1940) stressed the positive role that mestizos must play in developing a wide sense of Mexican nationality. He also became largely responsible for agrarian reform measures written into the Constitution of 1917, which institutionalized the long-range break up and redistribution of Mexico's latifundios.

. . . One can affirm that the unity of the ideal [of fatherland] in our country does not exist. Among all the units which make up the population occupying our land, there is, in effect, no unity of origin, of religion, of types, of customs, of language, of evolving development, nor of desires, of purposes, and of aspirations that determine in whole the unity of the ideal [of fatherland]. . . .

. . . Among the indigenous element and the *criollo* [native-born whites], there is a complete separation of origin; there is a complete difference of type; there is a complete opposition of customs; there are very great differences of language; there is an enormous evolutionary difference; and there is a true contradic-

Translated from Andrés Molina Enríquez, *Los grandes problemas nacionales* (Mexico: Imprenta de A. Carranza e Hijos, 1909), pp. 292, 306–8, passim.

tion of desires, of purposes and aspirations. The only common thing between them, and this under diverse forms, is the Christian Catholic religion, and in part, language. Between the indigenous element and the *mestizo* [mixed Indian and white] the differences are less, but also profound. . . .

. . . The *mestizos* are the most interesting ethnic element of our social composition. In them, indeed, exist the unity of origin, the unity of religion, the unity of type, the unity of language, and the unity of wishes, of purposes, and aspiration. The unity of origin is not rigorously absolute, but the circumstances of all them being hybrid products, emanating from the same historic period and without defined filiation makes them considered as one of the same birth. Neither is the unity of religion absolutely rigorous, but the form of Christianity that they observe in general and that they will study in a special mode later on is so proper and so characteristic of them that this form is one of the most salient features of unity which they present. The unity of type, like that of origin and of religion, is not absolutely rigorous in them because the races from which they come present many differences; but it is nevertheless enough that they can be recognized at first sight by their morphologic characteristics. The unity of language is greater than the latter, although neither is it absolute, because some anachronic differences in their own form of Spanish language and some differences of pronunciation can be noted. The unities that, indeed, are truly absolute are those of customs, of evolutionary age, and of purposes and aspirations . . . all the circumstances of unity expressed before are composed and translated in a firm, ardent, and resulute love of country. Among all the organic unities of the *mestizo* element exists the fact of community of sentiments, acts, and ideas proper for the members of a family . . .

. . . Does it seem to our readers that enough has been said to prove that the *mestizo* element is the most patriotic of those that compose the national population? Well then, if the *mestizo* is the strongest, most numerous, and most patriotic element of the country, then the government of the nation should continue in it; if in it is [to be found] the true fatherland, to transfer the direction of the national destiny to some other elements of the population is little less than treason to the fatherland. . . .

. . . Let us return to the fundamental base of our domestic policy. In order that our readers do not lose the thread of our ideas, we repeat here what in its time and place we said on this point. The fundamental and unavoidable base of all guiding work in the future for the well-being of the country has to be the continuation of the *mestizos* as the preponderant ethnic element and as the directive class of the population. This situation will permit three highly transcendental results to develop: first, that the population can elevate its census without necessity of supporting immigration; second, that this population can come to be a nationality; and third, that this nationality can fix with exactness the notion of its patriotism. All this will help create the Mexican fatherland and will save this fatherland from the dangers that will arise during the inevitable struggles with the rest of the peoples of Mexico.

READING 5 *Juan B. Justo and Argentine Socialism*

Introductory Note

These two selections by Juan B. Justo (1865–1928), the founder of the Argentine Socialist Party, suggest the philosophical underpinnings of the Argentine reformers. A physician, Justo was a very practical man. He urged his followers to apply the theories of socialism to their homeland and its problems. The first selection is a brief look at Justo's own view of socialism given as part of a speech in 1902. The second is a short essay on the history of socialism in Argentina, written in 1910.

SELECTION 5.1

What is socialism? The word is used to designate the labor movement on the one hand, and on the other, the idea of an egalitarian and communist society—narrow meanings that at times, by ignorance or design, are exaggerated to a ridiculous degree. For some employers, the most insignificant demand of the workers is socialism, and in form, the most dangerous; thus, a small farmer, on arriving in the kitchen of the peons, found written on the door the words "more bread," and excitedly returned to tell his wife that all the peons are anarchists. Or some look on socialism as

Selection 5.1: Translated from Juan B. Justo, *Discursos y escritos políticos* (Buenos Aires, 1933), pp. 91–2.

Selection 5.2: Translated from Juan B. Justo, *Socialismo* (Buenos Aires: Editorial La Vanguardía, 1920), pp. 101, 104, 107.

an illusion of some happy-go-lucky types who pass their time in dreams of a better world, overlooking the real life in homage to utopia. "Sleepers!" the Christians call us, hoping for paradise; and the patriots, satisfied with the constitution, speak of liberty, equality, and fraternity.

Partial and contradictory as the contemporary ideas of socialism are, they include, nevertheless, the essential elements of a synthetic formula: the proletarian agitation, the living force of the movement, and its ideal object.

In effect, socialism is the struggle to defend and elevate the working public, that, guided by science, is approaching the realization of a free and intelligent human society based on collective ownership of the means of production.

SELECTION 5.2

By 1885 there were a million European immigrants in Argentina of different nationalities and languages, men disciplined to work, with regular habits, with aspirations for a better life. Some became promoters, but many more remained wage-earners and displaced the less able workers of the country, at the same time increasing the viability of the *criollo* proletariat.

They had also brought with them their socialistic education, which led to the general practice of mutual aid among the immigrants—a practice little known to the people of Argentina. Many of those who came from the more advanced countries arrived with their new social ideas already shaped.

On January 1, 1882, the Germans in Buenos Aires formed the *Vorwärts* club with the objective of co-operating "for the realization of the principles of socialism." It was the first agitational group to be formed and, from 1886 on, it placed itself at the disposal of the workers in the few small conflicts with which the fight between capital and labor was begun in this country. In December of that same year the weekly *The Worker* appeared, the first herald of the fight of the proletariat.

It was truly an international movement. The public meetings

were conducted, in turn, in Spanish, Italian, French, and German. The committees chose to call themselves "international," and they sought to allow equal representation from each of the diverse tongues and nationalities. The very style of *The Worker* reflected the German origin of the engineer Ave-Lalleman and *of the workers* who printed it.

It was during this epoch that anarchism began to appear, with its honest extremism, its violence, and its ambiguous procedures; opposing all serious organization within the laboring class, and preaching absolute disregard for the law.

But circumstances were changing. *La Vanguardía,* put out primarily by Argentines, appeared in April 1894. In July the first local socialist group began to form, supported by men who spoke the language of the country. This gave new incentive to union activity. In 1895 the first executive committee of the newly founded Socialist Party resolved that its members would all be citizens, native or naturalized. . . .

Economic evolution has been the basis of Argentine history and the key to an understanding of its bright and dark phases. The most efficient political groups in our history are those who have represented the more general and best understood economic interests.

We have managed to break away from the simple formula and the schematic doctrine, and we are developing a popular method of historic action, vast and complex enough to meet the demands of circumstances. The problem of socialism is not, in this country or in any other, a matter of putting a definite, perfect plan of social organization into practice, as those who wish to see the people with their heads forever in the clouds suppose it is, and as those who are too lazy and cowardly for the necessary historical action say it is. . . . Here and everywhere, socialism presents problems that are infinitely more common and, hence, more transcendental: What types of individual and collective activity are needed to step up the physical and intellectual development of the masses? How can the tangible well-being of the workers be increased? . . . Only those changes that are statistically evident and which can be shown in diagrams should be considered: increased consumption, wage increases, more schools, a decrease in the rate of mortality.

Socialism is thus the coming of science to politics, the most advanced of all politics—not for what it foresees or promises, but for what it does. Socialism leads the people to the conquest of political power as an essential prerequisite to economic liberation—to gain control of the State in order to check capitalist exploitation up to its final abolition.

READING 6 *José Martí's Homage to Marx*

Introductory Note

José Martí (previously quoted in Reading One) eloquently called for social change and reform in Cuba, even if in hindsight some of his remarks were far less radical than those of mid-twentieth-century authors. He knew of Karl Marx's philosophy, but did not subscribe to it, although he wrote a eulogy when Marx died.

Here we are in the great hall. Karl Marx is dead. Because he sided with the weak he deserves honor. But he who yearns arduously for a remedy and only points out the injury does no good; the good lies in exercising a gentle remedy for the injury. The task of throwing men against men is a frightful one. The forced brutalization of some men for the benefit of others evokes our wrath. But to stop it we must find a way out for our wrath without provoking any rush or stampede. Karl Marx studied ways to place the world on new foundations. He awoke the sleepers and showed them how to cast down the broken pillars. But he walked in a hurry and somewhat in the shadow. He could not understand that no child can be born either at home from the womb of a woman or in history from the womb of a people without a natural and laborious gestation.

Here they are, the good friends of Karl Marx who was not only a titanic arouser of the European workers' anger, but also a profound analyst of the reasons for human misery and of human destiny. A man consumed by the desire to do good, he projected

Translated from José Martí, *Obras completas* (Havana: Editorial Lex, 1946), Vol. I, pp. 1517–18.

into everything that which was actually inside himself: rebellion, a way forward, struggle.

Here they are, a Lecovich, a man of the press. Listen to him. . . . He begins to speak in English; addresses others in German; "da, da!" his countrymen answer enthusiastically when he speaks in Russian. The Russians are the whip of the reform. But these impatient and generous men, darkened as they are by anger, are not the ones who are going to lay the foundation for the new world! They are the spur, and they come in time as the voice of man's conscience. But the steel that makes a good spur will not do for the builder's hammer.

READING 7 Positivism and Porfirism in Latin America

Introductory Note

Leopoldo Zea is one of Mexico's foremost philosophers. He was the pioneer of studies on Mexican positivism, and many subsequent writings on this subject have adopted Zea's method and conclusion. His classic works on the subject are El positivismo en México (*México, 1943*) *and* Apogeo y decadencia del positivismo en México (*México, 1944*).

The rule of General Porfirio Díaz in Mexico and the simultaneous influence of positivism, the accepted doctrine of the theorists of so-called Porfirism, form part of a remarkable experiment which was executed in more or less the same manner throughout Latin America.

When political independence from the Spanish Government was achieved the Latin American countries were quick to realize that this was not enough. The order imposed by the leaders of the emancipation differed very little from that which Spain had established. What had happened was a mere change of power; Creoles had taken the place of the Spanish ruling classes. But

From *Ideological Differences and World Order*, F. S. C. Northrup, ed. (New Haven: Yale University Press, 1949), pp. 166–91.

For an interesting critique of Zea's work on positivism, see William D. Raat, "Leopoldo Zea and Mexican Positivism: A Reappraisal," in *The Hispanic American Historical Review*, Vol. XLVIII, No. 1 (February 1968), pp. 1–18.

the social status remained as it had been in colonial times. Army and clergy enjoyed their old privileges—among them the right to rule the minds and bodies of their countrymen. . . .

Spain was present in every action of the Spanish Americans. Her habits, customs, ideas, and creeds were implanted in their minds. Those habits and customs had plunged them, once they were politically emancipated, into several decades of wanton bloodshed. In vain had the democratic idea which was written on their banners struggled to adapt itself to so hostile an environment. The authoritarianism inherited from Spain quelled all democratic intentions. The ideas proclaimed in those fratricidal fights were nothing but pretexts to justify strong impulses of personal rule. The ideas ceased to be valid norms and became embodied in the persons of the leaders who proclaimed them.

All Spanish America was divided into bands fighting against one another. In Mexico it was Centralists against Federals; in Argentina Unitarians against Federalists; in Chile *Pelucones* (big wigs) against *Pipiolos* (upstarts); and so on everywhere. But whoever won, the result was invariably the establishment of personal government. Some made no bones of their intention to re-establish the colonial order, with the one difference that the center was no longer Spain but the person of the respective rulers. Others, the enlightened ones, were all for democratic government; but, for the time being, while the masses were yet unfit for it, an equally personal government would see to their being prepared. There were those also who opposed central government for the sake of democracy but defended another of the political forms inherited from the colonial period: the cacicazgo or rule of local political bosses. . . .

The model for the new man of Spanish America was found in the Anglo-Saxon nations, England and the United States, particularly the latter, where the Spanish American reformers saw their ideals realized to an admirable degree. "In North America," said Sarmiento, "the settlers developed the economic life of the land; in South America they exploited it for the benefit of the mother country. . . . There the conquerors brought with them the ideal of labor; here they were satisfied to loaf as bureaucrats and parasites." One America had been colonized by Anglo-Saxons, inspired by the spirit of democracy, the other by a Latin race used to absolutism; hence the greatness of the first, the disgrace of the latter. Or in Lastarria's words: "In the North the people were supreme, actually and legally; they made the law and administered all its interests through their representatives. In Spanish America the people did not exist, society was alive only as far as it lived for the glory and benefit of its sovereign, an absolute ruler." With his accustomed impetuosity Sarmiento pointed out the remedy for Spanish American grievances: "Let us not detain the march of the United States! Let us catch up with the United States! Let us be America as the sea is the ocean! Let us be United States!"

In Mexico the admiration the United States enjoyed throughout Latin America was tempered by distrust, a consequence of the war of 1847. Mexico felt she was weak and inferior in comparison with the "Northern Colossus"; and this weakness and inferiority she blamed on the fact that she was a member of the Spanish or Latin race, an irrational, anarchic race incapable of such organization as had made North America a powerful nation.

To South Americans their own race appeared romantic, idealistic, given to utopias and to sacrificing reality to dreams. A race scorning material exertion and preferring to live suspended in a world of idealism without consequences. Nations founded by this race, the argument went on, could not but be inferior to those with a practical sense, such as England and the United States. History was on the side of the latter. England had defeated theocratic Spain, and in America the sons of England had defeated those of Spain. The United States had found itself pitted against a weak nation. And this weakness was due solely to racial defects. Since their independence Mexicans had done nothing but kill one another for ideas which were mere words and for leaders who claimed to represent those ideas. Hence the necessity of getting rid of so unfortunate a disposition.

To bring about the desired change no vehicle appeared more suitable than education. A doctrine had to be found, an idealogy, a body of thought, and it presented itself in the Comtian system.

Positivism was the philosophy of practical people like the Anglo-Saxons who had made great nations of their countries; it would make the Mexicans fit for true liberty and democracy.

Positivism would teach the Mexicans how to establish order, mental and social—order in their own minds being an indispensable presupposition of the direly needed social order. Philosophical doctrines or systems not grounded on positive principles were considered unsuitable for the Mexican mind. How can we expect to regenerate, asked Telesforo García, if we increase the defects of our race, yielding to them instead of checking them with the help of rationally erected dams? We Latin people are "given to dreams and mysticism"; under such circumstances is it not absurd that "instead of disciplining the mind with rigorous scientific methods, instead of directing our activity toward clearly defined, positive ends, we indulge in fantasies and dreams and take the zest out of labor through which man makes himself the master of nature?" . . .

Justo Sierra (1848–1912), one of the greatest educators of Mexico, made it clearer still that only through a mental and social change could Mexico survive in the struggle for life. A transition from the military era, the era of revolutions and continuous intestine wars, to the industrial era, the era of labor and a maximum personal effort, had to be achieved. And it had to be accomplished quickly, "for the giant nation that grows by our side and moves closer and closer in on us as a consequence of the industrial and agricultural prosperity of her border states and the extension of her railroads, threatens to absorb and dissolve us if she finds us weak." History had already spoken a few years before. Mexico had been defeated by the northern country—defeated, however, by a superior mental and social organization, not by a superiority of arms. In vain had the men of the liberal party endeavored to give the Mexican people a progressive education and organization; the old interests of the military and the clergy, a residue of colonial times, had proved stronger and had obstructed all progress. Those very interests had vanquished Mexico and not the arms of the North. Thus, when the war was over, the progressive party was firmly resolved to enforce a program that would put an end to such a situation. This program, said Sierra, proposed "to educate the people in absolute independence of the Church, to break down the barriers of religious intolerance, to release churchland from mortmain." Thus and thus only one might hope to build up what had been so badly missing in the war with the northern neighbor: national consciousness.

Such was the work to be accomplished by the generation that assumed political responsibility in Mexico from 1880 to 1910. Their aim was to establish order in Mexican minds and in Mexican society. They set up a new type of national education, and they endeavored to set up a new type of social order, claiming science as the foundation of both. Mental order was based on positivism, social order on Porfirism. . . .

Political evolution and evolution of political liberty had to be sacrificed for what Sierra called social evolution, that is, for that degree of social organization without which political evolution must remain a chimera. To wean the Mexicans from their habits of disorder proved a very difficult undertaking. "Those ingrained Mexican habits," says Sierra, "are a thousand times more difficult to get rid of than the old regime and the ruling classes it established. Nothing short of a total change in our working and living conditions can bring about a transformation of this order." Only a strong state could work such a miracle. Once a group or a party was able to maintain for some length of time a state of organization, political evolution would be set going. "And the mass of the people, which is more important in democracies than in aristocracies, will follow suit; for the function creates the organ." All political power and with it all political liberty were to be handed over to one strong man, General Porfirio Díaz. "To accomplish the great task enjoined on him," Sierra went on to say, "the President needed a maximum of authority, not only legal but political, social and moral as well." As to the first, he had to be in a position to take over the actual direction of political bodies: legislatures and governments of the states. As to the second, he must, with the consent of all, constitute himself the supreme justice of the peace of Mexican society. But all this renunciation and delegation of power to one man was to be compensated by the state's taking action in that matter on which Sierra, like all the champions of intellectual independence in Hispano-America, had set their high hopes: education. "To educate people," said Sierra, "means to make them strong. Liberty, collective and individual, is the patrimony of strong men only. The social evolution of Mexico will come to nothing unless it comes to this all-embracing end: liberty."

On November 26, 1876, General Porfirio Díaz, who had led a victorious revolution against the government of Sebastián Lerdo de Tejada with the battle cry "no re-election," was nominated provisional president. On December 6 of the same year he ceded the power to General Méndez, but took it back provisionally on February 16, 1877. On September 25, 1880, Manuel González was elected with the consent of Díaz; but in 1884 Díaz took office again, this time to stay until May 25, 1911, the day of the Mexican Revolution. All political forces of the country rallied around his person. He became the symbol of that peace and order the men educated in positivist ideas had so much at heart. A strong feeling of material well-being, which became more and more dehumanized, prevailed among the generation that supported him: industry, money, railways, more money. Mora's ideal seemed to be fulfilled; a new class, the bourgeoisie, seemed to determine the destinies of the country. Progress seemed to triumph, social evolution to advance with gigantic steps. But with all this well-being the purpose for which order had been established—liberty—fell into oblivion. People were content with a very special form of liberty: the liberty to get rich—a liberty in which not all classes could participate. Sierra himself had a premonition that the lack of true freedom would, in the end, undo what had been accomplished in the sphere of social evolution.

The new type of Mexicans emphasized their difference from the previous generation. "We are taken to task," they said, "because of our lack of faith, our positivism, our ill-concealed contempt for the institutions of the past." This was true, of course; and for reason for it was the different education they had received. "In philosophical matters," they told the old liberals, "you relied on Voltaire and Rousseau, on the Encyclopedists and the

Choix de Rapports of the French Revolution, and the most advanced of you studied high metaphysics from the works of the German School, while we have learned logic from Mill and Bain, philosophy from Comte and Spencer, science from Huxley, Tyndall, Virchow, and Helmholtz." So different an education could not but produce different people. "You stepped forth from college campuses," the positivists proceeded, "drunk with enthusiasm for the great ideas of 1789. Quoting Danton and the Girondists you dashed to the mountains to fight the ecclesiastics, you set up reforms, you brought down reactionaries, you moulded our laws on the pattern of beautiful utopias which, at that time, were honored as good money in philosophical transactions. Whereas we, less enthusiastic, more skeptical and perhaps more egoistic, dedicate ourselves to Newton's theory of gravitation, to natural selection, to sociological studies, and are concerned with our terrestrial destinies rather than with celestial spaces. We do not care for questions that cannot be subjected to the control of observation and experience. We disregard the portion of the world that cannot be investigated by means of telescopes or other instruments of scientific research. We do not arrive at our truths forthright; to attain them we need constant ardent efforts and patient, elaborate investigation."

These young positivists regarded themselves as destined to guide their country. Their methods were sure and precise—the methods of science learned in the new schools Barreda had reformed. This scientific method they intended to apply to all the problems of Mexico, in particular the political ones. In 1881, they spoke of nothing less than the "Scientific Political School of Mexico." In 1880 a number of the members of the new generation entered the Chamber of Deputies, among them Justo Sierra, Pablo Macedo, Rosendo Piñeda, Francisco Bulnes, and Jorge Hammeken Mexia. All of them except Mexia, who died prematurely, had a hand in setting up the new regime and initiating the epoch in Mexican history that has been given the name of Porfirism. . . .

What was happening? The opposite of what the pioneers who had fought for the creation of a new type of Mexicans were expecting. Positivist education had not produced men similar to those who had made great nations of England and the United States. Positivism had become another instrument serving the desire of power and dominion that had distinguished Spanish Americans at all times. Scientific absolution had superseded religious absolutism. And behind this phenomenon stood precisely those group interests Mora [José María Luis Mora, a liberal Mexican educator (1794–1850)] had battled against, except that the privileged classes were no longer the army and clergy but a new group that called itself the Mexican bourgeoisie—a group that had become narrower and narrower through the selection it practiced among its own ranks. A small but powerful oligarchy had formed around the President who had granted them the right of getting rich. This small group held all the wealth of the country; its members gave preference to their friends in the apportionment of prosperity. Cliques springing up in the shadow of local banks monopolized all profits and made of social progress but another legend. Blind to the problems of their country, those people were concerned with nothing but their own gains. And all this under the name of scientific and positivistic politics.

Social evolution, so dear to the disciples of Spencer, its impulses checked, was reduced to the evolution of middle-class wealth. The political and financial leaders of the country considered their own success the best index of progress. August science found itself harnessed to the interests of industrialists and financiers. Their methods lay beyond the reach of the great masses for which they felt an Olympian contempt. The people continued to be a minor that had to be ruled with an iron hand and could not be trusted with major liberties. Snobbism and luxury stood out against a background of general misery. The lower classes lived in utter poverty while the ruling classes arrogantly displayed their luxury. But had at least material progress been achieved, the indispensable requirement for the formation of a powerful bourgeoisie? Had the middle class been freed from its bonds to state and bureaucracy, as Mora had wished it to be?

No! The government continued to be the principal source of privileges; and the material progress that might have engendered a powerful bourgeoisie was not achieved. Despite all positive education middle-class mentality remained the same as in colonial times. The principal source of wealth remained the same: the exploitation of the rural worker. The social structure set up by Spain remained the same: on the one hand the great landowner, on the other the peasant who had no claim to the soil he tilled. It all boiled down to a political change: the colonial lord of the manor had given place to the Porfirian landowner. If there was progress, it worked toward greater efficiency in the methods of exploitation. Under Díaz the official machinery permitted the landed gentry to accumulate more acres than they could ever have held under the viceroys.

Industrialization, which Mora had regarded as the rightful source of middle-class power, never materialized. The Mexican bourgeoisie contented themselves with such income as they derived either from exploiting the land which, as often as not, they had never seen, or from speculating with the economy of the country. Instead of exploiting industry, they exploited peasants or the Treasury. Such industries as sprang up were due to the great European bourgeoisies, French and English in particular, to whom the progress of the country was of no concern. The Mexican bourgeoisie never got beyond playing the handmaiden to foreign interests. The brightest members of the generation which had been taught positive science took service with foreign enterprises. Instead of themselves exploiting the riches of the country, they turned them over to foreigners for exploitation. With all their education they had remained as unpractical as ever. As to order, which the positivists had so much at heart, reality was to reveal that it had not struck root in the Mexican mind. And it had not done so because that would have involved a change of mind impossible to bring about by mere teaching or training. The thesis that the function creates the organ turned out to be completely wrong. Thirty long years of dictatorial rule had failed to build up the desired order. The best procedure, so Mora, Barreda, and Sierra had taught, was to use persuasion, to have order accepted because it served the interests of the entire nation. But there was the rub: the nation would not let itself be persuaded that the order in question suited any interests except those of a small group which regarded itself as representative of all national interests. Nor was the progress those reformers had in mind the progress of the nation.

Discontent, not order, made itself felt in Mexican minds throughout the country—discontent and disgust at a doctrine the practical results of which had been nil; at a regime concerned with the interests of a very small circle of people; at a social situation which differed in no way from that of the colonial period. The next generation of intellectuals rebelled against education based on positive philosophy; and the people rebelled against Porfirist government. The order that had claimed to be everlasting was followed by one of the longest and most sanguinary revolutions. The entire political apparatus that bore the name of Porfirism was abolished as useless, and its downfall sealed the doom of the philosophical doctrine supporting it. Thus ended the great experiment of Mexican Porfirism.

READING 8 Gabino Barreda on Positivist Education

Introductory Note

Gabino Barreda (1820–81) headed the newly created National Preparatory School in 1868, where positivism, science, and precision were stressed in the curriculum. Many of the científicos, *the young lawyers and economists appointed by Porfirio Díaz to advise him during his reign of some thirty-four years (1867–1910), were strong positivists, and some of them, such as José Ives Limantour, were educated at the National Preparatory School. As the official philosophy of the* Porfirista *reign, positivism began to die out during the first decade of the twentieth century, as the social discontent behind Mexico's 1910 Revolution began to build up a head of steam.*

An education in which not one important branch of the natural sciences is omitted; in which all the phenomena of nature, from the most simple to the most complex, are studied and analyzed both theoretically and practically; an education in which understanding and the senses are cultivated at the same time, without the pledge to maintain by force this or that opinion, or this or that political or religious dogma, without fear of seeing the actions of this or that authority contradicted; an education, I repeat,

Translated from a letter by Gabino Barreda to C. Mariano Riva Palacio, Governor of the State of Mexico, dated 10 October 1870; in Gabino Barreda, *Estudios,* selección y prólogo de José Fuentes Mares (México: Ediciones de la Universidad Nacional Autónoma, 1941), p. 15.

undertaken upon such bases, and with only the desire to find the truth, that is, of finding that which really is, and not that which in our concept ought to be in the natural phenomena, would not be able to be less than, at the time the inexhaustible source of satisfactions, the most secure preliminary of peace and social order, because it will give all citizens the aptitude of appreciating all the acts of a similar nature, and at the same time, standardize opinions as much as possible. And the opinions of men are and will always be the motive of all their actions. The method is, without doubt, slow; but what does it matter if we are sure of its efficacy? What are ten, fifteen, or twenty years in the life of a nation, when it deals with laying the foundation of the only way of reconciling liberty with good will, progress with order? The intellectual order that this education would establish is the key to the social and moral order that we so greatly need.

II Mexican Nationalism: The Revolution of 1910

MEXICAN NATIONALISM

The Revolution of 1910 opened for the Mexican people an epoch of newly found pride in themselves and their country. Francisco I. Madero (1873–1913) early expressed this feeling in attacking the dictatorship of Porfirio Díaz (1876–1910) for its suppression of individual freedom. He demanded equality before the law through elections and presidential succession in his book, *La sucesión presidencial en 1910* (the Presidential Succession in 1910) which was published in its second edition in 1908 (Reading One). He affirmed his faith in the capacity of the Mexican people to exercise independent judgment. His book was the first of many patriotic appeals by Mexico's revolutionary leaders.

When Díaz failed to allow the legitimate expression of political democracy in the 1910 elections, Madero issued his *Plan de San Luis Potosí* (Reading Two). This document urged overthrow of the Díaz dictatorship. It appealed to the disenfranchised middle classes who could appreciate institutionalized democracy (compare Fidel Castro's statements, four decades later, espousing a return to elections and the Cuban Constitution of 1940, Part IV, Reading Ten; Part V, Reading One).

The Díaz government was overthrown and Madero became president. In February 1913 he and his vice-president, José María Pino Suárez, were killed and a counter-revolutionary coup led by General Victoriano Huerta (1854–1916) took control. In response, in March 1913, Venustiano Carranza (1859–1920), governor of the State of Coahuila, issued his *Plan de Guadalupe* reaffirming Madero's principles (Reading Three). These first three sources illustrate the emphasis in Mexico's early revolutionary nationalism on political rather than economic or social reform.

Other aspects of Mexican nationalism are to be found in the sources. Carranza's reactions against United States occupation of Veracruz (1914) show the omnipresent fear of North American power (Reading Four). They concentrate on territorial sovereignty, which was a reaction to Díaz's heavy foreign investment and to what seemed to many to be the presence of too many foreigners in Mexico. Given the loss of Mexican territory to the United States in years past, Carranza's reactions are understandable. Another force conditioning Mexican nationalism was the secular bias against clerical power in land holding, education, and politics; anti-clericalism permeates the Constitution of 1917 (Reading Five). Rigid enforcement of this secularism by President Plutarco Elías Calles (1877–1945) led to the great Church-State conflict during the late 1920s (Reading Six).

SOCIAL JUSTICE

The Mexican political system changed after 1910, offering new opportunities for the attainment of land, labor, and educational reforms. Unlike the closely centralized and authoritarian Díaz regime, the post-1910 government could de described as pluralistic. Pluralism made possible the expression of new social demands held in check during the Díaz epoch. This could be seen by late 1911 in the activities of syndicates of unions of tailors, bakers, bricklayers, shoemakers, mechanics, carpenters, painters, plasterers, stonecutters, and textile workers. New mutualist societies, groups not limited to one industry or trade, also developed during these months, such as the Grand Labor League and the National Labor Council. In 1912 the first major labor group that would give unity to the morass of smaller unions, the *Casa del Obrero Mundial* (House of the World Worker), was formed. Other groups that favored change were middle-class intellectuals, small landowners, the *campesinos* (farmers), and miners. Thus, new social groups were emerging as sources of political power for the governing revolutionary elite, thereby guaranteeing at least some implementation of basic social demands.

Madero's victory over Díaz did not, of course, bring immediate social justice to Mexico. He encouraged freedom of speech, of the press, and of labor to organize, but gave much less attention to economic objectives, particularly land reform. His inattention to the economic side of the revolution, and particularly to agriculture, prompted Zapata to issue his own *Plan de Ayala* (Reading Seven) which ordered the *campesinos* to take forceful possession of the lands. Carranza, like Madero, had paid scant attention to economic development; but under the pressure of competition for political power in late 1914 and early 1915 from Francisco (Pancho) Villa (1877–1923) and Emiliano Zapata (1880–1919), he issued strong reform promises to labor and *campesino* groups (Reading Eight). These promises were incorporated into the land and labor reform articles—27 and 123—of the 1917 Constitution which embodied key ideological norms for future presidential policies (Reading Nine).

Social reforms reached their peak during the presidency of Lázaro Cárdenas. Cárdenas (1895–) created two new nationalized workers groups from above: the *Confederación de Trabajadores Mexicanos* (Confederation of Mexican Workers or CTM) and the *Confederación Nacional de Campesinos* (National Confederation of Rural Workers or CNC), and brought them into the party structure. This was done partly to offset the still powerful system of ex-President Calles and partly as a dramatic implementation of Mexicanism which had been spelled out clearly in the party's Six Year Plan that Cárdenas followed (Reading Ten). Moreover, he particularly encouraged new attitudes toward work and achievement. In this attempt to modify Mexico's political culture, he amended the education article of the 1917 Constitution (Article 3) to give it a socialist framework (Reading Eleven). He also published government textbooks filled with themes of work, achievement, and participation in workers' syndicates (Reading Twelve).

NATIONALISM AND SOCIALISM IN MEXICO SINCE CÁRDENAS

Cárdenas represented a high point in Mexican national development. To be sure, later presidents espoused the principles of the Mexican Revolution.[1] Nationalism and socialism remained central virtues. But postwar leaders were interested in consolidation of revolutionary gains. They catered to industrial capitalists and the middle class unlike Cárdenas, who promoted vast agrarian reform and created national rural and urban labor organizations. They also moved away from the chauvinistic policy of Cárdenas's 1938 oil expropriations and began to encourage the return of foreign capital investments.

The postwar years represented a drive for industrialization by means of a mixed economy of both private and public sector ownership.[2] Peaceful transfers of political power through national, state, and local elections and more political participation came

1. Mexican presidents since Carranza are as follows:

President	*Dates in Office*
Venustiano Carranza	February 1915 to May 1920
Adolfo de la Huerta	May 1920 to November 1920
Álvaro Obregón	December 1920 to November 1924
Plutarco Elías Calles	December 1924 to November 1928
Emilio Portes Gil	December 1928 to February 1930
Pascual Ortiz Rubio	February 1930 to September 1932
Abelardo L. Rodríguez	September 1932 to November 1934
Lázaro Cárdenas	December 1934 to November 1940
Manuel Ávila Camacho	December 1940 to November 1946
Miguel Alemán	December 1946 to November 1952
Adolfo Ruiz Cortines	December 1952 to November 1958
Adolfo López Mateos	December 1958 to November 1964
Gustavo Díaz Ordaz	December 1964 to November 1970

2. See Stanford A. Mosk, *Industrial Revolution in Mexico* (Berkeley and Los Angeles: University of California Press, 1950); Raymond Vernon, *The Dilemma of Mexico's Development* (Cambridge: Harvard University Press, 1963); William P. Glade, Jr. and Charles W. Anderson, *The Political Economy of Mexico* (Madison: University of Wisconsin Press, 1963); Charles C. Cumberland, *Mexico: The Struggle for Modernity* (New York: Oxford University Press, 1968), Chapter 10; Victor Alba, *The Mexicans* (New York: Frederick A. Praeger, 1967), Chapter 11.

about through the *Partido Revolucionario Institucional* (Institutional Revolutionary Party or PRI) which was founded in 1929 as the *Partido Nacional Revolucionario* (National Revolutionary Party or PNR). After 1945 Mexico attained one of the highest rates of economic growth in Latin America. National policies became less combative and far less radical than Castro's model for change after 1959.

Social justice after 1945 was affirmed in national laws. They limited the scope of private business and allowed the executive branch to intervene in the state economy. Social security and minimum wages remained essential state guarantees. State investment in national industries and agricultural activities continued through *Nacional Financiera* (the public credit institution), the Agricultural Credit Bank, the *Banco de Crédito Ejidal* (Ejidal Credit Bank), and the Housing and Public Works Bank. Collective rather than individual rights remained a dominant force in shaping public policy under the direction of PRI presidential authority.

Mexican educational policy demonstrates the scope of postwar nationalism. For example, the unity of the Mexican people became a central theme in primary school textbooks after 1946 (Reading Thirteen). Gone was the doctrine of class struggle so characteristic of the 1930s. New official textbooks by 1959 emphasized values of class harmony and domestic unity. Themes of peaceful co-operation among nations replaced those of inevitable world conflict. Mexican patriotism, rather than class interests, were written into object lesson stories. Pictures of well-dressed boys and girls replaced the coverall-wearing little workers of the 1930s. There is little attempt to show class distinctions. The focus is upon a national community of Indians, *mestizos* and whites (Reading Fourteen).

These changes in educational policy were produced by the PRI. This party of the revolution, source of all Mexican presidents since its founding in 1929, is composed of leftist, centrist, and rightist groups brought together to pursue common goals associated with the "continuing revolution." The PRI system, with its powerful chief executive who symbolizes the nation, has worked remarkably well by and large and is often credited with bringing the Mexican people together. The extent of PRI identification with "revolutionary" nationalism and socialism is suggested by PRI's Declaration of Principles (Reading Fifteen).

The PRI's authority was challenged dramatically during the summer of 1968 for the first time in many years. University and high school students carried on a variety of anti-government demonstrations for two months, even daring to question President Gustavo Díaz Ordaz (1911–   ) himself. President Díaz Ordaz spent one hour of his September 1, 1968, State of the Union Address responding to the student demonstrations. His address, at once tough and conciliatory, attempted to show that the party was consistently dedicated to stability and continued major reforms (Reading Sixteen).

Discontent, by no means confined to students, had several causes. Mexico was still plagued with urban and rural poverty, high population growth, a lagging petroleum industry, underemployment, and low agricultural productivity. Consequently, criticism grew against PRI's tight political control and patronage system which discouraged opposition groups like the *Partido de Acción Nacional* (Party of National Action or PAN). The PRI had also become increasingly conservative over the years, moving toward intra-party compromise and rightist approaches to national problems. This trend continued with the election of Luis Echeverría Alvárez as president in 1970. Mr. Echeverría is associated with the "hard line" in PRI politics and is regarded as a conservative.

READING 1 *Madero's* La sucesión presidencial en 1910

Introductory Note

Francisco I. Madero (1873–1913) was a member of a wealthy landowning family in the northern state of Coahuila. He abhorred revolution, believing more in stability through laissez-faire liberalism. He entered politics, as the 1908 edition of La sucesión presidencial en 1910 *suggests, believing it possible to reform and replace the Porfirian dictatorship with democratic government. This first attempt at moral and political reform proved fruitless. Madero was jailed during the balloting in June 1910, while Porfirio Díaz and his unpopular vice-president, Ramón Corral, were "re-elected" for another six-year term.*

To the Heroes of our Country,
To the independent newspapermen,
To good Mexicans,

I dedicate this book to the heroes who won the independence of our country with their blood; who wrote the most brilliant pages of our history with their heroism and magnanimity; who, with their self-sacrifice, perseverance, and inspiration bequeathed us a code of laws so learned that they constitute one of our

Translated from Francisco I. Madero, *La sucesión presidencial en 1910: el partido democrático nacional* (México: Ediciones "Los Insurgentes," 1908), pp. 1–4.

most legitimate achievements of glory, and have allowed us to work all united, following the great principle of fraternity, in order to obtain, by means of liberty, the consummation of the magnificent democratic ideal, of equality before the law.

I have dedicated my book to these heroes at the outset because I have been taught to venerate them from my infancy, because in order to write it, I have been inspired in their pure patriotism, and because in their glorious example I have found the strength sufficient to undertake the difficult task that goes to the core of this work.

Through the study of history I have been able to strengthen my soul because I found it possible for us to breathe a different atmosphere from that which is currently breathed in the Republic; it is possible for us to breathe the spirit of liberty, saturated with the perfumes emitted by the plants which unfold only in this manner. This history gives us an idea more elevated than our miseries, teaching us that the great men whose admirable deeds, born in the same land as ours and which in their immense love of country is ours as well, found the necessary strength to save it from the greatest dangers, not vacillating in sacrificing for it, its well-being, its wealth, and its life.

In the second place, I dedicate this book to the Independent Press of the Republic which, with rare sacrifice, has sustained the unequal battle for more than thirty years against the ominous power which has centered in the hands of a single man; this press has waved the constitutional banner, has protested against all the abuses of power, has defended our insulted rights, our incarcerated Constitution, our mocked laws. . . .

Finally, I dedicate this book to all Mexicans in whom the notion of Country has not died and who nobly united this idea with that of liberty and of sacrifice; this planet of valiant defenders who have never failed the Nation in its days of trouble and who remain hidden because of their modesty, until the moment of battle arrives in which they will amaze everyone with their vigorous and energetic posture; to these valiant champions of liberty, who anxiously await the moment of battle; to these stoic citizens, who very soon will show to the world their fortitude and their energy; to all of them in whom vibrates some of the energy of the soul on reading this book, in which I will make an effort to speak the language of the fatherland. . . .

READING 2 *Madero's Plan of San Luis Potosí*

Introductory Note

Unimpressed by the challenge exerted by Madero, Porfirio Díaz (1830–1915) presided in 1910 over an enormous centennial celebration honoring the independence movement launched by Father Miguel Hidalgo in September 1810. The celebration reached its peak in mid-September and, soon after, Díaz allowed Madero to "escape" from his imprisonment in San Luis Potosí to exile in the United States. Madero's attempt at peaceful change had failed; he received an official 196 votes in the 1910 election as presidential rival, while Díaz received millions.

From his exile in Texas, Madero turned to new tactics. He issued the Plan of San Luis Potosí, *calling for nullification of the 1910 elections and for the Mexican people to stage a mass uprising against Díaz on November 20, 1910. This date signifies in Mexican history the beginning of the revolution.*

While the early revolutionary stages did not produce a huge popular uprising, they did produce sufficient strength to bring down the internally weak Díaz government. On May 25, 1911, Díaz resigned. He died later in Paris (July 1915), two years after Madero (February 1913).

United States, Congress, Senate, Subcommittee on Foreign Relations, *Revolutions in Mexico,* 62nd Cong., 2nd sess. (Washington: Government Printing Office, 1913), pp. 730–36.

Manifest to the Nation

Peoples, in their constant efforts for the triumph of the ideal of liberty and justice, are forced, at precise historical moments, to make their greatest sacrifices.

Our beloved country has reached one of those moments. A force of tyranny which we Mexicans were not accustomed to suffer after we won our independence oppresses us in such a manner that it has become intolerable. In exchange for that tyranny we are offered peace, but peace full of shame for the Mexican nation, because its basis is not law, but force; because its object is not the aggrandisement and prosperity of the country, but to enrich a small group who, abusing their influence, have converted the public charges into fountains of exclusively personal benefit, unscrupulously exploiting the manner of lucrative concessions and contracts.

The legislative and judicial powers are completely subordinated to the executive; the division of powers, the sovereignty of the States, the liberty of the common councils, and the rights of the citizen exist only in writing in our great charter; but, as a fact, it may almost be said that martial law constantly exists in Mexico; the administration of justice, instead of imparting protection to the weak, merely serves to legalize the plunderings committed by the strong; the judges instead of being the representatives of justice, are the agents of the executive, whose interests they faithfully serve; the chambers of the union have no other will than that of the dictator; the governors of the States are designated by him and they in their turn designate and impose in like manner the municipal authorities.

From this it results that the whole administrative, judicial, and legislative machinery obeys a single will, the caprice of Gen. Porfirio Díaz, who during his long administration has shown that the principal motive that guides him is to maintain himself in power and at any cost.

For many years profound discontent has been felt throughout the Republic, due to such a system of government, but Gen. Díaz with great cunning and perseverance, has succeeded in annihilating all independent elements, so that it was not possible to organize any sort of movement to take from him the power of which he made such bad use. The evil constantly became worse, and the decided eagerness of Gen. Díaz to impose a successor upon the nation in the person of Mr. Ramón Corral carried that evil to its limit and caused many of us Mexicans, although lacking recognized political standing, since it had been impossible to acquire it during the 36 years of dictatorship, to throw ourselves into the struggle to recover the sovereignty of the people and their rights on purely democratic grounds.

Among other parties that aimed at the same end, the National Antireelection Party was organized, proclaiming the principles of effective suffrage and no reelection, as the only ones capable of saving the Republic from the imminent peril by which it is menaced by a dictatorship daily growing more burdensome, more despotic, and more immoral.

The Mexican people effectively seconded that party and in response to the call made to it sent their representatives to a convention in which the National Democratic Party was also represented and which likewise interpreted the popular aspirations. Said convention designated its candidates for the presidency and vice presidency of the Republic, these nominations going to Dr. Francisco Vázquez Gómez and to myself for the offices of vice president and president of the Republic, respectively.

Although our situation is highly disadvantageous, because our adversaries counted upon the whole official element, upon which they relied without scruple, we believed it our duty to accept so honorable a designation in order to serve the cause of the people. Imitating the wise customs of republican countries, I traveled over a part of the Republic making a call to my fellow citizens. My trips were true triumphal marches; for everywhere the people, electrified by the magic words, effective suffrage and no reelection, gave evident proof of their unbreakable resolution to obtain the triumph of such redeeming principles. At last the moment came when Gen. Díaz understood the true situation in the Republic and realized that he could not fight advantageously against me in the field of democracy and ordered me put in prison before the election, which was carried out by excluding the people from the polls by violence, by filling the jails with independent citizens, and by committing the most shameless frauds.

In Mexico, as a democratic Republic, the public power can have no other origin nor other basis than the will of the people, and the latter can not be subordinated to formulas to be executed in a fraudulent manner.

For this reason the Mexican people have protested against the illegality of the last election and, desiring to use successively all the recourses offered by the laws of the Republic, in due form asked for the nullification of the election by the Chamber of Deputies, notwithstanding they recognized no legal origin in said body and knew beforehand that, as its members were not the representatives of the people, they would carry out the will of Gen. Díaz, to whom exclusively they owe their investiture.

In such a state of affairs the people, who are the only sovereign, also protested energetically against the election in imposing manifestations in different parts of the Republic; and if the latter were not general throughout the national territory, it was due to the terrible pressure exercised by the Government, which always quenches in blood any democratic manifestation, as happened in Puebla, Vera Cruz, Tlaxcala, and in other places.

But this violent and illegal system can no longer subsist.

I have very well realized that if the people have designated me as their candidate for the Presidency it is not because they have had an opportunity to discover in me the qualities of a statesman or of a ruler, but the virility of the patriot determined to sacrifice himself, if need be, to obtain liberty and to help the people free themselves from the odious tyranny that oppresses them.

From the moment I threw myself into the democratic struggle I very well knew that Gen. Díaz would not bow to the will of the nation, and the noble Mexican people, in following me to the polls, also knew perfectly the outrage that awaited them; but in spite of it, the people gave the cause of liberty a numerous contingent of martyrs when they were necessary and with wonderful stoicism went to the polls and received every sort of molestation.

But such conduct was indispensable to show to the whole world that the Mexican people are fit for democracy, that they are thirsty for liberty, and that their present rulers do not measure up to their aspirations.

Besides, the attitude of the people before and during the election, as well as afterwards, shows clearly that they reject with energy the Government of Gen. Díaz and that, if those electoral rights had been respected, I would have been elected for President of the Republic.

Therefore, and in echo of the national will, I declare the late election illegal and, the Republic being accordingly without rulers, provisionally assume the Presidency of the Republic until the people designate their rulers pursuant to the law. In order to attain this end, it is necessary to eject from power the audacious usurpers whose only title of legality involves a scandalous and immoral fraud.

With all honesty I declare that it would be a weakness on my part and treason to the people, who have placed their confidence in me, not to put myself at the front of my fellow citizens, who anxiously call me from all parts of the country, to compel Gen. Díaz by force of arms, to respect the national will.

The present Government, although it has its origin in violence and fraud from the moment it has been tolerated by the people, can have accepted from foreign nations certain titles of legality until the 30th of next month, when its powers expire; but as it is necessary that the new government, born of recent fraud, can not now assume power, or at best will find the greater part of the nation protesting against that usurpation, with arms in its hands, I have designated Sunday, the 20th of next November, for all the towns in the Republic to rise in arms after 6 o'clock P.M., under the following:

Plan

First. The elections for President and Vice President of the Republic, magistrates of the supreme court of justice of the nation, and deputies and senators, held in June and July of the current year, are declared void.

Second. The present Government of Gen. Díaz is not recognized, as well as all the authorities whose power ought to emanate from the popular vote, because, besides not having been elected by the people, they have lost the few titles of legality they might have by committing and supporting with the elements the people put at their disposal for the defense of their interests the most scandalous electoral fraud recorded in the history of Mexico.

Third. In order to avoid, as far as possible, the upheavals inherent in every revolutionary movement, all the laws promulgated by the present administration and their respective regulations, except those that are manifestly repugnant to the principles proclaimed in this plan, are declared to be in force, with the reservation to amend, in due time, by constitutional methods, those that require amendment. Likewise the laws, decisions of tribunals and decrees that approved the accounts and management of funds by the functionaries of the Porfirist administration in all its departments, are excepted; for as soon as the revolution triumphs the formation of investigating commissions will be initiated for the purpose of reporting as to the liabilities incurred by the functionaries of the federation, of the States, and of the municipalities.

In every case the obligations contracted by the Porfirist administration with foreign Governments and corporations prior to the 20th *proximo* [next] will be respected.

In abuse of the law on public lands numerous proprietors of small holdings, in their greater part Indians, have been dispossessed of their lands by rulings of the department of public development (*fomento*) or by decisions of the tribunals of the Republic. As it is just to restore to their former owners the lands of which they were dispossessed in such an arbitrary manner, such rulings and decisions are declared subject to revision, and those who have acquired them in such an immoral manner, or their heirs, will be required to restore them to their former owners, to whom they shall also pay an indemnity for the damages suffered. Solely in case those lands have passed to third persons before the promulgation of this plan shall the former owners receive an indemnity from those in whose favor the dispossession was made.

Fourth. Besides the constitution and existing laws, the principle of no reelection of the President and Vice President of the Republic, governors of the States, and municipal presidents is declared to be the supreme law of the Republic until the respective constitutional amendments are made.

Fifth. I assume the character of provisional President of the United States of Mexico, with the necessary powers to make war on the usurping government of Gen. Díaz.

As soon as the capital of the Republic and more than half of the States of the federation are in the power of the forces of the people the provisional President will issue a call for extraordinary general elections one month thereafter, and shall deliver the power to the President who is elected as soon as the result of the election is known.

Sixth. The provisional President, before delivering the power, shall make a report to the congress of the union of the use he has made of the powers the present plan confers upon him.

Seventh. The 20th day of the month of November, after 6 P.M., all citizens of the Republic will take up arms to remove from power all the authorities who now govern it. (The towns which are at a distance from means of communication will do so the day previous.)

Eighth. When the authorities offer armed resistance they shall be compelled by force of arms to respect the popular will, but in this case the laws of war shall be rigorously observed, attention being especially called to the prohibition against the use of expansive bullets, nor shall prisoners be shot. Attention is also called to the duty of every Mexican to respect foreigners in their persons and interests.

Ninth. The authorities who offer resistance to the realization of this plan shall be put in prison, to be tried by the tribunals of the Republic when the revolution is ended. As soon as each city or town receives its liberty the principal officer in command shall be recognized as the provisional legal authority, with power to delegate his functions to any other prominent citizen, who shall be confirmed in his office or removed by the provisional governor.

One of the first measures of the provisional government shall be to put all political prisoners at liberty.

Tenth. The appointment of the provisional governor of each State that has been occupied by the forces of the revolution shall be made by the provisional President. This governor shall be under strict obligation to issue a call for election of the constitutional governor of the State as soon as may be possible in the judgment of the provisional President. From this rule are excepted those States that have within two years had democratic campaigns for change of government, since in those States the person who was the candidate of the people will be considered as the provisional governor, provided he adheres actively to this plan.

In case the provisional President has not made the appointment of governor, this appointment has not reached its destination, or the person appointed does not accept for any reason, then the governor shall be designated by the vote of all the commanding officers who operate in the territory of the respective State, on condition that his appointment be ratified by the provisional President as soon as may be possible.

Eleventh. The new authorities will dispose of all the funds found in the public offices for the ordinary expenses of administration and for the expenses of the war, keeping accounts with due scrupulousness. In case the funds are not sufficient for the expenses of the war they shall contract for loans, either voluntary or forced, these latter only with citizens or national institutions. Of these loans scrupulous account shall also be kept and receipts in due form shall be given to the parties in interest, to the end that when the revolution triumphs the amounts loaned may be returned to them.

Transitory.—(a) The officers of the volunteer forces shall assume the grade that corresponds to the number of the forces under their command; in case military and volunteer forces operate together, the officer of the higher grade shall have the command of them, but in case both officers have the same grade the command shall belong to the military officer.

Civil officers shall have said grade while the war lasts, and, once it is ended, those appointments, on application of the parties in interest, shall be revised by the war department, which shall ratify them in their grade or reject them, according to their merits.

(b) All officers, civil as well as military, shall enforce the strictest discipline over their troops, and they shall be responsible to the provisional government for the misdeeds committed by the forces under their command, unless they show it was impossible for them to restrain their soldiers and that they had inflicted on the guilty the punishment they deserved.

(c) If the forces and authorities that sustain Gen. Díaz shoot prisoners of war, not for that reason nor by way of reprisal shall the same thing be done with theirs who fall in our hands; but, in exchange, the civil or military authorities in the service of Gen. Díaz who, once the revolution is started, have ordered, in any manner disposed, transmitted the order, or shot any of our soldiers shall be shot within 24 hours after a summary trial.

Not even the highest functionaries shall be exempted from this penalty. The only exception shall be Gen. Díaz and his ministers, on whom the same penalty shall be inflicted in case they order said executions or permit them, but after having been tried by the tribunals of the Republic, when the revolution has terminated.

In case Gen. Díaz orders that the laws of war be respected and that the prisoners who fall in his hands be treated with humanity, his life shall be spared, but in every event he must answer before the tribunals as to how he has managed the funds of the nation and as to how he has complied with the law.

(d) As an indispensable requisite in the laws of war that belligerent troops wear some uniform or distinguishing mark, and as it would be difficult to uniform the numerous forces of the people who are going to take part in the conflict, a tricolored ribbon on the hat or on the arm shall be adopted as the distinguishing mark of all the liberating forces.

Fellow citizens, if I call upon you to take up arms and overthrow the government of Gen. Díaz, it is not only because of the unwarranted act he committed during the last elections, but to save the country from the gloomy future that awaits it under his dictatorship and under the government of the nefarious scientific oligarchy which, without scruple and in great haste, are absorbing and wasting the national resources, and, if we permit him to continue in power, in a very short time they will have completed their work; they will have led the people into ignominy and will have degraded them; they will have sucked all their wealth and left them in the most absolute misery; they will have caused the bankruptcy of our finances and the dishonor of our country which, weak, impoverished, and manacled, will find itself without arms to defend its frontiers, its honor, and its institutions.

In so far as concerns me, I have a tranquil conscience, and no one can accuse me of promoting the revolution for personal ends, for it is within the knowledge of the nation that I did everything possible to reach a peaceable arrangement and was disposed even to resign my candidacy, provided Gen. Díaz had permitted the nation to designate although it be the vice president of the Republic; but, dominated by incomprehensible pride and unheard-of haughtiness, he did not heed the voice of the Fatherland and preferred to precipitate it into a revolution rather than yield a point; rather than return to the people an atom of their rights; rather than comply, even at the end of his life, with a part of the promises he made at Noria and Tuxtepec.

He himself justified the present revolution when he said, "Let no citizen impose and perpetuate himself in the exercise of power, and this will be the last revolution."

If the interests of the Fatherland had had greater weight in the mind of Gen. Díaz than the sordid interests of himself and his advisers, he would have avoided this revolution by making some concessions to the people; but, since he did not do so . . . so much the better; . . . the change will be more rapid and more radical, since the Mexican people, instead of lamenting like a coward, will accept the challenge like a brave man, and now, when Gen. Díaz proposes to rely on brute force to impose an ignominious yoke upon them, the people will have recourse to the same force to shake off that yoke, to eject that woeful man from power, and to recover their liberty.

San Luis Potosí, October 5, 1910. Francisco I. Madero.

READING 3 *Carranza's Plan of Guadalupe*

Introductory Note

With the death of Madero, Venustiano Carranza (1859–1920), governor of the state of Coahuila, issued his Plan of Guadalupe *on March 26, 1913. The Plan repudiated Victoriano Huerta's (1854–1916) assumption of power and designated Carranza as "First Chief" of a Constitutionalist Army. It marked the beginning of an anti-Huerta campaign by an unstable Constitutionalist coalition of regional forces which led to Huerta's resignation in July 1914. The plan is significant in that it refers even less to Mexico's social and economic problems than did Madero's* Plan of San Luis Potosí. *Carranza became president of Mexico in February 1915.*

Declaration to the Nation

Whereas, General Victoriano Huerta—to whom Francisco I. Madero, Constitutional President of Mexico, entrusted the defense of the institutions and the legality of his Government—on uniting with the rebel enemies in arms opposing the same Government, to restore the former dictatorship, committed the crime of treason to reach power, by arresting the President and Vice President, as well as the members of the Cabinet, forcing them under duress to resign their posts, as shown by messages addressed by the same General Huerta to governors of the States, advising them that he had the Chief Executive of the Republic and the Cabinet as his prisoners; and,

Papers Relating to the Foreign Relations of the United States (Washington: Government Printing Office, 1922), pp. 589–90.

Whereas, the legislative and judicial powers have recognized and protected General Huerta and his illegal and anti-patriotic proceedings, contrary to constitutional laws and precepts; and,

Whereas, several governors of States of the Republic have recognized the illegitimate government imposed by that part of the army which consummated the treason, headed by the aforesaid General Huerta, notwithstanding that the sovereignty of those very states, whose governors should have been the first to repudiate Huerta, had been violated—

We, the undersigned, chiefs and officers commanding the Constitutional forces, have agreed upon, and will sustain with arms, the following:

Plan

1. General Victoriano Huerta is hereby repudiated as President of the Republic.

2. The Legislative and Judicial Powers of the Federation are also hereby disowned.

3. The Governors of the States who still recognize the federal powers of the present administration shall be repudiated 30 days after the publication of this Plan.

4. For the purpose of organizing the army which is to see that our aims are carried out, we name Venustiano Carranza, now Governor of the State of Coahuila, as First Chief of the army, which is to be called Constitutionalist Army.

5. Upon the occupation of the City of Mexico by the Constitutionalist Army, the executive power shall be vested in Venustiano Carranza, its First Chief, or in the person who may substitute him in command.

6. The Provisional Trustee of the Executive Power of the Republic shall convene general elections as soon as peace is restored, and will surrender the power to the citizen who is elected.

The citizen who may act as First Chief of the Constitutionalist Army in the States whose governments may have recognized that of Huerta shall take charge of the provisional government and shall convene local elections, after the citizens elected to discharge the high powers of the federation have entered into the performance of their duties, as provided in the foregoing bases.

READING 4 *Carranza's Protests Against the Veracruz Occupation*

Introductory Note

During April 1914 the American military occupied Veracruz, not without casualties on both sides, including several Mexican naval cadets. Both Carranza and Huerta, political and military opponents during the revolution—then in its violent stages—issued strong denunciations of the occupation and demanded the withdrawal of American troops.

Carranza's statements reflect the underlying anti-foreign dimension of Mexican nationalism at the time. The Veracruz occupation is the central incident in United States-Mexican relations which undermined President Woodrow Wilson's attempts to establish a new basis for Pan-Americanism, based upon nonintervention.

In answer to the message of Secretary of State Bryan, which was communicated to me through you, please transmit to Mr. Bryan the following note addressed to President Wilson:

"Pending the action of the American Senate on Your Excellency's message directed to that body, caused by the lamentable incident which occurred between the crew of a whaleboat of the

Translated from Isidro Fabela, *Historia diplomática de la revolución mexicana* (México: Fondo de Cultura Económica, 1958), Vol. I, pp. 355–58.

cruiser Dolphin and the soldiers of the usurper Huerta, certain acts of hostility have been executed by the naval forces under the command of Admiral Fletcher at the port of Vera Cruz. In view of this violation of the national sovereignty, which the Constitutionalist Government did not expect from a Government which had reiterated its desire to maintain peace with the Mexican people, I comply with a duty of high patriotism in directing this note to you with a view of exhausting all honorable means before two friendly powers sever the pacific relations that still unite them.

"The Mexican nation—the real people of Mexico—have not recognized as their executive a man who has sought to blemish the national integrity, drowning its free institutions in blood. Consequently the acts of the usurper Huerta and his accomplices do not signify legitimate acts of sovereignty; they do not constitute real public functions of domestic and foreign relations; and much less do they represent the sentiments of the Mexican nation, which are of fraternity toward the American people. The lack of representative character in General Victoriano Huerta as concerns the relations of Mexico with the United States as well as with Argentina, Brazil, Chile, and Cuba has been clearly established by the justifiable attitude of these nations, that have refused to recognize the usurper, thus lending a valuable moral support to the noble cause that I represent.

"The usurped title of 'President of the Republic' cannot invest General Huerta with the right to receive a demand for reparation on the part of the Government of the United States, nor the right to grant a satisfaction if this is due.

"Victoriano Huerta is a culprit amenable to the jurisdiction of the Constitutionalist Government, today the only one, in the abnormal circumstances of our nation, which represents the national sovereignty in accord with article 128 of the Political Constitution of Mexico. The illegal acts committed by the usurper and his partisans, and those which they may yet perpetrate, be they of an international character such as those that recently occurred at the port of Tampico, or of a domestic character, will be tried and punished with inflexibility and promptness by the tribunals of the Constitutionalist Government.

"The individual acts of Victoriano Huerta will never be sufficient to involve the Mexican nation in a disastrous war with the United States, because there is no solidarity whatever between the so-called Government of Victoriano Huerta and the Mexican nation, for the fundamental reason that he is not the legitimate organ of our national sovereignty.

"But the invasion of our territory and the stay of your forces in the port of Vera Cruz, violating the rights that constitute our existence as a free and independent sovereign entity, may indeed drag us into an unequal war, with dignity but which until today we have desired to avoid.

"In the face of the real situation of Mexico—weak in comparison with the formidable power of the American nation and weaker than ever after three years of bloody strife—and considering the acts committed at Vera Cruz to be highly offensive to the dignity and independence of Mexico, contrary to your repeated declarations of not desiring to disturb the state of peace and friendship with the Mexican nation, and contrary also to the resolution of the American Senate, which has just declared that the United States does not assume any attitude inimical to the Mexican people and does not purpose to levy war against them; considering also that the hostile acts already committed exceed those required by equity to the end desired, which may be held to be satisfied; considering, furthermore, that it is not the usurper who should have the right to make reparation; I interpret the sentiment of the great majority of the Mexican people, so jealous of its rights and so respectful of the rights of foreigners, and invite you only to suspend the hostile acts already begun, to order your forces to evacuate all places that they hold in the port of Vera Cruz, and to present to the Constitutionalist Government—which I as Constitutional Governor of the State of Coahuila and First Chief of the Constitutionalist Army represent—the demand on the part of the United States in regard to acts recently committed at the port of Tampico, in the security that the demand will be considered in a spirit of elevated justice and conciliation.

V. Carranza,
The Constitutional Governor of the State of Coahuila,
and First Chief of the Constitutionalist Army."

READING 5 *The Mexican Constitution of 1917 and Anti-Clericalism*

Introductory Note

The secular overtones of Mexican nationalism are distinct in articles 3, 27, and 130 of the 1917 Constitution. Through article 3, the revolutionary leaders sought once and for all to reform Church control over the minds of children and to establish a new secular foundation for education and social change. Other issues at stake at this level of Mexican nationalism were clerical property rights and civil authority—also sharply proscribed by articles 27 and 130.

Revolutions are in part sustained by crystallized discontent and struggle against a common enemy. This proposition helps to explain anti-clericalism in Mexico which tended to unite revolutionary groups and give direction to the revolution.

ARTICLE 3 OF THE MEXICAN CONSTITUTION 1917 VERSION

Art. 3. Instruction is free; that given in public institutions of learning shall be secular. Primary instruction, whether higher or lower, given in private institutions shall likewise be secular.

Article 3, in its original form, is found in *Annals of the American Academy of Political and Social Science*, Supplement, May 1917, "The Mexican Constitution of 1917 Compared with the Constitution of 1857" (Philadelphia, 1917), p. 2; articles 27 and 130 are excerpted from *Political Constitution of the Mexican United States* (México: Cámara de Senadores, 1962), pp. 176–77; 231–32.

No religious corporation nor minister of any religious creed shall establish or direct schools of primary instruction. Private primary schools may be established only subject to official supervision.

Primary instruction in public institutions shall be gratuitous.

From Article 27

Religious institutions known as churches, regardless of creed, may in no case acquire, hold, or administer real property or hold mortgages thereon; such property held at present either directly or through an intermediary shall revert to the Nation, any person whosoever being authorized to denounce any property so held. Presumptive evidence shall be sufficient to declare the denunciation well founded. Places of public worship are the property of the Nation, as represented by the Federal Government, which shall determine which of them may continue to be devoted to their present purposes. Bishoprics, rectories, seminaries, asylums, and schools belonging to religious orders, convents, or any other buildings built or intended for the administration, propagation, or teaching of a religious creed shall at once become the property of the Nation by inherent right, to be used exclusively for the public services of the Federal or State Governments, within their respective jurisdictions. All places of public worship hereafter erected shall be the property of the Nation. . . .

Article 130

The Federal Powers shall exercise the supervision required by law in matters relating to religious worship and outward ecclesiastical forms. Other authorities shall act as auxiliaries of the Federation.

Congress cannot enact laws establishing or prohibiting any religion.

Marriage is a civil contract. This and other acts of a civil nature concerning persons are within the exclusive competence of civil officials and authorities, in the manner prescribed by law, and shall have the force and validity defined by said law. . . .

The law does not recognize any personality in religious groups called churches.

Ministers of denominations shall be considered as persons who practice a profession and shall be directly subject to the laws enacted on such matters.

Only the legislatures of the States shall have the power to determine the maximum number of ministers of denominations necessary for local needs.

To practice the ministry of any denomination in the United Mexican States it is necessary to be a Mexican by birth.

Ministers of denominations may never, in a public or private meeting constituting an assembly, or in acts of worship or religious propaganda, criticize the fundamental laws of the country or the authorities of the Government, specifically or generally. They shall not have an active or passive vote nor the right to form associations for religious purposes.

Permission to dedicate new places of worship open to the public must be obtained from the Secretariat of Government, with previous consent of the government of the State. There must be in every church building a representative who is responsible to the authorities for compliance with the laws on religious worship in such building, and for the objects pertaining to the worship. . . .

The formation of any kind of political group, the name of which contains any word or indication whatever that it is related to any religious denomination, is strictly prohibited. Meetings of a political character may not be held in places of worship.

A minister of any denomination may not himself or through an intermediary inherit or receive any real property occupied by any association for religious propaganda or for religious or charitable purposes. Ministers of denominations are legally incapacitated as testamentary heirs of ministers of the same denomination or of any private person who is not related to them within the fourth degree.

The acquisition by private parties of personal or real property owned by the clergy or by religious organizations shall be governed by Article 27 of this Constitution.

Trials for violation of the above provisions shall never be heard before a jury. . . .

READING 6 *Calles and Enforcement of Anti-Clericalism*

Introductory Note

In 1926 the government of Plutarco Elías Calles (1877–1945) began strict enforcement of the anti-clerical articles in the 1917 Constitution. Prior to this period, they had not been rigorously applied. In retaliation against Calles's prohibition against foreign priests, closure of religious schools, and requirement that priests register with local authorities, priests went on a three-year strike after 1926. They refused to perform traditional ceremonies of marriage, burial, or baptism; other pro-Catholic groups, including the Cristeros, launched a violent program of attacks on federal troops and school teachers throughout Mexico.

The ministry returned to its regular services in 1929, although Church-State relations were not stable until the presidency of Lázaro Cárdenas. The Calles government's view of the situation before and after 1926 is reflected partially in the following statement by Arturo M. Elias, consul-general of Mexico in the United States, 1926.

The incontrovertible evidence from the records of Mexican history shows that the century-long struggle of its people for freedom has always been opposed by the Church Hierarchy. Religious doctrines have never been involved, as they were in the

Arturo M. Elias, *The Mexican People and the Church* (New York: Published by the Author, December 1926), pp. 43–50.

Reformation in Europe. The Ecclesiastical Establishment sought to retain its special privileges gained under Spanish rule and thus to dominate the lives of the people of Mexico.

The same records show the Church Hierarchy to have supported every President or Dictator who opposed religious liberty and championed ecclesiastic privileges and to have opposed every President who in the slightest degree stood for religious liberty or any curtailment of the special privileges of the Church.

The records also show the Church Hierarchy in opposition to every attempt made to give the people a larger measure of control over their affairs, and reveal the clergy always on the side of centralized power as against the Federal system, such as exists in the United States of America. . . .

Then came the unexpected agrarian revolt in 1910 led by Madero, and the flight of Díaz, followed by the election of Madero as President. All the Democratic principles so obnoxious to the Clericals were championed by the new President. They threw all the power they had regained during the long rule of Díaz against the Madero administration, and when the agrarian leader was murdered, they supported the administration of the reactionary Victoriano Huerta, helping to supply him with funds.

But the rising tide of democracy had been only checked for a short period, and the Constitutionalists challenged the rule of the usurping militarist, Huerta, and drove him from the country. The Church Hierarchy was sternly dealt with, and edicts were issued against the exercise of their special privileges. When the new Constitution was adopted at Querétaro in 1917, the laws dealing with the Church as promulgated in 1857, 1859 and 1874 were reiterated and amplified. Some new provisions were added to meet new conditions. . . .

READING 7 *Zapata's Plan of Ayala*

Introductory Note

Where Madero neglected the social aspects of the revolution, Emiliano Zapata (1880–1919) demanded an immediate return of the village lands despoiled by the large landowners. Disillusioned by the Madero political reforms, Zapata determined to make his own decisions and refused to recognize the Madero government. On November 28, 1911, barely one month after Madero had been proclaimed president, Zapata issued his now famous Plan de Ayala. *He denounced Madero as a traitor for cooperating with Díaz politicians and wealthy hacendados, part of Madero's early program of building a coalition government.*

Liberating Plan of the sons of the State of Morelos, affiliated with the Insurgent Army which defends the fulfillment of the Plan of San Luis Potosí, with the reforms which it has believed proper to add in benefit of the Mexican Fatherland.

We who undersign, constituted as a revolutionary junta to sustain and carry out the promises which the revolution of November 20, 1910, just past, declare solemnly before the face of the civilized world which judges us and before the nation to which we belong propositions which we have formulated to end the

Translated from José D. Silva, *Fuente de Información de la Revolución Mexicana: Plan de Ayala* (México, 1957), pp. 30–33. A number of versions of Zapata's *Plan de Ayala* exist. These versions vary slightly in wording, spellings, grammar, and signatories, but they are essentially the same in content and emphasis. All are somewhat crudely written and this translation indicates something of the loose construction and unpolished nature of the Plan.

tyranny which oppresses us and redeem the fatherland from the dictatorships which are imposed on us, which are determined in the following plan:

1. Taking into consideration that the Mexican people led by Don Francisco I. Madero went to shed their blood to reconquer liberties and recover their rights, and not for a man to take possession of power, violating the sacred principles which he swore to defend under the slogans "Effective Suffrage" "No Reelection," outraging thus the faith, the cause, the justice, and the liberties of the people, taking into consideration that that man to whom we refer is Don Francisco I. Madero, the same who initiated the precipitated revolution, who as a man imposed his will and influence as a governing norm on the Provisional Government of the ex-President of the Republic Licenciado Francisco L. de la Barra, for having declared the freedom of the people, causing with this deed repeated sheddings of blood and many misfortunes for the fatherland in a deceitful and ridiculous manner, having no intentions other than satisfying his personal ambitions, his boundless instincts as a tyrant, and his profound disrespect for the fulfillment of the preexisting laws emanating from the immoral code of '57, written with the revolutionary blood of Ayutla;

Taking into account that the so-called Chief of the Liberating Revolution of Mexico, Don Francisco I. Madero, did not carry to a happy end the revolution which he gloriously initiated with the help of God and the people, since he left standing most of the governing powers and corrupted elements of oppression of the dictatorial government of Porfirio Díaz, which are not nor can in any way be the representation of National Sovereignty, and which, for being most bitter adversaries of ours and of the principles which even now we defend, are provoking the discomfort of the country and opening new wounds in the bosom of the fatherland, to give it its own blood to drink; taking also into account that the aforementioned Sr. Don Francisco I. Madero, present President of the Republic, tries to avoid the fulfillment of the promises which he made to the Nation in the Plan of San Luis Potosí, restricting the above-cited promises to the agreements of Ciudad Juárez, nullifying, pursuing, jailing, or killing revolutionary elements who helped him to occupy the high post of the President of the Republic, by means of false promises and numerous intrigues against the Nation.

Taking into consideration that the oft-mentioned Don Francisco I. Madero has tried to shut up with the brute force of bayonets and to drown in blood the people who ask, solicit, or demand from him the fulfillment of the promises of the revolution, calling them bandits and rebels, condemning them to a war of extermination without conceding or granting any of the guarantees which reason, justice, and law prescribe; taking equally into consideration that the President of the Republic Don Francisco I. Madero, making mockery of the people, has imposed against the will of the people Licenciado José María Pino Suárez in the vice-presidency of the Republic, or as governors of the State those designated by him, such as General Ambrosio Figueroa, scourge and tyrant of the people of Morelos, or entering into scandalous co-operation with the *Científico* Party, feudal landlords, and oppressive political leaders, enemies of the revolution which he himself proclaimed in order to forge new chains and follow the mold of a more shameful and more terrible dictatorship than that of Porfirio Díaz; for it has been clear and patent that he has outraged the sovereignty of the States, trampling on the laws without any respect for lives or interests, as happened in the State of Morelos, and others, leading them to the most horrendous anarchy which contemporary history registers.

For these considerations we declare the aforementioned Francisco I. Madero inept at carrying out the promises of the revolution of which he was the author, because he has betrayed the principles with which he tricked the will of the people and was able to get into power, incapable of governing, because he has no respect for the law and justice of the peoples; and a traitor to the fatherland, because he is humiliating Mexicans who want liberties in blood and fire, so as to please the *científicos* (a small coterie of advisers to Díaz), landlords, and political leaders who enslave us; and from today on we begin to pursue the revolution he began until we attain the overthrow of the dictatorial powers which exist.

2. Sr. Francisco I. Madero is disavowed as Chief of the Revolution and as President of the Republic, for the reasons which before were expressed, aiming at the overthrow of this functionary.

3. General Pascual Orozco, the second of the *caudillo* (political leader) Don Francisco I. Madero, is recognized as Chief of the Liberating Revolution, and in case he does not accept this delicate post, General Don Emiliano Zapata is recognized as chief of the Revolution.

4. The Revolutionary Junta of the State of Morelos manifests to the Nation under formal oath, that it takes as its own the plan of San Luis Potosí, with the additions which are expressed below in benefit of the oppressed peoples, and it will make itself the defender of the principles it defends until victory or death.

5. The Revolutionary Junta of the State of Morelos will not admit dealings nor compromises until it achieves the overthrow of the dictatorial elements of Porfirio Díaz and Francisco I. Madero, for the nation is tired of false men and traitors who make promises like liberators and on attaining power forget them and constitute themselves as tyrants.

6. As an additional part of the plan we invoke, we record: that the lands, forests, and water which the landlords, *científicos,* or political bosses have usurped, in the shadow of venal justice, the people or citizens who have the titles to those properties will immediately take possession of that real estate of which they have been deprived by the bad faith of our oppressors, maintaining at any price with arms in hand the mentioned possession; and the usurpers who consider themselves with a right to the properties will carry it to the special tribunals which will be established on the triumph of the revolution.

7. In virtue of the fact that the immense majority of the Mexican people and citizens are owners of no more than the land they walk on, without being able to improve their social condition in any way or to dedicate themselves to industry, or agriculture, because lands, forests, and water are monopolized in a few hands, for this reason the third part of those monopolies will be expropriated from their powerful proprietors, with prior indemnization,

in order that the people and citizens of Mexico may obtain *ejidos,* colonies, and legal rural property for peoples, or fields for sowing or tilling, and that the lack of prosperity and well-being of Mexicans may improve in all and for all.

8. The landlords, *científicos,* or political leaders who oppose the present plan directly or indirectly will have their goods nationalized and the two-third parts belonging to them will go for war indemnizations, pensions for widows and orphans of the victims who succumb in the struggle for the present plan.

9. In order to execute the procedures regarding the aforementioned properties, the laws of disamortization and nationalization will be applied as they coincide, as norm and example, will be those laws on ecclesiastical properties put in force by the immortal Juárez, which punished the despots and conservatives who in all time have tried to impose on us the ignominious yoke of oppression and backwardness.

10. The insurgent military chiefs of the Republic who rose up with arms in hand at the call of Don Francisco I. Madero to defend the plan of San Luis Potosí, and who oppose with force the present plan, will be judged traitors to the cause which they defended and to the fatherland, since at present many of them, to humor the tyrants, for a fistful of money, or for bribes or connivance, are shedding the blood of their brothers who claim the fulfillment of the promises which Don Francisco I. Madero made to the nation.

11. The costs of war will be taken in conformity with article 11 of the Plan of San Luis Potosí, and all procedures employed in the revolution we undertake will be in conformity with the same instructions which the mentioned plan determines.

12. Once the revolution which we are carrying along into the path of reality is triumphant, a Junta of the principal revolutionary chiefs from the different States will name or designate an interim President of the Republic, who will convoke elections for the organization of the federal powers.

13. The principal revolutionary chiefs of each State in Junta will designate the Governor of the State to which they belong, and this elevated official will convoke elections for the due

organization of the public powers, with the object of avoiding compulsory appointments which work the misfortune of the peoples, like the well-known appointment of Ambrosio Figueroa in the State of Morelos, and others who drive us to the precipice of bloody conflicts, sustained by the dictator Madero and the circle of *científicos* and landlords who have influenced him.

14. If President Madero and other dictatorial elements of the present and former regime want to avoid the immense misfortunes which afflict the fatherland and possess true sentiments of love toward it, let them make immediate renunciation of the posts they occupy and with that, they will close up the grave wounds which they have opened in the bosom of the fatherland, since, if they do not do so, the blood and the anathema of our brothers will fall on their heads.

15. Mexicans: consider that the cunning and bad faith of one man is shedding blood in a scandalous manner, because he is incapable of governing; consider that his system of government is choking the fatherland and trampling with the brute force of bayonets on our institutions; and thus, as we raised up our weapons to elevate him to power, we again raise them up against him for defaulting on his promises with the Mexican people and for having betrayed the revolution initiated by him; we are not personalists, we are partisans of principles and not of men!

Mexican People, support this plan with arms in hand and you will assure the prosperity and well-being of the fatherland.

Liberty, Justice, and Law.
Ayala, November 25, 1911.

READING 8 *Carranza's Land and Labor Decrees*

Introductory Note

Under intense competition for political and military support in late 1914 and early 1915, Carranza—with his back literally against the sea in Veracruz—issued his now famous decree of December 12, 1914. Article 20 of Carranza's program, which follows, indicates that, at last, the social reform motives of the revolution were given powerful political force, long after the Plans of San Luis Potosí and Guadalupe had paid them little attention (Selection 8.1). Later, Carranza authorized Álvaro Obregón (1880–1928) to enter into negotiations with the labor unions of Mexico City; he subsequently signed an agreement with them in February 1915 which also follows (Selection 8.2).

Selection 8.1: Article 20 of Carranza's Program

The first chief of the revolution in charge of the executive power will expedite and put in force during the struggle all the laws, measures, and means destined to give satisfaction to the economic, social, and political needs of the land, effecting the re-

Article 20 of Carranza's December 1914 decree and the "Agreement Between the Constitutionalist Government [Carranza] and the *Casa del Obrero Mundial* [House of the World Worker, Mexican Labor unions] may be found in English, in Frank Tannenbaum, *The Mexican Agrarian Revolution* (New York: The Macmillan Company, 1929), pp. 167–70.

forms which are demanded as indispensable by public opinion for the purpose of establishing a regime that will guarantee the equality of the Mexicans among themselves; agrarian laws favoring the formation of small property, dissolving the large estates and restoring to the villages the lands of which they were unjustly deprived; fiscal laws destined to obtain an equitable system of taxation for rural property; legislation for the purposes of bettering the condition of the rural *peón,* of the worker, of the miner, and in general of the working classes; the establishment of free municipal government as a constitutional institution; a basis for a new system for the organization of the army, electoral reforms for the purposes of obtaining effective suffrage, organization of an independent judiciary in the federal as well as in the state governments; revision of the laws relating to matrimony and the civil status of persons; measures that will guarantee the strict enforcement of the laws of reform; revision of the civil, penal, and commercial code to make more expeditious and effective the administration of justice; revision of the laws relating to the exploitation of mines, oil, water, forests, and other natural resources of the country for the purpose of destroying monopolies created by the ancient regime and to eliminate and to prevent the formation of others in the future; political reforms that will guarantee the true application of the constitution of the republic and in general all other laws that are necessary for the purpose of assuring to all the inhabitants of the land an effective and full enjoyment of their rights and their equality before the law.

Selection 8.2: Agreement Between the Constitutionalist Government and the Casa del Obrero Mundial

As the workers of the *Casa del Obrero Mundial* are supporting the Constitutionalist government headed by Citizen V. Carranza, we hereby declare that the following terms are to govern the relations between the said government and the workers and between them and it bearing on the manner in which the workers shall collaborate with the Constitutionalist cause: In witness whereof we subscribe our signatures to this document: For the *Casa del Obrero Mundial,* the citizens Rafael Quintero, Carlos M. Rincón, Rosendo Salazar, Juan Tudo, Salvador Gonzalo García, Rodolfo Aguirre, Roberto Valdéz and Celestino Gasca nominated on a sub-committee appearing before the First Chief of the Constitutionalist Army and exercising executive power conferred upon it by the Revolutionary Committee of Mexico City, which in turn represents the *Casa del Obrero Mundial,* and by Rafael Zubarán Capmany, Secretary of the government and representing the above-mentioned First Chief:

1. The Constitutionalist government reiterates its decree of November 4 of last year to include the conditions of the workers by the means of appropriate laws, enacting, during the struggle, every necessary law to carry out the said resolution.

2. The workers of the *Casa del Obrero Mundial* with the object of hastening the triumph of the Constitutionalists of the Revolution and of disseminating its ideals touching social reform and avoiding unnecessary bloodshed wherever possible, hereby declare the resolutions they have taken to collaborate in an effective and practical manner toward the triumph of the revolution, taking up arms both to garrison the towns in possession of the Constitutionalist government and to combat the reaction.

3. In order to carry out the proposed undertakings set forth in the two former clauses, the Constitutionalist government will attend with all the solicitude it has used up to date, to the workers' just claims arising from their labor contracts with their employers.

4. In towns occupied by the Constitutionalist army, and, in order that it may be free to attend to the needs of carrying on the campaign, the workers will organize in accordance with the military commander of each place, to hold it and preserve order. In case of the evacuation of towns the Constitutionalist government through the respective military commander will advise the workers of its intention, giving them every facility to reconcentrate in the places occupied by the Constitutionalist forces.

The Constitutionalist government in case of reconcentration will help the workers either by remunerating them for work actually done, or, under the caption of "solidarity" aid whenever work cannot be provided, so that they may attend to their principal means of subsistence.

5. The workers of the *Casa del Obrero Mundial* will draw up lists in every town where they are organized, and immediately in the City of Mexico, which lists shall include the names of all their comrades who agree to comply with the undertakings stated in clause 2; these lists, immediately upon completion, shall be sent to the First Court of the Constitutionalist government, so that this court may know the number of workers ready to take up arms.

6. The workers of the *Casa del Obrero Mundial* shall carry on an active propaganda to win sympathy for the Constitutionalist government among all the workers throughout the republic and the working-class world, pointing out to Mexican workingmen the advantages of joining the revolution inasmuch as it will bring about the improvement the working class is seeking through its unions.

7. The workers shall establish centers of revolutionary committees, in every place they deem it convenient to do so; these committees, besides doing propaganda work, will look after the organization of labor groups and toward their collaboration with the Constitutionalist cause.

8. The Constitutionalist government will establish, in case of necessity, labor colonies in the zones it may control to serve as places of refuge for the families of the workers who may have taken up arms or who may have in any other practical form shown their adhesion to the Constitutionalist cause.

9. The workers who take up arms in the Constitutionalist government, and also the female workers who perform service in aiding or attending the wounded, or other similar service, will be known under the one denomination whether organized in companies, battalions, regiments, brigades, or divisions, all will be designated as "reds."

Constitution and reform.
Rafael Zubarán Capmany
Rafael Quintero
Carlos M. Rincón
Rosendo Salazar
Juan Tudo

Health and Social Revolution.
Salvador Gonzalo García
Rodolfo Aguirre
Roberto Valdéz
Celestino Gasca

Veracruz, February 17, 1915.

READING 9 *The Constitution of 1917—Articles 27 and 123*

Introductory Note

The Constitution of 1917 gave legal expression to the social side of Mexico's Revolution and developing nationalism. It legitimized the agrarian reform drive, the rise of labor organizations, and the interest in secular education. These pressures for change fostered an open, ad hoc *nationalist ideology, characterized by a new emphasis on public policy, social justice, and social security in 1917.*

While the Constitution reiterates the objectives of democratic government enunciated in 1857, for example, freedom of association, speech, worship, universal suffrage, separation of power, and right to property, it modified these individual rights by a shift to collective social rights and state obligation to insure them. For the first time, essentially social guarantees were consigned to a Mexican constitution, and agrarian reform, labor reform, and education reforms replaced social privilege and laissez-faire individualism. The new orientation in democratic socialism well complemented the new faces of Mexican nationalism.

ARTICLE 27

Ownership of the lands and waters within the boundaries of the national territory is vested originally in the Nation, which has

Articles 27 and 123 are excerpted from *Political Constitution of the Mexican United States* (México: Cámara de Senadores, 1962), pp. 173–74; 176; 178–80; 224–26.

had, and has, the right to transmit title thereof to private persons, thereby constituting private property.

Private property shall not be expropriated except for reasons of public use and subject to payment of indemnity.

The Nation shall at all times have the right to impose on private property such limitations as the public interest may demand, as well as the right to regulate the utilization of natural resources which are susceptible of appropriation, in order to conserve them and to ensure a more equitable distribution of public wealth. With this end in view, necessary measures shall be taken to divide up large landed estates; to develop small landed holdings in operation; to create new agricultural centers, with necessary lands and waters; to encourage agriculture in general and to prevent the destruction of natural resources, and to protect property from damage to the detriment of society. Centers of population which at present either have no lands or water or which do not possess them in sufficient quantities for the needs of their inhabitants, shall be entitled to grants thereof, which shall be taken from adjacent properties, the rights of small landed holdings in operation being respected at all times. . . .

Legal capacity to acquire ownership of lands and waters of the Nation shall be governed by the following provisions:

I. Only Mexicans by birth or naturalization and Mexican companies have the right to acquire ownership of lands, waters, and their appurtenances, or to obtain concessions for the exploitation of mines or of waters. The State may grant the same right to foreigners, provided they agree before the Ministry of Foreign Relations to consider themselves as nationals in respect to such property, and bind themselves not to invoke the protection of their governments in matters relating thereto; under penalty, in case of noncompliance with this agreement, of forfeiture of the property acquired to the Nation. Under no circumstances may foreigners acquire direct ownership of lands or waters within a zone of one hundred kilometers along the frontiers and of fifty kilometers along the shores of the country. . . .

VII. The centers of population which, by law or in fact, possess a communal status shall have legal capacity to enjoy common possession of the lands, forests, and waters belonging to them or which have or may be restored to them.

All questions, regardless of their origin, concerning the boundaries of communal lands, which are now pending or that may arise hereafter between two or more centers of population, are matters of federal jurisdiction. The Federal Executive shall take cognizance of such controversies and propose a solution to the interested parties. If the latter agree thereto, the proposal of the Executive shall take full effect as a final decision and shall be irrevocable; should they not be in conformity, the party or parties may appeal to the Supreme Court of Justice of the Nation, without prejudice to immediate enforcement of the presidential proposal. . . .

X. Centers of population which lack communal lands (*ejidos*) or which are unable to have them restored to them due to lack of titles, impossibility of identification, or because they had been legally transferred, shall be granted sufficient lands and waters to constitute them, in accordance with the needs of the population; but in no case shall they fail to be granted the area needed, and for this purpose the land needed shall be expropriated, at the expense of the Federal Government, to be taken from lands adjoining the villages in question.

The area or individual unit of the grant shall hereafter be not less than ten hectares of moist or irrigated land, or in default of such land its equivalent in other types of land in accordance with the third paragraph of section XV of this article.

XI. For the purpose of carrying out the provisions of this article and of regulating laws that may be enacted, the following are established:

(a) A direct agency of the Federal Executive entrusted with the application and enforcement of the agrarian laws;

(b) An advisory board composed of five persons to be appointed by the President of the Republic and who shall perform the functions specified in the organic laws;

(c) A mixed commission composed of an equal number of representatives of the Federal Government, the local governments, and a representative of the peasants, to be appointed in the manner set forth in the respective regulating law, to function in each State, Territory, and the Federal District, with the powers and duties set forth in the organic and regulatory laws;

(d) Private executive committees for each of the centers of population that are concerned with agrarian cases;

(e) A communal office (*comisariado ejidal*) for each of the centers of population that possess communal lands (*ejidos*). . . .

Article 123

The Congress of the Union, without contravening the following basic principles, shall formulate labor laws which shall apply to:

A. Workers, day laborers, domestic servants, artisans (*obreros, jornaleros, empleados domésticos, artesanos*) and in a general way to all labor contracts:

I. The maximum duration of work for one day shall be eight hours;

II. The maximum duration of night work shall be seven hours. Unhealthful or dangerous work is prohibited for women in general and for young persons under sixteen years of age. Industrial night work is also prohibited for both these classes and they may not work in commercial establishments after ten o'clock at night.

III. Young persons over twelve and less than sixteen years of age shall have a maximum work day of six hours. The labor of children under twelve may not be the subject of a labor contract.

IV. For every six days of work a worker must have at least one day of rest;

V. During the three months prior to childbirth, women shall not perform physical labor that requires excessive material effort. In the month following childbirth they shall necesarily enjoy the benefit of rest and shall receive their full wages and retain their employment and the rights acquired under their labor contract. During the nursing period they shall have two special rest periods each day, of a half hour each, for nursing their infants;

VI. The minimum wage to be received by a worker shall be that which is considered sufficient, according to the conditions of each region, to satisfy the normal needs of his living, education, and honest pleasures, considering him as the head of a family. In every agricultural, commercial, manufacturing, or mining enterprise, the workers shall have the right to participate in the profits, which shall be regulated as indicated in section IX;

VII. Equal wages shall be paid for equal work, regardless of sex or nationality;

VIII. The minimum wage shall be exempt from attachment, compensation, or deduction;

IX. The establishment of a minimum wage and participation in profits, referred to in section VI, shall be done by Special Committees, to be formed in each Municipality, subordinate to the Central Board of Conciliation and Arbitration that shall be established in each State. In the absence of such Committee, the minimum wage shall be fixed by the respective Central Board of Conciliation and Arbitration;

X. Wages must necessarily be paid in money of legal tender and cannot be paid in goods, promissory notes, or any other token intended as a substitute for money;

XI. Whenever, due to extraordinary circumstances, the regular working hours of a day must be increased, one hundred percent shall be added to the amount for normal hours of work as remuneration for the overtime. Overtime work may never exceed three hours a day nor three times consecutively. Persons under sixteen years of age and women of any age may not be admitted to this kind of labor;

XII. In any agricultural, industrial, or mining enterprise or in any other kind of work, employers shall be obliged to furnish workmen comfortable and hygienic living quarters for which they may collect rent that shall not exceed one half percent monthly of the assessed valuation of the property. They also must establish schools, hospitals, and any other services necessary to the community. If the enterprise is situated within a town and employs more than one hundred workers, it shall be responsible for the first of the above obligations; . . .

XIV. Employers shall be responsible for labor accidents and for occupational diseases of workers, contracted because of or in the performance of their work or occupation; therefore, employers shall pay the corresponding indemnification whether death or only temporary or permanent incapacity to work has resulted, in accordance with what the law prescribes. This responsibility shall exist even if the employer contracts for the work through an intermediary;

XV. An employer shall be required to observe, in the installation of his establishments, the legal regulations on hygiene and health, and to adopt adequate measures for the prevention of accidents in the use of machines, instruments, and materials of labor, as well as to organize the same in such a way as to ensure the greatest possible guarantee for the health and safety of workers as is compatible with the nature of the work, under the penalties established by law in this respect;

XVI. Both employers and workers shall have the right to organize for the defense of their respective interests, by forming unions, professional associations, etc;

XVII. The laws shall recognize strikes and lockouts as rights of workmen and employers;

XVIII. Strikes shall be legal when they have as their purpose the attaining of an equilibrium among the various factors of production, by harmonizing the rights of labor with those of capital. In Public services it shall be obligatory for workers to give notice ten days in advance to the Board of Conciliation and Arbitration as to the date agreed upon for the suspension of work. Strikes shall be considered illegal only when the majority of strikers engage in acts of violence against persons or property, or in the event of war, when the workers belong to establishments or services of the Government;

XIX. Lockouts shall be legal only when an excess of production makes it necessary to suspend work to maintain prices at a level with costs, and with prior approval of the Board of Conciliation and Arbitration; . . . .

READING 10 *Policies of Cárdenas—1934-40*

Introductory Note

The Partido Nacional Revolucionario (National Revolutionary Party or PNR) met in late 1933 to endorse the chosen candidate for the coming presidential election—Lázaro Cárdenas. It also adopted a platform for his coming term, the Six Year Plan. While the Plan itself was an imprecise set of objectives, unclear as to how revolutionary goals would be obtained, it indicated a pattern of reform which provided Cárdenas with a basis to legitimize his subsequent programs. In addition to labor and land reform, it strengthened state control over education. The following document, outlining some of Cárdenas's central priorities, reflects the Six Year Plan.

Labor

The aspiration of the Revolution is that every man in every village shall find work, so that human life may be pleasanter, less miserable and nobler in this sense, in that it shall allow the individual to cultivate his physical and intellectual faculties, and therefore to achieve full realization of his own personality.

I should deem it very hard indeed to carry into effect the principles of the Six Year Plan, if I did not rely on the cooperation of organized rural industrial workers, disciplined and united.

The following are excerpts from speeches and declarations made by President Lázaro Cárdenas during his election campaign and during the first year of his term in office. They are in collected form in *Policies of the Present Administration of Mexico* (México: Government Printing Office, Ministry of Foreign Relations, 1936), pp. 11, 13, 17–18, 61–62.

Capitalism never fails to take advantage of a single conflict between labor unions.

Divisions between workers are criminal and sterile in results. Workers and peasants must remove all obstacles in the way of union between them. . . .

Agrarian Reform

The fundamental problem calling for immediate solution is the problem of the Land, as only when distribution of village common lands shall have been completed, and the needs of the villages be satisfied, will that spirit of unremitting effort essential to integral betterment of communities prevail.

The Six Year Plan deals in the first place with the Agrarian problem, and provides that land shall be available to the peasants, and to all men, in areas sufficient not only for solving the economic problems of every family by better diet, clothing and housing, but also to permit of education of children and adults, and to increase farming production as compared with that obtained or obtainable under the regime of land monopoly in few hands. . . .

Educational Reform

The mission of the school is not merely to furnish knowledge, pure and serene, but alien to the pain of the exploited, to the grave problems that affect our fatherland, for science in herself lacks human feeling. To realize this we need only remember the fact that scientific means (poison gas, the radio, all kinds of motors, aircraft, etc.) were all made use of in the great War for the destruction of humanity, which in the name of capitalistic 'justice" threw young men, peasants and workers, into a fight where no quarter was given and in which the sole gainers were commercial interests, that only lusted for power in order to continue to pile up more and more money.

We must stimulate that utilitarian and collectivist teaching that prepares pupils for production, that promotes in them love of work as a social duty; that will instill into them class consciousness so that they shall not forget that the spiritual heritage bestowed on them is intended for service to their class, for they must ever bear in mind that their education is but to fit them for the struggle, and for the success of organization.

Public education once recognized as not only a primary collective service on which depends unity of national feeling and action, but also economic redemption of the workers the State may not shirk its directing position in the revision of programs of educational institutions, both official and private. The Six Year Plan felicitously provides that intervention by the authorities shall not be confined to scientific and pedagogical supervision of school work, but that it shall also endeavor to extirpate that anarchy and ideological chaos provoked by the attacks of the defenders of the past and by the enemies of the tendencies of social solidarity imposed by the Revolution. . . . And consistently with revolutionary standards no religious groups will be allowed to continue to shed its influence over national education. . . .

Education

The amendment to the constitutional provisions governing education was made in 1934, but was not actually enforced until 1935. Said educational amendment makes the first and second stages of education an exclusive power of the State that may be delegated to private individuals, but always under official supervision. It demands, besides excluding all religious teaching, a truthful, scientific and rational answer to each and every one of the questions that must be solved by the mind of the pupils, so as to give them an exact and positive notion of the Universe and of man, as well as of the society in which they live. And the socialistic doctrine that the Mexican Revolution upholds is pointed to, as the official tendency of the education imparted by the State.

Former courses of study have been replaced by new, pursuant to the educational amendment.

During the first year of the present period 16% of the total Budget was appropriated for federal education, which means an increase of almost 50% over the average annual budget for the five previous years. The Six Year Plan provides for a progressive increase of almost 50% over the average annual budget for the amount to 20% of the total expenditures of the Nation.

During the first year of the present administration the number of rural schools was increased by 20% with respect to those existing prior to the taking effect of the Six Year Plan.

Twelve boarding schools for Indians were created, which added to the fifteen previously functioning, mean an increase of 80% in the number of this type of school.

159 schools of the type supported by the employers for their workers' children were created, in compliance with a provision of the Labor Law. There were previously 1980 schools of this class. The increase, in one year, amounts to 8%.

In the Capital of the Republic, the "Revolution School Center" was inaugurated. It is equipped with workshops and to handle a school population of no less than 5,000 children in the primary grades.

With a view to unification of primary educational systems throughout the country, agreements were made in the first year of the period between the Federal Ministry of Education and four local Governments, in addition to the five States that have placed their educational systems under federal control, pending conclusion of the necessary agreements.

All technical schools have been equipped with modern machinery.

The annual appropriation called for by the Six Year Plan was doubled, by founding six regional peasant schools.

Two industrial "Children of the Army" schools, have been established.

A National Council of Higher Education and Scientific Research has been formed that will be entrusted with the task of imparting ideological and pedagogical unity to the institutions for higher culture supported by the State in different parts of the country, and of promoting the advancement of science.

The number of readers at the libraries supported by the Ministry of Education increased by 100%, during the first year of the Six Year Period and two permanent and six traveling libraries have been created, the latter equipped with radio and cinema to tour through rural districts.

READING 11 *Socialist Education— The Cárdenas Years*

Introductory Note

Before a new version of article 3 had been approved by Congress, clear signs of a new political orientation were expressed by General Plutarco Elías Calles, "Supreme Chief" and maker of presidents, and by Lázaro Cárdenas who was designated presidential candidate for the 1934 elections. In July 1934 Calles argued that Mexico's children belonged to the revolution and the Mexican community which must in turn educate them rather than private Church schools. The aim was to forge a "new national soul." [1] *Meanwhile, Cárdenas began to use specific phraseology in citing new guidelines for educational planning. He urged the stimulation of a "utilitarian and collectivist, teaching" in order to prepare students for production and to encourage love of work as a social duty.*[2]

In September 1934 the PNR called for education to be imparted directly by the State and to be founded on the "orientations and postulates of the socialist doctrine that the Mexican Revolution

Translated from Camilo Arias Almaraz and Emma Martínez Dueñez, *Historia de la Educación en México* (México: Instituto de Capacitación del Magisterios, Secretaría de Educación Pública, 1962), Vol. II, pp. 63–64.

1. Partido de Acción Nacional (PAN), *Monopolio Educativo o Unidad Nacional Un Problema de México* (México: Editorial Jus, 1962), pp. 32–33.
2. See Reading Ten.

sustains."[3] *The final version of the 1934 amendment appears in the following document, suggesting that socialism as an ideology in Mexican reforms reached its highest point during the Cárdenas years. This specific version of article 3 was changed in 1946.*

Article 3

The education imparted by the State will be socialist, and in addition to excluding all religious doctrine, it will combat fanaticism and prejudice, for which it will organize its instruction and activities in a form to create in the youth a rational and exact concept of the Universe and of social life.

Only the state, federation, states, municipalities will impart primary, secondary, and normal education.

They may permit authorization to those private schools that wish to impart education in the forementioned grades, in accord in each case with the following norms:

I. The activities and instruction of private institutions will be adjusted, without any exception, to the precepts in the initial paragraph of this article, and they will be headed by persons that in the judgment of the State have sufficient professional preparation, agreeable morality, and ideology according to this mandate. In similar disposition, societies for exclusive or preferential action performing educational activities, and assocations or societies tied directly or indirectly with the propaganda of a religious creed, will not intervene in any form in primary, secondary, or normal school, nor will they be permitted to help them economically.

II. The formation of plans, programs, and methods of instruction belong in every case to the State.

III. Private institutions will not be permitted to function without having obtained previously, in each case, the expressed authorization of the public power.

IV. The State can revoke, at any time, the permitted authoriza-

3. *Diario de los Debates de la Cámara de Diputados del Congreso de los Estados Unidos Mexicanos,* XXVI Legislatura, Vol. I., No. 12 (September 26, 1934), p. 5.

tion. Against such revocation, there will be no recourse or judicial proceedings.

These same norms govern education of any type or grade that is imparted to workers and farmers.

Primary education will be obligatory and the State will impart it freely.

The State is permitted to revoke optionally at any time the recognition of official validity of studies conducted in private institutions.

The Congress of the Union, with a view to unifying and coordinating education throughout the Republic, shall issue the necessary laws designed to allocate the educational function among the Federation, the states, and the municipalities, to fix the fiscal appropriations corresponding to this public service, and for establishing the penalties applicable to officials who do not comply with or enforce the pertinent provisions, as well as the penalties applicable to all those who infringe such provisions.

READING 12 *Primary Textbooks Under Cárdenas*

Introductory Note

Once article 3 was amended in 1934 to support the "socialist doctrine" of the Six Year Plan, textbooks were published to correspond with constitutional law. These books incorporated new themes and images designed to stimulate "rational" concepts of the universe, a central objective of socialist education. The best organizing themes to achieve this end, in the opinion of Mexican educators, were those which emphasized economic interpretations of history, a point made in many introductions to the new texts. It was not unusual, then, to find in these books, topics like "the historic process of the Mexican worker," "the origin of colonial feudalism," "the immoderate wealth of the Church," and "the formation of national and foreign capitalism in Mexico." These topics are included in several of the textbooks from which some of the following excerpts are taken.

The selected passages from Mexican primary textbooks after 1934 suggest that Lázaro Cárdenas placed high priority on the

The citations on ancient history are translated from Luis Cháves Orozco, *Historia Patria* (México: Editorial Patria, 1934), pp. 114–15; the excerpts on economic determinism and class struggle are from Alfonso Teja Zabre, *Breve Historia de México* (México: Secretaría de Educación Pública, 1935), pp. 256–57; the selections on work are excerpted from textbooks published by the Cárdenas government, SERIE S.E.P., first, second, and third-year primary texts (México, 1938–40): p. 61, first-year; p. 11, second-year; and p. 54, third-year; the selection on Father's Syndicate is from the third-year textbook, SERIE S.E.P., p. 161.

motivation to achieve within the broader concept of Mexican nationalism. Primary textbooks were designed to instill equality, pride, and self-confidence in members of the Mexican working class and to motivate its future members to accomplish noble deeds through hard work and enterprise. Cárdenas presumably hoped to stimulate national development based in part upon new attitudes of self-reliance, self-confidence, and Mexican worker unity, attitudes significantly different from the fatalism and passiveness long associated with scholastic learning in pre-revolutionary days. For the first time in Mexico, the government determined to assume firm leadership in the process of socialization through publication of its own textbooks.

On Ancient History

The social organization of the Aztecs was equal to the Toltecs because the instruments of production were the same.

Among the Mexicans there were two social classes: the nobles and the plebeians.

The noble class was divided into two groups: the warriors and the priests.

The warriors and the priests succeeded in obligating the plebeians . . . to work for them.

Therefore, among the Mexicans, as exists today, there were exploiters and exploited. The exploiters of today are those who possess the instruments of production; the exploited are those who operate the instruments of production in exchange for a salary.

On Economic Determinism

Civilization and culture are results of the work of man over nature.

Work is the fundamental cause and the most approximate measure of value of useful things.

The social structure has as its base the organization of work, known as the techniques of production.

The principal historic factor is the struggle of the classes.

Social classes are formed according to their function in organized work of economic production. . . .

The struggle or contradiction is in general for the dominance of the instruments of production and for the profit of highest value, or in consequence, for the exploitation of man by man. . . .

The modern system of production creates the relations of capitalist character, evolving in the bourgeoisie world to high capitalism. In this cycle the social classes in contradiction or in struggle are the proletariat and the capitalist bourgeoisie. . . .

The struggle or contradiction for the dominance of the instruments of production is referred principally to land and machines and above all to the machines making machines.

On Class Struggle

Insurgency of the proletarian class searching for economic and effective equality.

Creation of a new State that can realize progressive socialization of the means of production.

But above all as supreme and final rule is this norm: the Mexican reality. That is the progress of the Revolution rooted in its own land and open to the future.

On Work

My Mexico is great, My Mexico is rich,
my Mexico is beautiful. If it is
beautiful, if it is rich, very rich
and extensive, I want my father, who
works much, to have a little piece
of the land of Mexico.

I want the poor to stop being poor.
I want all men to be equal.
I want my Mexico, very rich and
extensive, to be a strong country
of workers. . . .

My father is a bus driver. He drives the bus "Colonia Morelos." He is tall, strong, and very hard working. I want to be like him.

I will be a worker one day . . . I will have strong callouses and firm hands . . . I will have my overalls! And like my father I proudly shine with distinction of the worker.

Father's Syndicate

. . . Among other things represents the strength of the worker, organized with a noble and generous end: with the end of saving ourselves from exploitation. . . . The syndicates are united from factory to factory, from city to city, from country to country. Thus we are united and thus we struggle because we still do not have what we justly need. Some day all the world . . . will be but a great syndicate that will impose its conditions on the capitalists.

READING 13 *The 1946 Amendment to Article 3*

Introductory Note

The 1946 Amendment to article 3 constitutes the legal shift from socialist to democratic ideology as the basis for child indoctrination in the principles of Mexican nationalism. It was the basis for reorienting textbooks and teacher training away from aggressive radical nationalism, that is, class struggle of workers against capitalists and imperialists against socialists, toward themes of national unity, co-operation among classes, and respect for law. It was, like the 1934 amendment, anti-secular—although less so than in 1934—and based upon the continuing effort toward building a modern progressive Mexico.

ARTICLE 3

The education imparted by the Federal State shall be designed to develop harmoniously all the faculties of the human being and shall foster in him at the same time a love of country and a consciousness of international solidarity, in independence and justice.

I. Freedom of religious beliefs being guaranteed by article 24, the standard which shall guide such education shall be maintained entirely apart from any religious doctrine and, based on the results of scientific progress, shall strive against ignorance

Translated from *Political Constitution of the Mexican United States* (México: Cámara de Senadores, 1962), pp. 165–66.

and its effects, servitudes, fanaticism, and prejudices. Moreover:

(a) It shall be democratic, considering democracy not only as a legal structure and a political regimen, but as a system of life founded on a constant economic, social, and cultural betterment of the people;

(b) It shall be national insofar as—without hostility or exclusiveness—it shall achieve the understanding of our problems, the utilization of our resources, the defense of our political independence, the assurance of our economic independence, and the continuity and growth of our culture; and

(c) It shall contribute to better human relationships, not only with the elements which it contributes toward strengthening and at the same time inculcating, together with respect for the dignity of the person and the integrity of the family, the conviction of the general interest of society, but also by the care which it devotes to the ideals of brotherhood and equality of rights of all men, avoiding privileges of race, creed, class, sex, or persons.

II. Private persons may engage in education of all kinds and grades. But as regards elementary, secondary, and normal education (and that of any kind or grade designed for laborers and farm workers) they must previously obtain, in every case, the express authorization of the public power. Such authorization may be refused or revoked by decisions against which there can be no judicial proceedings or recourse. . . .

IV. Religious corporations, ministers of religion, stock companies which exclusively or predominantly engage in educational activities, and associations or companies devoted to propagation of any religious creed shall not in any way participate in institutions giving elementary, secondary, and normal education and education for laborers or field workers. . . .

READING 14 *Primary Textbooks in the Postwar Period*

Introductory Note

In "My Service to Mexico," which appears in the new official primary textbooks of the late 1950s, values of the national identity are paramount. The focus is on the unity of all Mexicans, not only worker unity as in the textbooks of the 1930s. Equality and collaboration replaced images of class struggle, conflict, or inequality—so characteristic of the late 1930s texts. Thus, both sets of textbooks (official textbooks of the 1930s and late 1950s) were used to introduce the younger generation to new national identities; the scope and depth of these identities differed before and after World War II. Both sets attempted to break patterns of traditional life—uncertainty, indecision, lack of political motivation, inferiority—by means of different degrees of national identification and unity.[1] *The result would be, hopefully, new achievement motivation and a modernized Mexico.*

The citations in this reading are translated from various textbooks as follows: "My Service to Mexico" appears in a number of textbooks issued between 1960 and 1963 by the Comisión Nacional de los Libros de Textos Gratuitos of the Secretaría de Educación Pública; the four citations on Mexico's nineteenth-century struggles are from the fourth-year textbook, *Historia y Civismo* (México: Secretaría de Educación Pública, no date), pp. 58, 94, 98; the citation on Madero, ibid., p. 161.

1. For studies on these traditional patterns of Mexican attitudes, see Dr. Vicente Suárez Soto, *Psicología Abismal del Mexicano* (México: Secretaría de Educación Pública, 1962), Vol. I, pp. 142–43; José Gómez Robleda, *Psicología del Mexicano* (México: Instituto de Investigaciones

My Service to Mexico

My country is Mexico. I must serve it always with my thought, with my words, with my acts.

In order to assure its good fortune and to increase its greatness, Mexico needs and requires the material and intellectual work of its children and the morality of all of them.

I must be dignified, just, generous, and useful. I will therefore honor my family, the society in which I live, my country, and humanity.

I will work always for the physical and mental health of the Mexican people in order that we can all benefit happily from the capacity to feel, to study, and to work.

Interpretations of Mexican history in the official primary textbooks urge the student to think in terms of patriotism and national community. The following passages, excerpts from the fourth-year text, *Historia y Civismo,* are examples of themes centering on unity, patriotism, and national strength.

On the War of Independence

Miguel Hidalgo y Costilla was the *Father of our Independence.* He loved the country, he battled for it, and he inculcated ideas of liberty and justice.

On the War of 1847 with the United States

The situation of Mexico in this epoch was thus:
1. The government lacked *money.*
2. There were no *great political leaders.*
3. There was no counting on *military organization* nor on *arms.*

Sociales, Universidad Nacional, 1962), pp. 68–75; Francisco Gonzáles Piñeda, *El Mexicano, Psicología de Su Destructividad* (México: Asociación Psicoanalítica Mexicana, Editorial Pax-México), pp. 202–3; Samuel Ramos, *Profile of Man and Culture in Mexico,* translated by Peter G. Eagle (Austin: University of Texas Press, 1962), p. 57.

4. The generals endowed with *skill* and *experience* did not occupy superior and *decisive* positions.
5. The gravest of all: there was no *peace* nor *union* among Mexicans who were divided by internal battles and almost always born with personal ambition and passion.

The goring that Mexico suffered in 1847 leaves us an experience that we must never forget: *union of all Mexicans* is indispensable because with domestic peace there is progress and with progress the strength capable of sheltering ourselves from abuses and injustices. We must be industrious, energetic, conscious of our responsibility, and *unite ourselves in order to strengthen our fatherland each day.*

Restoration After the French Intervention

Thanks to the *patriotism* and *strength* of Benito Juárez, and to the heroic perseverance of the soldiers of the Republic, he saved the *sovereignty of Mexico,* awoke the *national conscience,* and obtained the *political unification of the country.*

The new textbooks of the 1950s were much more sympathetic to Madero than the texts of the 1930s which denigrated him. A fourth-year text published in the SERIE S.E.P. of 1939 said of Madero that he "did nothing to improve the conditions of the workers, wages or to resolve the agrarian problem." The postwar texts read as follows:

Madero became President on 6 November 1911. He was a man of great nobility and of very good intentions. His situation on occupying the government did not permit him to realize then what the Revolution represented.

READING 15 *The Revolutionary Party in the Postwar Period*

Introductory Note

The Partido Revolucionario Institucional (*Institutional Revolutionary Party or PRI*) *is the party of the Mexican Revolution. Its members, particularly the upper echelon decision-makers, pay constant homage to the revolution with its deeply carved reform objectives. Today the party consists of three major sectors—farm, labor, and popular—held together by an umbrella organization designed to provide the consensus required for stability and on-going permanent reforms. That it is geared to national and social change which make up the "continuing revolution" is suggested by the following document.*

In conformity with the prescription of Section VI of Article 29 of the present Federal Electoral Law, the Institutional Revolutionary Party declares that the essential and governing principles of its activities are the following:

Definition of the Party

I. The Institutional Revolutionary Party is a political organization which supports the principles of the Mexican Revolution. Its basic

Translated from *Declaración de Principios* (México: Partido Revolucionario Institucional, 1963), pp. 5–10.

objective is to acquire and maintain political power by means of the vote and through its permanent action in the struggle for democratic improvement and social justice, with the goal of conserving political stability and accelerating the social and economic development that the nation demands.

Simultaneously, it drives and channels the force of the Mexican people, inspired in their major historical traditions, with the goal of constructing a new society characterized by the complete enjoyment of the material and cultural comforts required by man in order to live in liberty and dignity; the constant participation of the people in the government, the absolute dominion of the nation over its natural resources and the rational use of them; maximum development of the productive forces, the planned intervention of the State in economic activities in order to conserve and increase the national patrimony, and the just and equitable distribution of the wealth and revenue.

Given the historical experience of the country, the struggle of the people to forge this new society should be realized through peaceful means and by way of political, legislative, and administrative procedures, under the protection and in fulfillment of the Constitution. Such is the Mexican way of development.

In order to pursue these propositions, the Party depends on the organizations of *campesinos*, workers, civil servants, technicians, professionals, artists, and intellectuals; businessmen, industrialists, farmers, and small stock farmers; unsalaried workers, women, and young revolutionaries, social groups that constitute the major productive force of the national wealth. It accepts, moreover, the following of each citizen who truly contributes to the development of the nation, which should be realized in an atmosphere of independence, democracy, peace, and social justice.

Party members, grouped in the Agrarian, Worker, and Popular sectors, find themselves firmly united in respect of these principles, which should always be interpreted and applied in a dynamic and revolutionary form.

On the other hand, the Party recognizes that the armed forces formed by its own people, author of the Mexican Revolution, understand that its highest mission consists in guaranteeing the integrity and independence of the country, the rule of the Constitution, and domestic peace.

National Conscience

II. The Party affirms the necessity of strengthening the consciousness of our nationality, understood as a collectivity of men's lives that have a common territory, history, culture, economic and social life, and language, and which progresses peacefully toward its social transformation.

It acknowledges that nationalism will strengthen, encouraging in all Mexicans a love of country by virtue of the active participation of all of them in the resolution of general problems; the elevation of the sentiment of social solidarity; the tightening of moral, cultural, and material bonds which give cohesion to the community; the respect and reciprocal understanding of their rights and problems and the preservation of the positive aspects of the tradition and historic legacy of the preceding generations, drawing from them the most highly valued ideas in order to meet the pressing needs of the people.

The Constitution as the Banner

III. The Party declares that the Political Constitution of the Mexican United States, in addition to being the fundamental juridical law of the nation, constitutes the basic program of the revolutionary governments for shaping the ideals of the people and channels the social transformation of the country which will be attained with greater speed, fewer disputes and sacrifice, by means of its just performance.

Moreover, it will demand that the Constitution be respected and obeyed because it represents the most complete juridical, political, and social expression of our national existence and structures the system of government anchored in the reality of our people. At the same time, it will struggle energetically against all tendency that would detract from the natural and democratic goals of the Mexican State.

It declares that the Magna Carta of 1917 is the banner of the people and the source of inspiration in its revolutionary struggle, assurance that through its consistent application the highest goals will be reached through proper and effective solutions, in accord with our particular temperament.

As faithful interpreter of the interests and aspirations of the people, it reaffirms its inviolable purpose of defending the law of constitutional order.

Fundamental Goals

IV. The Party will struggle for the sovereignty and territorial integrity of the Republic; for the submission of governments and governors to constitutional rule, for the preservation of liberties of thought and belief, speech, press, work, and other individual guarantees to man and citizen; for the effectiveness and development of social guarantees; for the right of the people to education and culture; for collective interest prevailing always over individual interest; for the creating of favorable conditions so that the *campesinos*, the workers, the popular sector, and the people in general benefit from a just social life; for an accelerated economic development by means of economic and social planning; for the perfecting of democracy; for the establishment of an international order based upon the principles of self-determination, nonintervention, juridical equality of nations and peace founded in justice, the observance of legal and freely contracted international agreements, and the harmony among all countries independently of their social and political systems. . . . *[This document goes on to outline party responsibilities in the specific areas of social security, public health, popular education, public morals, economic development, agrarian reform, indigenous communities, worker reforms, youth activities, women's organizations, foreign policy, and the electoral system.]*

READING 16 *Diaz Ordaz's 1968 State of the Union Address*

Introductory Note

President Gustavo Díaz Ordaz (1911–   ) delivered his annual State of the Union Address on September 1, 1968. In it, he outlined Mexico's continued path of development along principles of the permanent revolution, but he responded as well to the recent student riots of the summer 1968. The speech is significant in its references to revolutionary progress and for the amount of space given to the summer events, which challenged public consensus on PRI leadership.

We are making every effort to insure the rapid progress of the agrarian program.

We would like to take care of a greater number of farm workers; we want everyone to have plots of land; but there are areas in which it is becoming increasingly difficult to find lands that can be distributed.

When a public statement has been made to the effect that in a certain region no more land is available, this does not mean that we intend to give up, even in that region, this first step in Agrarian Reform. Within the norms established in Article 27 of the Constitution and in the Code of Agrarian Laws, we shall continue to concern ourselves with finding, even there, extensions of land that can be used by *ejido* members.

Gustavo Díaz Ordaz, "State of the Union Address" of September 1, 1968, official English translation, pp. 5–7, 20–24, 27–28, 36–40.

The latifundium has been a perpetual obstacle in Mexico's march forward. Our internal struggles are marked by the various forms it assumes in the different stages in the life of the country. For this reason, the Mexican Revolution is essentially and basically anti-latifundium. . . .

Today, 25 years after its establishment, the social security system in Mexico covers more than 8 million of our people. All persons obliged to belong to the Social Security under the law must become affiliates.

Our national solidarity will have to be put to the test at the proper time in order that other sectors, which do not come under labor legislation begin to enjoy similar benefits. . . .

The most important factor in progress is education. More and better teachers with more and better schools will enable us to achieve our highest aspirations in the training of youth, who will one day take over the direction of the future course of the nation.

Total enrollment of children in the federal, state, and private elementary schools and kindergartens is 8,542,000 or 24.8 per cent higher than in 1964. . . .

There are 178,000 students in the schools and faculties of higher education. Of these, 33,000 are in federal institutions, 51,000 in the National Autonomous University of Mexico, 70,000 in state schools, and 24,000 in private schools. . . .

The program for the training of engineering and technological professors (UNESCO Plan) was initiated this year at a cost of 40 million pesos, including workshop and laboratory equipment. . . .

An increase of 4.2 million pesos in the investment program of the National Indian Institute, made an expenditure of 500,000 pesos possible for starting work on a new coordinating center in the Sierra Nahuatl-Totonaca in the State of Puebla. . . .

The theory of overall development for our people considers the terms justice and equality of the foremost importance. We not only want to increase the wealth but also to assure its adequate social distribution. We not only seek an increase in the production of goods and services, but also want these to satisfy the growing needs of the majority so that these benefits are distributed among all our fellow citizens, especially among the most needy sectors.

Beyond any other considerations, the governments of the Mexican Revolution are chiefly concerned with the individual and his full development in all aspects. Humanism has been guide and goal of the three basic movements of the country, Independence, Reform and Revolution, and continues permanently to inspire our economic, social and political action. . . .

Educational Reforms

Let us now examine, briefly, the real background of the problem: the urgent need for a profound educational reform. This problem is not limited to Mexico; the crisis in education is worldwide.

The general concept on which Mexican education is based is only a partial answer to the pressures of our time, and it has not been possible to apply it fully. In speaking of educational reform I believe that it should begin in the home, continue in kindergarten, primary and secondary school, extend to preparatory school, professional and even post-graduate studies, and at each stage establish the foundations for attitudes toward life and conduct toward our fellow human beings. Education is continuous: it never ends.

It is absurd for juvenile minds to acquire knowledge, often outdated, with a useless overburdening of the memory. It is necessary to select the material and present it in a coordinated manner, to adopt modern teaching methods which arouse interest and curiosity and to eliminate obsolete and overly detailed programs, to replace them by others of less quantity but more quality.

I am aware of the enormous difficulties of such an undertaking; the advances of science and technology are dizzying. What may be at this moment the latest discovery may be outmoded by a new invention at the next. Consequently, there is no time to make a careful synthesis, and even less time for a complete synthesis of the material which might serve as the basis for teaching. Furthermore, philosophy and politics cannot keep up with scientific and technological advances. They cannot explain to the youth the up-to-date "whys" and "wherefores."

The revolution in knowledge that transformed the Ministry of Instruction into the Ministry of Education was absolutely intentional.

Perhaps we have paid too much attention to teaching and too little to education. We should teach how to think, to understand, to act, to tolerate and, what is extremely important, we should teach how to learn.

Among both children and adults, we should spread the principle of fraternity with our fellow man.

We must set aside all dogmatism. We adults were first given orders, and later, occasionally, an explanation. Today, we should explain first, try to persuade, not to impose ourselves. We should suggest, without attempting to dominate.

At the same time, great care should be taken to insure that the child or youth is not left without guidance, abandoned to his natural, rash impulses. Those best able to do so, shall have to decide, and, further, clearly define—objectively, without regard for transitory situations, and as a permanent guide—whether the teacher should be deprived of all authority over the student, and whether all administration of the schools should be abolished; or whether each classroom and each educational institution can achieve the difficult, but not impossible combination, of order with freedom.

We should not give complicated lessons in civics; we should make the student understand that he is not permitted to do everything, that his rights are limited by the rights of others; that to live within society means practicing tolerance, in order to be tolerated: that every right carries with it a corresponding obligation that not all the responsiblity for the acts of a minor falls on the parents or society, as we are so frequently told, but rather that we all are responsible, at least in part, for our actions, and that as we grow, so grows our responsibility.

It should always be remembered that to enroll in a school is to confess that one does not know; it is an act of humility that does not degrade, but rather exalts, because it carries with it the lofty aim of learning.

He should be left with the clear idea that no single individual, no group, no social class—no matter how wealthy or powerful they may be or try to be—controls the destiny of Mexico; that sovereignty lies only in the people and is exercised through majority decision.

In the national interest and for the benefit of the majority of young people we must take into account the requirements of our economic development in restructuring the educational system. However, as I stated at Punta del Este: "Let us ensure that education is not merely bookish nor solely utilitarian. Education for production and education for culture; without humanist content, economic development means nothing in the history of a people."

The task consists of "harmoniously developing all the faculties of the human being and fostering in him both love of country and an awareness of international solidarity, in independence and in justice."

The goal is to form men, true men, both free and responsible.

A Call to the People

From this high tribunal of the Nation, in this solemn hour, I call all the Mexican people to the most noble of missions: that of seeking and finding the pathways to be followed by our children; pathways that will lead them to true and worthy goals; sure pathways that can be traveled in freedom and responsibility to reach the goal with the greatest of satisfactions: to have contributed one's own part to the growing advance of the Nation.

There is room for all: there are no insignificant Mexicans in the task of forging the future of the Nation. Young and old, technicians and scientists, teachers and researchers, all can contribute their interests, their knowledge and talent, not only to criticize what is useless and should be cast out but, principally, to choose what should be utilized in order to create a new educational structure.

Because the task is so arduous and complex, neither effort nor experience nor erudition will suffice; all will be sterile unless the best men put forth the most worthy aspect of their being: the passion to serve Mexico.

Youth should have a dream—but they should not let themselves be deluded.

We have several examples of youths who, deceived by the mirage of believing themselves great heroes, soon discovered that their heroism was false; they could have been useful to Mexico, but they lost their way through the bitterness of their frustration.

The spirit of youth desires adventure and heroism. Do they wish to set out on a great adventure, be truly and grandly heroic? Then they have the great opportunity to participate in the fascinating adventure of building a better Mexico each day, a greater and more generous Mexico. Here they can exercise their heroism, an unspectacular but noble heroism, which will give them great satisfaction: knowing that they have forged themselves by enriching their spirit with knowledge and tempering their character by the education of the will in order to taste the greatest joy of all, that of working for one's own benefit and for the aggrandizement of the nation.

We agree with youth that they should not passively accept our society as it is; but we do not agree that they should simply resign themselves to rejecting it thoughtlessly or rebelling against it with no awareness of what they want and what they will build to replace what they try to destroy.

Serious damage is being done by the modern philosophers of destruction who are against everything and in favor of nothing.

They are right not to like this imperfect world that we will leave them. But we have no other. Not without studies, without education, without discipline, without ideals—and merely with disorder and violence—are they going to improve it.

Life does not and should not stagnate, because all stagnation is unhealthy. It is a historic law that life develops in stages that escape the boldest will to transform, and that each human wave forces the preceding one to increase the pace.

Each wave should be a new and dynamic contribution to the fortunes of Mexico, not a heavy burden. The younger generation will have to consider, in the depths of its being, that the senseless attack does not correspond to its responsibility, and that Mexico does not accept solutions that go against its own nature.

Any disagreement produced in the heat of the eternal yearning for renewal and justice is welcome. Any disagreement that helps and does not impede the achievement of a better Mexico is welcome.

Gratefully I accept the messages of vigorous encouragement from a young worker of the capital and a young farmer from the arid fields of Zacatecas.

With the first I believe that the impulses of the new generation should be channeled toward the achievement of the highest destinies of our country, uniting all its will and all its effort in the daily forging of the Nation.

With the second I know, as he tells me, that the young farmers of the country are fully engaged in a struggle, their weapons in hand, but that their struggle is the work in the fields and that their weapons are the hoe, the pick, the shovel, the plow handle and the steering wheel of a tractor.

I am filled with emotion as I pay homage to those hands that seldom handle currency, that rarely feel the joy of a caress.

Those same rough and suffering hands raised a cudgel or a lance at the call of Hidalgo and Morelos; those that ignored the immensity of the desert when they hauled the carriages of Benito Juárez' glorious army; the same hands that grasped the rifle or machete under the flag of Madero, Carranza, or Zapata.

Youth Suffrage

Shortly, I shall submit the bill for amending Article 34 of the Constitution. I remain confident that the rights and duties of citizenship will be honorably exercised and complied with by youth, that they will contribute to the process, and that their presence as citizens, their anxieties and convictions to the electorate will emphasize the real and dynamic sense of our Revolution.

Our ancestors refused to make the right to vote dependent on economic status, property or income, or even on literacy, and thus they prevented the formation of two Mexicos—one legal, composed of a small minority enjoying all privileges, and the other real, composed of the great majority deprived of all rights. In opposition to the inclination of those who wished to make the vote a burden, our ancestors decided that, as the essence of democracy, the vote should simply be counted; because there can be no government for the people if it does not come from the people. The course of history confirms the correctness of their course. Today it is our wish to continue on this same road that marks the progress of Mexico.

In its institutional stage the Revolution granted women the right to vote despite pessimistic predictions, and the active and legal participation of women in politics has resulted in the improvement of our system.

Just as the women of yesterday, the youth of tomorrow will strengthen those institutions that all Mexicans must protect and they will maintain and improve the rules for harmony among all within the framework of a free and orderly society.

Party Responsibility

In perfecting our democracy, a primary function and a grave responsibility is placed upon our national political parties.

Respect for law, choice of the best men, the creation of programs best suited to Mexico, and acceptance of the decision of the majority, are essential for the consolidation of our political system.

It is the duty of all political parties, not only the majority party, to work tirelessly for civic progress, to eliminate outmoded procedures, and by these means to prevent ideological differences from disrupting national unity. The play of political parties, as the representative of the people, within the law strengthens their liberties and confidence.

There is ample liberty to seek and propose solutions to problems that afflict the various sectors of our society, and also for the majority of the citizens to solve them.

Confidence in our institution, in our revolutionary tradition and in the principles derived therefrom, are enough to support our conviction that the open discussion of ideas, as opposed as they may be, not only does not impede the progress of the nation, but accelerates, consolidates, and enriches it. Only he who lacks confidence in his own ideas fears the ideas of others.

The various steps that have led to greater participation in public affairs by political groups whose ideas differ from those of the government are the fruit of a maturity that the people are in the process of achieving, and that the Revolution has had the wisdom to harvest.

They imply a responsibility for all: those who created them must try to perfect them; those who are now employing legal instruments to oppose the government must give up those that are outside the law. Since there are means for forming legal opposition, there is no valid reason now for illegal or subversive opposition.

We have been making steady progress in perfecting our democratic institutions.

The form in which various electorial procedures have been carried out; the increasingly evident civic maturity of the Mexican people reflected in numerous political activities; the atmosphere of calm and respect for mutual rights which has existed in the majority of these actions; the liberty with which people of different ideological persuasions active within the country have been able to express themselves—all these show us that we are walking with sure steps along the road of our democratic consolidation.

If we have demonstrated immaturity in exceptional cases, or if we have regressed at times, this does not invalidate the general evaluation that there have been many positive actions and few negative ones.

The Mexican Revolution

This step forward in the democratic process is a direct result of the profound social and economic changes brought about by the Mexican Revolution which have given a new aspect to the country. If present-day Mexicans are more politically aware, and our increasing participation in public affairs gives meaning to the overall system of our institutions, it is because the changes derived from the Revolution have brought us broader liberties, greater material well-being, more education, better conditions in the fields of health, security, communications and other areas.

The Revolution is a long process which renews itself at every stage at great risk and peril and, as a result, demands constant vigilance and strict adherence to its principles and program of action, all the more so by those of us who have reached the higher levels of responsibility.

On assuming the Presidency I stated, "From the broad use of our liberties, our unity is born, and from our unity comes all we have achieved and ought to achieve.

"What has been won in so many years of effort can be lost if we do not carefully protect it each and every day."

Let us make our unity continue to be the result of the broad use of our liberties and let it go on to mean not resignation, not ambiguity, not surrender, but persistence in one's own firm convictions and respect for those of others, within the law.

III The Inter-war Period

Aside from the Mexican Revolution, Latin America produced no titanic upheaveals during the first part of the century. The numerous strikes, demonstrations, and governmental overthrows that occurred seldom touched more than small segments of the population. The general trend throughout the hemisphere was toward strong dictatorships which brooked very little change. Yet underneath this calm exterior there was a growing restlessness.

For example, social reformers in Peru had been calling for change for decades before the start of the century. Manual González Prada (1846–1918), who had been a writer of literary criticism in his early years, began offering trenchant criticism of existing political, economic, and social conditions at the turn of the century. Luis Alberto Sánchez (1897–   ), the Peruvian writer, said of González Prada that "he molded the mind of Peruvian youth."[1] His ideas also spread beyond Peru's borders. But of even greater importance were the works of José Carlos Mariátegui (1894–1930), a brilliant Peruvian whose writings heralded the social reform movements which swept his Andean nation in the years between the two World Wars. A member of the small Peruvian middle class, he became a Marxist with unique Peruvian views. After traveling in Europe after World War I, he returned to Peru preaching socialist theory and urging the youth to adopt socialism. His *Siete ensayos de interpretación de la realidad peruana* (Seven Interpretive Essays of the Peruvian Situation) was probably the most important document on Marxist

1. Luis Alberto Sánchez, *Historia de la literatura americana* (Santiago de Chile, 1937), p. 365.

theory produced in Latin America prior to the Cuban Revolution. He was also sharply critical of the United States's economic investment in Latin America (Reading One).

Mariátegui served as the key forerunner of the social reform movement of Víctor Raúl Haya de la Torre (1895–), which became known after a time as Aprismo, taking the term from the initials of Haya de la Torre's party, the *Alianza Popular Revolucionario Americana* (American Popular Revolutionary Alliance or APRA). One student of Haya de la Torre writes: "The term *Aprismo* is one which has acquired a varied ideological content during the past ten years." [2] Not only does it apply to the political tenets and programs of APRA, "but also to the philosophies, theories, and ideals set forth by a very able group of writers who look to Haya de la Torre as party chief and intellectual guide."

World Communism was also influential in Latin America during the inter-war years. Communist Parties were formed in most countries. Dissident socialists in Argentina formed the *Partido Socialista Internacional* (International Socialist Party or PSI) in 1918—a group which in 1920 became the *Partido Comunista Argentina* (Argentine Communist Party or PCA). Mexican, Chilean, Brazilian, and Cuban parties followed in quick succession.[3] Other parties were formed out of workers' syndicates and student groups.[4] In large measure, they followed the dictates of Moscow in connection with strategy. In 1928, when the Comintern proposed a policy of radicalization and the adoption of hard-line tactics, most of the parties agreed. Late in 1935, the Communists surveyed their activities and reception in Latin America and criticized their past policy (Reading Two). As a result, they

2. Robert E. McNicoll, "Intellectual Origins of Aprismo," in Paul Kramer and Robert E. McNicoll, eds., *Latin American Panorama: An Anthology* (New York: G. P. Putnam's Sons, 1968), p. 266.
3. For surveys of Latin American Communism see Robert J. Alexander, *Communism in Latin America* (New Brunswick, N.J.: Rutgers University Press, 1957); and Luis E. Aguilar, ed., *Marxism in Latin America* (New York: Alfred A. Knopf, 1968). Professor Aguilar's book contains an excellent introduction to Communism in the hemisphere.
4. Aguilar, op. cit., pp. 10–20.

urged a softer approach and common front tactics on the parties, and, again, most went along.[5]

The *Partido Comunista Cubana* (Cuban Communist Party or PCC) came in for some of the sharpest criticism in the article (Reading Two), for it had pushed the radicalization theme further than most of the other parties. The PCC had tried during the early 1930s to win hemisphere Communist support for its position. Consistent with the international Communist line, the PCC had argued for the formation of soviets on the island and attacked almost every other political force from right to left (Reading Three).

But if the Cuban party took a hard line, the *Partido Comunista Chileno* (Chilean Communist Party or PCC) had shown itself to be the most flexible party in Latin America during that era of radical tactics. In the 1920s its members won several seats in the legislature. The party was divided during this period between the hard-liners and those who favored greater flexibility in policy. But when the Chilean Communists did in 1938 align themselves somewhat in a common front with other leftist and radical parties to help secure the presidential election of a moderate leftist, it appeared to some observers that the groundwork laid earlier in the hard-line years had paid off. The PCC position was not one of wholeheartedly supporting the government, but rather one of supporting and criticizing selectively (Reading Four).

Of importance during those years for the Communist movement was Luís Carlos Prestes's (1908–   ) assumption of party leadership in Brazil. He dominated his party's apparatus much more than party leaders in other countries dominated theirs. At the same time, Prestes was regarded as closer to Moscow than most other leaders of Latin American Communism.[6] This can be seen in his support of unity with the Western Allies in World War II (Reading Five) and his later praise of the United States for some of its international policies.

Prestes spent much of his time either in flight or in prison be-

5. For details, see Alexander, op. cit., pp. 107–183.
6. Ibid., pp. 1–8.

cause Getúlio Vargas (1883–1954), Brazil's strongman in the 1930s, saw Prestes as a threat to his rule. Vargas was Brazil's president from 1930 to 1945, and again from 1950 to 1954. The Vargas years were stormy ones. He and his plans for an *estado novo* (new state) may never have been fully developed, but Vargas left his imprint on Brazil and raised his vast nation, Latin America's largest, to world recognition. Parts of Vargas's *estado novo* were embodied in the Constitution of 1934 which provided for a strong executive and protection for workers. But the concept was not a detailed economic and social program, appearing instead in piecemeal fashion through Vargas's writings and speeches (Reading Six). His support came, in part, from the growing armies of workers in Brazil who regarded him as a leader with their interests at heart.

That support from the populace was not enough to keep Vargas in power, however, for the military forced him to resign in 1945. Yet Vargas had a hand in Brazilian politics for the next five years, serving a term in the Senate, and then running for the presidency and winning in the 1950 election. Workers and businessmen alike supported his constitutional return to power. But the army, many of the liberal, democratic elements in the country, and the coffee barons of São Paulo worked to block his government and, as calls for his resignation grew, Vargas took what he believed to be the only way out: suicide. In his suicide note, he sharply criticized his opponents and eloquently defended his policies (Reading Seven).

Part of Vargas's troubles were inspired by the coffee plantation owners—particularly from São Paulo state. They had dominated Brazilian economic life for many years and, according to many writers, had prevented any change in Brazilian conditions from colonial times on. Celso Furtado, the noted Brazilian economist, shares this view (Reading Eight).

READING 1 *Yankee Capitalism Denounced*

Introductory Note

José Carlos Mariátegui (1895–1930), a leading Peruvian Communist, was an outspoken critic of "Yankeeland." A onetime associate of Víctor Raúl Haya de la Torre (1895–), the founder of Peru's Alianza Popular Revolucionario Americana, *Mariátegui became a Communist when the two parted company. Mariátegui founded a literary journal,* Amauta, *in 1925 and edited it until his death five years later. Earlier he had traveled in Europe and made contact with socialists and others in France and Italy. Returning to Peru, he became a firm and ardent advocate of socialism and later of Communism.*

Until recently, industrial development in the United States depended entirely on the vigorous rate of consumption of the American population. But ever since production began to exceed consumption, this development has come to depend heavily on the conquest of external markets. The accumulation of the larger part of the world's gold supply in the Yankee reserves has created the problem of the exportation of capital. It is not enough for the United States to dispose of its excess production; it also needs to dispose of its gold surplus. The country's industrial development can no longer absorb all of its financial returns.

Before the war, Yankee industry was a good target for European investors. Profits from wartime production, however, made it possible for Yankee industry to become completely independ-

Translated from José Carlos Mariátegui, *Defensa del marxismo* (Lima: Biblioteca Amauta, 1959), pp. 137–39.

ent of European banking. The United States was transformed from a debtor to a creditor nation. During the postwar period of economic crisis and revolutionary agitation, on the other hand, the United States was forced to discontinue its loans. The European nations had to organize their financial affairs before they could apply for credit to the New York banks. Likewise, with regard to private investments, the threat of the Communist revolution, toward which poverty-stricken Europe seemed to be heading, warned the North American capitalists to exercise utmost care. For this reason, the United States did its best to put the Dawes Plan [a plan to ease the payment of reparations by Germany after World War I] into effect in Europe. It did not succeed until Poincaré suffered his political defeat in the Ruhr in 1923. From then on, under stipulated conditions governing the payment of German reparations and the Allied debt to the Yankee treasury, Yankeeland has extended numerous credits to Europe. It has made loans to countries to help them stabilize their exchange rates; it has lent funds to private industries for the reorganization of their plants and policies.

A great number of stocks and titles have passed into Yankee hands. But such investing has its limits. United States capital cannot be used to finance European industry without creating the risk of European production cutting into the United States-controlled markets. On the other hand, these investments help the European economy in a manner that is beneficial to the North American economy. The Dawes Plan and its sequel of financial agreements and settlements have put Europe into a period of capitalistic—and democratic—stability, which the reactionary apologists call the work of fascists. But, as the last Economic Conference demonstrated, Europe has not yet reached her equilibrium.

Trotsky has made a singularly penetrating and objective study of Yankee capitalism today. "Gold inflation," observed the Russian leader, "is as dangerous to an economy as currency inflation. One can die of overeating as well as of starvation. A superabundance of gold prevents an increase in profits, reduces the interest on capital, and in this way brings about an irrational increase in production. Producing and exporting for the purpose of hoarding gold in cellars is tantamount to dumping merchandise into the sea. For this reason, America finds it necessary to expand more and more, that is, to convert her excess funds into investments in Latin America, Europe, Asia, Australia, and Africa. But this course causes the European economy as well as other economies to become more and more an integral part of the United States economy." . . .

The empire of the United States assumes . . . all the responsibilities of capitalism. And, at the same time, it faces all its contradictions, which are precisely from what socialism gains its strength. The destiny of North America can be considered only on a worldwide plane. And on this plane, North American capital, still internally vigorous and prosperous, ceases to function as a national, autonomous phenomenon and is converted into the culmination of a world phenomenon, subordinated to an inescapable historical destiny.

READING 2 Whither Communism in the 1930s

Introductory Note

Latin America's Communist Parties underwent a number of changes in the 1930s, moving from the hard line espoused during the 1920s to the concept of the common front, of working with other political forces of the left. An interesting evaluation, a sort of self-analysis, of the Communist Party apparatus throughout Latin America is contained in the following document prepared in 1935 at the time the hard line was replaced with the popular front concept.

During the period that has elapsed since the Sixth Congress of the Comintern (1928), the Communist movement in Latin America has achieved considerable success. At the time of the Sixth Congress, there were Communist parties and Communist groups in twelve countries in Latin America, while at the present time they exist in nineteen countries. Communist parties have been founded in Peru, Paraguay, Venezuela, Costa Rica, Panama, Puerto Rico, and Haiti, and Communist groups in Bolivia and Santo Domingo [sic]. In 1933 the Communist Party of Paraguay, which ceased to function in 1930, was reorganized. The Communist Party of [El] Salvador, which arose in 1930 and in 1932

"Struggles of the Communist Parties of South and Caribbean America," *The Communist International*, Vol. XII, No. 10 (May 20, 1935), pp. 564–76.

was crushed by the government, at the present time is also being rebuilt. The Communist Party of Guatemala, which was formed prior to the Sixth Congress, had practically collapsed by 1932. It is also now being revived. Thus the only countries without Communist organizations in 1934 were Nicaragua, [British] Guiana, and the West Indies.

The sharpening of class contradictions accelerated the bankruptcy of those petty bourgeois organizations that had tried to lead the mass revolutionary movement. Thus the petty bourgeois elements in the Mexican Revolution displayed their inability to solve the revolutionary tasks and slid into the camp of bourgeois national reformism, which is irreconcilably hostile to the agrarian revolution. In 1930 the process of disintegration of "Prestism" in Brazil led to the situation where the greater part of the leaders passed over to the side of various landlord parties, while the minority, headed by Prestes, came into the ranks of the Communist Party. In Nicaragua, where the rebel bands of Sandino had since 1927 carried on the struggle against the armed intervention by the United States, in 1933 the struggle ended by the capitulation of Sandino and his passage over to the side of the counter-revolutionary government of Sacasa.

The rapid radicalization of the masses and the sharp intensification of the class struggle accelerated and deepened the process of disintegration of the traditional parties, and the differentiation of the liberal bourgeois landlord parties and the petty bourgeois groups. Their upper ranks, openly leaning on imperialism, support the reactionary governments (e.g., the support of the Justo government by the Alvearist wing of the Argentine Radicals, the support of Benavides in Peru by the top leaders of the APRA [Alianza Popular Revolucionaria Americana], etc.). At the same time a considerable part of these parties are striving to widen their influence on the masses by resorting to national reformist maneuvers, and even the "socialist" camouflage (the declaration of a "Socialist Republic" by the Grove government in Chile). Finally, petty bourgeois trends arose in the traditional parties ("Radical Bolsheviks" in Argentina, "Left" Batllistas in Uruguay,

Socialist groups in Brazil, "Apro-Communists" in Peru, "Guiteristas" in Cuba, etc.) wavering between national reformism and the anti-imperialist and anti-feudal revolution.

Since the Sixth Congress the influence of anarcho-syndicalism within the working-class movement in Latin America has considerably decreased. In some countries, the best elements came over to the Communist movement as in Argentina, Brazil, Paraguay, and Cuba, where the revolutionary trade-union amalgamation, which is under the leadership of the Communist Party, has taken in a considerable majority of the former anarcho-syndicalist workers. In other countries the weakening of anarcho-syndicalist influence is accompanied by a strengthening of the Socialist and reformist organizations (Argentina), the national reformist parties (National Revolutionary Party in Mexico; "Revolutionary Party" of Grau San Martín in Cuba).

In spite of the successes that have been attained, the main reason that the development of the revolutionary crisis in Latin America is being delayed is the fact that the Communist parties continue to lag behind the big tasks that are called forth by the level of development of the mass movement, and that the proletariat is poorly organized. The Communist parties are not sufficiently ready for decisive revolutionary struggles for power.

In some countries (e.g., Colombia, Ecuador, and Panama) the Communist parties are still greatly contaminated with hostile class elements, and their activity is not yet of a consistent Communist character. In a number of countries, the Communist parties have still very weak contacts with the masses and have by no means eliminated their sectarian tendencies (especially in Mexico).

Even the strongest and most firmly welded Communist parties are characterized by more or less considerable fluctuation of membership, inadequate ideological maturity of the leading cadres, insufficient ability to consolidate successes organizationally. Work in the mass organizations, especially in the reformist and anarcho-syndicalist trade unions, is weak in most cases. In some countries regression is even to be observed. In the vast majority of the countries, our opponents, the leaders of the reformist, anarchist, governmental, and other trade unions still succeed in carrying with them the vast majority of the organized workers. At the same time the majority of the Communist parties still carry on poor work in the countryside, especially among the Indian peasants.

Not a single Communist party has yet adapted itself sufficiently to illegal conditions and at the same time has not been able to make full use of legal possibilities.

The basic weakness of the Communist parties of Latin America have made themselves particularly sharply felt in the carrying out of the united front. The work in the opponent mass organization is very weak and divorced from the struggle for the united front. In a number of cases the adoption of the tactics of a united front has met with direct resistance from various elements and units of the Communist parties and was subjected to the grossest right and left opportunist distortions. When carrying on joint activities with reformist organizations, the Communist parties and the revolutionary trade unions often prove to be incapable of keeping the leading role (e.g., in Mexico in 1932).

On the question of national reformism, the inability of these parties to correctly distinguish and differentiate the role of the various bourgeois and petty bourgeois parties in the growing anti-imperialist and agrarian revolution led occasionally to the revolutionary perspectives being toned down and to an overestimation of the forces of the counter-revolution. The bourgeois and petty bourgeois parties, which differed in the political role they played, in their class character and social composition, were regarded as a simple reactionary front which would inevitably take action against the anti-imperialist revolution. The Communist parties underestimated the special importance of bourgeois national reformism, which has great influence over the petty bourgeoisie, peasantry, and even over the working class in Latin America. As a result of this, they frequently adopted a "neutral" position when big mass struggle took place, fell into a passive attitude, and isolated themselves from the masses of the toilers at times when big political events took place.

At the very moment when a very wide revolutionary upsurge

of the people was taking place, accompanied by a tremendous strike struggle waged by the proletariat and directed against American imperialism and its local reactionary agents, the Communist Party of Cuba absolutely incorrectly raised the question of differentiating between the camp of counter-revolution and the camp of the national liberation struggle, characterizing the national revolutionary Guiteras group, as parties moving in the direction of fascism.

READING 3 *Cuba's Radical Communist Party*

Introductory Note

During the 1930s when most of Latin America's Communist parties were vacillating in their stands on many issues, including the establishment of Communist governments, the Partido Comunista Cubano (*Cuban Communist Party or PCC*) *was taking a militant, radical stand. In resolutions adopted at the 1934 Congress of the PCC, the party defended its position in firm language.*

All the governments which have succeeded one another in power since the overthrow of Machado [Gerardo Machado, dictator of Cuba from 1925 to 1933] have demonstrated equally their incapacity to solve even a single one of the problems created by the crisis.

The bourgeois-landlord government of Grau San Martín, who was placed in the presidential chair on the fourth of September, 1933, by the petty bourgeoisie, principally the students, by workers who were under the influence of the petty bourgeoisie, and by the army, failed because it could not fulfill its mission of curbing the revolutionary movement of the masses. It failed because it could not solve the problems of the crisis, having subsequently lost the support of the petty bourgeoisie, and because, although a government which defended the interests of the

"The Present Situation, Perspectives and Tasks in Cuba," *The Communist*, Vol. XIII, No. 3 (1934), pp. 875–79, 1158–67.

bourgeoisie, the landlords, and the imperialists, as well as their dictatorship, against the masses, it did not gain the confidence of Yankee imperialism nor the native ruling classes, precisely because it could not curb the developing revolution.

The advent to power of the Mendieta-ABC-Batista government on January 18, 1934, is a factor tending to deepen the crisis. It signifies the triumph of the policy of Yankee imperialism by setting up a government of concentration whose mission is to unleash a decided offensive, through methods of violence and terrorism, against the revolutionary movement of the toiling population.

The Mendieta government, faithful executor of the Yankee plans of slavery, not only puts them into practice, but is making enormous expenditures for its apparatus of repression in preparing for war to help Yankee imperialism in the next imperialist slaughter.

Our Party has made great and unquestionable progress since its birth and development during the eight years of the Machado dictatorship, living under the most difficult conditions of white terror.

Our Party was able to convert itself from a group of Communists centered in Havana in 1925, struggling against ferocious persecution, imprisonments, tortures, and assassinations, into a national Party with organizations throughout the country, having thousands of members and leading hundreds of thousands of workers.

On the road toward this development the Party has had to combat and conquer alien class influences which filtered into our ranks. The Party has dissipated the influence of the anarchists and liquidated the opposition to the Party, purging itself of Trotskyite elements and strengthening its own ranks with the enrollment of new members and the forging of better discipline. The Party has liquidated the serious mistakes which were committed in the trade union field, especially relative to the liquidation of the united front tactic, and the policy of "joint committees" which were the expression of the united front from the top and not from below. . . .

The Party must have the perspective of establishing Soviet

power on a local scale in exact proportion to the maturing of the revolutionary situation.

It is necessary to loose a systematic and implacable struggle against all the measures of the counter-revolutionary concentration government, particularly against the white terror.

We must advance a simple program which will convince the masses of the possibility of maintaining a soviet government in Cuba. We must take advantage of the example of Soviet China, whose Red Army has driven back the sixth offensive of the Kuomintang.

We must convince the masses that there is no other way out except the agrarian anti-imperialist revolution, that, is, the overthrow of the power of the exploiters, the complete independence of Cuba, the immediate withdrawal of armed Yankee forces from Cuban waters and from Guantánamo naval base; the confiscation and nationalization of all the means of economic power in the hands of foreign capitalists; the confiscation of the land of the *latifundistas* and their delivery without cost to the peasants; the establishment of a government based on soviets (councils) of delegates of workers, peasants, soldiers, and sailors; the arming of the broad masses and the formation of a Red Army of Workers and Peasants.

We must show the masses that the revolution in Cuba is not an isolated event, but constitutes part of the world revolution and develops in conditions marked by the growth of the world revolutionary crisis. . . .

The Cuban soviet government will recognize and enter into negotiations with the U.S.S.R., exchanging sugar for wheat, oil, machines and other products. The Cuban soviet government will organize the economic basis of Cuba, stimulating the production of products that will assure the feeding of the population in spite of a possible economic blockade from the outside. . . .

We must strengthen the work in the army and navy and other armed forces. The Party must seriously begin to penetrate the mass of soldiers and sailors. At the same time, we must unmask the betrayal of their struggles by Batista and the new officers, and popularize the instances of fraternization.

The Party will not be able to face these great tasks if it does not undertake serious work for its Bolshevization, for its conversion into a mass Communist Party, endowed with an iron discipline and with a strong sense of responsibility on the part of each active member.

We must liquidate the danger of right opportunist tendencies expressed in the lack of faith in the revolution, in defeatism and irresponsibility.

At the same time, we must combat the leftist tendencies to set a fixed time for revolution, to talk loosely of taking power while we are isolated from the daily struggles. It is necessary to liquidate through merciless struggle all the alien class influences in the Party.

Only with iron discipline, Communist strategy, and correct tactics, forged in the fire of struggle, with a Bolshevik line, will the Party be able to lead the masses along the road of the agrarian anti-imperialist revolution.

READING 4 *Chile's Popular Front*

Introductory Note

When the Communist movement in Latin America eschewed the hard line for common front approaches, the Partido Comunista Chileno *(Chilean Communist Party or PCC) moved quickly to work out common front arrangements with other political forces of the left. Not only did Chile have a tradition of easy-going political debate, but also the recent political climate in the nation provided a ready mood for such common front approaches.*

In the presidential election of 1938, a Popular Front candidate, Pedro Aguirre Cerda, defeated the candidate of the established, traditional parties—and the Communists who had supported Aguirre Cerda claimed some of the credit. After the election, the PCC called on the government to initiate a number of reforms and wrote its own program of action for the victory of the Popular Front in subsequent elections.

. . . The Communist Party calls upon the people to organize and to mobilize, and to demand of the government and state authorities the adoption of the following measures:

Establishment of an effective control on the part of the state over the operations of all banks in the country, with the object of preventing new frauds and utilizing the credit for the benefit of the independent industrial development of Chile, to the advantage of the small farmers, miners, merchants, and industrialists.

Nationalization of those foreign enterprises which are involved

"A Program of Action for the Victory of the Chilean People's Front," *The Communist*, Vol. XX, No. 2 (1941), pp. 20–22.

in the stock swindle and which are accused of having meddled in internal affairs, to the detriment of the people and of democracy.

Maintenance of the act prohibiting the return of the fascist conspirators Ibáñez and Herrera.

Support of the president of the republic in his veto of the rightist plot to outlaw the Communist Party and, in general, to limit the free expression of political opinions, in order to prevent the throwing of light upon the crimes of the oligarchy. Defense of the election of the Communist members of Parliament.

Formation of a true Popular Front government through the elimination of those ministers who display a conciliationist, anti-Popular Front tendency, and their replacement by men who are disposed to support the Popular Front by speeding the realization of an immediate plan of economic and social action, based upon the Popular Front program.

The Communist Party calls upon the people to organize and mobilize in order that they may obtain these measures of national salvation. Once again, the Communist Party addresses itself to the workers, peasants, professionals, and honest intellectuals, to all those progressive individuals who are devoted to the fatherland and who are desirous of seeing Chile freed of the shameful scars inflicted upon it by the land-owning oligarchy; they are urged to group themselves in committees with a Popular Front base, in shop, commune, city ward, and on landed estate, with the object of struggling for the adoption of the measures indicated, for their own demands, and for the effective and rapid fulfillment of the 1938 program. . . .

The Popular Front will triumph, and the people of each commune, organized in committees of struggle, will remain vigilant in seeing to it that the Popular Front program is carried out.

READING 5 Prestes and Brazilian Communists

Introductory Note

Luís Carlos Prestes, the Brazilian Communist leader, was freed from prison in 1945 and immediately began a review of the direction of his party. In a book published that year, he wrote of the need to support the concepts of Pan-Americanism and of limited good relations with the United States. His words were, in part, the residue of good feeling for the Allies which had characterized much of the Communist approach during the war years.

His analysis of the Brazilian Communist Party, part of his 1945 book, called for the re-creation of the party more in the mold of the developments in 1945.

. . . The effects of the 1935 defeat on our Party are well known. In the fire of events, our Party was revealed in its true nature—a small party, only feebly linked to the masses, infiltrated by alien ideologies that employed ill-chosen methods of organization, and therefore incapable of surviving the brutality of reaction, which brought it to almost total extinction. But the very struggle revealed what there was of courage and self-sacrifice in a small number of Party cadres. These were elements that had been forged during the years of reaction and terror, and that had succeeded in maintaining their links with the masses, rebuilding

Translated from Luís Carlos Prestes, *Os comunistas na luta pela democracia* (Rio de Janeiro: Edições Horizonte, 1945), pp. 9–12.

the Party and, in practice, fighting against "liquidationism" and other forms of enemy infiltration into the ranks of the revolutionary movement. They succeeded in gradually restoring the Party to its legitimate role as the organized vanguard of the working class, and more specifically as the leaders of our people in the war on Nazism and the fifth column in our country.

Our Party's legal activity is itself a new factor in accelerating political definitions. Reactionaries and leftists of all shades are tearing off their masks, to reveal in their hatred of our Party the real value of the democracy they pretend to defend. In the very same newspapers, they accuse us of being Communists, the enemies of God, country, and family, and at the same time, through the spokesmen of the Trotskyite rabble, of not being Communist enough, or of having betrayed Marxism-Leninism. . . . What they all want, it is clear, is to divide the people, to set up obstacles to their progress to democracy, to turn Brazilian against Brazilian once again to the benefit of the worst exploiters both inside and outside the country, the fascists and their fifth column within the country.

There are still many patriots under the malevolent influence of the enemies of national unity. Accordingly, it is up to us to redouble our efforts to enlighten the largest possible number—not only the rural and urban workers but also the intellectuals, who are the favorite target of the leftists and the Trotskyites.

Instead of the small, illegal party that carried on agitation and spread the general idea of Communism and Marxism, we now need a great party, authentically linked to the working class and the decisive forces in our country, a party that will include the best, the most advanced, the most honest intellectuals, a party that will draw in the best elements of the rural masses, a party that by virtue of its broad social composition will in fact have the necessary power and ability to lead our people in the fight for progress and independence, for liberty and social justice, for popular democratic government.

Finally, we need a party quite different from our old and glorious Party, in which we old militants became the better and more valuable fighters the more we succeeded in resisting persecution by the police and in living incognito among the masses of the people. Today, we need a new-style party, a great party closely linked to the masses; and all of us need to adapt ourselves to the new conditions, to develop the new qualities that our Party, now expanded and legalized, is going to demand from each of its militants.

Our success is going to depend on the capacity we develop to carry out the Party's political line, on our ability to fight for national unity without sacrificing the Party's class independence, to defend its role of leadership in the struggle of the working class and the broadest possible spectrum of workers in the country. Our Party, the vanguard of the working class, must lead; it must not let itself be swept along by the spontaneous movement of the popular masses, by "public opinion," which is in general nourished by the bourgeois press in order to drag the masses in the direction of its class interests. Those who "preach passivity are the carriers of that bourgeois policy which condemned the proletariat to the role of an instrument in the hands of the bourgeoisie," as Stalin has said.

This is the great peril that threatens us in the period through which we are now passing. If we let ourselves be carried along by the spontaneous movement of the masses—whose discontent, as a result of the economic crisis and after so many years of reaction was, and still is, readily exploited by fascism and its fifth column—we would unconsciously serve their ends and would be guilty of the greatest of all crimes against our people.

This is what is being done by all those who allow themselves to be swept along by events and who, however much they claim that they are Communists, are still under the influence of ideologies alien to the proletariat, not to mention those who employ leftist arguments and are nothing more than mouthpieces of the Trotskyite rabble. We must therefore make the most vigorous efforts to steer our Party cadres through these shoals—which will only be accomplished by resolutely and speedily raising the political and theoretical level of the entire Party, and above all, of its more responsible cadres.

READING 6 *Vargas and the* Estado Novo

Introductory Note

During the fifteen years from 1930 to 1945, Brazil was dominated by one man, Getúlio Vargas (1893–1954), who probably more than anyone else must be credited with unifying the nation. While ruling his vast nation, Vargas evolved his concept of a new Brazil, a Brazil that was no longer dominated by strong regional sentiments. His concept of an estado novo *must be gathered from his speeches, interviews, and other appearances, a selection of which is included here. The design of the* estado novo *was loosely written into the Constitution of 1937. Reduced to its essentials, the concept meant political order and economic progress for Brazil—and for Brazilians. While the* estado novo *was never spelled out in full, even in the 1937 Constitution, it was nevertheless implicit in the wording of that document which was issued as the Statute of November 10, mentioned in the following selection.*

The new government is above all else the adaptation of the political system to the realities of Brazil. It integrates all the forces of the collective into a framework of order, social cohesion, and governmental authority. It assures the historical fundamentals of the nation, its essential elements for existence, and its claims to progress menaced, compromised, and sacrificed by the old order which was not only incapable of defending them but permitted and even stimulated factious disturbances, armed regionalism irreconcilable with national unity, and the

Translated from Getúlio Vargas, *A Novo Política do Brasil* (Rio de Janeiro: José Olympio, 1938), Vol. V, pp. 188–89, 196, 259–60.

formation of parties of an aggressive character, refractory by nature to the democratic processes, of the kind that aimed at territorial dismemberment and the subversion of society. . . .

Conserving the traditional lines of organic federation and what existed substantially in that system, such as the autonomy of the states, the democratic form, and the representative process; the Statute of November 10 created, nonetheless, a new legal structure. Among the profound changes brought about by the new regime are: the limitation of direct, universal suffrage, applicable only to specific questions of pertinence to all citizens thus making representation more valid; the municipality as the nuclear base of the political system; the substitution of the principle of the independence of powers by the supremacy of the Executive; the strengthening of the power of the Union; the effective and efficient participation of the economy, through its own organizations, in the constructive and integrating work of the government.

The new system consecrates a government of authority by instituting as law the legislative decree, by giving to the President of the Republic powers to expedite law decrees when Congress is not in session, by attributing to him the prerogative of dissolving it in special cases, and by taking from the Judiciary the privilege of supreme interpretation of the constitutionality or unconstitutionality of the laws which involve public interests of great importance. These new powers, placed under the guard of the government, always overcome private interests.

Profoundly nationalistic, the regime insures and consolidates national unity and formally restricts the autonomy of the states by suppressing regional symbols, extending intervention, establishing the supremacy of federal over local laws in the case of concurrent legislation by attributing to the central government the power to requisition the state militias at any time, etc.

The professions are represented in their own, independent chamber with consultative functions in all the projects concerning the national economy, and eventually it will have legislative functions. . . .

The movement of November 10th was, without doubt, brought

about by the national will. We had need of order and security in order to carry on; conspiring against that was the critical state of political decomposition to which we had arrived. Slowly our public life had been transformed into an arena of sterile struggles where plots, clashing interests of the oligarchy, personal competitions, and differences in personal interests were decided. Men of character without ambition to govern drew away from it nauseated, leaving the field open to political professionals and to demagogic and audacious adventurers. It was thus that Communism succeeded in infiltrating and came to be at one time a national danger. Defeated in its violent attempt to seize power, it continued, nevertheless, its work of undermining authority by utilizing as its weapons the other evils that make the situation of the nation so unstable and chaotic: the weakness of political parties, regional jealousies, and dictatorial flights of fancy. Those three evils are in the final analysis simply the result of a single general cause, well-formed and known: the sterility and depletion of the sources from which the agents of stimulation and renovation of public life ought to come. The political parties had abdicated their social function. They survived at the cost of electoral exploitation and they proliferated often with a predominately local character using old political formulas, foreign to the modern contingencies throughout the world and to the national realities. Foresight of the danger in which we found ourselves and which was felt by all caused us decisively to favor the political unification of the nation, which is precisely why the regime was established on November 10th. The Estado Novo embodies, therefore, the will and ideas which oppose and work against all the factors tending to weaken and dissolve the fatherland—extremes, sabotage, and compromise. It is ready to fight against those evils. It will mobilize all the best that we possess in order to make our nation strong, dignified, and happy. . . .

READING 7 *Vargas's Suicide Note*

Introductory Note

Getúlio Vargas returned to the presidency in 1950, having been elected by the voters of the country. Yet he found it difficult to rule, and demands for his resignation were heard from many quarters. Ironically, he was attacked by groups and individuals upon whom he had formerly relied during the fifteen years he had been dictator.

Rather than resign, however, Vargas committed suicide on August 24, 1954. He left two notes, one of which merely said: "To the wrath of my enemies I leave the legacy of my death. I carry with me the sorrow of not having been able to do for the humble all that I desired. Getúlio Vargas."[1] *The other note, which is reprinted here, has been subjected to intense scrutiny and there are some who doubt that Vargas actually wrote it. In it, Vargas severely criticized the role of international economic interests and thus indicated that he held them responsible for Brazil's poor economic situation.*

Once more, the forces and interests which work against the people have organized themselves afresh and break out against me.

They do not accuse me, they insult me; they do not fight me, they vilify and do not allow me the right to defend myself. They must silence my voice and impede my actions so that I shall not

Reprinted from John W. F. Dulles, *Vargas of Brazil: A Political Biography* (Austin: University of Texas Press, 1957), pp. 334–35.

1. Jordan M. Young, *The Brazilian Revolution of 1930 and the Aftermath* (New Brunswick, N.J.: Rutgers University Press, 1967), p. 103.

continue to defend, as I have always defended, the people and especially the humble. I follow my destiny. After decades of domination and plunder on the part of international economic and financial groups, I placed myself at the head of a revolution and won. I began the work of liberation and I installed a regime of social freedom. I had to resign. I returned to the government on the arms of the people. The underground campaign of international groups joined that of the national groups which were working against the regime of assuring employment. The excess-profits law was held up by Congress. Hatreds were unleashed against the just revision of minimum wages. I wished to bring about national freedom in the utilization of our resources by means of Petrobrás; this had hardly begun to operate when the wave of agitation swelled. Electrobrás was obstructed to the point of despair. They do not want the worker to be free. They do not want the people to be independent.

I assumed the government in the midst of an inflationary spiral which was destroying the rewards of work. Profits of foreign companies were reaching as much as 500 per cent per annum. In declarations of import values, frauds of more than $100 million per year were proved. Came the coffee crisis and the value of our main product rose. We tried to defend its price and the reply was such violent pressure on our economy that we were forced to give in.

I have fought month after month, day after day, hour after hour, resisting constant, incessant pressure, suffering everything in silence, forgetting everything, giving myself in order to defend the people who now are left deserted. There is nothing more I can give you except my blood. If the birds of prey want someone's blood, if they want to go on draining the Brazilian people, I offer my life as a holocaust. I choose this means of being always with you. When they humiliate you, you will feel my soul suffering at your side. When hunger knocks at your door, you will feel in your breast the energy to struggle for yourselves and your children. When you are scorned, my memory will give you the strength to react. My sacrifice will keep you united and my name will be your battle standard.

Each drop of my blood will be an immortal flame in your conscience and will uphold the sacred will to resist. To hatred, I answer with pardon. And to those who think they have defeated me, I repay with my victory. I was a slave of the people, and today I am freeing myself for eternal life. But this people whose slave I was will no longer be slave to anyone. My sacrifice will remain forever in their souls and my blood will be the price of their ransom.

I fought against the spoliation of Brazil. I fought against the spoliation of the people. I have fought with my whole heart. Hatred, infamy, and slander have not conquered my spirit. I have given you my life. Now I offer you my death. I fear nothing. Serenely I take my first step toward eternity and leave life to enter history.

READING 8 *Obstacles to Change in Brazil*

Introductory Note

Explaining in some ways the problems that Getúlio Vargas faced in Brazil and those that have faced the nation's leaders since his suicide is the following analysis by Celso Furtado, the noted Brazilian economist.

Furtado, who was at one time a prominent figure in Brazilian politics as head of the development agency for the impoverished Northeast, has written extensively on Brazil and on Latin America, and now living in exile, sounds a note of strident criticism of Brazil's present military government.

Brazil's economic system and social structure of 1930 differed little from what they had been in the 19th century. Her economy was still based on the export of a narrow range of raw materials, chiefly coffee, and the national revenue was still mainly drawn from taxes levied on foreign trade. Production, be it of coffee, sugar, cocoa or other natural products, was organised on the basis of estates, and the estate was still the basic social and economic institution of the country. Some four-fifths of the population was rural, and economically and socially organised around these estates. These were sometimes extremely large, embracing several thousand people. About four-fifths of the population was also illiterate, and then, as now, such people were constitutionally without political rights. Those who participated effectively in the

Celso Furtado, "Political Obstacles to Economic Growth in Brazil," *International Affairs,* Vol. 41, No. 2 (April 1968), pp. 261–64.

electoral process comprised scarcely more than 1 per cent. of total population of the country. For the great mass of the people the state existed only in its most obvious symbolic forms, such as the person of the President, who, to them, had merely taken the place of the Emperor. Local authorities, even when forming an integral part of the machinery of federal government, were in effect controlled by the big landowners. The ballot was open, and votes were controlled by trusted representatives of the local *grands seigneurs.* Finally, a mechanism existed whereby the electoral results could be altered by the central authorities. Thus those who were in power were equipped with all the necessary means to maintain themselves in it.

From the point of view of the humble countryman, living his whole life on a great estate, the only meaning of 'power' was that exercised by the local estate owner. The state itself as a national political entity had hardly any meaning for the mass of the populace since its prime function was to finance the military machine and the civil service. Control of the latter was for all practical purposes in the hands of local rulers forming a seigniorial class, whose traditionally accepted authority was, as its name implies, based on the ownership of land. Brazil was an oligarchic republic on a seigniorial basis. The struggles for power between regional oligarchal factions were kept under discipline and restraint by the personal writ of the Emperor, who was the keystone of national unity. The republican régime, installed in 1889, strengthened the hand of the local oligarchic groupings. However, at this stage the coffee-growing section enjoyed undisputed pre-eminence, and continued to wield power uninterruptedly for the first 40 years of the Republic.

Alongside this essentially stable society, whose system of power merely reflected its patriarchal structure, there grew up a source of instability in the form of an urban population engaged in activities connected with foreign trade, government work and services in general. This section of the population had greater opportunity for education, even in its higher forms, and was much influenced by foreign ideas. It was this class that was most adversely affected by the exchange policy traditionally followed by the government to defend the interests of the exporters. Whenever the foreign market prices of Brazilian exports fell, the currency was devalued, and a substantial proportion of the real loss of income was transferred to the importers. Since these urban populations relied quite considerably on imports, even for their food, prices rose sharply in all major cities and towns whenever the country was faced with a decline in prices for its exports. Conditions such as these tended to create a feeling of unrest in the towns which found frequent expression in local revolts. Nevertheless, the urban population was really no more than an appendage of the rural economy, from which, indirectly, it earned its living. The leading strata of urban society were composed for the most part of members of the great landowning families.

Stagnation in the agricultural export sector, concentration of investment in the main population centres, chiefly in manufacturing projects, and finally, the rapid growth of state activities, combined to cause considerable changes in the social structure of the country whose most obvious outward and visible sign was a rapid process of urbanisation. According to the census of 1920 (there was none in 1930) the population of Brazil was about 30m., of whom 7m. lived in the towns. Today the population figure is up to 80m., of which the towns account for no less than 35m. Since the urban population has a far higher percentage of literacy than the rural, it is clear that the political centre of gravity has undergone a radical displacement, at least in so far as the electoral process is concerned. . . .

Brazilian industrialisation, child of the last three decades, is a typical example of what may be termed development on the basis of import-substitution. Its rapid and precocious growth during the period ushered in by the 1929 crisis is, in Latin America, peculiar to Brazil. The great coffee plantations formed under the stimulus of the high prices prevailing in 1927–29 started production in 1931 and plunged the country into a crisis of overproduction just at the time when coffee prices had fallen by two-thirds on the world market. Thus Brazil found herself facing a dual crisis: one which forced her to cut her imports by half, and the other, internal, resulting from the need for financing large stocks of unmarketable coffee. The extent of the strain involved may be gathered from the fact that the value of coffee that had to be bought for stocking or destruction exceeded, in some years, 10 per cent. of the gross national product. This was a policy inspired by the coffee interests, or designed to appease them.

The more the government bought up coffee for stocking or destruction, and thus inflated the internal economy, the more did the Brazilian currency depreciate in relation to foreign currencies; this process also favoured the coffee-growers, because the price of coffee continued to rise in depreciated national currency even while the world price was steadily falling. The consequences of such a policy were, however, much more far-reaching than could be foreseen at the time. In seeking to maintain money incomes in the country under conditions of declining import capacity, the policy of favouring the coffee sector became, in the final analysis, one of industrialisation. With the rapid devaluation of the currency, the relative prices of imported goods rose, thereby creating extremely favourable conditions for home production. Since profits from the cultivation of coffee were now declining, because the favoured treatment shown by the government to the growers only partly compensated for the fall in the real value of their exports, consumer goods production for the home market became the most attractive field of investment in the Brazilian economy. In this way investment was deflected from the traditional export sector, principally that of the production and marketing of coffee, and channelled into the manufacturing industries. During the period 1929–37, total imports declined by 23 per cent. and industrial production rose by 50 per cent.

The second phase of Brazilian industrialisation, that of the post-war years, is no less interesting from the point of view of the policy followed and the results achieved. In order to protect coffee prices on the world market whilst there were still enormous stocks in Brazil, the government in 1946 maintained the wartime rate of exchange of the *cruzeiro* [the Brazilian unit of currency] in spite of the fact that the level of prices had risen much more in Brazil than in the United States. By then it was known from experience that devaluation of the *cruzeiro* would mean an immediate fall in the world price of coffee and adverse repercussions on the country's balance of payments. In pursuing this policy, which meant low prices for imported goods, the Brazilian Government completely disregarded the interests of industry, particularly as the Brazilian tariff was specific, and in no way geared to price-rises on the world market.

The indirect consequences of this policy were unexpected. Imports rose rapidly, exhausting the reserves of foreign exchange accumulated during the war, and leading, as early as 1948, to the formation of short-term debt. Preoccupied with the price of coffee, particularly in view of the increasing adverse trade balance, the government preferred to introduce a system of import-restriction rather than to devalue the *cruzeiro*. In rationing the available foreign exchange, the authorities were in practice compelled to give general priority to the import, first, of raw materials and intermediate products in order to maintain the level of employment in existing industries, and, secondly, of plant and equipment. The import of anything 'superfluous' became exteremely difficult. Thus, under cover of maintaining the external price of coffee, a dual protection of industry was created whereby the import of foreign-made equivalents was virtually prohibited, while the necessary exchange was made available for the import of raw materials and plant at subsidised prices. The government's firm adherence to this policy was one of the causes of the marked rise in the world coffee price that was a feature of 1949. Conversely, this rise in price created conditions which encouraged the government to persist in this policy. In this manner a substantial proportion of the income generated by the improvement in the terms of trade between 1949 and 1954 was transferred to the industrial sector in the form of deliveries of plant and intermediate products at relatively low prices. In these conditions, and in view of the fact that the demand for finished goods remained inflated, industrial investments were bound to show a rising yield. . . .

Industrialisation in Brazil thus was a by-product of measures taken to favour the traditional agricultural export-economy. However, industrialisation produced important repercussions within those institutions upon which the traditional system of power was based.

IV The Postwar Period

The post-World War II years in Latin America were tumultuous. Not only did Fidel Castro come to power in Cuba and Eduardo Frei Montalva in Chile (dealt with respectively in Parts V and VI), but much of the hemisphere showed a much clearer trend toward change and reform than it had in earlier decades.[1]

MOVEMENTS OF THE DEMOCRATIC LEFT

One of the most significant movements in the period after 1945 was the rise of the democratic left, a loosely knit structure which embraced governments in half a dozen countries. Its leaders were men who came to power in the 1950s bringing with them new democratic ideas and reformist policies. Key figures included Venezuela's Rómulo Betancourt (1908–   ), who more than anyone else came to personify the democratic left, and Costa Rica's José Figueres (1912–   ), who offered his country and his ranch as a haven for many Latin American politicians in exile. Betancourt spent time in Costa Rica with Figueres, as did Juan Bosch (1905–   ), the Dominican author and politician who was the leading opponent of long-time Dominican dictator Rafael Leonidas Trujillo Molina (1896–1961).[2]

Betancourt had briefly been a Communist in his younger days, but in 1941 he founded a non-Communist political force known

1. See, for example, Arthur P. Whitaker and David C. Jordan, *Nationalism in Contemporary Latin America* (New York: The Free Press, 1966).
2. Bosch later became president of his nation, but its military leaders overthrew his government in 1963. When forces loyal to Bosch staged a revolt in 1965 in hopes of returning him to power, United States military intervention eventually ended the revolt and Bosch was subsequently defeated for the presidency in a 1966 election.

as *Acción Democrática* (Democratic Action). AD, as it is popularly known in Venezuela, actually succeeded in winning the presidency in 1948 for Venezuela's noted novelist, Rómulo Gallegos (1884–1969),[3] but he was overthrown after nine months by the nation's military. The ensuing ten-year dictatorship under Colonel Marcos Pérez Jiménez (1909–), forced *Acción Democrática* underground for ten years. AD and other parties overthrew the Pérez Jiménez regime in 1958 and the following year Betancourt himself became president. He served his full term, and in 1964 handed over the presidential sash to his colleague and fellow AD member, Raúl Leoni (1914–). Betancourt's most famous work appeared in 1956—*Venezuela: Política y petróleo* (Venezuela: Politics and Petroleum)—a book that contained his hopes for Venezuela (Reading One).

Puerto Rico's Governor Luis Muñoz Marín (1898–) was part of the democratic left.[4] Although his island is not an independent nation and has commonwealth status with the United States, Muñoz Marín became an effective part of the movement because of his role as a bridge between the English-speaking United States and Spanish-speaking Latin America and because of his friendship with other members of the group. A sampling of his writings suggests how keenly he felt that the Puerto Rican experiment as a commonwealth in association with the United States was beneficial to Latin America in general (Reading Two).

To Bolivia, the only country other than Mexico and Cuba regarded as having had a valid social revolution in this century, the year 1952 brought the start of a profound change in the nation's political and economic structures. Under Víctor Paz Estenssoro (1908–), Bolivia's *Movimiento Nacional Revolucionario* (National Revolutionary Movement or MNR) began a series of major reforms, including nationalization of the nation's tin mines, an agrarian reform measure designed to redistribute huge tracts

3. Rómulo Gallegos was Venezuela's leading writer in the first part of the century, author of the noted novel *Doña Bárbara*, published in 1929.
4. For short biographical essays on some of the leaders of the democratic left, see Robert J. Alexander, *Prophets of the Revolution: Profiles of Latin American Leaders* (New York: The Macmillan Company, 1962).

of land to the impoverished peasantry, and a variety of educational improvements aimed at ridding the nation of its staggering illiteracy. Not all the programs were successful. The tin nationalization, with its padded payrolls and overbearing bureaucracy, has long since been recognized as an unfortunate move.[5]

The MNR, as one of its cardinal propositions, promised to give the land back to the Indians.[6] The program of the party in this connection stated as far back as 1942 that:

> We demand a law regulating the work of the peasant, in accordance with the peculiarities of each region without modifying the customs imposed by geographical conditions, but guaranteeing the health and the satisfaction of the needs of the Bolivian workers. We demand that every work of colonization show recognition of the need to make every Bolivian, man or woman, a landholder. . . .
>
> We demand the study on a scientific basis of the Indian agrarian problem so as to incorporate in the national life the millions of peasants now outside of it, and to obtain an adequate organization of the agricultural economy so as to obtain the maximum output.[7]

Once in office, the MNR carried out its promise. Paz and his associates pushed through an agrarian reform law which was one of the most advanced in Latin America (Reading Three).[8]

THE PEACEFUL COMMUNIST PATH

Traditional Latin American Communist Parties have remained

5. See Robert J. Alexander, *The Bolivian National Revolution* (New Brunswick, N.J.: Rutgers University Press, 1958); and Harold Osborne, *Bolivia: A Land Divided* (London: Oxford University Press for the Royal Institute of International Affairs, 3rd edition, 1964).
6. Abraham Maldonado, *Derecho Agraria* (La Paz, 1955), p. 312.
7. Ibid., p. 312.
8. For a study of agrarian reform in Latin America, see T. Lynn Smith, ed., *Agrarian Reform in Latin America* (New York: Alfred A. Knopf, 1965). This volume contains, in addition to Professor Smith's valuable introductory essay, a collection of some of the best writing on the subject. Among the essays are three on Bolivia's program.

strikingly consistent in advocating peaceful struggle based upon the broadest possible anti-imperialist and anti-oligarchic fronts. Of course, Castro's more militant stand in Cuba and the revolutionary and guerrilla stand of Ernesto Che Guevara are exceptions to this pattern. Moreover, some small Communist Parties—the *Partido Comunista Venezolana* (Venezuelan Communist Party or PCV), the *Partido Guatemalteco de Trabajo* (Guatemalan Labor Party or PGT), and the *Partido Comunista Colombiano* (Colombian Communist Party or PCC)—have been linked with recent urban and rural insurgency; but the main thrust of the larger parties in Chile, Brazil, and Argentina has been toward peaceful change.[9]

The strategy of building peaceful alliances with non-Communist nationalist groups allowed for variations of tactics within and among countries. The policies of the Chilean party have evolved—to cite one example—from the broad Popular Front in the 1938 and 1946 elections to the present uneasy alliance with the socialists in the *Frente de Acción Popular* (Popular Action Front or FRAP). This Marxist alliance, more limited than the earlier Popular Front, put up its own candidate in the 1964 presidential elections. The two other leftist, but non-Marxist parties, the Radicals and the Christian Democrats, did not support FRAP's socialist candidate.

Unlike the Chilean Communist Party (Reading Four), the

9. For background on this point, see Ernst Halperin's monograph series on recent Chilean elections (issued by M.I.T. Press) and his *Nationalism and Communism in Chile* (Cambridge: M.I.T. Press, 1965). The estimated membership for the PCV in 1966–67 was 10,000, the PCC's (Colombia) was 8000. PCV membership is concentrated in urban students, intellectuals, workers, and newspapermen. The Chilean Party's membership for the same years was estimated at 30,000; the Argentine Party's at 60,000; and the Brazilian Party's at something under 40,000. While not the largest numerically, the Chilean Communists are regarded as the strongest and most politically successful in Latin America. These figures come from a study prepared at the request of the United States Senate Subcommittee on American Republics Affairs of the Committee on Foreign Relations. See *Survey of the Alliance for Progress: Insurgency in Latin America* (Washington: Government Printing Office, January 15, 1968).

Brazilian and Argentine parties operated illegally. They attempted to peacefully forge an alliance which would draw support away from the established governments (Readings Five and Six). Like most orthodox Communist Parties in Latin America, both parties based their thought upon Marxist-Leninist philosophy, rather than an indigenous national ideology. In this sense, they are less nationalist than those parties advocating Christian Democracy (Chile's Christian Democrats and the Social Christians or COPEI in Venezuela), indianismo (Peru's *Alianza Popular Revolucionaria Americana*), or revolutionary nationalism (Mexico's *Partido Revolucionario Institucional* or Bolivia's *Movimiento Nacional Revolucionario* from 1952 to 1964).

Another tactical change emerged in the 1960s. Since the Cuban Revolution—which had massive peasant support—the peaceful path has been expanded to include not only organized labor, students, and the petty bourgeoisie, as in the past, but also rural peasant groups. The urban proletariat is most often acknowledged by the larger parties to be the most powerful social class within this alliance, an ideological point perfectly consistent with the traditional Marxist doctrine, and the proletariat is the class by which the revolution is to be carried out. The history of the Latin American Communist movement demonstrated little interest in the rural areas before the 1959 Cuban Revolution.[10] Yet after 1959, the Communist Parties increasingly turned their attention toward building a mass rural following, as the Chilean example suggests (Reading Seven).

Pursuing this tactical change, at least three small parties—those of Venezuela, Guatemala, and Colombia—began to give heavy support to rural insurgency. The Venezuelan Party began to abandon the violent road in 1966 (Reading Eight), and the Colombian and Guatemalan Parties appear to be following a dual policy of tacit support for insurgency while officially holding that participation in elections and other overt legal activity are ap-

10. See Rollie Poppino, *International Communism in Latin America: A History of the Movement, 1917–1963* (London: The Free Press of Glencoe, 1964), p. 101.

propriate steps in preparing the masses for revolution—a "preparation" process in effect for years (Reading Nine).

The "dual policy" of smaller Communist Parties underlines two of the many problems that plague Communist groups in Latin America: internal factions (the "soft" vs. "hard"-liners) and the absence of rigid organizational discipline. They have tended to be organizationally and politically weak (Chile is an exception), as well as less determined to gain power at any risk, and much less cohesive than their European counterparts. They operate in a political and cultural setting where personalism, emotionalism, and traditional social values tend to condition the process of political activity. Latin American attitudes and values—not conducive to tight discipline and ideological commitment but amenable to opportunism and splintering—appear to be more conservative and conformist at all levels of society than "revolutionary" in the Marxist sense. This helps explain the absence of a revolutionary tradition among the orthodox pro-Moscow parties and their tendency to play the normal game of opportunist politics: co-operation with both dictators and democrats for limited benefits.

THE GUERRILLAS

While guerrilla warfare conducted by small insurgent groups has a long history in Latin America, it became increasingly popular after Fidel Castro's successful overthrow of Fulgencio Batista (1901–   ). Castro, of course, did not begin as an open advocate of guerrilla war. Indeed, his early statements between 1956 and 1958 focused upon "moderation" and constitutionalism. When he landed in Cuba from Mexico in December 1956, he apparently had no plans or elaborate theory for an extended struggle but he began to engage in guerrilla warfare with hopes of instigating a mass rebellion against the existing regime (Reading Ten).

Once in power after January 1959, Castro and his close associate, Ernesto Che Guevara (1928–67), an Argentine, began to popularize the idea that Cuba's had been an "agrarian revolution" with the fundamental struggle centered in the countryside and led by guerrilla fighters (Reading Eleven). Although their writings and speeches may have been misleading about the urban middle class's role in the revolution, they constitute the basis for later guerrilla warfare movements in the hemisphere.[11]

Two central points distinguish the guerrillas from the orthodox Communist Parties. Firstly, they disagree on the issue of revolutionary timing. Historically, the Communists have concentrated on preparing the masses for revolution, waiting for the proper conditions to cause an eruption. In contrast, the guerrillas are action-oriented. They emphasize—in accordance with both Castro and Guevara—that in many countries it is unnecessary to wait for a spontaneous revolution. Instead, they argue, revolutionary leadership must be prepared to initiate and engage in armed struggle. Where objective conditions do not exist, the guerrillas can create them.

Secondly, the guerrillas tend to focus more on the tactical theory of guerrilla war, with its emphasis on armed struggle, than on Marxism-Leninism. To be sure, words like "imperialism" and "class struggle" are used and references to Marxism are made, but the main interest is not in dialectics but in immediate armed struggle. Indeed, Régis Debray (1931–   ), the young French Marxist captured in Bolivia for alleged participation in the guerrilla insurgency, argues in his book, *Revolution in the Revolution?* that guerrillas do not require a Communist Party, since they need maximum flexibility in the countryside and will form their own organization, the nucleus for a new party.[12]

Several interviews in the late 1960s with guerrilla leaders docu-

11. See Theodore Draper, *Castroism: Theory and Practice* (New York: Frederick A. Praeger, 1965), pp. 57–134. A useful article, putting the guerrilla situation in historic perspective, is Edward Bernard Glick, "Isolating the Guerrilla: Some Latin American Examples," *Orbis*, Vol. VII, No. 3 (Fall 1968), pp. 873–86.
12. Régis Debray, *¿Revolución en la Revolución?* (Havana: Casa de las Américas, 1967). For a variety of comments on Debray's thesis, see Leo Huberman and Paul M. Sweezy, eds., *Regis Debray and the Latin American Revolution: A Collection of Essays* (New York: Monthly Review Press, 1968). Debray's book has been put out in an English edition under the title *Revolution in the Revolution?* (New York: Monthly Review Press, 1967).

ment the degree of attention paid to radical nationalism rather than Marxism-Leninism (Reading Twelve). Many of the guerrilla leaders have visited Cuba and follow the "guerrilla war" strategy put forward by Castro, Guevara, and Debray, but they seldom follow sectarian ideologies or belong to the traditional Communist Party. They come from many backgrounds, but are united in the belief that the status quo must be overturned in the quest for social justice and national development.

The guerrilla movements suffered a number of setbacks in the late 1960s. Peruvian and Dominican Republic movements were quickly squashed. A Brazilian movement collapsed of its own weakness in 1967. Guerrillas were captured in Argentina and Paraguay in 1964 and 1965. Guevara's death in Bolivia, in October 1967, produced serious reverses there and undoubtedly worried guerrillas elsewhere. Other causes for concern were itemized in Guevara's diary, including sickness, lack of men, the difficulty of making contact with outside help in order to replace arms, ammunition, and medical equipment, and—perhaps most important of all—the extremely frustrating inability to establish a peasant base for future mobilization (Reading Thirteen).

PAN-AMERICANISM

Numerous hemisphere statesmen have urged multinational cooperative action to bring about reform and change in Latin America. This approach, already evident before the turn of the century, gained its biggest impetus in post-World War II years. Spokesmen for the democratic left were generally sympathetic to the idea. And the conversion of the old Pan-American Union into the Organization of American States in 1948 marked a significant turning point in the hemisphere's multinational efforts.

But the organization did not become a major factor in the quest for change until the last years of the 1950s, when the hemisphere nations, gathered in Bogotá, the Colombian capital, agreed on the establishment of the Inter-American Development Bank. The bank's charter authorized it to promote the investment of public and private capital for development purposes.

The bank grew steadily, although its beginnings were on

a rather inauspicious scale. Hemisphere statesmen, including the former president of Colombia, Alberto Lleras Camargo (1901–), spoke out in behalf of the bank and urged its expansion. Felipe Herrera (1922–), president of the bank from its inception and a former finance official in Chile, has seen his role as one of educating the public of the Americas to the bank's activities and its possibilities (Reading Fourteen).

The great impetus to regional hemispheric action on the issue of change and reform came with President John F. Kennedy's call for an *alianza para el progreso* in a 1961 speech. Latin America and the United States subsequently set up the framework for the Alliance for Progress at Uruguay's Punta del Este in August of the same year. But the Alliance idea had its first major articulation in a 1958 letter sent by Brazil's President Juscelino Kubitschek (1902–) to President Dwight D. Eisenhower (1890–1969) calling for a hemisphere-wide attack on backwardness in Latin America. Terming his proposal "Operation Pan-America," Kubitschek's letter was in part inspired by the difficult experiences encountered by then Vice-President Richard M. Nixon on a Latin American tour in 1958 (Reading Fifteen).

The story of the years of the Alliance have been told and retold, and the Alliance itself has received repeated comment—both favorable and unfavorable.[13] The criticism has come both from those who support its basic goals and from those who are its sharpest detractors. While the nations of the hemisphere have made some headway in regearing their economic and social structures under the aegis of the Alliance, it seems clear to most analysts that the Alliance has not lived up to the goals originally set for it (Reading Sixteen). It may be that the goals were too high in the first place. Whatever the problems, efforts to revitalize and rekindle the Alliance spirit were begun in the late 1960s.

Chile's reformist President Eduardo Frei Montalva (1911–)

13. See Lincoln Gordon, *A New Deal for Latin America: The Alliance for Progress* (Cambridge: Harvard University Press, 1963); and John C. Dreier, ed., *The Alliance for Progress: Problems and Perspectives* (Baltimore: Johns Hopkins University Press, 1962).

sought to shore up the Alliance with new stress on multinational projects, regional economic agreements, and overall hemisphere economic integration. In a 1966 article Frei spoke eloquently of his goal of bringing the nations of the hemisphere closer together, particularly in the economic sphere, as a means of reforming and regearing their economies to the needs of the present century. Frei argued for regional planning and a "sense of common destiny" to achieve the goals (Reading Seventeen).

A POTPOURRI OF REFORM

Although the movements of the democratic left, the Communists, the guerrillas, and the inter-American system are easy to define, it is difficult to label the other efforts at change in the early postwar years. These efforts include a variety of elements —Juan Domingo Perón's social legislation in Argentina, the end of the Getúlio Vargas years in Brazil and eventually the establishment of a military government there, growing nationalism in such countries as Bolivia and Peru, the emergence of a new bloc of Latin American nations in the English-speaking Caribbean.

The Argentina of the 1930s was conservative, often intolerant of labor, and, in many ways, quite undemocratic. Elections were tightly controlled by the conservative-military alliance of these years in order to maintain itself in power. The years from 1930 to 1943 have been called by some the Era of Infamy. These years of increasing governmental control of the economy, of banking, of provincial politics, explain in some measure, the climate that allowed a Perón (1895–   ) to emerge. The political and economic uncertainties of pre-Perón years help explain not only how Perón could come to power in 1943 and begin his long hegemony, but also the general climate of malaise felt in Argentina since World War II.[14]

Estimates of the Perón years now suggest that history will

14. For analyses of the Perón years, see Joseph R. Barager, ed., *Why Perón Came to Power: The Background to Peronism in Argentina* (New York: Alfred A. Knopf, 1968). Also, George Pendle, *Argentina* (London: Oxford University Press for the Royal Institute of International Affairs, 3rd edition, 1963).

judge them as a mixed blessing. While Perón did move the nation toward solving some of Argentina's long-standing ills, his years also created new problems. Perón correctly saw the need to further the economic development of Argentina through nationalization and industrialization policies. But although he was furthering the development of mineral resources in the interior and the growth of important provincial towns, he was also allowing the rural areas to languish somewhat, and agriculture did not keep pace with the advances he was fostering in other areas. Much of Peróns's support came from the lower classes, particullarly the urban *descamisados* (literally, the shirtless ones), who had helped bring him to power in the first place and among whom there is still a sharp longing to return to the Perón years that ended in his overthrow in 1955.

It seems clear that the lower classes benefited in the Perón era—more so in the early years than in later years—from his program of social legislation. "Social justice" was a hallmark of Peronist philosophy in these years. Perón and his followers called it *justicialismo,* and they spoke much of forming a state based on this philosophy. Yet the theory that Perón and his wife, Eva (1919–52), devoted themselves unstintingly to the welfare of the *descamisados* overstates the case. By favoring the *descamisados,* Perón set class against class and created imbalances in Argentine society which remain today. Moreover, a lowering of moral standards, corruption, and gangsterism were part of the Perón years and legacy. Yet Perón responded to the problems facing one group of Argentines and they still do him homage in regularly voting *Peronista.*

Perón's philosophy is scattered throughout his writings and speeches, a few of which are excerpted here. His wife Eva, who was a strong asset to Perón in his rise to power and his maintenance of power, also spelled out some of this philosophy (Reading Eighteen). Post-Perón problems were many. They have been analyzed over and over again by Argentine commentators including one of Perón's successors, Arturo Frondizi (1908–), who warned the Argentine people that they must tighten their belts and live in austerity if they were to lift themselves out of the economic and political morass into which they had gotten themselves (Reading Nineteen).

In the English-speaking Caribbean, constitutional developments in the early postwar years and the yearning of many black peoples to set up their own governments and to be free from Britain led to the establishment of black, semi-self-governing states. A British plan to federate the Caribbean islands in one regional grouping before granting independence failed when the two largest islands, Jamaica and Trinidad, opted out, partly in fear of the consequences of being saddled with the economic backwardness of the smaller islands. Both Jamaica and Trinidad became independent, as did Barbados and Guyana (which had formerly been British Guiana).

For some time, British Guiana was under the leadership of Marxist-leaning Cheddi B. Jagan (1923–   ) who, together with his American-born wife, Janet (1929–   ), worked to create a Marxist nation out of the colony. Under new voting arrangements, Forbes Burnham (1925–   ), a onetime Jagan associate, won the prime ministership in 1964 and formed a government in coalition with a third political group, the United Force. Complicating the picture were two main racial groups represented, respectively, by Jagan and Burnham. Conflict arose between them over race. Jagan was the leader of the colony's East Indians, descendants of the indentured servants brought to the Caribbean by the British following the end of slavery, while Burnham represented the Africans, descendants of the original slaves brought to the New World by the British.

Burnham, after the 1964 election victory, led the colony into independence in 1966 and won another election victory in 1968, using constitutional provisions that permitted overseas Guayanese to vote. Both Jagan and Burnham believe in broad social legislation to help the mainland nation's 650,000 people share a better way of life. The Burnham government has introduced a variety of social welfare projects (Reading Twenty).

In other parts of the onetime British American empire, black leaders are beginning to be heard. The eloquence of Lynden O. Pindling (1927–   ) in the Bahamas, for instance, appeals to the island-nation's dominantly black population (Reading Twenty-one).

Returning to Spanish-speaking America, the rise of military government and new forms of militarism in the late 1960s appears to be part of a new nationalist urge on the part of Latin Americans. What is going on in Peru, under a military government which came to power in October 1968, is illustrative (Reading Twenty-two), as are the similar efforts in neighboring Bolivia under a military government.

READING 1 *Betancourt's Hope for Venezuela*

Introductory Note

Rómulo Betancourt (1908–   ), the founder and longtime leader of Venezuela's most important post-World War II political force, Acción Democrática (Democratic Action), spent much of his early life in opposition to the dictatorial regimes governing his native land. A writer of some prominence in Venezuela and elsewhere in the hemisphere, Betancourt's most famous book is Venezuela: Política y petróleo, *the first edition of which, published in Mexico in 1956, is something of a collector's item. In it he called on Venezuela to use its rich petroleum reserves for the betterment of the masses and his political movement promised, once in office, to do just that.*

Betancourt was elected president in 1958 and following his inauguration early the next year embarked on an ambitious economic development program that included industrial expansion, agricultural education, and the improvement of communications —all of them points outlined in his noted book.

One might suppose that the possibility of reestablishing and stabilizing a civilized system of government in Venezuela is remote indeed. The uninterrupted flow of petroleum, with the financial returns which come from this export, and the inter-

Translated from Rómulo Betancourt, *Venezuela: Política y petróleo* (México: Fondo de Cultura Económica, 1956), pp. 768–70, 774.

national complicities which have been an effective support for dictatorial regimes in our country, seem to guarantee a rosy future for dictatorship in Venezuela. This conclusion is the result of a hasty analysis. In Venezuela the collective will to recover lost liberties, encouraged and channeled by the political forces organized by the parties, has not died out. And history proves that in any country where numerous groups within the population, with moral and intellectual fibre, persevere in their resistance to institutionalized arbitrariness, these groups always succeed eventually in imposing democratic norms of government and administration.

This is what Andrés Eloy Blanco [a Venezuelan poet who helped Betancourt found his party] said, in the well-chosen words of a great poet and intuitive politician, in the lecture which was his last will and testament, given a few hours before he died, before the members of *Acción Democrática* in exile in Mexico: "It is necessary to acknowledge the importance of the economic realities, but we must also remember the reality of our people. They are as a people economically backward and resplendent in their epic struggle; underdeveloped by any economic criterion and millionaires in human wealth; small in number but great in their heroism. Among the people emotional values and above all the human factor are vital. Our prime material and our greatest wealth is our human wealth."

But other tendencies, which also go toward putting an optimistic face on the political future of Venezuela, should be noted. Some of these are related to the national reality itself; others result from recent historical events, universal in scale, which have occurred within the American scene.

Regarding Venezuela, it is coming to be realized that the regime imposed upon the nation without its consent is a historical anachronism, which goes against the degree of development already achieved by the country. Its empiric administrative systems and its daring disdain of all norms of good government are as contrary to the needs of a highly evolved society as its police methods of dealing with the citizenry are repugnant to the entire population. The fact is that Venezuela is no longer what she was in the days of Castro and Gómez [early Venezuelan dictators], when she had scarcely two million inhabitants and was a backward, bucolic nation, without industries, isolated from the world in an era of difficult communication, and with a population scourged by yellow fever and lack of culture. Today we form part of a modern nation, a nation which has passed through the industrial revolution of the twentieth century with a national territory largely made safe from tropical diseases, and with a population which exceeds five million, of whom half a million are workers living in industrial and extractive centers. Large segments of this population are cultured and there is a numerous, well-informed middle class. The nation is no longer a walled island but, on the contrary, due to its geographic location and its economic potential, it is a plexis of aereal and maritime intercommunications. The radio had nullified the attempts of the governors to isolate us from the world as Paraguay was isolated in the nineteenth century under Francia. Thus one can understand why the determining majority of Venezuelans, apart from the ideological positions of the various social groups, is against a regime which makes every effort to continue to apply the tribal methods of Cipriano Castro and Juan Vicente Gómez to an adult nation in the process of accelerated growth. . . .

And if the Venezuelan nation is different today from what it was in the times of Gómez, today's army is also distinct from the mountaineers of that era, a primitive horde commanded by ignorant cut-throats. The requirements of national growth itself and the technological complexity of modern arms have forced the rise of groups of officials possessing appreciable personal culture in some branches of the armed forces, especially the Navy and the Air Force.

It was groups from among these cultivated sectors of the armed forces who have contributed to the changes overcoming anti-democratic situations in some Latin American countries. . . .

Our reasoned and profound conviction is that it will be possible to create a stable form of government in our country which will respect popular liberties, and among them the fundamental right of suffrage; a government concerned to resolve by modern and rational means the problems of the collectivity; a government honorable in its handling of public moneys and disposed to convince foreign investors that their capital may enter the nation for the purpose of legal business, and not to despoil our natural resources and trample upon the rights of the Venezuelan worker. In short, a government capable of orienting and conducting the national democratic revolution that is at the present moment a historical necessity for Venezuela, and which can no longer be postponed.

READING 2 *Muńoz Marín and Puerto Rico's Democracy*

Introductory Note

Luis Muñoz Marín, Puerto Rico's longtime governor (1948–64), was a leader of Latin America's democratic left during the 1950s and early 1960s. A strong advocate of Puerto Rico's close relationship with the United States, he was the architect of the island's unique commonwealth status.

The son of the Puerto Rican patriot Luis Muñoz Riverd, Muñoz Marín was born to politics and to his island's status as a dependency of the United States. He early advocated independence for Puerto Rico which had come under United States rule at the end of the Spanish-American war, but he later decided the island was not ready either for independence or for statehood. It was during the 1940s that he evolved the concept of commonwealth status for Puerto Rico and won Washington's acceptance of the idea. It was also in this period that he began "Operation Bootstrap," a program of accelerated economic growth and development for the island which has brought a degree of prosperity to his people.

I believe that basically the democracy of Puerto Rico has contributed to the democracy of the Western Hemisphere a new form of political party, to which I have the honor to belong, the

Speech by Luis Muñoz Marín to the Inter-American Press Association, October 16, 1957. Mimeographed, pp. 1–4, passim. Reprinted by permission.

Popular Democratic Party. I say that this is a new form of political party because it has brought about, and is still carrying on, a peaceful revolution in Puerto Rico by completely legal processes. It is doing this, not by propounding doctrines, but by facing with open heart and open mind the great problems that for so many years have burdened my Puerto Rican compatriots in their daily lives. This is a revolution that is a contribution of considerable value to democracy. . . .

One method which we have finally developed in order to keep the political parties free of the influence of money is a law which provides that all political parties shall receive from public funds the legitimate expenses which a party must incur in its work in a democracy; these funds are provided in equal amounts to all political parties. To the party of which I have the honor to be the leader, which received 64 per cent of the votes in the last election, exactly the same amount is contributed for its expenses as is given to the smallest party, which obtained only 12 or 14 per cent of the votes at the last election. This frees the political parties from any ties or obligations of any kind to the economic interests that normally have to provide the campaign funds for political parties, and I believe that this is another important contribution that Puerto Rico has made to democracy.

Still another contribution which Puerto Rico is making to democracy is the creation of a new form of poltical association in a federal system of government. Since the first steps were taken and this new form of association established, Puerto Rico's relationship with the United States has been based on a pact which was approved both by the Congress and the President of the United States and by the electorate of Puerto Rico by direct ballot. Under this pact Puerto Rico is associated with the United States within a federal system of government on a basis of common citizenship, a common market, common currency, common defense, and common international political relation. In the field of culture Puerto Rico maintains relations with other countries but in its political relations it is part of the federal union. This system, under which all of the internal government of Puerto Rico is vested in the people of Puerto Rico, according to the constitution that was written and approved by that same people, is a creation that leaves the way open for new political forms.

Puerto Rico and its people are not working toward—and I should like my Latin American friends to understand this thoroughly, since at times it is a little difficult for them to grasp the matter because of the different historical traditions that exist in other parts of Latin America—Puerto Rico, I repeat, is not working toward independence; the Commonwealth is not an expedient that is to lead to independence. Neither is Puerto Rico going to become a federated state of the Union; the Commonwealth is not a way station along the road to that political status. It is a political creation, constitutional in itself. It is new, but it is not doomed to remain static; it can develop, it can grow, but it is my opinion and apparently the opinion of most Puerto Ricans that it will have to grow of its own nature toward independence and not toward statehood. I want to tell you my friends, that if the people of Puerto Rico were to find that the alternative to independence was colonialism, then they would dauntlessly face all the economic dangers of independence, because there is no colonialist spirit among them. What they have done is to create a new form of freedom that suits their own special needs, economic as well as cultural. And that is why we feel proud to be the creators of the plan for a commonwealth in voluntary association with the United States of America. But please note that it is a form of freedom; if it were not, we would not be in favor of it.

READING 3 *Bolivia's Agrarian Goal*

Introductory Note

Among the key features of Bolivia's national revolution of 1952 was its effect on the rural areas, particularly in its agrarian reform activities. It took time to work out the details of the agrarian reform law, but on August 2, 1953, Víctor Paz Estenssoro issued the law. It was a detailed document, starting out with an outline of the history of land and its use in Bolivia from the time of the Incas. It also contained a breakdown of land divisions in effect at the time of the 1950 census. Some of the salient features of this document are reprinted here, including a list of objectives in agrarian reform which forms a sort of preamble to the document itself.

A. To distribute the arable land to the peasants who do not have enough, on condition that they work it, expropriating for this purpose the lands of the latifundists who have them in excess or receive an income without any personal work in the fields;

B. To restore to the Indian communities the lands which were taken from them and co-operate in the modernization of cultivation; respecting, and where possible making use of, collectivist traditions;

C. To free the agricultural workers from their conditions of serfdom, proscribing gratuitous personal obligations and services;

D. To stimulate increased productivity and commercialization

Translated from the agrarian reform law, published in *La Revolución Nacional a través de sus decretos más importantes—tercer año de la victoria nacional de abril* (La Paz, 1955), pp. 46–47, passim.

of agriculture and grazing, aiding the investment of new capital, respecting the small and medium cultivators, encouraging agrarian co-operatives, lending technical assistance, and opening up the possibilities of credit;

E. To conserve the natural resources of the country, adopting indispensable scientific and technical methods;

F. To promote currents of internal migration of the rural population, now excessively concentrated in the Inter-Andean region, with the objective of obtaining a more rational distribution of the population, strengthening national unity, and connecting the Eastern and Western parts of Bolivian territory. . . .

Article I. . . . the soil, the subsoil and the waters of the territory of the Republic belong originally to the Bolivian Nation. . . .

Article II. The State recognizes and guarantees private property when this fulfills a useful function for the nation; it plans, regulates, and rationalizes the use of the land and supports the equitable distribution of the land, to assure the freedom and the economic and cultural welfare of the Bolivian population.

READING 4 The Chilean Communist Party

Introductory Note

Long before the issue of peaceful vs. violent change began to split Latin American Communism, the Chilean Communists had opted clearly for the peaceful path.[1] *They justified their support for peaceful change with the argument that the Chilean masses simply were not prepared for revolution. It should also be noted that Chile, unlike many other Latin American countries, has enjoyed an established system of democratic government for decades—complete with many political parties and regular elections. In short, Chile has historical traditions and political attitudes that are not amenable to armed warfare.*

When Peking broke with Moscow, the Chilean Communist Party naturally followed the Soviet line. The similarities between the adherents of peaceful change and Moscow's policy were indicated in the speech of Luis Corvalán, Secretary General of the

1. For an analysis of the evolving position of the Chilean Communists, see Ernst Halperin, *Nationalism and Communism in Chile* (Cambridge, Mass.: M.I.T. Press, 1965). See also the following two monographs by Professor Halperin mentioned on p. 164, footnote 9: "The Sino-Cuban and the Chilean Communist Road to Power: A Latin American Debate" (February 1963) and "Sino-Cuban Trends: The Case of Chile" (March 1964).

Translated from *Principios,* No. 113 (May-June 1966), pp. 114–20, passim. *Principios,* published in Santiago, the Chilean capital, is the theoretical organ of the Central Committee of the Chilean Communist Party. The complete text of the article was also published in *Pravda* on April 3, 1966.

Partido Comunista Chileno (*Chilean Communist Party or PCC*), *at the Twenty-Third Congress of the Communist Party of the Soviet Union in April 1966.*

Dear comrades: The Party of Lenin celebrated its First Congress with nine delegates, today it is celebrated with almost 5000. . . .

Without overlooking every possible effort, we maintain and will continue to maintain close relations with all Communist Parties. The result of this and similar efforts by other vanguard groups, was the presence at our aforementioned Congress, of representatives from thirty-four sister parties. Unfortunately, our relations with the Chinese comrades, which were once active and fruitful for both parties and for everyone, are today practically nonexistent. We have publicly expressed our desire to renew these relations on the basis of the principles and the rules of noninterference, of equality, and the independence of the parties, which we all accepted when we prepared and signed the Moscow Declaration of 1960.

And with regard to the relations among parties, we support the proposal of comrade Brezhnev with respect to the fact that no party may assume hegemony. Each Communist Party determines its own line and the line common to all is the one that has been elaborated and can be elaborated by all the parties.

No one but each party is more aware of its own reality. Each party has its own experience, and the duty to learn from the experiences of others, as well as the duty to transmit with Communist modesty its own experiences, rather than to pontificate.

We believe that no matter how sharp the discrepancies, and despite differences of opinion on circumstantial matters, it is imperative to impose unity of action among all the Communist Parties, and among all the revolutionary forces. No conscientious worker in our country would ever harbor the idea that he might aid the common cause by granting primary importance to that which disunites rather than to that which unites.

When it is daytime in Vietnam it is night in Chile. For an

inhabitant of Hanoi or Saigon, our country is far away overseas, on the other side of the world. But no matter the distance, in Chile, as in all corners of the earth, the barbarous crimes of the Yankee imperialists create deep indignation and repudiation, and there is great admiration for the heroic struggle of the Vietnamese people. As in many other countries, we in Chile have begun to organize material aid for the glorious combatants. We are therefore fully in agreement with comrade Gomulka [Wladyslaw Gomulka, first secretary of the Polish Communist Party], with regard to the co-ordination of the actions of all the socialist countries and all the Communist Parties in the manner of concrete aid.

The aggressive policy of Yankee imperialism is also waged in a brutal form against the peoples of Latin America. Cuba and Santo Domingo have suffered it in the flesh. The so-called Johnson Doctrine and the plans designed to create an interventionist inter-American force, demonstrate that the sovereignty and independence of each Latin American nation are seriously threatened.

In the face of the revolutionary wave that is rising in Latin America, the North American imperialists have stated that they will not permit another Cuba. But whether they like it or not, there will be a second Cuba, and a third, and many more, as many as there are countries in our continent. Each according to its own national characteristics, with methods and forms that will correspond to each particular reality, the Latin American peoples, some first and others later on, will all in the end follow the example of Cuba.

We are confronted with an implacable enemy, and the task will be arduous, complex, and more or less prolonged. Since the time of Hitlerite Fascism there has never been a greater danger for the independence, liberty, and life of our peoples. But this very fact demands and makes it possible for us to unite and mobilize sufficient forces, from the most diverse national sectors, for a victorious struggle against imperialism. This action requires the participation of both socialists and nonsocialists, all of us moved by the desire to safeguard or to rescue the sovereignty of our fatherlands. We cannot allow ourselves the luxury of losing a single ally, nor of forgetting the national liberating anti-imperialist nature of the period in which we are living, a period that is indispensable to our struggle for socialism.

As comrade Brezhnev [Leonid I. Brezhnev, first secretary of the Soviet Communist Party] has said: "To lead the class struggle is a great and complicated art, and in our time, perhaps it is more complicated than ever. The conditions under which the sister parties struggle are all very different. The revolutionary struggle has incorporated new social sectors and whole peoples, whose traditions, economic conditions and combat experiences are different. This also puts its stamp on the activities of the Communist Parties."

Just a little over a year ago, the Christian Democratic Party came to power in our country. This is a large and heterogeneous party whose basic objective is to impede the popular revolution and socialism, with the particular difference that it is attempting to achieve this with new methods, by working within the bosom of the masses, promoting agrarian reforms and other changes, while at the same time granting concessions to imperialism and attacking, sometimes violently, the positions and gains of the proletariat.

Under these circumstances, and in view of all the contradictions of various types, the situation demands a full knowledge and power over the new social processes, and that we never lose sight of the principal enemies—imperialism and the oligarchy—and support certain aspects while combating other activities of the government. We must also promote a common action by all the parties committed to radical changes, whatever may be their present political orientation, and above all we must expand the activities of the masses and undertake the job of organizing the masses on a much greater scale than has been customary, for the purpose of achieving leadership of the working class.

In its activities, admittedly not without errors and weaknesses, our party had enjoyed significant successes. It had been transformed into a party of national importance, whose opinion and conduct no one may ignore. Together with the Socialist Party we have obtained up to one million voters in an electorate of two and a half million. We cannot foresee all the situations of the future. But the fact we have pointed out demonstrates that a Communist–Socialist alliance constitutes an alternative road to power, the only revolutionary alternative.

We have not forgotten the need to correctly assess the situation, the need to discard subjectivism and to correctly consider the fact that the enemy will not spare any efforts in their desire to isolate us, to bar the road to us, and to defend their privileges. But we also know that with the realistic guidance of the Communists, and by unifying the majority of the people with the working class, the latter can conquer the sky. The new Five Year Plan of the USSR strengthens the historic optimism of the Communists and of the working class of the whole world.

Many are the contributions of the Soviet Union to the cause of mankind's liberation. But none is greater than the construction of Communism. The building of Communism will make the Soviet Union even more powerful, this immense multinational nation, bulwark of peace and champion of the liberation of all peoples.

The ideas of Communism, with the force of its example, will continue to exert a truly decisive influence in the awakening of awareness in millions and millions of workers in all countries, who will thus take part in the struggle.

Your successes have been, are, and will continue to be the successes of the Communists and proletarians of the whole earth.

Long live the Five Year Plan of the Soviet Union!

Honor and glory to the builders of Communism!

Yankees, get out of Vietnam!

Honor and glory to the Vietnamese fighters!

Long live the unity of the anti-imperialist actions of all the Communist Parties and all the revolutionary forces!

Long live peace and Communism!

READING 5 *The Argentine Communist Party*

Introductory Note

The Partido Comunista Argentino (*Argentine Communist Party or PCA) is one of the largest in Latin America, but it has not achieved substantial political success. After enjoying legal status from 1945 to 1959 during which time the PCA participated in elections, the administration of Arturo Frondizi curtailed its operations in 1959 and 1960. The government of José María Guido formally outlawed the party and its front organizations in mid-1963.*

With the restraints of illegality producing a sharp drop in membership, the military-dominated government of General Juan Carlos Onganía tightened the restrictions on Communist activities even more in August 1967. President Onganía signed into law an anti-Communist bill which defined a Communist "as one who carries out activities that are proved to be undoubtedly motivated by Communist ideology." [1] *While the law did not make it illegal to believe in Marxism, those judged true believers or Communists were to be prohibited from teaching in public or private schools, holding public office, owning property in*

1. Quoted in a Buenos Aires dispatch by Barnard L. Collier in *The New York Times,* October 3, 1967.

Pauline González Alberdi, "Anti-imperialist struggle in Argentina and the Communist Party," *World Marxist Review,* Vol. 11, Nos. 10–11 (October-November 1968), pp. 77–78, 80, passim.

specified security zones, disseminating information, or holding a union or professional office. Under the law, a "Communist" convicted of spreading his beliefs could be sentenced to as much as forty years in prison.

The following selection by Paulino González Alberdi of the Argentine party indicates the traditional Moscow-oriented Communist position in Argentina. It discusses the military coup by which General Onganía came to power—a coup which unseated the constitutional government of Arturo U. Illia.

The struggle of the working class of the country and of all democratic sections of the population against the military dictatorship installed after the coup of June 28, 1966, is gaining momentum. The coup, it will be recalled, was masterminded by fascist-like Army generals subservient to the Pentagon, who had the full backing of the *latifundist* oligarchy and big capitalists, not to mention the head of the Catholic church and other clerical dignitaries.

In his report to the Seventh National Conference of the Communist Party, Victorio Codovilla, Chairman of the Party, described the situation as follows:

> At the time of the coup the objective conditions had matured in the country for effecting deep-going changes in its socio-economic structure, and also in its political superstructure, towards an agrarian, democratic and anti-imperialist revolution. Also the subjective conditions were maturing which would have made these changes possible: the struggle of the workers and of the masses was mounting, there was a broader united action by the working class and all democratic sections pressing for profound changes in the social, economic, political and cultural life of the country.

The success of the coup in these conditions, followed by the establishment of a dictatorship headed by General Onganía, was due, on the one hand, to the fact that Dr. Illia's government of the

Civil Radical Union, instead of relying on the support of the workers and the popular masses, and taking measures against the putschists, yielded to the pressure of the latter, and, on the other, to the support given by the Peronist and "Independent" leaders of the CGT (General Confederation of Labor) and by Perón [Juan Domingo Perón, the former dictator] himself.

Shortly before the coup, on May 1, 1966, the CGT leaders, under mass pressure and on the insistence of the Communists and the Movement for Trade Union Unity and Coordination (MUCS), had signed a program-document aimed at promoting united working-class action. The CGT leadership was reorganized accordingly to include Peronists, "Independents" and Communists. Uniting most of the working people, this organization was on the way to becoming a real center coordinating the mass struggle and anti-imperialist actions. Its leaders, however—with the exception of Communist and some other officials—had meanwhile been busy contacting the military, the architects of the coup, and subsequently supported it.

As for the leaders of the various bourgeois and petty-bourgeois political parties, they adopted a wait-and-see attitude, preferring not to come out openly against the military dictatorship.

The Communist Party found itself isolated, the masses in a state of confusion because of the Peronist leader's policy. In these conditions the Party decided not to expose its vanguard, not to throw it alone into battle, but to intensify its work among the people, explaining the character of the coup and the military dictatorship set up as a result. This dictatorship, the Party explained, would pursue a reactionary anti-labor policy, a policy in the interests of the oligarchy and imperialism; the Party called on the people to prevent, through unity and struggle, consolidation of the dictatorship. It outlined its attitude in a statement published 24 hours after the coup. . . .

The facts confirm that the Communist Party acted correctly in June 1966 when it decided not to throw its vanguard into battle against the dictatorship. This Leninist position enabled the Party to regroup broad sections of the population and direct them in a struggle which in the present conditions is more and more closely related to the problem of the conquest of power. The Communist Party is working for labor unity and, more particularly, for a broad front of struggle against the dictatorship, and for the fundamental changes sorely needed by the country and which ever broader sections of the population are demanding. We have in mind an anti-imperialist, democratic and anti-*latifundia* front, a front of struggle for peace which would unite diverse forces, ranging from the working class to the national bourgeoisie. This front would make it possible to end the dictatorship and form a broad democratic coalition government which would include also the Communist Party and democratic-minded patriotic military.

This coalition could resolve the urgent problems of the day and convene a constituent assembly based on proportional representation, that is to say that every party or group would be represented in accordance with its weight in society. The constituent assembly would begin to effect the fundamental changes needed in the economic, political, social and cultural life of the country. The Communists would participate in such a government with their program for agrarian reform, expropriation of monopoly-owned enterprises, etc. Basing themselves on this program, the Communists would support a constitution under which a one-chamber parliament as the principal organ of administration would appoint the President, the Council of Ministers and the Supreme Court. A multi-party system would be envisaged.

The Communist Party is preparing for all conditions of struggle—for those which will not necessitate insurrection and those that might call for armed action. The Party realizes that this will depend on the concrete conditions, that in Argentina it is a question of mass action or gamble, and not of armed or unarmed struggle. The Party is guided by the slogan advanced by its Twelfth Congress: "Through mass action to conquest of power."

The Communist Party is winning support thanks to its decisive role in the struggle, to its propaganda and political education of the working people. It is working to free the masses from the paralyzing influence of bourgeois nationalism, expressed mainly in the ideology of Peronism. Bourgeois nationalism acts from Right positions, but even more so from those of the ultra-Left groups which direct their fire against the Communist Party, against the Soviet Union, and which try to oppose the so-called third world to the socialist camp. . . .

READING 6 *The Brazilian Communist Party*

Introductory Note

Once the largest Communist Party in Latin America with a membership of 150,000, the Brazilian Communists have suffered a steady decline in fortunes since their party was outlawed in 1947. Its present membership is estimated at under 40,000.[1] *The party continues to follow the peaceful line and is, from available sources of information, unconnected with guerrilla war outbreaks.*[2] *The following document by the party's secretary general, Luís Carlos Prestes, outlines the party's program for building a pacific anti-imperialistic front.*

Last December [1967] the Communist Party of Brazil held its Sixth Congress which rounded off the discussion that had been followed with keen attention not only by Party members and sympathizers, but also by other of the country's revolutionary

1. Rollie Poppino, *International Communism in Latin America: A History of the Movement, 1917–1963* (London: The Free Press of Glencoe, 1964), p. 13.
2. United States Subcommittee on American Republic Affairs of the Committee on Foreign Relations, *Survey of the Alliance for Progress: Insurgency in Latin America* (Washington: Government Printing Office, January 15, 1968), p. 28

Luís Carlos Prestes, "Political line and tactics of Brazilian Communists in the new conditions," *World Marxist Review,* Vol. 11, No. 6 (June 1968), pp. 31–33, 35–36, passim.

circles and political forces. The Congress discussed the current situation in Brazil, the work of the Party and its Central Committee, analyzed the causes that had made possible the military coup of 1964 [which ousted President João Goulart], and approved a political line corresponding to the new situation. . . .

The discussion before the Congress evolved in the final analysis as a struggle between two opposite concepts of revolution: the Marxist-Leninist concept which regards revolution as part of the mass movement that arises whenever the necessary objective and subjective conditions are created, even though these are shaped by the character of the historical period and place, and the non-Marxist, petty-bourgeois concept of the "guerrilla center," which regards revolution as an impulsive act by a courageous minority, able by the example of its armed actions to enlist the masses in revolutionary struggle, irrespective of the concrete situation. It was these two concepts that touched off the debate especially on issues that particularly interested the rank and file, namely, the causes for the defeat in April 1964 and the political and tactical line in the new situation.

The Congress held that the April defeat was due primarily to the change in the political attitude of the national bourgeoisie and urban petty bourgeoisie, particularly beginning with the second half of 1963. As a result, by March 1964 the political climate in the country was the very reverse of what it had been at the beginning of 1963.

To understand the change that took place in the political attitude of the national bourgeoisie and urban petty bourgeoisie we shall review the economic, social and political processes in the three years preceding the military coup.

The year 1961 was one of big gains for the nationalist movement which had been on the upswing since November 1955 when War Minister, General [Henrique] Teixeira Lott, headed the actions of the democratic forces who ousted the president and, later, the acting president when they refused to hand over the administration to Juscelino Kubitschek, the newly-elected president. The objective antecedents of these gains lay in the economic and political process in the country and in its impact on the socio-political thinking of big sections of the people. These gains reflected, in the final analysis, the clash between Brazil's developing productive forces on the one hand, and U.S. imperialism and the reactionary classes on which it relies to exploit Brazil and preserve its domination over it, on the other.

That same year a new type of people's movement emerged and began to play a leading role in political life. It was the fruit of an alliance of the working class—in the shape of its trade unions—and some sections and groups of the urban petty bourgeoisie, primarily students and civil servants. This movement, which made its first contact with the nascent union movement in the countryside, began to exert influence in the army, airforce and navy who were already fighting, within the framework of their corporate organizations, for their demands.

Despite the fact that the Party was outlawed, Communists openly engaged in political activity, strengthened their contact with various mass movements, reinforced their underground organization with thousands of new members. The Party became an influential political force among the other organizations and trends in the democratic and anti-imperialist movement.

Progressive, anti-imperialist trends appeared in all the bourgeois political parties, forming a nationalist group of 100 deputies and senators in parliament.

These different mass movements and political trends began to establish contact with each other and to take a common stand on important issues. In some cases they created definite organizational forms of unity, taking joint actions of a democratic and anti-imperialist character. Never before in the history of our country had the theses of the Brazilian revolution gained such wide currency.

The upsurge of the working-class, nationalist and peasant movements represented—despite their weakness—a potential threat to imperialism, the reactionary bourgeoisie and *latifundists.* The reactionaries did everything to halt and reverse this process. The democratic movement was able to gain ground mainly because of the relative political freedom in the country. The reactionaries sought above all to destroy this freedom.

In 1962–63 U.S. imperialism and its local allies set up in Brazil a ramified apparatus of propaganda, corruption and political pressure; they launched a broad anti-Communist, anti-labor and anti-Goulart campaign aimed at intimidating the national bourgeoisie and urban and rural petty-bourgeoisie with the bogey of a communist revolution and a so-called syndicate republic, and at winning these sections over to their side.

As long as the economy was on the upgrade, the national bourgeoisie was not afraid of the immediate effects of the labor and mass movements and resisted the reactionaries. The bourgeoisie needed popular support to resist the pressure of the imperialists and the *latifundists* who wanted to halt the process of industrialization or, at any rate, to subordinate it to the interests of U.S. imperialism and its local agents. The national bourgeoisie therefore advocated democratic liberties and supported the Goulart government whose policy furthered its interests.

The petty bourgeoisie, too—as long as the economic situation favored it, and its economic and social positions remained stable—advocated observance of constitutional rights and supported Goulart.

The results of the plebiscite in January 1963 when, despite an intensive propaganda campaign, four-fifths of the electorate favored a return to the presidential form of government as against parliamentary government which reduced the powers of President Goulart, showed that right up till then the correlation of forces was clearly in favor of the democratic, anti-imperialist camp. The vote for a return to presidential government was an unequivocal vote of confidence in Goulart or, at any rate, a clear expression of agreement with his policy. The national bourgeoisie and the petty bourgeoisie likewise voted for the most part for a return to presidential government.

However, starting with 1962 the economic situation began to deteriorate. Growth of industrial production declined, inflation spiraled intensifying the action of factors which led to a further decapitalization of the bourgeoisie and to a sharp drop in the standard of living of the urban middle sections who, unlike the working class, did not have unions to fight against the worsening of their conditions. Industrial growth which was 7.7 per cent in 1961, dropped in the next two years, first to 5.2 per cent, and then to 2.2 per cent. Thus by 1963 per capita growth in industry had ceased, since annual growth of population averaged 3.2 per cent. Simultaneously the cost of living, already up by 24 per cent, rose to 70 per cent in 1963, and showed every tendency of doubling in the following year. . . .

As the years of the chronic industrial depression under the dictatorship subsequently showed, Brazil was rapidly approaching a situation where her problems could be solved effectively only through profound, radical reforms, that is, through revolutionary transformations which would eradicate the causes of the structural crisis and, in the first place, the exploitation of the national economy by the U.S. monopolies and the *latifundia* system of land ownership. The Communist Party had long since made this proposal, and the labor, nationalist, and peasant movements began to advance this demand as their banner of struggle. The need for a revolutionary solution took deeper root in the minds of the people. . . .

Critically examining the objective economic, social and political processes in Brazilian society up to the time of the 1964 military coup, the Sixth Congress made a Marxist analysis of the basic reasons for the defeat of the democratic and anti-imperialist forces. It rejected the thesis of those who, adhering to the petty-bourgeois concept of revolution, denied the existence of objective circumstances for the victory of the reactionaries and gave as the reason the Party's unpreparedness for armed struggle which, they maintained, was the consequence of a rightist political line, of class illusions in relation to the bourgeoisie. . . .

Congress proceeded from these conclusions in working out its tactics:

(a) the dictatorship is impairing the interests of the nation and is an insult to the people's civic dignity. Also, it is damaging the interests of a large section of the national bourgeoisie, and even those of the big landowners and the reactionary bourgeoisie. This means that broad social forces have a stake in fighting the dictatorship.

Consequently, the most important political task is to build a front of political and mass action embracing all these forces and depriving the dictatorship of mass support, thus facilitating and expediting its overthrow. All trends and groups, all political and public leaders willing to fight against the dictatorship should be enlisted, regardless of their having collaborated with or supported the regime in the past. How consistent their opposition to the regime may be at present is also irrelevant. The main thing is to enlist all who are prepared to do something, no matter how little, against the dictatorship.

(b) The anti-dictator front is an alliance of heterogeneous socio-political forces. Therefore, its member groups cannot have the same ultimate aim or tendency. The only forces interested in totally uprooting the dictatorship and restoring democracy are the working class, the small urban bourgeoisie and the peasants. Hence, it is up to the Communists to weld into the anti-dictator movement the political trends representing these classes and groups, notably the various trends of the Left movement, the political, public and religious groups and leaders championing peasant interests, those of the small urban bourgeoisie and all people of labor. This integration of the Left may produce a center that will unite all the anti-dictator forces.

(c) The people's struggle and the efforts of the united democratic and patriotic forces will ultimately destroy the dictatorship. Active opposition and vigorous mass actions will reduce the regime's socio-political basis and could lead to its defeat by non-violent means. Democratic action can compel the reactionary and defeatist minority to retreat and restore democratic rights. But events may turn out differently: the dictatorship may resort to force, precipitating an armed rising or civil war. It is therefore essential for the Communists to prepare the Party and the masses for this contingency and to secure mutual understanding among the various groups in the anti-dictator front. . . .

(d) In the present stage, the Communist Party is working for a revolutionary, democratic and anti-imperialist government that would break the way for socialism. The overthrow of the present semi-fascist political regime may be followed by a further advance; abolition of the regime of capitalists and landowners subservient to the imperialists. . . .

READING 7 *Chilean Communism and Agrarian Reform*

Introductory Note

Once in power after November 1964, the Chilean Christian Democrats began their agrarian reform program through the Corporación de la Reforma Agraria (*Agrarian Reform Corporation or CORA*). *CORA could expropriate poorly used or abandoned land and was to organize the* campesinos *on the land into* asentamientos (*co-operative societies*). *By June 1967, 478 farms had been expropriated and 400* asentamientos *had been created to accommodate 12,000 families.*

In addition, the government amended the Constitution so that property was no longer inviolate; and agrarian reform and peasant union laws, also passed in 1967, began to strengthen the reform movement. These developments, in combination with Fidel Castro's consistent emphasis on the importance of the rural peasant, led the Chilean Communists to concentrate tactics more upon rural areas. The following selection is indicative of this new interest.

Chile's economic crisis is clearly the result of the semi-feudal pattern of agriculture: a tiny group of big landowners control about 80 per cent of the country's farmland.

Enrique Avendano, "Agrarian reform movement in Chile," *World Marxist Review,* Vol. 11, Nos. 10–11 (October-November 1968), pp. 59–61, 63, passim.

Agricultural output is not keeping pace with growth of population—an average of two per cent in 1939–65 compared with a 2.6 per cent annual population rise. This has meant spending more foreign exchange on imports, though the country is in a position to meet all its farm-produce requirements.

The big landowners have been steadily raising farm prices on the pretext of stimulating output. And using the same excuse they have been demanding, and getting, generous credits, which in many instances are used for travel abroad, new villas, speculation and other purposes wholly unrelated to agriculture.

Agriculure accounts for 35.6 per cent of all development credits, but, as the statistics show, the credits are granted strictly on a class basis. For instance, 2,480 big landowners averaged 57,286 *escudos* [the Chilean unit of currency] each, 10,198 middle landowners 7,040 *escudos,* 24,965 small landowners only 577 *escudos,* while 80,000 smallholders received no credits at all.

Despite these and other privileges for the *latifundists,* agriculture is in a state of decline. This is apparent from the fact that in 1964 Chile spent more than $160 million on agricultural imports and earned only $39 million from agricultural exports, leaving the treasury with a deficit of $120 million. Agricultural imports over the past 14 years add up to more than $1,000 million.

Of Chile's 74 million hectares (exclusive of the Antarctic zone) only 30 million are suitable for farming and 21 million are forest. Of the 30 million, only 11 million are productive land, of which only 6 million are classed as fertile, and slightly more than one-third is actually cultivated.

These figures, too, are part of the semi-feudal land-tenure system, with large areas concentrated in the hands of a tiny group, while thousands of peasant families have very small plots or none at all.

Of the 350,000 rural families, 185,000 are tenant farmers, sharecroppers or farm laborers. About 53 per cent of the peasant population is landless.

Census figures show that out of 165,000 land-owning families, 127,000 have either subsistence or smaller plots. This poses the problem of *minifundia,* that is, plots too small to provide food for the family cultivating them. In most cases these *minifundia* are in the poor-soil areas on the mountainous coastal strip or in the Andes foothills.

Then there are these figures: of the 38,000 landowners with farms larger than subsistence plots, 6,326 own 40 per cent of all the land, or nearly 75 per cent of the cropland and pasturage, including the most fertile and irrigated lands.

This land-tenure system is a major obstacle to Chile's economic, political and social development.

The peasants, who make up nearly a third of Chile's population, are concentrated in the 17 predominantly farming central and northern provinces, which, however, account for only eight per cent of the national income.

To say that the peasants have no access to the benefits of civilization would be a gross understatement. A survey conducted by the Ministry of Agriculture and the Catholic University of Chile revealed that most of the rural population has work only 180–200 days a year and earns less than the minimum cost of living. About 36 per cent of the adult population is illiterate. Housing conditions are spelled out in the following figures: in 90 per cent of the houses covered by the survey, there were 2–6 people to a room and 4 people to a bed; 75 per cent of all the houses lacked electricity and elementary sanitation. In most rural areas there is a shortage of drinking water and only 1.5 hospital beds per 1,000 of the population. Rural Chile has the highest infantile mortality rate, and 40 per cent of the population suffer from chronic malnutrition.

Rural poverty is aggravated by gross mishandling of social insurance funds. Most are appropriated by the *latifundists* who, incidentally, make no contribution to the fund. Peasants and farm laborers are thus deprived of medical care and sick benefits. Farm owners are supposed to pay social insurance benefits to their tenants and workers, but in most cases they use the money to pay wages or for speculation. The new result is that an increasing number of pension-age farm workers are compelled to continue to work in the hope of eventually getting a pension.

For more than 40 years our Party has been fighting for transfer of the land to those who till it and for economic and social rights for the peasants. Many Party members have been murdered by *latifundists* when they tried to organize the peasants.

We Communists feel that liquidation of the present semi-feudal structure would go a long way towards victory in the fight against Chile's other enemies, American imperialism and the monopoly oligarchy.

A few years ago the Communist Party was the only organization campaigning for agrarian reform. Now it is a national issue, one that is causing anxiety among every section of the population. There have been demonstrations, conferences, discussions in the press, on the radio and television. And there is a growing realization that the solution of Chile's economic problems lies through liquidation of the *latifundia*. . . .

Our Party is exerting every effort in support of the peasants. A new development is the recent organization of a United Front in Defense of the Agrarian Reform, which has been joined by peasant organizations, the United Trade Union Center and the Student Federation. Its purpose is to assure that the agrarian reform is consistently carried out in every part of the country.

Rural Chile is today the scene of tense struggle. The enemy is still strong, but our Party, jointly with the working class and all progressive forces, will perform its historic mission of abolishing all the *latifundia* and transferring the land to those who till it.

READING 8 The Venezuelan Communist Party

Introductory Note

The Partido Comunista Venezolano (*Venezuelan Communist Party or PCV*), *like the Chilean Party, is oriented toward unified integration of anti-imperialist national leftists. But unlike the party in Chile, the PCV's adherence to peaceful change is of recent origin.*[1] *During the early 1960s it joined the* Movimiento Izquierda Revolucionario (*Movement of the Revolutionary Left or MIR*) *and other radical leftist groups to advocate rural guerrilla fighting and urban terrorism. The declared purpose of this policy was to overthrow the government of Rómulo Betancourt, leader of* Acción Democrática (*Democratic Action*) *and president from 1959 to 1964.*

Internal disagreement within the party over peaceful vs. violent change as well as increasing antagonism on the part of the Venezuelan masses led the PCV to abandon in 1966 the "violent

1. For an analysis of the split within the PCV over peaceful vs. violent change, see Martin D. Gensler, "Los Aliados Incompatibles," in *Problemas del Comunismo,* Vol. XIV, No. 4 (July–August 1967), pp. 49–63; Kevin Devlin, "Castro and Communism," *Problems of Communism,* Vol. XVII, No. 1 (January–February 1968), pp. 1–11; James Petras, Revolution and Guerrilla Movements in Latin America: Venezuela, Colombia, Guatemala, and Peru," in Petras and Maurice Zeitlin, eds., *Latin America: Reform or Revolution* (Greenwich, Conn.: Fawcett World Library, 1968), pp. 329–69.

Translated from *Ultimas Noticias* (Caracas), May 17, 1967, paid advertisement.

change" thesis in favor of developing a broader national movement. This change in position, with justifications for it, is outlined in the Resolutions of the Eighth Plenum of the Central Committee of the PCV (1966) which follows:

The Central Committee has met to reaffirm the Leninist principles of organization and leadership of the party; to defend internal unity; to initiate a process of criticism and self-criticism; to analyze the process experienced since the third congress; and to formulate a policy of recovery and of unity of the people's forces in the struggle to defeat Betancourtism and prevent the continuity of the reactionary leadership of the AD along the road to a nationalist change that will restore complete respect for democratic freedoms, improve the living conditions of the popular masses, and establish the bases for the independent development of Venezuela.

The party has successfully endured one of the hardest tests to which its unity and its very existence as an independent Marxist-Leninist party of the working class has been subjected. Disguising itself with ultra-radical language, acting as alleged defenders of the Third Congress, spreading slanderous statements to distort our policy and discredit the leading cadres, a splinter group has been organized—encouraged from abroad—which set itself the task of assaulting the organizations of leadership and imposing a policy of anarchy and terror and of liquidation of the party. For a time they lied, concealing their divisionist maneuvers and justifying themselves in the name of the "armed struggle." When their plans were revealed and the party tried to reestablish its discipline and authority, the splinter group rebelled openly and took the road of anti-party activity. The concepts contrary to Marxism-Leninism and the typically terrorist-type actions have made manifest the adventurist nature of the anti-party group. Its conduct serves, objectively, the reactionary and Betancourtist ruling clique of the government, not only against our party and the Venezuelan people, but also against the international Communist movement and, especially, against the Cuban Revolution.

Playing the *gorilla* [derisive Latin American term for military leader] game has once again confirmed the Leninist truth that the path of the ultra-leftist deviations coincides with the positions of the right. Unwittingly or not, the action of the anarchy-terrorist group today serves gorillaism and the imperialist interest in extending reactionary hegemony and isolating and destroying the revolutionary movement. . . .

The period between 1958 through 1966 has been the richest period of activities and experience in the history of the party and the Communist Youth (JC). To the PCV and the JC, which performed with honor the mission of leading the popular insurrection of January 23rd, fell the role of vanguard in the great struggles waged in defense of democratic achievements and to win a nationalist and revolutionary policy. The rise to power of Rómulo Betancourt and the reactionary clique of the AD leader was a harsh blow to the popular movement. The Betancourtist government adhered to the U.S. policy requiring anti-Communist measures, the breakup of the unity of January 23rd, and the alignment of Venezuela against the Cuban Revolution, thus opposing the democratic majority of our country.

The acute antagonism between Betancourtist policy and the sentiments and interests of the Venezuelan people, in addition to the grave economic problems faced by the masses, created an inevitable political and social conflict between the popular sectors of the government, a conflict which reached all national levels, especially the working class, the urban middle class, the youth, the patriotic sectors of the armed forces, and so forth. . . .

The present Venezuelan situation is characterized by the following fundamental facts:

(a) U.S. domination and penetration have increased. . . .

(b) The hegemony of the *gorilla*-Betancourtist clique is being maintained, and it is today the principal political instrument of U.S. intervention. . . .

(c) The conflict still exists between different ruling class groups and cliques over control of the greatest amount of power in the Venezuelan government and state. . . .

The *gorilla* military groups are not discarding the possibility of a coup d'état in view of the government's lack of mass support, the weakening of the AD as a popular party, and the pressure of certain economic sectors, which do not conceal their ambition to replace the AD with a more reactionary formula which would better safeguard their interests. . . .

The Central Committee, on the basis of the current correlation forces and the characteristics of this political moment, agrees to focus the tactics of the party in the following direction: to promote the development of a broad national movement in favor of a progressive, nationalist, and democratic change. The points of the minimum program approved by the seventh plenum can serve for co-operation, agreement, and discussion with all the democratic forces in the country. . . .

The Central Committee will adopt new tactical measures for the party in the immediate future, in the knowledge that the electoral process and the struggle to prevent the continuity of the reactionary AD leadership will become the great central goal of the real nationalist and democratic forces. This tactic will always be in the service of the general strategic objectives of the Venezuelan Revolution.

The Central Committee, in raising, more vigorously than ever before, the slogan that the fundamental problems of Venezuela are to end its dependence on U.S. imperialism, overcome backwardness, and win complete political and economic independence, does not forget that this is impossible to achieve through elections. But it is no less true that one cannot scorn the importance of an electoral defeat of the reactionary AD leadership, particularly if it comes about as the result of a mass movement with the active participation of the left and the PCV. The removal of the ruling reactionary AD leadership would mean the creation of a new political picture, a change in the correlation of forces favorable to the revolutionary movement, and the expansion of the possibilities for more profound changes in national life.

READING 9 *The Colombian Communist Party*

Introductory Note

Although the Partido Comunista Colombiano (*Colombian Communist Party or PCC*) *is oriented toward the peaceful road, its position on armed struggle is not as clear as the Chilean or Venezuelan Communist Parties. Operating legally and enjoying the support of dissident labor and student groups, the party's rank and file does not appear to be large—certainly smaller than the Chilean Party, the largest in Latin America. In the March 1966 presidential elections the PCC supported the maverick Liberal Party candidate, Alfonso López Michelson, who lost to the regular Liberal candidate, Carlos Lleras Restrepo.*[1] *In spite of its open and legal activities, the party appears willing to philosophically and tactically support the armed struggle path, as the following statement by Jaime González suggests.*

1. The PCC must operate under the rules of the *Frente Nacional* (National Front) system which for sixteen years (1958–74) alternates the presidency between the Conservative and Liberal Parties. Only candidates bearing the label may run in elections. In the March 1966 elections, over 65 per cent of the electorate abstained from voting in what many regarded as a means of protest against the two-party arrangement which grew out of an agreement between the two parties at the end of the Gustavo Rojas Pinilla dictatorship. In addition to alternating the presidency, the system provides for parity arrangements in the legislature and other branches of government.

Jaime González, "Colombia: Communist election tactics," *World Marxist Review*, Vol. 11, No. 6 (June 1968), pp. 85–88, passim.

Politically oriented guerrillas in rural Colombia appear to be connected with the Communist Party. This connection underlay the March 1967 round-up and jailing of Communist Party leadership, including its secretary general, Gilberto Vieira, in response to a pay car mining by allegedly Communist-led guerrillas in the jungle Magdalena lowlands. By jailing the Communists, the government of President Lleras Restrepo hoped to encourage Moscow, with which it was negotiating a trade agreement at the time, to force the pro-Soviet Colombian Communists to cease whatever aid they were giving to the guerrillas. Also, such use of government force might have produced a split between the legal Communists and the subversive guerrillas. The statement by González suggests that this hope was not realized. Yet, there was subsequent evidence of a division between rural-based Communists, who advocate armed struggle, and urban-based Communists who follow the electoral process and are partly aligned with progressive Liberals.[2]

The position of the PCC is obscured further by the political history of Colombia, so different from Chile and Venezuela. Since 1948 Colombia has experienced civil war, banditry, and bloodshed—all part of la violencia *(the violence) which has claimed over 300,000 lives. The story of the Communists' role in this complex postwar setting is yet to be written.*

. . . Ever since 1948 Colombia has been living in an atmosphere of terror, with occasional pauses followed by savage repressions thinly veiled by a semblance of "law and order." This is part of the "secret war" which the government censorship so zealously tries to keep out of the public eye. President Lleras Restrepo has succeeded, to some extent, in concealing his repressive policies

2. See James Petras, "Revolution and Guerrilla Movements in Latin America: Venezuela, Colombia, Guatemala, and Peru," in Petras and Maurice Zeitlin, eds., *Latin America: Reform or Revolution* (Greenwich, Conn.: Fawcett World Library, 1968), p. 356. See also Alan Young, "Revolutionary Parties in Contemporary Colombia," mineograph paper (Stanford, Calif.: Institute of Hispanic American and Luso-Brazilian Studies, Stanford University, 1963).

by a series of bogus reforms, and is determined to continue that tactic. His Big Business government is primarily concerned to isolate the proletariat and its vanguard, the Communist Party. That was its purpose in seeking to destroy the LRM [Liberal Revolutionary Movement]—suppress the forces advoating renewal and carry out a few paltry reforms in an attempt to breathe new life into what is essentially a sick organism.

The Communist Party is working towards a united front by strengthening contacts with old allies and winning new ones. In a situation when "legal" repression alternates with an outright war of annihilation, the Party must utilize every respite, every pause between two rounds of terror, to bring together all the progressive forces that can contribute to the struggle. And from this follows that we should not underestimate the opportunities for legal work, which can bring us thousands of new supporters.

For a long time we have heard insistent voices urging the Party to abandon legal activity and concentrate on the armed struggle. But the people's war we are now waging is bound to be long and tortuous, nor would we underrate the strength of our adversary.

The Communist Party knows only too well that the country's vital problems cannot be resolved through parliamentary activity, which, however, can be an auxiliary factor. The Central Committee said on this score:

> The Tenth Party Congress established that the problems of the Colombian people cannot be solved by peaceful means. Consequently, we do not regard the elections, which are a peaceful form of mass struggle, as a means of attaining our revolutionary goals. They can only carry us one step forward. . . . In pursuance of our policy of combining all forms of struggle, we must make use—despite all difficulties and restrictions that are part of the two-party system—of the election discussions to awaken to action the masses misled by the leaders of the so-called traditional parties, and also to impede the work of the machine of government.

In deciding to contest the elections, we were mindful of the probable course events would take, namely, aggravation of the crisis of the regime, and "siege" of the traditional system, for which the Party has been patiently and consistently preparing. . . .

The Central Committee formulated these basic provisions of the electoral alliance:

> Elected candidates shall be committed to the following program:
>
> (1) Repeal of martial law and an end to all repressive measures in rural areas;
>
> (2) Abolition of the parity system; free nomination of candidates by all political parties and their share in branches of government;
>
> (3) Immediate release of trade union leaders and political detainees and termination of political trials; reinstitution of civil courts to try civilians;
>
> (4) Moratorium of the foreign debt and withdrawal from the International Monetary Fund;
>
> (5) Expulsion of the U.S. Military Mission;
>
> (6) Repeal of decree 939 of 1966, which bans strike action and imposes compulsory arbitration; withdrawal of the labor reform and development fund bills envisaging deduction from wages to finance social services; a higher minimum wage;
>
> (7) Constitutional reform envisaging more effective civil rights guarantees, restoration of parliament's legislative initiative and establishment of control over the executive to prevent the imposition of martial law and guarantee trade unions and other mass organizations full and unhampered exercise of their rights, particularly the right to organize and strike;
>
> (8) Effective diplomatic, trade and cultural ties with the socialist countries.

In short, the Communist Party has countered the bourgeois alternative with a common-denominator election platform. In contrast to constitutional reform that would only harden the two-party system, in contrast to "solution" through a military coup, the Communist Party calls for democratic transformations as the prelude to fundamental change. . . .

The Central Committee resolution is based on the premise that Colombia is in the pre-revolutionary stage and that the policy must be to accelerate the maturing of a revolutionary situation. This calls for mobilization of all the anti-regime forces. . . .

READING 10 Castro in the Sierra Maestra

Introductory Note

Fidel Castro's contemporary emphasis on guerrilla warfare as the key to revolutionary victories in Latin America obscures one underlying fact: he did not begin his campaign with this strategy in mind.[1]

Both in 1953 and 1956, Castro planned to build urban bases in Oriente Province which could lead to sabotage, agitation, and popular uprisings. In 1956 he had set up no organization in the Sierra Maestra before his boat, "Granma," landed; it was flight from capture that drove twelve of the original eighty-two men into the Sierra Maestra where they found each other and began new plans. In short, the goal of building an urban base in Oriente Province—far from the capital—fell through and, as Theodore Draper puts it, "Castro, in effect, backed into guerrilla warfare after all his other plans had failed."[2]

Castro's views on armed struggle, guerrilla warfare, and revolution were aired in February 1957 in a series of articles by Herbert L. Matthews, a New York Times *correspondent. Matthews's reports indicate that two years before Castro was to*

1. Theodore Draper, *Castroism: Theory and Practice* (New York: Frederick A. Praeger, 1965), pp. 21–26.
2. *Ibid.*, p. 24.

Excerpted from series of three articles by Herbert L. Matthews, *The New York Times*, February 24, 1957, pp. 1, 34; February 25, 1957, pp. 1, 11; February 26, 1957, p. 13.

defeat Fulgencio Batista (January 1959), he held strong views on restoring "liberty, democracy, social justice, . . . the Constitution [and] . . . elections" to Cuba; his guerrilla movement was not Communist-inspired nor anti-imperialist, according to Matthews who traveled into the Sierra Maestra to interview Castro.

To many who read the articles Castro came forward as a nationalist, even as his later Marxist-Leninist policies indicated. Matthews's reports captured the genesis of guerrilla warfare in modern Cuba which later had a dramatic impact on Latin America. Matthews managed to get through government road blocks with the help of Castro's contact men. He interviewed Castro in the Sierra Maestra mountains.

. . . Throughout Cuba a formidable movement of opposition to General [Fulgencio] Batista has been developing. It has by no means reached an explosive point. The rebels in the Sierra Maestra cannot move out. The economic situation is good. President Batista has the high officers of the Army and the police behind him and he ought to be able to hang on for the nearly two years of his present term that are still left.

However, there are bad spots in the economy, especially on the fiscal side. Unemployment is heavy, corruption is rife. No one can predict anything with safety except that Cuba seems in for a very troubled period.

Fidel Castro and his 26th of July Movement are the flaming symbol of this opposition to the regime. The organization, which is apart from the university students' opposition is formed of youths of all kinds. It is a revolutionary movement that calls itself socialistic. It is also nationalistic, which generally in Latin American means anti-Yankee.

The program is vague and couched in generalities, but it amounts to a new deal for Cuba, radical, democratic and therefore anti-Communist. The real core of its strength is that it is fighting against the military dictatorship of President Batista. . . .

From the looks of things, General Batista cannot possibly hope to suppress the Castro revolt. His only hope is that an Army column will come upon the young rebel leader and his staff and wipe them out. This is hardly likely to happen, if at all, before March 1, when the present suspension of constitutional guarantee is supposed to end.

Fidel Castro is the son of a Spaniard from Galicia, a "Gallego" like Generalissimo Francisco Franco. The father was a pick-and-shovel laborer early in this century for the United Fruit Company, whose sugar plantations are on the northern shores of Oriente Province. A powerful build, a capacity for hard work and a shrewd mind led the father up in the world until he became a rich sugar planter himself. When he died last year each of his children, including Fidel, inherited a sizeable fortune.

Someone who knew the family remembers Fidel as a child of 4 or 5 years, living a sturdy farm life. The father sent him to school and the University of Havana, where he studied law and became one of the student opposition leaders who rebelled against General Batista in 1952 because the General had staged a garrison revolt and prevented the Presidential election of that year.

Fidel had to flee from Cuba in 1954 and he lived for a while in New York and Miami. The year 1956, he announced, was to be the "year of decision." Before the year ended, he said, he would be "a hero or a martyr."

The Government knew that he had gone to Mexico and, last summer, was training a body of youths who had left Cuba to join him. As the end of the year approached the Cuban Army was very much on the alert, knowing that something would be tried and that Fidel Castro was coming back. He was already, in a measure, a hero of the Cuban youth, for on July 26, 1953, he had led a band of youths in a desperate attack on the Moncada Barracks in Santiago de Cuba.

In the fighting then about 100 students and soldiers were killed, but the revolt failed. The Archbishop of Santiago, Msgr. Enrique Pérez Serantes, intervened to minimize the bloodshed and got Señor Castro and others to surrender on promises of a fair trial. Fidel Castro was sentenced to fifteen years in prison but there was an amnesty at the time of the Presidential elections of Nov. 1, 1954, and he was let out. It was then he crossed to the continent and began to organize the 26th of July Movement. It is under this banner that the youth of Cuba are now fighting the Batista regime.

The blow, which at the time seemed an utter failure, was struck on Dec. 2, 1956. That day a 62-foot diesel-engined yacht, the Gramma [sic], landed eighty-two young men, trained for two months on a ranch in Mexico, on the Oriente shore below Niquero at a spot called Playa Olorada. The idea had been to land at Niquero, recruit followers and lead an open attack by a Cuban Naval patrol boat. Planes flew in to strafe and the men on the yacht decided to beach her.

Playa Olorada, unhappily for the invaders, was a treacherous swamp. The men lost their food and most of their arms and supplies and soon were being attacked by Army units. They scattered and took to the hills. Many were killed. Of the eighty-two no more than fifteen or twenty were left after a few days.

President Batista and his aides were remarkably successful from then on in hiding what happened. The youths they captured were forced to sign statements saying that they had been told Fidel Castro was on the Gramma with them but that they had never seen him. Thus doubt was cast that he had ever come to Cuba.

Because of the complete censorship, Havana and the other Cuban cities crackle with the most astonishing rumors; one constantly encouraged by the Government has been that Fidel Castro is dead. Only those fighting with him and those who had faith and hope knew or thought he was alive—and those who knew were very few and in the utmost peril of their lives if their knowledge was traced.

This was the situation when the writer got to Havana on Feb. 9 to try to find out what was really happening. The censorship has been applied to foreign correspondents as well as Cuban. What everybody, even those who wanted to believe, kept asking was: "If Fidel is alive, why does he not do or say something to show that he is." Since Dec. 2 he had kept absolutely quiet—or he was dead. . . .

The part of the Sierra we were in grows no food. "Sometimes we eat; sometimes not," one rebel said. On the whole, they obviously keep healthy. Supporters send in food, the farmers help, trusted couriers go out and buy supplies, which the storekeepers sell them at great risk and against Government orders.

Raúl Castro, Fidel's younger brother, slight and pleasant, came into the camp with others of the staff, and a few minutes later Fidel himself strode in. Taking him, as one would at first, by physique and personality, this was quite a man—a powerful six-footer, olive-skinned, full-faced, with a straggly beard. He was dressed in an olive gray fatigue uniform and carried a rifle with a telescopic sight, of which he was very proud. It seems his men have something more than fifty of these and he said the soldiers feared them.

"We can pick them off at a thousand yards with these guns," he said.

After some general conversation we went to my blanket and sat down. Someone brought tomato juice, ham sandwiches made with crackers and tins of coffee. In honor of the occasion, Señor Castro broke open a box of good Havana cigars and for the next three hours we sat there while we talked.

No one could talk above a whisper at any time. There were columns of Government troops all around us, Señor Castro said, and their one hope was to catch him and his band.

The personality of the man is overpowering. It was easy to see that his men adored him and also to see why he has caught the imagination of the youth of Cuba all over the island. Here was an educated, dedicated fanatic, a man of ideals, of courage and of remarkable qualities of leadership.

As the story unfolded of how he had at first gathered the few remnants of the Eighty-two around him; kept the Government troops at bay while youths came in from other parts of Oriente as General Batista's counter-terrorism aroused them; got arms and supplies and then began the series of raids and counter-attacks of guerrilla warfare, one got a feeling that he is now invincible. Perhaps he isn't, but that is the faith he inspires in his followers.

They have had many fights, and inflicted many losses, Señor Castro said. Government planes came over and bombed every day: in fact, at 9 sharp a plane did fly over. The troops took up positions; a man in a white shirt was hastily covered up. But the plane went on to bomb higher in the mountains.

Castro is a great talker. His brown eyes flash: his intense face is pushed close to the listener and the whispering voice, as in a stage play, lends a vivid sense of drama.

"We have been fighting for seventy-nine days now and are stronger than ever," Señor Castro said. "The soldiers are fighting badly; their morale is low and ours could not be higher. We are killing many, but when we take prisoners they are never shot. We question them, talk kindly to them, take their arms and equipment, and then set them free.

"I know that they are always arrested, afterward and we heard some were shot as examples to the others, but they don't want to fight, and they don't know how to fight this kind of mountain warfare. We do.

"The Cuban people hear on the radio all about Algeria, but they never hear a word about us or read a word thanks to the censorship. You will be the first to tell them. I have followers all over the island. All the best elements, especially all the youth, are with us. The Cuban people will stand anything but oppression."

I asked him about the report that he was going to declare a revolutionary government in the Sierra.

"Not yet," he replied. "The time is not ripe. I will make myself known at the opportune moment. It will have all the more effect for the delay, for now everybody is talking about us. We are sure of ourselves.

"There is no hurry. Cuba is in a state of war, but Batista is hiding it. A dictatorship must show that it is omnipotent or it will fall; we are showing that it is impotent."

The government, he said with some bitterness, is using arms

furnished by the United States, not only against him but "against all the Cuban people."

"They have bazookas, mortars, machine guns, planes and bombs," he said, "but we are safe here in the Sierra, they must come and get us, and they cannot."

Señor Castro speaks some English, but he preferred to talk in Spanish, which he did with extraordinary eloquence. His is a political mind rather than a military one. He has strong ideas of liberty, democracy, social justice, the need to restore the Constitution, to hold elections. He has strong ideas on economy, too, but an economist would consider them weak.

The 26th of July Movement talks of nationalism, anti-colonialism, anti-imperialism. I asked Señor Castro about that. He answered, "You can be sure we have no animosity toward the United States and the American people."

"Above all," he said, "we are fighting for a democratic Cuba and an end to the dictatorship. We are not anti-military, that is why we let the soldier prisoners go. There is no hatred of the Army as such, for we know the men are good and so are many of the officers.

"Batista has 3,000 men in the field against us. I will not tell you how many we have, for obvious reasons. He works in columns of 200; we in groups of ten to forty, and we are winning. It is a battle against time and time is on our side."

To show that he deals fairly with the *guajiros* [countryside peasants] he asked someone to bring "the cash." A soldier brought a bundle wrapped in dark brown cloth, which Señor Castro unrolled. There was a stack of peso bills at least a foot high—about $4,000, he said, adding that he had all the money he needed and could get more.

"Why should soldiers die for Batista for $72 a month?" he asked. "When we win, we will give them $100 a month, and they will serve a free, democratic Cuba."

"I am always in the front line," he said, and others confirmed this fact. Such being the case the Army might yet get him, but in present circumstances he seems almost invulnerable.

"They never know where we are," he said as the group arose

to say good-by, "but we always know where they are. You have taken quite a risk in coming here, but we have the whole area covered, and we will get you out safely."

They did. . . .

[February 24, 1957]

* * * * * *

President Fulgencio Batista of Cuba is fighting off a revolutionary offensive. As of today he has the upper hand, and with any luck he can hang on until his Presidential term ends in February, 1959.

The economy is good and most workers are contented. There are profitable sugar, coffee and tobacco crops. Tourism has been satisfactory. Investments from the United States are high and General Batista has been made to feel he has the United States behind him. The upper echelons of the Army and the police are his men and they give him his power.

Yet the President needs luck, for Cubans are a violent, unpredictable people, and the forces lined up against General Batista are strong and getting stronger every day.

Those and other developments have been hidden by the strictest censorship ever imposed in Cuba. Even the best-informed Cubans do not know what is happening outside their immediate circles.

This has been the case since Jan. 15, at which time constitutional guarantees were suspended for forty-five days in all of Cuba. It is still true, though censorship on outgoing dispatches of foreign correspondents was eased on Thursday [Feb. 21, 1957]. The only way to get complete information about Cuba today is to go there, as this writer did, to talk with every type of Cuban and to travel around the island. One must then leave the country to write the story.

On such a trip one gets to understand why President Batista is so generally unpopular and why such a formidable opposition is building up against him. The dictator has lost the young generation of Cuba. The group of young rebels, led by a former law student, Fidel Castro, that dominates the Sierra Maestra at the eastern end of the island and that is fighting off successfully the cream of General Batista's army is only one element—the most dramatic one—to prove this.

Señor Castro's men, the student leaders who are on the run from the police, the people who are bombing and sabotaging every day, are fighting blindly, rashly, perhaps foolishly. But they are giving their lives for an ideal and for their hopes of a clean, democratic Cuba. . . .

It is universally agreed that there is more corruption than ever under the Batista regime, and this is saying a great deal in Cuba. The enormous peculations, in which President Batista is said by everyone to take a large share, is more concentrated now, being mostly in the hands of Army generals and public works contractors. There is smuggling on a great scale, and Havana is becoming a wide open city for gambling.

With all the advantages he has had, President Batista merely had to avoid mistakes to coast through this term of office, to which he was elected Nov. 1, 1954. However, he has made bad mistakes and seems rattled. Otherwise he would not have introduced the tightest of all Cuban censorships, which has been proving such a boomerang that the people have even doubted that the economic situation was good. The rumors going around Havana and the other Cuban cities are all far worse than the reality.

The Cubans are a volatile, tough and brave people. Their anger and disappointment have been rising steadily. It is being said in Cuba that because of this the future looks more hopeful.

[February 25, 1957]

* * * * * * * * *

The old, corrupt order in Cuba is being threatened for the first time since the Cuban Republic was proclaimed early in the century. An internal struggle is now taking place that is more than an effort by the outs to get in and enjoy the enormous spoils of office that have been the reward of political victory.

This is the real and deeply significant meaning of what is happening in Cuba today, and it explains the gravity of the menace in the military dictatorship of President Fulgencio Batista.

This writer has studied Cuban affairs on repeated visits since General Batista seized power by a garrison revolt on March 10, 1952, and he has just spent ten days in Cuba talking to all sorts of conditions of men and women, Cuban and American, in various parts of the island.

At last one gets the feeling that the best elements in Cuban life—the unspoiled youth, the honest business man, the politician of integrity, the patriotic Army officer—are getting together to assume power. They have always made up the vast majority of Cubans, but Cuba has never had majority rule, least of all since General Batista interrupted a democratic presidential election in 1952 to take over by force. The Cuban people have never forgiven him for that. . . .

It is disturbing to find that the opposition, which contains some of the best elements in Cuban life, is today bitterly or sadly anti-United States. This is a recent development in Cuba and it is one of the sharpest impressions a visitor from the United States now gets. It does not, of course, apply to United States tourists, who are not held responsible for the situation and who meet unfailing friendliness.

The opposition says there is an infinitely harder problem because Washington is backing President Batista, and many "proofs" are offered. The first is the public cordiality and admiration for General Batista expressed on frequent occasions by United States Ambassador Arthur Gardner. Another is the friendliness of the United States investors and business men who, despite their misgivings, naturally want to protect their investments and businesses. "We all pray every day that nothing happens to Batista," one of the most prominent directors said to me. They fear that the alternative would be much worse, at least in the beginning, perhaps a military junta, perhaps a radical swing to the left, perhaps chaos.

There is also bitter criticism in Cuba, as in all Latin American dictatorships, over the sale of United States arms. While I was there, seven tanks were delivered in a ceremony headed by Ambassador Gardner. Every Cuban I spoke with saw the delivery as arms furnished to General Batista for use in bolstering his regime and for use "against the Cuban people."

Also while I was there, the United States aircraft carrier Leyte came on an official visit with four destroyers, and this, too, was taken as evidence that the United States was displaying its support of President Batista.

An appeal in English was circulated in Santiago de Cuba during my visit, "To the People of the United States From the people of Cuba."

"We do not wish to harbor resentment against you, our good neighbors of the North," it said. "But do give us your understanding and fairness when considering our crisis."

A movement of civic resistance has been formed in Santiago, which is the capital of Oriente Province at the eastern end of the island where Fidel Castro, the rebel leader, is fighting a guerrilla war in the Sierra Maestra. Business and professional men of the highest type are the leaders. The women of Oriente have cooperated so impressively that for many weeks they have refused to send their children to school. The University of Oriente is closed.

A similar movement of civic resistance is getting under way in Havana. It is a non-violent movement of influential citizens in support of honesty, decency, democracy, apart from the political parties and movements, which are hopelessly divided and discredited, and also apart from the Army. The citizens want to demonstrate to the decent, patriotic elements in the Army that the people of Cuba, moderate, bourgeois people, will support them against the regime as the Argentine people did their Army and Navy against General Juan D. Perón.

In this struggle one other element of prime importance must be added—the Cuban university students with their long traditions of struggle against Spanish oppressors and Cuban dictators.

The directorate of the Federation of University Students has been on the run from the police for many weeks, thus far successfully. The authorities accuse them of complicity with Fidel Castro, with whom they signed a pact in Mexico City, but they say they are fighting a parallel, separate fight for the same goals. The real reason the police want them is that they are out for trouble, and the Superior Council of the University of Havana, headed by the rector, Clemente Inclán, whom I saw, is clearly afraid to reopen the university in present circumstances. . . .

So one sees three elements lining up against President Batista today—the youth of Cuba, led by the fighting rebel, Fidel Castro, who are against the President to a man; a civic resistance formed of respected political, business and professional groups, and an honest, patriotic component of the Army, which is ashamed of the actions of the Government generals. Together these elements form the hope of Cuba and the threat to General Fulgencio Batista.

[February 26, 1957]

READING 11 Che Guevara on Guerrilla Warfare

Introductory Note

Perhaps the most colorful and legendary figure in postwar Latin America, Ernesto Che Guevara was born in Rosario, Argentina, June 14, 1928. He died in Bolivia as a leader of a guerrilla band on October 9, 1967, after rising to international prominence as a leader of the Cuban Revolution with Fidel Castro.

In Cuba he achieved high posts in the government and in the directorate of the Cuban Communist Party, as Fidel Castro's right hand man. Then, strangely, Guevara disappeared from Cuba in March 1965. This disappearance coincided with a period when Castro appeared to be compromising on his earlier strict adherence to the armed struggle thesis which Guevara supported strongly.[1]

Such a compromise brought Cuba closer in line with Moscow and split it away from the Chinese and pro-Chinese leftists in Latin America; it also repudiated Che's thesis of the priority on "armed insurrections" and reaffirmed the traditional Latin American Communist line of "broad united fronts" and peaceful change.

Guevara's disappearance raised numerous speculations. The rumors included that he was executed after a quarrel with Fidel Castro, that he was in the Dominican Republic involved in a civil war, that he had departed for Vietnam or Algeria, that he

1. See D. Bruce Jackson, "Whose Men in Havana," *Problems of Communism,* Vol. XV, No. 3 (May–June 1966), pp. 1–10.

Translated from Ernesto Che Guevara, "Guerrilla Warfare: A Method," *Cuba Socialista,* Año III, No. 25 (September 25, 1963), pp. 55–70.

was somewhere in Latin America as an underground organizer, and finally, that he had died in Havana after an asthma attack.

While no single statement by Guevara captures his adventurous and idealist sentiments, it is easier to document his firm belief in armed struggle and revolution as the best means to break what he regarded as "Yankee imperialism" and oligarchic domination in Latin America. The following selection indicates his adherence to the armed struggle thesis.

. . . We consider that the Cuban Revolution made three fundamental contributions to the laws of the revolutionary movement in the current situation in America. They are: firstly, people's forces can win a war against the army. Secondly, we need not always wait for all the revolutionary conditions to be present; the insurrection itself can create them. Thirdly, in the underdeveloped parts of America the battleground for armed struggle should in the main be the countryside. (*Guerrilla Warfare*)[2]

Such are the contributions to the development of the revolutionary struggle in America, and they can be applied to any of the countries on our continent where guerrilla warfare may be developed. . . .

We shall start from this basis to analyze the whole question of guerrilla warfare in America.

We have asserted that it is a means of struggle to achieve an end. Our first concern is to analyze the end and to see whether the winning of power here in America can be attained in any other way than by armed struggle.

Peaceful struggle can be carried out through mass movements and can—in special situations of crisis—compel governments to yield, so that the popular forces eventually take power and establish a proletarian dictatorship. Theoretically this is correct. When analyzing this on the American scene we must arrive at the following conclusions: Generally speaking, on this continent

2. This introductory passage is quoted from Guevara's book, *Guerrilla Warfare*, the English edition of which was issued by Monthly Review Press in 1963.

there exist objective conditions which impel the masses to violent actions against the bourgeois and landlord governments; in many other countries there exist crises of power and some subjective conditions too. Obviously, in the countries where all these conditions are given, it would be criminal not to act to seize power. In others where this situation does not occur, it is right that different alternatives should emerge and that the decision applicable to each country should come out of theoretical discussion. The only thing history does not permit is that the analysis and executors of proletarian policy should blunder. No one can claim the role of vanguard party as if it were a university diploma. To be a vanguard party means to stand in the forefront of the working class in the struggle for the seizure of power, to know how to guide this struggle to success by short cuts. That is the mission of our revolutionary parties, and the analysis should be profound and exhaustive in order that there will be no mistakes. . . .

That is to say, we should not be afraid of violence, the midwife of new societies; only such violence should be unleashed precisely at the moment when the people's leaders find circumstances most favorable.

What will these be? Subjectively, they depend upon two factors that are complementary and that in turn deepen in the course of the struggle: the consciousness of the necessity of change and the certainty of the possibility of this revolutionary change. These two factors, coupled with the objective conditions—which in nearly all of America are highly favorable for the development of struggle—with the firm will to attain it as well as the new correlation of forces in the world, determine the form of action. . . .

Why do we think that guerrilla warfare is the correct way in the present situation in America? There are fundamental arguments which in our opinion determine the necessity of guerrilla action as the central axis of the struggle in America.

First, accepting as true that the enemy will struggle to maintain itself in power, it is necessary to consider destroying the oppressor-army. To do this, it is necessary to confront it with a people's army. This army is not born spontaneously; it must be armed from the enemy's arsenal and this demands a long hard struggle in which the people's forces and their leaders will always be exposed to attack by superior forces and be without adequate conditions of defense and maneuverability. . . .

Secondly, the general situation of the Latin American peasantry and the increasingly explosive character of its struggle against feudal rule in the framework of an alliance between local and foreign exploiters. . . .

At the outset of the past century, the peoples of America freed themselves from Spanish colonialism, but they did not free themselves from exploitation. The feudal landlords assumed the authority of the governing Spaniards, the Indians continued in their painful serfdom, the Latin American man remained a slave one way or another, and the minimum hopes of the peoples died under the power of the oligarchies and the tyranny of foreign capital. This is the truth of America, to one or another degree of variation. Latin America today is under a more ferocious imperialism, more powerful and ruthless than the Spanish colonial empire.

What is Yankee imperialism's attitude confronting the objective and historically inexorable reality of the Latin American revolution? To prepare to fight a colonial war against the peoples of Latin America; to create an apparatus of force to establish the political pretexts and the pseudo-legal instruments underwritten by the representatives of the reactionary oligarchies, in order to curb, by blood and by iron, the struggle of the Latin American peoples.

This objective situation demonstrates the latent, unused strength in our peasants and the necessity to utilize it for the liberation of America.

Thirdly, the continental character of the struggle.

Could this new stage of the emancipation of America be conceived as a confrontation of two local forces struggling for power in a given territory? Hardly. The struggle between all the forces of the people and all the forces of repression will be a struggle to the death. . . .

READING 12 *The Venezuelan Guerrillas*

Introductory Note

The Venezuelan guerrilla movement has been one of shifting strategies and personnel since its formative years following the Cuban Bay of Pigs episode in April 1961. The Fuerzas Armadas de Liberación Nacional (*Armed Forces of National Liberation or FALN*) *began in early 1963 as a group composed of the membership of the* Partido Comunista Venezolana (*Venezuelan Communist Party or PCV*) *and the* Movimiento Izquierda Revolucionario (*Movement of the Revolutionary Left or MIR*). *It first attempted to stimulate massive peasant uprisings—a policy which fits its view of what had transpired in Cuba under Castro's leadership; this failing, it next turned towards a campaign of urban terror. Through these tactics, it hoped to force the military to intervene and seize power, thus defeating the December 1963 presidential elections and setting up the conditions for a popular uprising leading toward socialist government. The elections were held,* Acción Democrática (*Democratic Action or AD*) *remained in power, and the FALN once again reversed its policy and returned to rural guerrilla warfare.*

Douglas Bravo was leader of the hard-line faction which refused to follow the PCV's new peaceful orientation in 1966. He and four other guerrilla commanders determined to reorganize the FALN—formerly merged with the PCV—under separate

Interview with Douglas Bravo, Havana Domestic Radio Broadcast, December 24, 1966. See also text of the interview conducted by Mario Menéndez Rodríguez, in *Sucesos* (Mexico City), December 10, 17, and 24, 1966. Interview with Luben Petkoff, Havana Domestic Radio Broadcast, January 23, 1967.

leadership, an act which earned him suspension from the party's Central Committee and eventual expulsion from the party itself. The following interviews with Bravo and Luben Petkoff, second in command of the FALN in 1966–67, indicate their radical nationalist perceptions and rationale for adopting guerrilla warfare tactics instead of opting for peaceful change tactics as did the PCV.

Bravo: We can say that the Armed Forces of National Liberation are composed of four elements: the rural guerrilla forces, the guerrillas of the mountains, who constitute the axis of the entire Venezuelan armed movement; the urban guerrilla fighters, whom we call the UTS, which consists of tactical sabotage units; the patriotic officers in the garrisons; and the suburban guerrilla movement. The basic organic power of the FALN rests upon these four pillars. . . .

It has often been said that only communists are in the FALN. Some say that the armed forces are composed of members of the Movement of the Revolutionary Left. Those who say this are wrong. The FALN is composed of Communists, members of the MIR, the Democratic Republic Union [URD], . . . and of patriots belonging to all groups. I shall tell you something that will surprise you: the FALN, and you can verify it right here among the guerrilla fighters, are composed of men who belong to the Democratic Action Party, the COPEI [the Social Christian Party], and the URD. These are the parties that have been in power for the past seven years. This is to prove that we are speaking of a broad and vast liberation movement which embraces all factions seeking national liberation. . . .

There have been countless movements in Latin America, Asia, and Africa which failed for lack of a vanguard movement with a revolutionary doctrine and an advanced doctrine. There have been liberation movements in Latin America like the one in Bolivia where the workers virtually seized power and where the popular militia were created. They defeated the army, but the leadership of the Nationalist Revolutionary Movement, which directed the Bolivian Revolution, did not have a revolutionary and radical program. Its men lacked a radical philosophy which could have brought about the transformation desired by the Bolivian people. The FALN are composed of groups with different beliefs, but the leadership believes in a doctrine of radical changes as have come about in other revolutionary movements, such as in Cuba.

Question: Why did you select the path of arms to obtain the liberation of Venezuela?

Bravo: I believe I am no different from the hundreds of Venezuelan patriots who have resolutely taken up weapons against the Betancourt and Leoni governments, and who will continue under arms until a truly patriotic, revolutionary, nationalist, and progressive government is achieved. All of us who have taken up arms in the rural areas and the cities, in the barracks, the universities, and the schools are inspired, naturally, by the idea of liberating the country. I must confess to you that these things also inspired me, but that, I can also tell you, I have never been a partisan of bad things—injustices, and I have always tried to rebel against all that is bad or unjust.

In the specific case of our country, about why I took up arms, why others have taken up weapons, that is an answer I must give you based on the reality of the Venezuelan nation, based on the living conditions of the workers, peasants, students, and progressive intellectuals. In short, the answer lies in the afflictions, the sufferings, and the bitterness of the popular masses. Therefore, when we rose up in arms, it was because we had reached the alternative of either taking the road of U.S. domination, the road of servitude, the unpatriotic road; or the resolute road of national liberation, which, inevitably, requires taking up weapons. . . .

That is to say that taking up arms against an oppressor is the basic characteristic of all revolutionaries. It is the basic characteristic of the men who aspire to great changes. . . .

We are pacifists, but, understand, not pacifists in the political sense, as is the usual explanation, that is, by the sector that opposes the development of the armed struggle. We are fighters for peace in the broadest sense, the philosophical sense, the deepest sense. But it is precisely the fighters who love peace and who aspire to a new and different world, and that is why we take up weapons to win that world; that is precisely why we revolutionaries do not spare any effort in going out with our weapons in hand to make the changes the peoples demand, to reply to the enemies, to reply with weapons to the aggressors who use weapons. . . .

Question: Why have you chosen the armed method as the only way to achieve the political, economic, and social liberation of Venezuela?

Answer: Since we are speaking about national liberation, the words themselves explain the reason why the armed method must necessarily be the one used to wage the revolution in Venezuela, and not only in Venezuela but also in all Latin America. When we speak of national liberation, we mean fighting U.S. imperialism, and fighting U.S. imperialism today means taking up arms against it. It has been proven—imperialism itself has proven it—that it is impossible for the Latin American people and for the people of Venezuela specifically to rid themselves of the imperialist oppression and tutelage except by taking up arms against it.

We are not fighting to replace one group of men by another. Our struggle is between two different social systems. Naturally, this is the meaning we give to the liberation of Venezuela. . . . We are convinced that armed struggle is the only method that can be used by the Venezuelan Revolution and the Latin American Revolution because this is what U.S. imperialism wants. U.S. imperialism is using a global strategy that includes all Latin America. We can see how it interferes in the domestic policy of the American states, with its organizations, such as the Organization of American States, the Inter-American Defense Board, and so forth. Imperialism uses these organizations to violate the sovereignty of the other states, to interfere in the policy of the other countries, and to give orders to the puppet governments still prevailing in Latin America.

We can see what happened in Santo Domingo, where U.S.

imperialism wanted to set up a "representative democracy" government. They intervened militarily to stop Dominicans from setting up the government they wanted. This is true not only in the Dominican Republic but also in other countries of Latin America. It is so because that is what Johnson and top-ranking officials of the U.S. State Department want. They have said that the same thing will happen in any other Latin American country that wants to set up the form of government demanded by the people. . . .

In spite of the fact that we firmly maintain that the only means open to the Venezuelan Revolution is the armed method, we do not disregard other methods of struggle used in combination with this fundamental and principal method of struggle. We believe that all methods within reach must be used in the struggle for national liberation. Thus, we must combine, or know how to combine, the activity of unarmed mass movements, peaceful mass movements, and traditional popular demonstrations with that of armed organizations. We must use both clandestine and open methods, legal and illegal means. However, we must keep clearly in mind that armed struggle is the fundamental and principal way to achieve final liberation. There can be no other way. . . .

Question: What assistance do the peasants give the guerrillas?

Answer: First of all, it consists of their incorporation into guerrilla ranks, bearing arms along with the guerrillas. This is assistance in its highest form. The assistance of the peasant in obtaining food supplies is also fundamental. The peasant also plays an important role in obtaining information for us. Through the peasant we are able to learn when the enemy is coming, where he is going, and the size of his forces. . . .

Even those peasants who are afraid to help us do not help the enemy. They do not inform him of our movements. They say they are for neither side. With this kind of people we are patient. With them we are doing successful political work. Every day we win over more peasants of this kind. . . .

Question: How do you Venezuelans view the Cuban Revolution?

Answer: We see in the Cuban revolutionary and in the development of the Cuban Revolution a development of socialism in Cuba. We see in the ideas of the Communist Party of Cuba, in the ideas of its maximum leader, Fidel Castro, with regard to the really revolutionary interpretation of the meaning of world proletarianism, a real example for everyone, particularly for the socialist camp. . . .

READING 13 *Guevara and Guerrilla Warfare in Bolivia*

Introductory Note

In 1967, Ernesto Che Guevara turned up in Bolivia as head of a guerrilla band trying to set up a new front in South America. His presence was not at first detected, but as the Bolivian Army repeatedly engaged the guerrilla forces in small, often insignificant skirmishes, the suspicion mounted that Guevara might indeed be the leader of the guerrillas. He had been missing for more than two years with some observers thinking him dead and many speculating about him in the world press.

At the Havana-sponsored meeting of the Organización Latino Americana de Solidaridad *in August 1967, a letter purportedly written by Guevara from somewhere on the battlefield of world revolution heightened speculation that Guevara was in Bolivia.*[1]

1. The message to the Tricontinental was issued in a pamphlet by the *Organización de la Solidaridad de los Pueblos de Africa, Asia, y América Latina* (Organization of the Solidarity of the Peoples of Africa, Asia, and Latin America or OSPAAAL), the official name of the Tricontintental organization. Reprinted in John Gerassi, ed., *Venceremos! The Speeches and Writings of Ernesto Che Guevara* (New York: MacMillan Co., 1968), pp. 413–24.

Daniel James, ed., *The Complete Bolivian Diaries of Che Guevara and other Captured Documents* (New York: Stein and Day, 1968), pp. 151–52, 176–77, 202, 219–20. There are a number of English translations of Guevara's diary available. In addition to the James version, which contains an introduction by the editor, the most prominent English translation is one containing an introduction by Fidel Castro. See Robert Scheer, ed., *The Diary of Che Guevara–Bolivia: November 7, 1966–October 7, 1967* (New York: Bantam Books, 1968). This version appeared originally in *Ramparts,* Vol. 7, No. 1 (July 27, 1968), composing the whole issue.

But final confirmation of his presence was not made until October 9, when Bolivian soldiers who had captured Guevara the day before, killed him apparently on orders from General René Barrientos Ortuño (1922–69), the Bolivian president. The following brief excerpts are from several monthly summaries of activities contained in the diary he wrote while leading the guerrillas. The excerpts tell something of the many problems he faced.

[April] Things are normal, although we suffered two great losses: Rubio and Rolando. The death of the latter is a severe blow since I planned to leave him in charge of the eventual second front. We had four additional actions, all of these with positive results in general and one very good: the ambush in which Rubio died.

On another plane: the isolation continues to be complete, sicknesses have undermined the health of some comrades, forcing us to divide forces, which has greatly diminished our effectiveness. As yet we have been unable to establish contact with Joaquín. The peasant base has not yet been developed although it appears that through planned terror we can neutralize some of them; support will come later. Not one enlistment has been obtained, and apart from the dead we have lost Loro, who disappeared after the action at Taperillas.

Concerning the points noted regarding the military strategy, it can be emphasized: (a) the controls have not been effective to date and they cause us some annoyance but they allow us to move around because of their slight mobility and their weakness. In addition, following the last ambush against the dogs and their handler, they can be expected to be very careful not to enter the woods. (b) The clamor continues but now on both sides, and after the publication of my article in Havana there must not be any doubt about my presence here. It appears certain that the Americans will intervene here strongly and they are already sending helicopters and, apparently, Green Berets, although they have not been seen around here. (c) The Army (at least one company or two) has improved its technique; they surprised us at Taperillas and did not become demoralized on Mesón. (d) Peasant mobilization is nonexistent, except in regard to intelligence tasks, which are rather bothersome to us. But they are not very fast or efficient; they can be neutralized.

The status of Chino has changed and he will be a combatant until a second or third front is formed.

Dantón and Carlos fell victim to their own haste, their near desperation to leave, and my lack of energy to stop them, so that communication with Cuba (Dantón) has been cut and the plan of action in Argentina (Carlos) is lost.

In short: A month in which everything resolved itself in the normal manner, considering the necessary hazards of guerrilla warfare. The morale is good among all the combatants who have passed their preliminary test as guerrillas.

* * * * * * * * *

[June] The negative aspects are: the impossibility of making contact with Joaquín; and the loss of our men, the loss of each of which constitutes a serious defeat, even though the Army does not know this. We have had two small battles during the month, causing the death of 4 Army troops and wounding three others, according to their own reports.

The most important items are:

(1) The total lack of contacts, which leaves us with only 24 fighting men, and with Pombo wounded our movements have become very slow.

(2) The lack of peasant recruits continues. It is a vicious circle: to get this enlistment we need to settle in a populated area, and for this we need men.

(3) The legend of the guerrilla movement continues to grow. Now we are the super-men guerrillas.

(4) Our lack of contact extends even to the Party; although we have tried to make a contact here through Paulino, which might work out.

(5) Debray continues to be news, but now it is more related

to my case. I now appear as the leader of this movement. We shall see what results from this step of the government, whether it will be negative or positive for us.

(6) The morale of the guerrilla group continues to be good, and their willingness to fight keeps increasing. All the Cubans are excellent in combat, and we only have two or three lazy Bolivians.

(7) Militarily the Army's action has been nil, but they are working on the peasants in a way that we must be very careful of as they can change a whole community into informers, either through fear of our aims or through trickery.

(8) The massacre in the mines has cleared the picture for us; and if the proclamation can be spread, it will bring endorsements.

Our most urgent task is to establish contact with La Paz and get military supplies and a doctor. Also to enlist 50 or 100 more men from the town, although the number of combatants would be reduced in action to 10 or 25 men.

* * * * * * * * *

[August] It was, without a doubt, the worst month we have had so far in this war. The loss of all the caves with the documents and the medicines was a hard blow, especially psychologically. The loss of two men in the latter part of the month and our subsequent march on a horse-meat diet demoralized the men, leading to the first case of desertion, Camba, which would constitute a net gain except under these circumstances. The lack of contact with the outside or with Joaquín plus the fact that the prisoners taken from Joaquín may have talked, also demoralized my force a little. My illness caused uncertainty in several others and all these factors were reflected in our only encounter in which we should have inflicted several casualties on the enemy but wounded only one. Finally, the difficult march through the hills without water brought out the worst in my men.

The most important factors:

(1) We still have no contact of any kind and have no reasonable hope of establishing any in the near future.

(2) We still have not incorporated the peasants, which is logical when one considers the little contact we have had with them in recent weeks.

(3) There is a decrease, I hope temporary, in the fighting spirit.

(4) The Army does not improve in effectiveness nor in combativeness.

We are in a period of low moral and revolutionary spirit. The most urgent tasks continue to be the same as last month, that is: Reestablish contacts. Enroll combatants. Supply ourselves with medicine and equipment.

I should mention that Inti and Coco are becoming ever more steadfast revolutionary and military cadres.

* * * * * * * * *

[September] It should have been a month of recuperation and it was just about to be, but the ambush in which they got Miguel, Coco, and Julio ruined everything and we have been left in a dangerous position, losing also León; as far as Camba is concerned, that is a net gain.

We had small skirmishes in which we killed a horse, killed and wounded a soldier, and Urbano exchanged shots with a patrol, and the fateful ambush at Higuera. We already left the mules and I think it will be a long time before we will use this type of animal unless I start having bad asthma attacks again.

Further, there may be truth in some of the news about deaths in the other group which can be considered liquidated, although it is possible that there is a little group of survivors wandering about, avoiding contact with the Army, because the news of the simultaneous death of all seven may be false or at least exaggerated.

The situation is the same as last month except that now the

Army appears to be more effective in its actions, and the peasants do not give us any help and are turning into informers.

The most important task now will be to sneak out and look for favorable areas, and then make the contacts, even though they have wrecked the entire apparatus in La Paz where they have given us some hard blows.

The morale of the rest of the men remains fairly high, and I am only doubtful about Willy, who may take advantage of a skirmish to try to escape alone unless we talk to him.

READING 14 *The Inter-American Bank*

Introductory Note

Organized in 1960 to foster the economic and social progress of Latin America, the Inter-American Development Bank (IADB) became the instrument during the 1960s for a variety of development projects throughout the hemisphere. Its president, Felipe Herrera (1922–), has argued persuasively through both North and South America for the bank and its purpose, and did so in a 1959 speech from which this selection has been taken.

The Inter-American Development Bank is a cooperative effort of the Inter-American System. It can never be the particular property of any of its members.

The Bank was intended to accelerate the balance and well-ordered growth of all the countries of the Hemisphere. By definition, it must transcend the narrow limits of nationalism. . . .

The Bank is fundamentally a financial and banking institution, whose operations will be oriented by the strictest standards of sound and productive credit. In this sense we must profit by the great experience of other financial institutions, especially the International Bank for Reconstruction and Development. The Bank will also, through a Fund for Special Operations, be in a position to meet the needs of countries and enterprises that

Speech by Felipe Herrera before the closing session of the committee drafting the agreement which set up the Inter-American Development Bank, in Washington, April 8, 1959. From *The Inter-American Bank: Instrument for Latin American Development* (Washington: Inter-American Development Bank, 1962), pp. 2–3, passim.

cannot meet the rigid requirements of international public credit institutions. This is a problem that was of major concern and dominated most of our discussions [on the formation of the bank]. We feel that we have arrived at a happy formula, combining the principles of sound financing with the possibilities of credit for projects of an essentially social nature. . . .

The Bank will consider only those projects and proposals that are adequately presented by the member countries, but will contribute, according to the Agreement, by assisting in formulating projects. This is why we have given such great importance to technical assistance, not only in drawing up projects but in training specialists. I think we shall be able to apply the thought of José Martí to the training functions of the new institution—"He who sows schools will reap men."

READING 15 Operation Pan-America

Introductory Note

Brazil's president in the late 1950s was something of a visionary not only for his own vast nation, but also for the hemisphere as a whole. Juscelino Kubitschek captured something of the frontier spirit in his construction of Brazil's interior capital, Brasília, which he hoped would serve as a catalytic agent for moving some of the sea-coast oriented Brazilian population into the interior.

On the international front, his travels and his actions as president attracted new interest in Brazil. While Kubitschek's reputation was world-wide, his special interests centered on the Western Hemisphere. In numerous speeches during the years just before his presidency (1956–60) and then during his period in office, Kubitschek spoke out frequently on the need for greater hemispheric unity. He also began to preach a reformist policy not only for Brazil, but for both the Americas.

Written in May 1958, the Kubitschek proposal for Operation Pan-America "was the seed from which the Alliance for Progress took its origin" as one scholar has noted.[1]

Mr. President [Dwight D. Eisenhower]:

I want to convey to Your Excellency, on behalf of the Brazilian people as well as for myself, an expression of sentiments of

1. Lincoln Gordon, *A New Deal for Latin America: The Alliance for Progress* (Cambridge, Mass.: Harvard University Press, 1963), p. 6.

From Francisco Medaglia, *Juscelino Kubitschek, President of Brazil: The Life of a Self-Made Man* (New York: Brazilian Government Trade Bureau, 1959), pp. 121–22.

solidarity and esteem, the affirmation of which is become necessary in view of the aggressions and vexations undergone by Vice President Nixon, during his recent visit to countries in Latin America.

The widespread reaction of aversion on the part of the governments and of public opinion in the very nations in which occurred those reprovable acts against the serene and courageous person of the Vice President, constitutes proof that such demonstrations proceed from a factious minority.

Nonetheless, it would be hardly feasible to conceal the fact that, before world opinion, the ideal of Pan American unity has suffered serious impairment. Those disagreeable events, which we deplore so much, have nevertheless imparted an inescapable impression that we misunderstand each other on this Continent. The propaganda disseminated by the tools of anti-Americanism is apparently now directed toward presenting such supposed misunderstandings as actual incompatibility and even enmity between the free countries of the American community. Fortunately, this is far from being the truth.

It appears to me, Mr. President, that it would be utterly inconvenient and unfair to allow this false impression to prevail, morally weakening the cause of democracy, to the defense of which we are pledged.

In addressing these words to Your Excellency, my sole purpose is to acquaint you with my deepseated conviction that something must be done to restore composure to the continental unity. I have no definite and detailed plans to that effect, but rather ideas and thoughts which I could confide to Your Excellency should an early opportunity to do so arise.

I might venture at this juncture, however, that the hour has come for us to undertake jointly a thorough revision of the policy of mutual understanding on this Hemisphere and to conduct a comprehensive reappraisal of the proceedings already in motion for the furtherance of Pan American ideals in all their aspects and implications. The time has come for us to ask ourselves the pertinent question as to whether or not all of us are doing our utmost to weld the indestructible union of sentiments, aspirations and interests called for by the graveness of the world situation.

As a soldier who led democracy to victory, as an experienced statesman and, above all as a man sensitive to the ways of truth, Your Excellency is in a unique position to evaluate the seriousness of the question which I postulate with the exclusive purpose of defining and subsequently eliminating an entire range of misunderstandings that are easily capable of being removed at this moment but which may perhaps suffer a malignant growth should we fail to give it proper and timely attention.

It is hoped that the unpleasant memory of the ordeal undergone by Vice President Nixon will be effaced by the results of earnest efforts towards creating something deeper and more durable for the defense and preservation of our common destiny.

As I have already said to Your Excellency, it is advisable that we correct the false impression that we are not behaving in a fraternal way in the Americas; but beside this corrective effort, and in order that it be durable and perfect, we must search our consciences to find out if we are following the right path in regard to Pan Americanism.

It is my earnest hope that Your Excellency will feel that this letter was written under the impulse of a desire to reaffirm the warm and sincere fraternal sentiments which have always bound my Country to the United States of America, in perfect attunement with the ideas outlined by Your Excellency on the occasion of the meeting of the Chief Executives of the American nations in Panama.

May God guard Your Excellency and the people of the United States of America.

Juscelino Kubitschek

READING 16 *Declaration of the Alliance*

Introductory Note

Sparked by President John F. Kennedy's call for an alianza para el progreso, *the nations of the Western Hemisphere met in the Uruguayan beach resort of Punta del Este August 5 to 17, 1961. Ministers of finance or economy led the national delegations to the session.*

Out of the two-week meeting came two basic documents—the Declaration to the Peoples of America (which follows) and the Charter of Punta del Este, which spelled out in concrete detail the goals of the Alliance planners. The Declaration takes note of the charter of the Organization of American States, the regional hemisphere organization, Juscelino Kubitschek's Operation Pan-America, and the Act of Bogotá of 1960 which puts emphasis on four types of social investment: education, public health, housing, and improvement of rural living standards. All of these points are key parts of the fabric of the Alliance for Progress and are implicit in its charter.

Assembled in Punta del Este, inspired by the principles consecrated in the Charter of the Organization of American States, in Operation Pan America and in the Act of Bogotá, the representatives of the American Republics hereby agree to establish an Alliance for Progress: a vast effort to bring a better life to all the peoples of the Continent.

This Alliance is established on the basic principle that free men working through the institution of representative democracy

Official Text, Alliance for Progress News Team, pp. 1–4.

can best satisfy man's aspirations, including those for work, home and land, health and schools. No system can guarantee true progress unless it affirms the dignity of the individual which is the foundation of our civilization.

Therefore the countries signing this declaration in the exercise of their sovereignty have agreed to work toward the following goals during the coming years:

To improve and strengthen democratic institutions through application of the principle of self-determination by the people.

To accelerate economic and social development, thus rapidly bringing about a substantial and steady increase in the average income in order to narrow the gap between the standard of living in Latin American countries and that enjoyed in the industrialized countries.

To carry out urban and rural housing programs to provide decent homes for all our people.

To encourage, in accordance with the characteristics of each country, programs of comprehensive agrarian reform, leading to the effective transformation, where required, of unjust structures and systems of land tenure and use; with a view to replacing *latifundia* and dwarf holdings by an equitable system of property so that, supplemented by timely and adequate credit, technical assistance and improved marketing arrangements, the land will become for the man who works it the basis of his economic stability, the foundation of his increasing welfare, and the guarantee of his freedom and dignity.

To assure fair wages and satisfactory working conditions to all our workers; to establish effective systems of labor-management relations and procedures for consultation and cooperation among government authorities, employers' associations, and trade unions in the interests of social and economic development.

To wipe out illiteracy; to extend, as quickly as possible, the benefits of primary education to all Latin Americans; and to provide broader facilities, on a vast scale, for secondary and technical training and for higher education.

To press forward with programs of health and sanitation in

order to prevent sickness, combat contagious disease, and strengthen our human potential.

To reform tax laws, demanding more from those who have most, to punish tax evasion severely, and to redistribute the national income in order to benefit those who are most in need, while, at the same time, promoting savings and investment and reinvestment of capital.

To maintain monetary and fiscal policies which, while avoiding the disastrous effects of inflation or deflation, will protect the purchasing power of the many, guarantee the greatest possible price stability, and form an adequate basis for economic development.

To stimulate private enterprise in order to encourage the development of Latin American countries at a rate which will help them to provide jobs for their growing populations, to eliminate unemployment, and to take their place among the modern industrialized nations of the world.

To find a quick and lasting solution to the grave problem created by excessive price fluctuations in the basic exports of Latin American countries on which their prosperity so heavily depends.

To accelerate the integration of Latin America so as to stimulate the economic and social development of the Continent. This process has already begun through the General Treaty of Economic Integration of Central America and, in other countries, through the Latin American Free Trade Association.

This declaration expresses the conviction of the nations of Latin America that these profound economic, social, and cultural changes can come about only through the self-help efforts of each country. Nonetheless, in order to achieve the goals which have been established with the necessary speed, domestic efforts must be reinforced by essential contributions of external assistance.

The United States, for its part, pledges its efforts to supply financial and technical cooperation in order to achieve the aims of the Alliance for Progress. To this end, the United States will provide a major part of the minimum of twenty billion dollars, principally in public funds, which Latin America will require over the next ten years from all external sources in order to supplement its own efforts.

The United States will provide from public funds, as an immediate contribution to the economic and social progress of Latin America, more than one billion dollars during the twelve months which began on March 13, 1961, when the Alliance for Progress was announced.

The United States intends to furnish development loans on a long-term basis, where appropriate running up to fifty years and in general at very low or zero rates of interest.

For their part, the countries of Latin America agree to devote a steadily increasing share of their own recources to economic and social development, and to make the reforms necessary to assure that all share fully in the fruits of the Alliance for Progress.

Further, as a contribution to the Alliance for Progress, each of the countries of Latin America will formulate a comprehensive and well-conceived national program for the development of its own economy.

Independent and highly qualified experts will be made available to Latin American countries in order to assist in formulating and examining national development plans.

Conscious of the overriding importance of this declaration, the signatory countries declare that the inter-American community is now beginning a new era when it will supplement its institutional, legal, cultural and social accomplishments with immediate and concrete actions to secure a better life, under freedom and democracy, for the present and future generations.

READING 17 *Frei's Hemisphere Reform*

Introductory Note

Eduardo Frei Montalva (1911–   ), who became president of Chile in 1964, has probably been the most consistent supporter of the Alliance for Progress and yet one of its sharpest critics on the questions of performance. In speeches and articles, published both in Latin America and in the United States and Britain, Frei has called for greater togetherness on the part of Latin America as the only means of achieving the economic and social reforms which the hemisphere so desperately needs.

The pressure for accelerated development is universal, and expresses itself in different forms in all nations. Latin America is no exception, and each country in the hemisphere is vitally committed to plans for the betterment of its economic and social conditions. This pledge, both of peoples and governments, originates not only in the will to increase their well-being and improve their standard of living, but also in the conviction that the very existence of democracy depends upon its fulfilment.

In the world as a whole, the growth of closer international relations has brought about a process of integration which increases the interdependence of nations. Frontiers no longer limit the movement of people, ideas, goods, capital and aid; many important aspects of life in all countries are decided within international organisations or through multilateral contracts of every kind.

Eduardo Frei Montalva, "Latin America in the World of Today," *International Affairs,* Vol. 42, No. 3 (July 1966), pp. 373–80, passim.

There is, therefore, a double reason for impetus to be given to economic and social development. On the one hand there is the duty and the need to give to all peoples living conditions in accord with modern possibilities and the requirements of human dignity; on the other hand, States, as representatives of national communities, must be given the opportunity for adequate expression and for a share in decisions which, being international, affect directly or indirectly all the countries of the world. . . .

Contemporary history provides evidence of the many dangers and tensions which arise when there are disparities in the level of development within the same region, and when there are fundamental and organic differences in the political systems adopted by various nations for the furtherance of economic growth. Given this situation, our economic and social progress cannot remain either isolated or unaffected by what happens in the rest of Latin America. It is not only cultural and geographical links, together with a common origin, which give to all Latin Americans mutual interests and objectives; it is also the certainty that the only solid basis for economic growth and social betterment, in conformity with freedom and the respect for human rights, is that the same process should take place throughout the whole of Latin America, with the same basic outlines, and with the conviction that it is a common task for the benefit of the whole Continent.

That is why one of the essential objectives of our foreign policy is the integration of Latin America—by which we mean the elimination of economic and political barriers between all our countries, so that united in a joint effort, more rapid economic and social development would be possible for each, through the development of Latin America as a whole.

The economic aspects of integration have been the subject of profound study. However, a brief summary of the most important characteristics may be appropriate. Although there are occasional boom periods in export, the general trend of Latin-American foreign trade does not allow for a constant and sufficient inflow of the foreign currencies which would enable us to obtain the necessary capital goods and equipment needed for the industrialisation and growth of the economies of the Latin-American countries. One need only mention that the trade deficit for Latin America will be 1,500 million dollars in 1970, and that in the event of a breakdown in the programmes for the substitution of imports, the deficit will reach 4,300 million dollars. For this reason it is necessary to hasten the process of substitution of imports. This substitution can make no further progress in limited national markets, for modern techniques of greater efficiency need a high output level, which is only possible for Latin America if national markets are integrated on a continental scale.

Our Continent, furthermore, has few capital resources, and its limited capacity for investment is inefficiently applied. There is great duplication of effort in industries which, owing to the smallness of available national markets, make minimum use of capital and modern techniques and only survive with a very low level of productivity. Such, for example, is the case with the steel and non-ferrous metals industries, advanced chemicals, the motor industry, certain agricultural products and others of lesser importance.

It is necessary, therefore, that Latin America should, through integration, promote joint planning arrangements in order to avoid such duplication, and to allow for a wider and more efficient employment of its resources. Planned readjustment of its industries is especially necessary, and the goal must be a massive industrial expansion; this is imposed on us by the rapid growth of population, by the interdependence of our countries and their industries, and by the insufficient contribution of foreign capital. In Latin America economic integration is the only rational answer to these urgent problems and needs.

In other words, integration must use the modern techniques created and developed in more advanced countries to satisfy the demands of large markets and societies of a more homogeneous nature and less attached to traditional customs.

The capacity for development may be defined as the capacity to absorb modern techniques, and for this it is necessary not only to have available the capital goods which are involved in modern methods, but also to change the existing economic and social structure, and systems and habits of production and consumption. These changes are closely linked with economic integration.

Technical progress applied in more extensive markets, and the consequent increase in productivity, will promote the distribution of the national product among larger groups, and if this occurs throughout the whole Continent social advances will become possible, with the consequent modernisation of the present structure of production and consumption. In addition, it is evident that closer contacts between the Latin-American countries will encourage the mutual understanding of habits and customs, will increase the exchange of ideas and technical know-how, and thus enable the countries concerned to reach a standard of living more in keeping with the adoption of technical advances characteristic of modern societies and economies.

In this way, a higher production of consumer goods, both durable and non-durable, will be possible; adequate amounts of processed foodstuffs will be available; demand for, and so the production of, textiles will increase; marketing methods will improve. Obviously this process, already begun in Latin America and urged forward by integration, will create the necessary conditions for the expansion of heavy industry, the processing of metals, the manufacture of machine tools and of industrial equipment in general.

Integration, therefore, signifies not only quantitative changes in Latin American markets, but qualitative changes as well, and both are necessary for the development of the Continent.

The validity of the economic arguments for integration is indisputable; however, although they have been less emphasised, political arguments are equally, or more, fundamental.

Because the world is becoming progressively more interdependent, international relations now have greater influence on the political, economic and social conditions of individual nations. The decisions of a small group of powerful countries react upon all other nations, and on their capacity to achieve progress, to assert their national identity and culture, to preserve their autonomy, or to express themselves in the world at large. In the councils of nations, where the future of thousands of millions of human beings is decided—as for example, on issues of disarmament or international liquidity, the prerogative belongs only to a few countries which have assumed the right to pronounce on problems which are of concern to and affect all nations.

This is a recognised fact, based on the conditions which define the power of nations, and the capacity and opportunity which they create for themselves in order to exercise that power.

Such a state of affairs has a double consequence: it is an important cause of the present anarchy in international relations, and it prevents due consideration of the interests of the weaker nations, which are also the most numerous. . . .

In the particular case of Latin America, the isolated voices of individual countries will never command a receptive world audience. Our nations will never have the capacity to influence world affairs and decisions while they remain disunited, while they do not define a common expression of their interests, aims and policies.

In the future, more than today, the world forum will belong to the great nations or to large communities of nations. What possibility will Latin America have to make herself heard if she continues to be divided?

From this point of view, the integration of Latin America is also an historic responsibility, which has already begun in the economic plane and which must be simultaneously intensified within the proper political sphere, through which the independence of each nation will be preserved within a framework of political interdependence mutually agreed. . . .

There are various causes for the relative slowness in achieving integration in Latin America, many of which have been mentioned in different papers and studies. But it is necessary to examine two important aspects of the problem which have not been sufficiently analysed.

Latin America is a continent comprising countries in very different stages of development. As well as those having modern industrialised sectors, with high productivity and a structure for production which will enable them, in a relatively short space of time, to reach satisfactory levels of development, there are others with all the circumstances and problems which are typical of underdevelopment. Progress and backwardness co-exist in our continent, and this is the main reason for our slow advance in achieving real integration.

Some countries, for sound reasons, are not prepared to take part in a process of integration which would endanger advances which are possible for them through their own efforts. The elimination of Latin-American barriers can even, in certain cases, consolidate the weaknesses and backwardness of some countries and perpetuate the existing economic malformations. The mere creation of an economic area, through a commercial policy, does not ensure a balanced and harmonious development; on the contrary, it may enlarge the gap between developed regions and those which are less advanced. . . .

Solidarity and the sense of common destiny can better create conditions for a successful collective effort than a mere reciprocity of benefits.

There is a second difficulty with which the process of integration must contend; this concerns the kind of activities undertaken by the intergovernmental organisations of LAFTA [Latin American Free Trade Association]. Hitherto, these have dealt in practice only with the examination and solution of differences between the member countries. Limited almost entirely to settling transitory problems, the negotiating machinery is unsuitable for implementing bolder plans of action. Because of this, it is necessary that the permanent authorities of LAFTA, duly reorganised should study what kind of precise measures might be undertaken to solve problems common to the area. Its efforts to change the present structure of international commerce and of world finance are of enormous interest to our countries. The organs of LAFTA can analyse the position of our nations and present these to outside countries and international bodies, thus giving all of us in LAFTA and Latin America a greater capacity for negotiation. Above all, they should create, in the sphere where negotiations for integration are taking place, a sense of destiny and common permanent interests which, because of their importance, take precedence over the smaller problems of zonal interchange.

There is an aspect of integration which should be considered as fundamental in the Latin-American countries, as in all the developing parts of the world; it relates to the human element. Generally one emphasises financial resources and capital goods, but not enough emphasis is given to the need to take the fullest advantage of human resources.

In the last resort, underdevelopment is a human rather than an economic condition. The leading issue in Latin-American countries is the co-existence of small groups which have achieved a level of adequate knowledge alongside large masses of population which have not. This situation produces a near-vacuum in place of what should have been the middle sectors of society, and so reduces the number of those able to carry out resolutions and policies. Integration should lead to a better employment of human resources and to a wider and more specialised division of labour.

Provincialism lessens and divides. A wider policy, the possibility of maintaining a better level of higher education, the utilisation of new techniques in a dynamic economy, would also raise the level of political contest. There would be greater stability in political conduct and in the efforts to introduce the necessary structural changes; there would be a better yield from the enormous potential of the hemisphere.

Integration, therefore, not only relates to economic and social development; it is also basically related to human development. One is not possible without the other. Integration, if it only means interchange of goods and merchandise, is slow and limited, and will never receive the support of the people, nor will it break down the opposition of established interests which always resist change, even if only through inertia. Confidence and support will be forthcoming and resistance will lessen if it is understood that integration implies a change of mind and the opening up of new horizons.

Having considered the problem as a whole, in the light of historical evolution, we must ask ourselves some basic questions: Can the urgent and inevitable social changes be realised without creating the conditions inherent in integration? Social change in

Latin America cannot be deferred; pressure will increase at the rate at which the masses of peasants and labourers, living on the margins of the regional economy without power and without organisation, make themselves felt. This process is already taking place, and it is inevitable.

Can the reasonable and legitimate aspirations of these masses be satisfied without an end to inflation, without agrarian reform, without creating new employment through a more rapid industrial development; without increased investment in education, housing, health; without a better distribution of our available resources?

In the world of today all these things have only limited possibilities at a national level. This fact has been understood by others. It is a fact which Latin America has an ever more urgent need to understand.

READING 18 *Perón and Peronism*

Introductory Note

Long before Juan Domingo Perón (1895–   ) came to power, he had earned a considerable reputation as a theorist and as a lecturer on history. An army officer, he possessed considerable charm and had early demonstrated in his career that he had a facility for arousing the enthusiasm of his fellow officers—from whom he emerged as leader—and from vast numbers of the Argentine people.

Perón and his wife, María Eva (Evita) Duarte (1919–52), a young radio performer, were both of rather humble social origin, Perón having been the son of a small farmer of Italian extraction, Evita, born out of wedlock on a farm outside Buenos Aires. This humble origin helped establish their popularity with the masses.

Perón's philosophy was one that evolved over the years. There is no single document that can be considered the key one. His political, social, and economic policies—those which make up Peronism—must be garnered from a number of sources.

Agrarian Policy

A policy like this shows that the object of the State in taking over the commercialization of the grain production, is not to obtain

Items 1–4 are from Juan Domingo Perón, *The Voice of Perón* (Buenos Aires: Secretaría de Informaciones de la Presidencia de la Nación Argentina, 1950), pp. 17, 20, 25; item 5 is from Juan Domingo Perón, *Perón Expounds His Doctrine* (Buenos Aires, 1948), pp. 146–47. The passages from Eva Perón are from the English translation of her autobiography, *La Razón de Mi Vida: Eva Perón, My Mission in Life*, translated by Ethel Cherry (New York: Vantage Press, 1955), pp. 20, 107–8.

substantial benefits from it. We have a far greater and nobler purpose which is to establish the prices of farm and agricultural products on a remunerative level and to ensure the normal and continual development of this basic activity for the National economy.

[April 3, 1949]

A New Argentina

We are forming a new Argentina, so that there is no place for the outworn oligarchy that betrayed the country. The last place, the most modest place, corresponds to the soldiers of this cause who are striving, precisely, to reconquer what that oligarchy had delivered into alien hands.

[May 20, 1947]

A New Stage

We are living in a new stage in our history. What a lot of Argentines do not realise is that we are living in an epoch making period in our history. Those Argentines who have not understood it as such, are men who are at the level of the times they live in.

They existed before and they still exist, but I can assure you that this movement might fail if it was lacking in support. We should make sure that it receives this support.

[February 23, 1948]

Balance of Power

The fact that the Church has nothing to do with the Governing of the State does not mean that the State can do without the Church. And that necessity to include the Church in the National life, to uphold Roman Catholicism, and that the President should be of the Catholic faith, is one of the most praiseworthy clauses in our Magna Charta, because those who approved it in spite of their broad outlook which is reflected in all their actions, were bound to acknowledge that the Government of nations must be based on principles of morality, and these moral principles must stem from religious precepts. This idea is not without importance in the growth of a nation, for although there are moral principles which are common to all religious sects, there are others which differ widely.

Equal consideration for man and woman in the family, the sacred nature of marriage, respect for individual freedom, certain ideas about the rights of property and labour relations, like many other Christian principles, are not shared by men of other religions.

[November 5, 1947]

Immigration

The New Argentina we are building can and will give a home to millions of men from other nations who wish to make a future for themselves under the protection of our blue and white flag, symbol of liberty and justice.

For this reason, and fulfilling the principles of our Constitution, we have made a call to all the men of good will who, animated by the purpose of collaborating in the common work and of building their own future, wish to make their home on the Argentine soil, prodigal in spiritual blessings.

[May 1, 1948]

Industrialization

From today onwards we shall industrialize the country so that our work may be done by Argentine workers and so that they may earn what foreign workers earned before. This is what industrialization means to us. To accomplish this cycle we shall complete and intensify the economic cycle of production and consumption, we shall produce more, and value that production in view of our own industrialization and commerce, avoiding exploitation and increasing the consumption. When this cycle is closed, we shall be able to provide our country with 80 or 90 per cent of our production and we shall only export 10 or 20 per cent, because it is necessary to convince ourselves that the money of a man from Catamarca or Santiago del Estero is worth as much as that of the English, Americans or Japanese. All this problem is in itself simple if one tries to solve it, but it gets complicated when one cannot or does not want to solve it. We have our orientation clearly defined and a plan of action that will take us directly to the achievement of the objectives we are looking for.

[July 30, 1947]

Eva Perón on Perón

. . . What he was about to accomplish in my country was nothing less than a revolution.

When the thing to be accomplished is a revolution, the group of men capable of following its course to the end sometimes diminishes to the vanishing point.

Many revolutions have been started here and in every country of the world. But a revolution always entails a new path whose course is difficult, and which is meant only for those who feel the irresistible attraction of dangerous enterprises.

That is why revolutions wished for by the people, and even carried out with their entire support, have failed, and continue to fail.

When the Second World War somewhat loosened the influence of the imperialists protecting the oligarchy enthroned in the government of our country, a group of men decided to bring about the revolution that the people wanted. . . .

From the day I approached Perón I was aware that his struggle for social justice would be long and difficult.

As he went on explaining his purposes to me (and his purposes were nothing less than changing an entire economic capitalistic system into one more worthy and more human, and thus more just), my forebodings were confirmed: the struggle would be long and difficult!

I saw a spectacle of many millions of Argentines awaiting justice; and at their head Perón, wishing to give to all that which was due to each.

And at the same time fighting against the forces conjured up by the unpatriotic and by powers foreign to the nation, determined to go on exploiting the good faith and the generosity of our people.

Although I believed in Perón, perhaps more than he himself believed in his own strength, I could never imagine that the greater part of his dreams—and what dreams they were—would be realized so quickly in my country.

His reasoning was simple. Perhaps too simple to convince ordinary men, who, as Perón is apt to say, "go in flocks like sparrows and fly low."

He used to tell me in 1945:

"Social justice demands a redistribution of all the riches of the country so that thus there may be fewer rich and fewer poor.

"But how can a government which has not the control of economic power redistribute the riches of the country?

"That is why it is needful for me to dedicate all my efforts to assuring the economic power of the country! Everything that is a means of economic dependence will have to be nationalized; and all that which forms an unnecessary expenditure of national riches. In this way there will be more riches for the people!

"In this way the people will have what they need, or at least all that belongs to them!

"All this, obviously, will take time . . . and many Argentineans will still die without being able to see the hour of justice!" . . .

READING 19 *Uncertainties after Perón*

Introductory Note

The overthrow of Juan Domingo Perón's government in 1955 was not unexpected. But it set the stage for a ten-year period of political and economic uncertainty for the Argentines. Perón was blamed in some quarters for the economic chaos which enveloped Argentina during these years. Yet the Argentine nation and more importantly the nation's military leaders found themselves unable to make up their minds about the direction of the government.

One of the half dozen men to occupy the Argentine presidency in this era was Arturo Frondizi (1908–), a Radical Party politician whose political and economic policies grew to be detested by many Argentines.

Frondizi's messages to the Argentine people were seldom hopeful in the short run, although they held out hope for a better tomorrow, if the Argentine nation would accept reform. He often issued warnings which were stern in tone and distasteful in their implications, as in the address which follows.

Frondizi weathered a number of cabinet crises, street rioting and violence, and serious economic grumbling over his stabilization and austerity programs for a nation that had never before found itself so severely limited on the economic front. In the end, because the military saw the specter of Peronism rising anew, the military overthrew Frondizi in 1962.

From Lewis Hanke, *South America* (Princeton: D. Van Nostrand Company, 1959), pp. 162–65, translated from *La Prensa* (Buenos Aires), December 30, 1958. Reprinted by permission.

I am addressing the Argentine people in order to inform them of the transcendental economic decisions that have been made by the National Government. These are decisions which affect life throughout the country and which, therefore, interest all and each one of its inhabitants. I have chosen this opportunity to make this announcement, precisely at the end of the year that is coming to an end and just before a new year, because these decisions of an economic character also point out the end of an era and mark the beginning of what must be a new life for the whole of the nation. But it will be an arduous dawn and one full of disagreeable surprises, because this is also one of the most serious and hazardous moments of our national existence. . . .

The time has come to face facts and to adopt heroic measures. As from January 1, 1959, the country will begin a new phase, under a program of financial-economic stabilization, which will allow the full implementation within two years of the program of national expansion we have already started. . . .

During the last fifteen years, Argentina has spent much more than it has produced, has not maintained basic capital investments, and has gone severely into debt abroad. Towards the end of the last war, reserves of gold and foreign currency held by the Central Bank surpassed by $1,300 million the foreign debt. On the other hand, towards the end of the present year, it was the foreign debt which surpassed by $1,100 million the nation's reserves of gold and foreign currency. . . .

Since January 1, 1955 until the end of 1958, the country has accumulated a deficit of more than $1,000 million in its foreign trade. State enterprises lose many million pesos per year. The railways alone lose annually 14,000 million pesos, for income is about 6,000 millions and expenses 20,000 millions without amortization or replacement of equipment. From 1946 to date, the Treasury of the Nation has withdrawn from the Retirement Funds more than 55,000 million pesos and many of these funds lack the money to face their obligations. This is proof of the extent to which the country has been living at the cost of consumption of its own savings. Not even the savings of the worker, deposited in the Retirement Funds, which should protect him against accidents in his work and give him peace of mind in his old age, have escaped this.

The Nation, the Provinces and Municipalities have 1,800,000 officials, employees, and workers which, with their families, mean seven million inhabitants. More than 30 per cent of the State's income is spent on wages and this explains why there is no money to build houses, roads, schools, or even to repair pavements or give more light to our dark streets.

But this is not all. The National Government alone costs the country more than 100,000 million pesos. Only about half of that amount is covered by income from taxation and other contributions. The rest must be covered by means of borrowing or new currency, or in other words, the public administration spends double what it collects. . . . Thus is explained the fact of the constantly increasing cost of living and that in only ten years from 1948 to date it has increased more than 600 per cent. We live in permanent deficit and if we do not react in time future generations will never forgive us the crime we are committing against their welfare and even against their freedom.

The basic problem which affects the Argentine economy is a process of gradual impoverishment, due to the fact that the productive capacity of the country has not kept up with the growth of the population and social level. As was the case thirty years ago, the country depends on the exploitation of agriculture and livestock, which each year supplies smaller and less valuable exportable surpluses. Exploitation of petroleum and coal has been delayed, as well as the creation of new sources of electric power, utilization of mineral deposits, and development of steel and heavy industry. The material and financial resources which might have been used to fulfill these objectives were applied to unproductive investments and to maintaining levels of consumption which exceeded the true capacity of production of the country. . . .

Argentina has receded and lost position in the international picture. It has delayed its progress, increased its divisions, and compromised its destiny. We Argentines are frustrating the marvellous future assigned to us by Providence when it endowed these lands with so many riches and so many possibilities. The spectacle of our cities without light, our streets impassable, ever dirtier and more gloomy, shows an absurd decadence of a young and potentially rich people. We have, however, moral and material reserves to make Argentina truly a land of promise and, moreover, we have the necessary willpower to apply them to their full extent in order to overcome the present situation. . . .

Hard times are ahead of us, but the better the understanding and contribution of all, the briefer and less heavy will be the period of reaching stabilization. There will be two years of work and sacrifice, which the Argentines will face with faith and serenity, because they know that without economic stabilization there will be no material progress, no peace, no quiet, nor any true labor union life. Without stabilization there will be no freedom or democracy in the country.

The program of stabilization is a supreme effort to prevent the present dramatic situation from releasing an economic, social, and political crisis of painful consequences for the Argentina people. . . .

The situation is serious and all and each one of the Argentines must bear the consequences of a process which cannot be modified in a short time. There is no magic process by which the country can avoid its own reality. The Stabilization Program will prevent a total economic crisis and will thus keep the people from excessive suffering. But it cannot replace what no longer exists nor distribute more than there is, nor suppress the consequences of an already notorious impoverishment. The Argentine living standard must go down during the next 24 months, due to the simple reason that we shall not be able to keep consuming more than we produce. But the standard of living will rise to unexpected heights when the productive effort, in which all efforts are now being placed, is translated into greater wealth for distribution. . . .

We are also clearly conscious that Argentine responsibility spreads outside our borders. The success of the effort we are carrying out will contribute to the promotion of a true awakening of the sister nations of America, which today are going through situations similar or worse than ours. . . .

READING 20 *Divided Guyana*

Introductory Note

Of all the formerly British Caribbean lands which have become independent in the postwar years, Guyana has probably posed the greatest concern for both the United States and Great Britain. Although it has been under the somewhat gentle hands of Forbes Burnham and his black-dominated People's National Congress (PNC) since 1964, the legacy of racial strife, economic upset, and political turmoil which accompanied the decade of Cheddi B. Jagan's premiership is still very much with the Guyanese.

Burnham represents the black community, some 40 per cent of the population, while Jagan, as leader of the People's Progressive Party (PPP) symbolizes the nation's East Indians (composing some 45 per cent of the population). Burnham has tried to broaden the base of his government, getting it away from being simply a black government, and he has been somewhat successful. But at first he had to attempt to do so in coalition with the United Force (UF), an essentially white party led by Guyanese of Portuguese extraction.

This potpourri of the races lives in uneasy peace under Burnham, who spoke of his hopes for governing Guyana after he won the December 1964 election (Selection 20.1). Burnham was prime minister when the nation became independent in May

Selection 20.1 is from a speech by Forbes Burnham on December 19, 1964, following the election and his formation of a minority government.

Selection 20.2 is from the party platform of the People's Progressive Party for the 1968 election, contained in a pamphlet entitled *For Honest and Progressive Government, Vote P.P.P.* (Georgetown: People's Progressive Party, 1968), pp. 4, 7–8, 13.

1966. Selection 20.2 is the platform of Jagan's PPP for the 1968 parliamentary elections which Burnham won with the help of the overseas Guyanese vote (which is largely black and therefore presumably pro-Burnham).

Selection 20.1: Burnham on the Future

The election is now over. A hard and at times bitter campaign has come to an end. On the results the People's National Congress, in the interests of peace and stability in Guyana, has agreed with the support of the United Force to form the Government. One of the more serious tasks facing us is the attainment of independence at the earliest point in time.

One of the disturbing features of the election which we have noted is the apparent cleavage existing in our society brought about by colonialism and seven years of mismanagement and misrule.

It has come to our knowledge that despite the years of disaster suffered by the people of this country a large section of the electorate was persuaded against its best interests to vote for the party formerly in power as a result of the dishonest and opportunist propaganda that unless *that* party was returned to power those people would suffer.

The new government headed by me intends to show by its actions in the immediate future and indeed throughout its term of office that this is not true.

The problem of racial cleavage, racial antagonism, and distrust which the last government allowed to develop during its term of office is still with us, but our government recognizes this as a challenge which it intends to accept and which it is determined to overcome. . . .

We are fully aware that attempts will be made in the future as in the past to create disturbances. All of us know who are likely to create disturbances and who think that they have some benefit to be derived from chaos and violence. We have no benefit to derive from such things and we will stamp out firmly and ruthlessly any disruption of the calm and studied and steady progress which we are determined to establish and maintain in this country for the good of all.

We wish to let our Indian citizens know therefore that they can depend upon this government as they could not upon the previous administration for justice and fair play, peace and security, ordered progress and economic advance. . . .

All intelligent Guyanese know that the previous administration has by its actions deliberately prevented the attainment of independence by this country, so that today we are one of the few remaining colonial peoples. Indeed it is now clear that far from wanting freedom the previous government was bent upon creating those conditions calculated to delay the transfer of power from British to Guyanese hands until such time as they were able at the bidding and under the tutelage of their *foreign* totalitarian masters to introduce the form of tyranny and slavery which is *their* conception of freedom.

We know that more than ever these people will seek the delay of independence and anyone who by word or deed contributes toward the delay of independence for even one day, is an ally of those who would enslave us [underscore from official text].

SELECTION 20.2: JAGAN'S PROGRAM

The People's Progressive Party is the political vanguard of the Guyanese working-people uniting in its ranks workers, farmers, students, youth and progressive sections of the intelligentsia, and is guided by the revolutionary principles of scientific socialism.

The PPP is proud of its record, from its inception in 1950 to the present time, as the vanguard of the struggle of the Guyanese people for independence, freedom and socialism.

In the face of difficulties, obstacles and setbacks, the Party has consistently fought for independence for this country, and has unswervingly advocated the establishment of a socialist society only through which equality, justice and the creation of a prosperous Guyana is possible.

The PPP has never failed to uphold steadfastly the demand for self-determination of the people of Guyana, while the reactionary leadership of the East Indian Association, the League of Coloured People, the UDP, NLF, PNC, UF, TUC and ASCRIA has resolutely opposed this. Even now, efforts of some of these right-wing puppet leaders are preventing the realization of genuine independence.

In the present context of Guyana, the Party's efforts are directed towards the conquest of political power by the people in order to bring about the socialist transformation of the entire society. . . .

A PPP, broad-based government will be a regime committed to the defence of freedom and democracy. It will:

—Work out a democratic Constitution that will fully embody all fundamental rights and give expression to the national aspirations of the Guyanese people, and be subjected to ratification by the people by means of plebiscite.
—Uphold and honour the fundamental rights laid down in our Constitution; and enforce broad democratic freedoms, including those of speech, press, publication, assembly, association (trade unions, political parties), creed, and demonstration.
—Guarantee to all citizens inviolability of the person and the home, secrecy of correspondence, freedom of movement, freedom to work and rest, and the right to study.
—Abolish all repressive, anti-democratic and anti-national laws and regulations made by the coalition.
—Dismantle the fraudulent electoral arrangements and restore its Constitutional functions to the Elections Commission. . . .
—Discard the policy of economic enslavement which benefits U.S. imperialism and the foreign monopolies.
—Nationalize the key sectors in industry, agriculture, banking, insurance, and foreign trade.
—Make the people prosperous and the country powerful and independent by planned proportional development of the national economy. . . .

The PPP believes that Guyana should pursue a policy of non-alignment. A PPP Government therefore will:

—Establish with all countries not founded on racism and regardless of their social systems, diplomatic, trade and cultural relations based on the principles of mutual respect, sovereignty and integrity, non-interference and mutual benefit.

—Promote international co-operation in economic, technical, educational, health, and scientific fields; and actively support the national liberation struggles of the people of Africa, Asia and Latin America and the principle of self-determination.

—Vigourously oppose the policies of apartheid, racism, imperialist aggression and plunder.

—Abolish all agreements and commitments entered into by the coalition government which are inimical to the interests of the Guyanese people.

—Recognize the People's Republic of China [Communist China], the German Democratic Republic, North Korea, North Vietnam, and others, and promote trade and cultural relations.

—Refrain from joining the U.S.-dominated Organisation of American States. In the Caribbean area, the PPP will work for genuine co-operation with all other Caribbean countries so as to overcome the legacy of the colonial past.

—Seek a permanent and honourable solution of the spurious territorial claims of Venezuela and Surinam, without compromising the territorial integrity and sovereignty of Guyana.

In general, the foreign policy of the PPP will be founded on the pillars of strict non-alignment, active support of national liberation struggles, recognition of the socialist countries and unreserved opposition to neo-colonialist policies of plunder and aggression.

READING 21 *Bahamas for the Black Man*

Introductory Note

Lynden O. Pindling (1927–   ) is the first black man to serve as prime minister of the Bahamas. After winning a narrow election victory in January 1967, over the white-dominated United Bahamian Party (UPB), Pindling fourteen months later went on to win a substantial victory for his Progressive Liberal Party (PLB). Although the party is not entirely black, the overwhelming majority of its members are, reflecting the 95 per cent of Bahamians who are black.

Prior to Pindling's 1967 victory, the islands had been in the hands of a white group known as the "Bay Street Boys" after the main street in Nassau, the capital, where the banks and financial institutions of the islands have their offices. Graft, corruption, and political looseness characterized previous governments—a situation which Pindling promised to clean up while not adding taxes [as his opponents said he would] to the island picture. His enemies also said he would lead the islands into what they regarded as a "disastrous independence," and although he has moved the Bahamas to semi-independence, he had not by the end of 1969 shown much inclination to go the full way.

One of Pindling's prime campaign themes was a desire to do more for the predominant black population. Charging that their lot was poor, Pindling promised changes and reforms, some of which he outlines in the following speech, given as he wound up his successful campaign to remain in office in 1968.

From a speech by Prime Minister Lynden O. Pindling, March 28, 1968.

The year is 1967; the month is January. It is the 10th day of that first month of the year. Yes, you remember; it was on that day that you placed the first Progressive Liberal Party Government in office. It was on that day that the first Government of the people, for the people and by the people, began to take shape and form and, six days later, began to do the people's bidding and their own.

Many of you across these lovely Islands had been falsely led to believe that the members of my great Party were incapable, were inexperienced, and could get nothing whatever done. Many of you were told that the Progressive Liberal Party had nothing to offer and could do nothing for you.

Our political enemies prophesied doom: they said that the tourist would go home and stay away; that investors would pack up and leave; that jobs would run out of money and close down; they said that unemployment would be rife and that we would have to eat grass.

I can thank God tonight that you and I, my political friends and my political enemies, are alive at this time so that it can be seen who was telling the truth. I can thank God tonight that the Progressive Liberal Party did have much to offer and did do a great deal—and in a short space of time too.

With the new Progressive Liberal Party Government that you elected, things took an immediate turn for the better, not for the worse; things started to look up, not down; and once they started to look up, they've been moving up ever since. Do you wish to turn back now? I do not think so. Do you wish to return to the days of corruption, of conflict of interest in the Cabinet? No, I really do not think so. . . .

I will, for the record's sake, make a few comparisons between the last and best year of the U.B.P. [United Bahamian Party] and the first and only-the-beginning-year of the Progressive Liberal Party.

In 1966, the U.B.P. installed 350 street lights. In 1967, the P.L.P. installed 1081, an increase of 208.85%. 2400 more street lights will be installed in 1968, and 800 of these have already been installed in January and February.

Was your pathway to progress one of those that was lit?

In 1966, the U.B.P. awarded 22 University Scholarships. In 1967, the P.L.P. awarded 58 Scholarships, an increase of 163.64%. 100 University Scholarships will be awarded this year, 1968.

Will your son get one?

In 1966, the U.B.P. granted 139 High School Scholarships. In 1967, the P.L.P. granted 479, an increase of 244.6%. In 1968, it will be 550, as free high school education spreads further and further.

Will your boy or girl be in the honoured list?

In the civil service in 1966, the U.B.P. provided for 11 promotions of Bahamians to the rank of Assistant Secretary and over. In the year 1967, the P.L.P. provided for 46, an increase of 318.18%.

In 1966, the U.B.P.'s promotional efforts were instrumental in bringing 822,317 tourists to our beautiful Bahama Islands. In 1967, the P.L.P. was responsible for 915,273, an increase of 11.3%. There will be more than a million in 1968. . . .

I hope you will agree with me that that was not a bad first effort. . . .

I believe the Party has proven it could do it; I believe the Party has proven it could do it better, and I believe that the Party has proven it has not let you down.

If it's integrity you want, vote P.L.P.
If it's performance you want, vote P.L.P.
If it's moving on you want, vote P.L.P.

The Progressive Liberal Party will continue its upward forward march on behalf of the Bahamian people, and I give you my pledge that the Progressive Liberal Party will not seek Independence and will not introduce the income tax.

[The remainder of the speech to the accompaniment of soft martial music.] Already some of the 'Egyptians' whom we had seen, have quit and we shall see no more. I hear their chariots roll behind us, but have no fear, God's willing, soon, very soon, we shall see the rest of them no more. . . .

READING 22 *New Economic Nationalism*

Introductory Note

In October 1968, Peru's military under General Juan Velasco Alvarado (1914–) unseated the government of President Fernando Belaúnde Terry (1912–) and set in motion a vigorous form of economic nationalism aimed at "solving our national problems and ridding bad government from the people." The tone of the military government was clearly nationalist with the military men promising Peru's twelve million citizens new economic programs aimed at improving the economic well being of the people.

One of the first steps taken by the military men was seizure of the International Petroleum Company, the Peruvian subsidiary of Standard Oil of New Jersey. The action brought Peruvian-United States relations to a new low and demonstrated the limitations placed on United States ability to influence events in Latin America. Despite United States protests, the military government made it clear that it wanted no interference from that country.

To support its case and to show that, in its view, the Peruvian people would benefit from the expropriation, the government issued a pamphlet on "Petroleum in Peru." Excerpts from the pamphlet and remarks made by General Velasco suggest the tone of Peruvian nationalism.

Selection 22.1 is extracted from *Petroleum in Peru: For the World to Judge, The Case History of a Unique Case* (Lima: General Bureau of Information), pp. 51–54.

Selection 22.2 is from a speech by President Juan Velasco Alvarado, February 6, 1969.

Selection 21.1: Peru's case on Nationalization

. . . The juridical nature of the act of expropriation of the industrial installations owned by International Petroleum Company, has been erroneously interpreted abroad as a "confiscation" or "seizure" of foreign property.

This belief is far from true.

Prior to the Revolution, the Department of State of the United States was already taking an active part in negotiations leading to International Petroleum Company's obtaining an agreement fully satisfactory to its interests.

Unofficially, the Department of State informed the Peruvian Government that economic aid might be reduced if the petroleum matter did not obtain a solution which was favorable to the viewpoints of the International Petroleum Company.

The deposed administration, devoted to the execution of public works, made Peru dependent on North American credit. Undoubtedly, the fear of losing such aid led to excessive tolerance towards the demands of the Company and undue pressures.

During the month of August 1968, the United States Ambassador to the Organization of American States, Mr. Sol Linowitz, visited Lima. Mr. Linowitz's visit was for the purpose of forcing an arrangement in favor of International Petroleum Company, which unfortunately was accepted by the deposed Government, who carried out the Acts of August 12 and 13, 1968, rejected by public opinion.

What was gained with Mr. Linowitz's visit?

International Petroleum Company undertook to turn over to the Government of Peru, as a compensation for the outstanding debt, the installations for the extraction of crude oil and natural gas. Likewise, it ceded the surface ownership of the La Brea y Pariñas estate, with due respect to the rights of third parties. The Government thus unconstitutionally condoned the outstanding [debt] and granted to International Petroleum Company the right to retain the refinery and annexes thereto, including petroleum pumping equipment, storage tanks, oil pipelines, etc.

On August 13, 1968 the so-called "Act of Talara" was signed. That day, the country learned of one part of the arrangement. Days later, there began to appear further concessions to International Petroleum, which had not been communicated to the public. This attitude led to an increase of national opposition, especially when it became known that the Government had granted the following concessions:

1. Concession for 80 years for petroleum refining at Talara.
2. Concession for 80 years to manufacture oils and fuels.
3. Concession for 80 years to maintain the monopoly on marketing.
4. The commitment had also been undertaken to grant an area of one million square hectares in the Peruvian jungle zone.

With the knowledge of the reserved agreements, which the Government had not informed to the country, an agitated national debate took place, with the censure of all sectors towards the attitude of the Government. The scandal reached its peak when the President of the Empresa Petrolera Fiscal [Peru's national oil enterprise] denounced the fact that one page had been subtracted from the contract for the sale of crude oil, signed as part of the agreement of August 13, 1968.

The duty to protect the interests of the State led the Armed Forces to make a military pronouncement on October 3. President Belaúnde was deposed and the Congress was closed down. Six days later, and fulfilling its commitment to the country, the Revolutionary Government took possession of the La Brea y Pariñas oilfields and expropriated the Talara industrial complex, leaving in the hands of International Petroleum Company the product marketing network and 50% of the "Concesiones Lima," which said enterprise held in partnership with Empresa Petrolera Lobitos, a subsidiary of the Lobitos Oilfield of England.

The decision of the Revolutionary Government to expropriate the industrial installations of the International Petroleum Company at La Brea y Pariñas, precipitated the cooling off of relations between Peru and the United States of America. . . .

Selection 22.2: General Velasco Speaks Out

No conscientious person, no country, nor government or any justice tribunal could approve the stripping of the national resources of a generous nation that has always granted, and shall continue to give the security offered by its laws to foreign investors, who have come, are coming and shall come to live and work honestly in our land. . . .

The case of the International Petroleum Company is the problem of a company that has transgressed and offended our laws, usurped our rights by using all available means and one that is determined to create conflict between two friendly governments. The case of the International Petroleum Company is unique, it is a singular case. . . .

Wherefore the revolutionary government declares before the world that any foreign investor needs not entertain the smallest concern, in spite of the deceitful and costly—in the millions!—campaign which the International Petroleum Company has once again unleashed in foreign countries, thus revealing its undesirable character.

v *Cuban Nationalism: The Revolution of 1959*

CUBAN NATIONALISM

In statements before the revolution, Fidel Castro (1927–) expressed pride in Cuba and concern for its lower classes but his political program was vague. In 1953 he called for a return to Cuba's 1940 Constitution, thereby showing faith in representative government, although he knew that the 1940 Constitution had not guaranteed democratic rights to weak and powerless groups. This led him to attack all vested interests, promising vast social reforms—also outlined in the 1940 Constitution—through centralized political power (Reading One). In 1957 Castro issued a statement promising to restore constitutional freedoms and to hold elections one year after the provisional government assumed power, a promise he did not keep. Two years after toppling the dictatorship (1952–59) of Fulgencio Batista (1901–), he declared himself a Marxist-Leninist (Reading Two). Since then, Castro's political ideology has been phrased in Marxist-Leninist terms, although he has developed his own nationalist version of "Marxism."[1]

1. Most students of Cuban political development agree that loyalty to Castro supersedes loyalty to Marxism-Leninism in priority for membership in top party organizations. Another aspect of the "neo" side to Castro's Marxism-Leninism is his implementation of Guevara's ideas about "moral incentives" rather than Soviet "material incentives" (Socialist Emulation); also Cuban textbooks and manuals began to replace Soviet copies. For a discussion of these and other indications of neo-Marxism-Leninism, see W. Raymond Duncan, "Moscow and Cuban

A new national social ethic has permeated the writings and speeches of Castro, Ernesto Che Guevara (1929–67), and other leading members of the Cuban Communist Party since 1959. The key values of this ethic—work, unity, struggle, dignity, and commitment to Cuban development—are expressed in militant and aggressive terms designed to eliminate traditional attitudes of fatalism and apathy long associated with Cuban underdevelopment (Reading Three). By promoting the values of the new ethic, with emphasis on instilling them in the young, the leaders are trying to create a "New Man" who will possess cultural and technical skills combined with political responsibility and dedication to Cuban development. The Marxist-Leninist ideology, linked as it is with imperialism, class struggle, socialist unity, and economic determinism, is a convenient and natural vehicle through which to communicate the new social ethic, which is an expression of essentially nationalist attitudes and objectives (Reading Four). Cuba is on a wartime footing, with the "guerrilla spirit" of combat aimed not only at traditional national values and poverty, but also toward the "imperialist" United States and "corrupt" governments in other Latin American countries.

Given Cuba's past dependency, first on Spain and later on the United States, it is not surprising to find sovereignty and political independence stressed in contemporary Cuban nationalism. Through Castro's controlled communications media, this emphasis appears in at least three distinct forms: (1) anti-imperialist polemics against the United States (Reading Five), (2) a call for independence from all powers, including Moscow (Reading Six), (3) public glorification of such figures as Carlos Manuel de Céspedes (1819–74), Antonio Maceo (1848–96), Máximo Gómez (1839–97), and José Martí (1853–95), Cuban heroes who struggled against outside powers well before the turn of the century (Reading Seven).

These themes display the nationalist, rather than the purely Marxist-Leninist, dimension of Cuba's Revolution. They also con-

---

Radical Nationalism," in *Soviet Policy in Developing Countries* (Boston: Blaisdell Press, 1970).

dition relations with Moscow and Washington, since, in Castro's view, both great powers pose critical threats to Cuban sovereignty.

One of Castro's national development objectives is implicit in the new social ethic and in his emphasis on Cuban sovereignty: an independent Communist society whose citizens form a unified national community—a "revolutionary family"—motivated by a sense of destiny and purpose and conscious of past and present struggles. Castro's speeches also repeat the goals of a rising and equitable standard of living, eradication of the vestiges of capitalism, and dramatic expansion of education and cultural life. These goals are to be attained through development of Cuba's agricultural (especially sugar production) and technical capacity. Finally, Castro is determined that all Cubans be "workers, students and soldiers" so the nation will be strong enough to deter potential United States aggression through a new sense of self-sacrifice and individual commitment (Reading Eight).

Because Cuba's guiding ideology is a form of Marxism-Leninism, Cuban nationalism has a distinctly international tone. Castro's polemics against United States foreign policy, other Latin American governments, and the Organization of American States illustrate the point. He has unmitigated scorn for "reformist" parties in Latin America, such as *Acción Democrática* in Venezuela. Castro pledges Cuba repeatedly to the spirit, if not the practice of revolutionary internationalism. All over Latin America, people are able to hear Castro on the radio urging armed struggle, although these broadcasts began to abate somewhat during the late 1960s. And he has demonstrated his willingness to host international conferences of Latin American Communists and left-wing extremist groups. Until 1967 Castro generally disavowed direct aid to militant groups in Latin America, but after May of that year he openly offered Cuban aid (Reading Nine). Although Moscow and Havana do not agree on the roads to change in Latin America, Moscow is not unaware of the international significance of Cuba's Revolution. Former Soviet ambassador to Cuba, Aleksandr Alekseyev, stated in early November 1966:

> The achievements of socialism are a magnificent testimonial of its indivisibility and vitality. Socialism, on emerging from the limits of a single country, became a world system embracing more than a third of humanity. Socialism triumphed in several countries in Europe, Asia and it waved its banners over the Western Hemisphere in Cuba. All these facts demonstrate the international significance of the October Revolution and prove the power of socialism and its great froce to attract.[2]

CASTRO'S STRATEGY FOR CHANGE

Castro's strategy for change, although not always clearly spelled out, depends upon the integration of Cuban society by new organizations closely tied to the Cuban Communist Party (PCC). All Cubans are affected by the operation of the central administrative apparatus, which is controlled by Castro himself. The numerous "committees" and "groups" set up by Castro do not serve as vehicles for the free expression of particular interests; rather, they work to implement governmental directives and to absorb elements potentially hostile to the regime (Reading Ten). This kind of organization allows Castro to play the traditional role of *caudillo* (political leader) through a political system that still relies on authoritarian inter-personal relations characteristic of Cuban political culture and associated with the concepts of *personalismo* (personalism), and *machismo* (male virility).

Castro's elaborate system of political integration includes the *Union de la Juventud Comunista* (Union of Communist Youth or UJC), the *Asociación Nacional de Agricultores Pequeños* (National Association of Small Farmers or ANAP), the *Federación de Mujeres Cubanas* (Federation of Cuban Women or FMC), and the *Comites de Defensa de la Revolución* (Committees for the Defense of the Revolution or CDR). Mexico has remarkably similar organizations although the ideologies behind them are, of course, radically different.

Political socialization in Cuba—the process of inducting all members of society into operative patterns of authority, beliefs, and values deemed important by the national leadership—is vital

2. Havana Domestic Radio Broadcast, November 9, 1966.

to Castro's overall strategy for change. The socialization process helps guarantee continued loyalty to Castro, to the party, to the ideology of neo-Marxism-Leninism, and to official national goals. It is added insurance against future revolts.

The instruments of political socialization include mass rallies, the communications media, Committee meetings, the activities of party cadres, and state-controlled education (Reading Eleven). Thus all Cubans, particularly young people, are exposed to Castro's version of the new Communist society. This is why substantially more political integration and socialization has taken place in the Cuban Revolution than in the revolutions in Bolivia (1952) and Mexico (1910).

Most students of Cuban affairs believe that Castro's revolution has had more impact in rural than in urban areas. He was not able to move swiftly toward industrialization, as Guevara indicates in one of the selections in Reading Twelve, yet the base for future industrialization—increased agricultural productivity—is being laid (Reading Twelve). The agricultural phase of Castro's development program is vital to economic modernization. In theory, it should expand the size of the internal market, produce the food required by a rising population, and become a new source of national income through exportation.

Cuba's agricultural revolution aims at increasing productivity through (1) expanded and more efficient land use, and (2) modernized farming. It is difficult to determine whether Cuba has made any progress toward either of these goals, because statistics on production frequently are not available and the use of Marxist terminology makes the measurement of production rather vague. In any case, Castro has made clear that Cuban economic development revolves around a five-year plan intended to boost sugar production to ten million tons by 1970. In January 1969, he announced that by 1970 Cuba's agricultural production would be double its pre-1959 figure; thereafter it would increase at an average annual rate of about 15 per cent. Castro attributed increased productivity largely to an expansion of agriculturally productive land. In the early stages of the revolution he had expropriated large domestic and foreign land holdings and this was followed by extensive clearing and planting projects. Massive work brigades were put to work day and night including Sundays to cultivate sugarcane, tobacco, coffee, rice, and vegetables. Because land use came directly under state control, Castro was able to expedite his agricultural program.

The modernization of farming in Cuba requires extended use of fertilizer, artificial insemination, new irrigation and drainage systems, hill terracing, and construction of roads and railroads in farm areas. During the first decade of Castro's rule, each year was given a revolutionary name. The importance of agriculture is suggested by the names of three of the years: 1960, the "Year of the Agrarian Reform"; 1965, the "Year of Agriculture"; 1969, the "Year of Decisive Endeavor," referring to the 1970 sugar harvest goal.[3]

The success of Castro's agricultural and industrial plans depend on raising Cuba's scientific competence. Since this task in turn depends on an increase in literacy and technical training, party cadre activities and official state publications enncourage such education (Reading Thirteen). Their efforts point up another imperative of Castro's national social ethic: the duty to develop technical skills and to use them.

3. The other national dates are:
1959: Year of Liberation
1960: Year of the Agrarian Reform
1961: Year of Education
1962: Year of Planning
1963: Year of Organization
1964: Year of Economy
1965: Year of Agriculture
1966: Year of Solidarity
1967: Year of Heroic Vietnam
1968: Year of Heroic Guerrilla
1969: Year of Decisive Endeavor

READING 1 *Fidel Castro's* History Will Absolve Me

Introductory Note

Castro's "History Will Absolve Me" speech is generally considered a landmark statement in the revolution. It was delivered before the Court of Justice which was trying him for the July 26, 1953 attack on the Moncada Army barracks at Santiago de Cuba. In pleading his defense on October 16, 1953, Castro enumerated Cuba's national problems, designating six areas that required immediate attention: the land-holding system, industrialization, housing, unemployment, education, and health. Castro's later emphasis on these problems can be traced to this 1953 statement of beliefs.

The speech also called for restoration of the 1940 Constitution as supreme law of the land. Thus, it could have appeal to the discontented middle classes who wished to return to constitutional government and to the impoverished lower classes attracted to the concept of government-sponsored social and economic change. The reader should note that it is far more comprehensive in its social and economic proposals than was Francisco Madero's Plan of San Luis Potosí *in Mexico.*

Fidel Castro, *History Will Absolve Me* (Havana: Guairas Book Institute, 1967), pp. 59–67, 69, 79–83. (Originally published in Spanish as *La historia me absolverá.*) *Caballerías* and *arrobas,* to which Castro refers in this section, are units of measure in Cuba. A *caballería* is a measure of land equal to 33⅓ acres. An *arroba* is roughly 25 pounds.

As soon as Santiago de Cuba was in our hands, we would immediately have readied the people for war. Bayamo was attacked precisely to locate our advance forces along the Cauto River. Never forget that this province, which has a million and a half inhabitants today, is undoubtedly the most resistant and most patriotic of Cuba.

It was this province that continued the fight for independence for thirty years and paid the highest tribute in blood, sacrifice, and heroism. In Oriente, you can still breathe the air of that glorious epic. At dawn, when the cocks crow as if they were bugles calling soldiers to reveille, and when the sun rises, radiant over the rugged mountains, it seems that once again we will live the days of Yara or Baire. I stated that the second consideration on which we based our chances for success was one of social order because we were sure of the people's support. When we speak of the people we do not mean the comfortable ones, the conservative elements of the nation, who welcome any regime of oppression, any dictatorship, any despotism, prostrating themselves before the master of the moment until they grind their foreheads into the ground. When we speak of struggle, the people means the vast unredeemed masses, to whom all make promises and who all deceive; we mean the people who yearn for a better, more dignified and more just nation; who are moved by ancestral aspirations of justice, for they have suffered injustice and mockery, generation after generation; who long for great and wise changes in all aspects of their life; people, who, to attain the changes, are ready to give even the very last breath of their lives, when they believe in something or in someone, especially when they believe in themselves. In stating a purpose, the first condition of sincerity and good faith, is to do precisely what nobody else ever does, that is, to speak with absolute clarity, without fear. The demagogues and professional politicians who manage to perform the miracle of being right in everything and in pleasing everyone, are, of necessity, deceiving everyone about everything. The revolutionaries must proclaim their ideas courageously, define their principles and express their intentions so that no one is deceived, neither friend nor foe.

The people we counted on in our struggle were these:

Seven hundred thousand Cubans without work, who desire to earn their daily bread honestly without having to emigrate in search of a livelihood.

Five hundred thousand farm laborers inhabiting miserable shacks, who work four months of the year and starve during the rest, sharing their misery with their children; who have not an inch of land to till, and whose existence would move any heart not made of stone.

Four hundred thousand industrial laborers and stevedores whose retirement funds have been embezzled, whose benefits are being taken away, whose homes are wretched quarters, whose salaries pass from the hands of the boss to those of the money-lender, whose future is a pay reduction and dismissal, whose life is eternal work and whose only rest is in the tomb.

One hundred thousand small farmers who live and die working on land that is not theirs, looking at it with sadness as Moses looked at the promised land, to die without ever owning it; who, like feudal serfs, have to pay for the use of their parcel of land by giving up a portion of its products; who cannot love it, improve it, beautify it, nor plant a lemon or an orange tree on it, because they never know when a sheriff will come with the rural guard to evict them from it.

Thirty thousand teachers and professors who are so devoted, dedicated, and necessary to the better destiny of future generations and who are so badly treated and paid.

Twenty thousand small business men weighted down by debts, ruined by the crisis and harangued by a plague of grafting and venal officials.

Ten thousand young professionals; doctors, engineers, lawyers, veterinarians, school teachers, dentists, pharmacists, newspapermen, painters, sculptors, etc., who come forth from school with their degrees, anxious to work and full of hope, only to find themselves at a dead end with all doors closed and where no ear hears their clamor or supplication.

These are the people, the ones who know misfortune and, therefore, are capable of fighting with limitless courage!

To the people whose desperate roads through life have been paved with the bricks of betrayals and false promises, we were not going to say: "We will eventually give you what you need," but rather—"Here you have it, fight for it with all your might, so that liberty and happiness may be yours!"

In the brief of this case, the five revolutionary laws that would have been proclaimed immediately after the capture of the Moncada barracks and would have been broadcasted to the nation by radio should be recorded. It is possible that Colonel Chaviano may deliberately have destroyed these documents, but even if he has done so I remember them.

The First Revolutionary Law would have returned power to the people and proclaimed the Constitution of 1940 the supreme Law of the State, until such time as the people should decide to modify or change it. And, in order to effect its implementation and punish those who had violated it, there being no organization for holding elections to accomplish this, the revolutionary movement, as the momentous incarnation of this sovereignty, the only source of legitimate power, would have assumed all the faculties inherent in it, except that of modifying the Constitution itself: in other words, it would have assumed the legislative, executive and judicial powers.

This approach could not be more crystal clear nor more free of vacillation and sterile charlatanry. A government acclaimed by the mass of the rebel people would be vested with every power, everything necessary in order to proceed with the effective implementation of the popular will and true justice. From that moment, the Judicial Power, which since March 10th has placed itself against the Constitution and outside the Constitution, would cease to exist and we would proceed to its immediate and total reform before it would again assume the power granted to it by the Supreme Law of the Republic. Without these previous measures, a return to legality by putting the custody of the courts back into the hands that have crippled the systems so dishonorably would constitute a fraud, a deceit, and a new betrayal.

The Second Revolutionary Law would have granted property,

non-mortgageable and non-transferable, to all planters, non-quotaplanters, lessees, share-croppers, and squatters who hold parcels of five *caballerías* of land or less, and the State would indemnify the former owners on the basis of the rental which they would have received for these parcels over a period of ten years.

The Third Revolutionary Law would have granted workers and employees the right to share 30% of the profits of all the large industrial, mercantile and mining enterprises, including the sugar mills. The strictly agricultural enterprises would be exempt in consideration of other agrarian laws which would be implemented.

The Fourth Revolutionary Law would have granted all planters the right to share 55% of the sugar production and a minimum quota of forty thousand *arrobas* for all small planters who have been established for three or more years.

The Fifth Revolutionary Law would have ordered the confiscation of all holdings and ill-gotten gains of those who had committed frauds during previous regimes, as well as the holdings and ill-gotten gains of all their legatees and heirs. To implement this, special courts with full powers would gain access to all records of all corporations registered or operating in this country, in order to investigate concealed funds of illegal origin, and to request that foreign governments extradite persons and attach holdings rightfully belonging to the Cuban people. Half of the property recovered would be used to subsidize retirement funds for workers and the other half would be used for hospitals, asylums and charitable organizations.

Furthermore, it was to be declared that the Cuban policy in the Americas would be one of close solidarity with the democratic peoples of this continent, and that those politically persecuted by bloody tyrants oppressing our sister nations would find generous asylum, brotherhood, and bread in the land of Martí; not the persecution, hunger, and treason they find today. Cuba should be the bulwark of liberty and not a shameful link in the chain of despotism.

These laws would have been proclaimed immediately, as soon

as the upheavals were ended and prior to a detailed and far-reaching study. They would have been followed by another series of laws and fundamental measures, such as the Agrarian Reform, the integral Reform of Education, electric power nationalization of the trust and the telephone trust, refund to the people of the illegal excessive rates this company has charged and payment to the Treasury of all taxes brazenly evaded in the past.

All these laws and others would be based on the exact fulfillment of two essential articles of our Constitution: one of them orders the outlawing of large estates indicating the maximum area of land any person or entity may own for each type of agricultural enterprise, by adopting measures which would tend to revert the land to the Cubans. The other, categorically orders the State to use all means at its disposal to provide employment to all those who lack it and to insure a decent livelihood to each manual or intellectual laborer.

None of these articles can be called unconstitutional. The first popularly elected government would have to respect these laws, not only because of moral obligation to the nation, but because when people achieve something they have yearned for throughout generations, no force in the world is capable of taking it away again. . . .

The problem concerning land, the problem of industrialization, the problem of housing, the problem of unemployment, the problem of education and the problem of the health of the people: these are the six problems we would take immediate steps to solve along with the restoration of public liberties and political democracy. . . .

A revolutionary government with the backing of the people and the respect of the nation, after cleaning the various institutions of all venal and corrupt officials, would proceed immediately to industrialize the country, mobilizing all inactive capital, currently estimated at about 150 million dollars, through the National Bank and the Agricultural Industrial and Development Bank, and submitting this mammoth task to experts and men of absolute competence completely removed from all political machinations, for study, direction, planning, and realization.

After settling the one hundred thousand small farmers as owners on land which they previously rented, a revolutionary government would proceed immediately to settle the land problem. First, as the Constitution ordains, we would establish the maximum amount of land to be held by each type of agricultural enterprise and would acquire the excess acreage by: expropriation, recovery of the lands stolen from the State, improvement of swampland, planting of large nurseries, and reserving of zones for reforestation. Secondly, we would distribute the remaining land among peasant familites with priority given to the larger ones, and would promote agricultural cooperatives for common use of expensive equipment, freezing plants and a single technical, professional directing board in farming and cattle raising. Finally, we would provide resources, equipment, protection, and useful guidance to the peasants.

A revolutionary government would solve the housing problem by cutting all rents in half, by providing tax exemptions on homes inhabited by the owners; by tripling taxes on rented homes; by tearing down hovels and replacing them with modern multiple-dwelling buildings; and by financing housing all over the island on a scale heretofore unheard of; with the criterion that, just as each rural family should possess its own tract of land, each city family should own its home or apartment. There is plenty of building material and more than enough manpower to make a decent home for every Cuban. But if we continue to wait for the miracle of the golden calf, a thousand years will have gone by and the problem will still be the same. On the other hand, today possibilities of taking electricity to the most isolated spots of Cuba are greater than ever. The use of nuclear energy in this field is now a reality and will greatly reduce the cost of producing electricity.

With these three projects and reforms, the problem of unemployment would automaticlly disappear and the task of improving public health and to fight against disease would be made much less difficult.

Finally, a revolutionary government would undertake the integral reform of the educational system, bringing it in line with the foregoing projects with the idea of educating those generations who will have the privilege of living in a happy land. Do not forget the words of the Apostle:

> A grave mistake is being made in Latin America: in countries that live almost completely from the produce of the land, men are being educated exclusively for urban life, and are not trained for the farm life. The happiest country is the one which has best educated its sons, both in the instruction of thought and the direction of their feelings.
>
> An educated country will always be strong and free.

The soul of education, however, is the teacher himself and in Cuba the teaching profession is miserably underpaid. Despite this, no one is more dedicated than the Cuban teacher. Who among us has not learned his ABC's in the little public schoolhouse? It is time we stopped paying pittances to these young men and women who are entrusted with the sacred task of teaching the young. No teacher should earn less than $200, no secondary professor should get less than $350, if they are to devote themselves exclusively to their high calling without suffering want. Moreover, all rural teachers should have free use of the various systems of transportation; and, at least every five years, all teachers should enjoy a sabbatical leave of six months with pay so they may attend special refresher courses at home and abroad to keep abreast of the latest developments in their field. In this way, the curriculum and the teaching system may be constantly improved.

Where will the money be found for all this? When there is an end to embezzlement of government funds, when public officials stop taking graft from the large companies who owe taxes to the State, when the enormous resources of the country are brought into full use, when we no longer buy tanks, bombers and guns for this country (which has no frontiers to defend and where these instruments of war, now being purchased, are used against the people) when there is more interest in educating the people than in killing them there will be more than enough money.

Cuba could easily provide for a population three times as great as it now has, so there is no excuse for the abject poverty of a single one of its present inhabitants. The markets should be overflowing with produce, pantries should be full, all hands should be working. This is not an inconceivable thought. What is inconceivable is that the majority of our rural people are now living in worse circumstances than were the Indians Columbus discovered in the fairest land that human eyes had ever seen.

To those who would call me a dreamer, I quote the words of Martí:

> A true man does not seek the path where advantage lies, but rather, the path where duty lies, and this is the only practical man, whose dream of today will be the law of tomorrow, because he who has looked back on the upheavals of history and has seen civilizations going up in flames, crying out in bloody struggle, throughout the centuries, knows that, without a single exception, the future lies on the side of duty. . . .

READING 2 *Castro's* Second Declaration of Havana

Introductory Note

Many of Castro's proposed social and economic reforms hardly changed after he came to power. What did change was the political ideology and system designed to legitimize and implement them. Instead of building on political democracy, constitutionalism, elections, and a parliament—suggested in his statements before 1959—Castro turned to the Communist Party and adopted Marxism-Leninism as the official Cuban ideology. The Communist Party under Castro's direct leadership became the means to organize Cubans into a radically new, single-party political system and to forge new nationalist identities vis-à-vis Yankee imperialism and through internal struggle for development.

These uses of Marxism-Leninism are clear in Castro's Second Declaration of Havana *delivered February 4, 1962, shortly after Castro officially adopted that ideology. Excerpts from it follow.*

Martí, as far back as 1895, pointed to the danger hanging over America and called imperialism by its name: imperialism. He warned the peoples of America that they, more than anyone, were obligated that Cuba not yield to the greed of the Yankee who despised the peoples of Latin America. With his own bloodshed

Fidel Castro, *Second Declaration of Havana* (Havana: Imprenta Nacional Unidad, 1962), pp. 6–7, 10–12, 15–18, 31, 33, 35, 37.

for Cuba and for America, he endorsed the posthumous words which today the people of Cuba endorse at the beginning of this declaration, as homage to his memory.

Sixty-seven years passed. Puerto Rico was converted into a colony and still is a colony filled with military bases. Cuba also fell into the clutches of imperialism, whose troops occupied our territory. It imposed the Platt Amendment on our first Constitution, a humiliating clause which gave it the odious "right" of outside interference. Our wealth passed into their hands; they falsified our history, our administration, and molded our politics to the interests of the intruders; the nation was subjected to 60 years of political, economic and cultural asphyxia.

But Cuba rose, Cuba was able to redeem itself from this bastard tutelage. Cuba broke the chains which tied its fortune to the oppressing empire; Cuba regained its riches, recovered its culture and raised its sovereign flag as the Free Territory and the Free People of America.

The United States will never again descend on America utilizing the strength it gained by oppressing Cuba; on the other hand, the United States is trying to descend on Cuba, using the strength gained by dominating most of the countries of Latin America.

What is Cuba's history but that of Latin America? What is the history of Latin America but the history of Asia, Africa and Oceania? And what is the history of all these peoples but the history of the cruelest exploitation of the world by imperialism?

At the end of the last century and the beginning of the present, a handful of economically developed nations had divided the world among themselves, subjecting two thirds of humanity to their economic and political domination. Humanity was forced to work for the dominating classes of the group of nations which had a developed capitalist economy.

The historic circumstances which permitted certain European countries and the United States of North America to attain a high industrial development level, put them in a position which enabled them to subject and exploit the rest of the world.

What motives lay behind this expansion of the industrial powers? Were they moral, "civilizing" reasons, as they claimed? No: their motives were economic.

The discovery of America sent the European conquerors across the seas to occupy and to exploit the lands and peoples of other continents; the lust for riches was the basic motivation for their conduct. America's discovery took place in the search for shorter ways to the Orient, whose products Europe valued highly.

A new social class, the merchants and the producers of articles manufactured for commerce, arose from the feudal society of lords and serfs in the latter part of the Middle Ages.

The lust for gold promoted the efforts of the new class. The lust for profit was the incentive of their behavior throughout its history. As industry and trade developed, the social influence of the new class grew. The new productive forces maturing in the midst of the feudal society increasingly clashed with feudalism and its serfdom, its laws, its institutions, its philosophy, its morals, its art and its political ideology. . . .

It was inevitable that imperialism and colonialism should enter into a deep and unescapable crisis. The general crisis began right after the First World War; the revolution of the workers and peasants overthrew the Czarist empire in Russia and, under the most difficult conditions of blockade and capitalist aggression established the first socialist State in the world, thus beginning a new era in human history. Since then and up to the present day, the crisis and corruption of the imperialist system have deepened incessantly.

The Second World War was unleashed by the imperialist powers. Criminally invaded, the Soviet Union and other nations of Europe and Asia were dragged into a bloody fight for freedom. The war ended with the defeat of fascism, the formation on a world scale of socialism, and the struggle for sovereignty by the colonial and dependent nations. Between 1945 and 1957, over 1 billion 200 million human beings attained independence in Asia and Africa. The people's blood was not shed in vain.

The movement of the dependent and colonialized peoples is

a universal phenomenon shaking the world. It marks the final crisis of imperialism. . . .

But History's development, the upward march of humanity, can never cease nor can it be stopped. The forces that move the people, the true creators of history, are determined by the material conditions of existence and the aspiration to achieve the highest goals of well-being and freedom. These forces arose and were made possible by man's progress in the scientific, technical and cultural fields; they prevailed over the terror unleashed by dominating oligarchies.

The subjective conditions in each country, the factors of consciousness, of organization, of leadership, can accelerate or delay revolution, depending on the state of their development. Sooner or later, in each historic epoch, as objective conditions ripen, consciousness is acquired, organization is achieved, leadership arises, and revolution is produced.

Whether this takes place peacefully or comes to the world after painful labor, does not depend on the revolutionaries; it depends on the reactionary forces of the old society; it depends on their resistance against allowing the new society to be born, a society produced by the contradictions of the old society. Revolution, in history, is as the doctor who assists at the birth of a new life. It does not use forceps unless it is necessary, but it will unhesitatingly use them every time labor requires them. A labor that brings the hope of a better life to the enslaved and exploited masses. Revolution is inevitable in many countries of Latin America. Nobody's will determines this fact. It is determined by the frightful conditions of exploitation which afflict mankind in America. It is determined by the development of the revolutionary consciousness of the masses, by the world crisis of imperialism and by the universal movement of struggle of the world's subjugated peoples.

The restlessness felt today is an unmistakable symptom of rebellion. The very entrails are shaking of a continent that has witnessed four centuries of slavery, semi-slavery and feudal exploitation of man, from its aboriginal dwellers and the slaves brought from Africa, to the national groups arising later: White, Negroes, Mulattoes, Mestizos and Indians who today are made brothers by Yankee scorn, united under the humiliation and the Yankee yoke, as they are united in the hope of a better tomorrow.

At the outset of the past century, the peoples of America freed themselves from Spanish colonialism, but they did not free themselves from exploitation. The feudal landlords assumed the authority of the governing Spaniards, the Indians continued in their painful serfdom, the Latin American man remained a slave one way or another, and the minimum hopes of the peoples died under the power of the oligarchies and the tyranny of foreign capital. This is the truth of America, to one or another degree of variation. Latin America today is under a more ferocious imperialism, more powerful and ruthless than the Spanish colonial empire.

What is Yankee imperialism's attitude confronting the objective and historically inexorable reality of the Latin American revolution? To prepare to fight a colonial war against the peoples of Latin America; to create an apparatus of force to establish the political pretexts and the pseudo-legal instrument underwritten by the representatives of the reactionary oligarchies, in order to curb by blood and by iron, the struggle of the Latin American peoples.

United States intervention in the internal affairs of Latin American countries continued more openly and at an unbridled tempo. The Inter-American Defense Council, for example, was, and continues to be, the nest wherein the most reactionary and pro-Yankee officers of the Latin American armies are hatched, in order to be used later as repressive instruments at monopoly's behest. The U.S. military missions in Latin America are a permanent espionage force in every nation, linked closely to the Central Intelligence Agency. They teach the most reactionary concepts to the officer groups, seeking to subvert the armies into instruments of their political and economic interests. . . .

U.S. imperialism's avowed policy of sending soldiers to fight the revolutionary movement in any Latin American country, to kill workers, students, peasants, to kill Latin American men and women, has no other purpose than to maintain its monopolistic interests and the privileges of the treacherous oligarchies which support the monopolies.

It can now be clearly seen that the military pacts underwritten by the United States and Latin American governments were pacts secretly arrived at behind the backs of the peoples. They invoked imaginary outside dangers that nobody ever saw anywhere and had the sole and exclusive purpose of preventing the struggle of the peoples. They were pacts against the peoples, whom they regarded as the only danger; the danger, within, of a liberation movement which would imperil Yankee interests. Naturally, the peoples asked: Why such military pacts? For what purpose these arms shipments that are technically inadequate for modern war, but are, on the other hand, sufficient to smash strikes, repress popular demonstrations, and spread bloodshed through the land? For what purpose, the military missions, the Rio de Janeiro Treaty, the thousand and one international conferences?

Since the end of the Second World War, the Latin American nations are becoming pauperized constantly. The value of their exports keep diminishing, costs of imports increase, the per capita income falls. The dreadful percentages of child death rate do not decrease, the number of illiterates grows higher, the peoples lack employment, land, adequate housing, schools, hospitals, communication systems and the means of subsistence. On the other hand, North American investments exceed 10 billion dollars. Latin America moreover supplies cheap raw materials and pays high prices for manufactured articles. Like the first Spanish conquerors, who exchanged mirrors and trinkets with the Indians for silver and gold, so United States trades with Latin America. To hold on to this torrent of wealth, to take greater possession of America's resources and to exploit its long-suffering peoples: this is what is hidden behind the military pacts, the military missions and Washington's diplomatic lobbying. . . .

As to the accusation that Cuba wishes to export its revolution, we reply: Revolutions are not exported; they are made by the peoples.

What Cuba can give and has already given to the peoples is its example.

And what does the Cuban Revolution teach? That revolution is possible, that the peoples can make it, that in today's world there is no force strong enough to impede the people's liberation movements.

Our victory would never have been possible if the revolution itself had not been inexorably destined to arise from the conditions which existed in our economic-social reality, a reality which pertains even to a greater degree in a goodly number of Latin American countries.

It happens inevitably that in those countries where Yankee monopolist control is strongest, where exploitation by the reigning few is most unrestrained and where the conditions of the masses of workers and peasants are most unbearable, the political power becomes more vicious, states of siege become habitual, all expression of mass discontent is suppressed by force, and the democratic channels are closed off thereby revealing more plainly than ever the kind of brutal dictatorship assumed by the dominating classes. That is when the people's revolutionary breakthrough becomes inevitable.

And while it is true that in America's underdeveloped countries the working class is in general relatively small, there is a social class which because of the sub-human conditions under which it lives constitutes a potential force which—led by the workers and the revolutionary intellectuals—has a decisive importance in the struggle for national liberation: the peasantry.

In our countries two circumstances are joined: underdeveloped industry, and an agrarian regime of a feudal character. That is why no matter how hard the living conditions of the workers are, the rural population lives under even more horrible conditions of oppression and exploitation. But, with few exceptions, it also constitutes the absolute majority, sometimes more than 70 percent of Latin American populations. . . .

Wherever roads are closed to the peoples, where repression

of workers and peasants is fierce, where the domination of Yankee monopolies is strongest, the first and most important lesson is to understand that it is neither just nor correct to divert the people with the vain and fanciful illusion that the dominant classes can be uprooted by legal means which do not and will not exist. The ruling classes are entrenched in all positions of state power. They monopolize the teaching field. They dominate all means of mass communication. They have infinite financial resources. Theirs is a power which the monopolies and the ruling few will defend by blood and fire with the strength of their police and their armies.

The duty of every revolutionary is to make revolution. We know that in America and throughout the world the revolution will be victorious. But revolutionaries cannot sit in the doorways of their homes to watch the corpse of imperialism pass by. The role of Job does not behoove a revolutionary. Each year by which America's liberation may be hastened will mean millions of children rescued from death, millions of minds freed for learning, infinitudes of sorrow spared the peoples. Even though the Yankee imperialists are preparing a bloodbath for America they will not succeed in drowning the people's struggle. They will evoke universal hatred against themselves. This will be the last act of their rapacious and cave-man system.

No one people of Latin America is weak, because all are part of a family of 200 million brothers who suffer the same miseries, harbor the same sentiments, face the same enemy. All dream alike of a happier fate and all can count on the solidarity of all honorable men and women throughout the world.

The epic of Latin America's independence struggles was great, and that fight was a heroic one. But today's generation of Latin Americans is summoned to write a greater epic, one even more decisive for humanity. The earlier fight was to free ourselves from Spanish colonial power, from a decadent Spain which had been invaded by Napoleon's armies. Today the liberation struggle confronts the strongest imperial land in all the world, the most significant power of the world imperialist system. Thus we perform an even greater service for humanity than did our ancestors.

This struggle, more than the first, will be conducted by the masses, by the peoples. The people will play a far more important role than they did then. Individual leaders matter less in this fight than in that.

This epic we have before us will be written by the hungry masses of Indians, of landless peasants, of exploited workers. It will be written by the progressive masses, the honest and brilliant intellectuals of whom we have so many in these suffering lands of Latin America. A battle of masses and of ideas, an epic borne onward by our peoples who have been ignored until today and who now are beginning to make imperialism lose its sleep. They thought us to be an impotent, submissive herd, but now they are beginning to fear that herd. It is a thundering herd of 200 million Latin Americans among whom Yankee monopoly capital already spies its gravediggers. . . .

READING 3 *A New National Social Ethic of Work*

Introductory Note

Castro does not refer officially to a new "national social ethic," but his emphasis on the values of work, unity, struggle, self-dignity, austerity, and commitment to Cuban development suggest that such a national ethic exists. The following speech, made July 26, 1967 in Santiago de Cuba's José Martí Plaza marking the fourteenth anniversary of the attack on the Moncada barracks, clearly identified the "revolution" with "work."

With missionary zeal, Castro and the Communist Party leaders appear dedicated to implanting their own version of the Protestant ethic in traditional Hispano-Catholic soil, where "work, thrift, austerity" were not always popular values, although some commentators of the revolution have suggested that Castro's stress on "work" is designed to shore up flagging revolutionary momentum.

Many will ask themselves, or some may ask themselves: What do these forces and movements represented here have in common with our people? It is that in any order, between the European sculptor, the artist, the poet, and the sculptors of this revolution, the ones who write a glorious page in history, the ones who create wealth with their hands to consolidate the revolutionary ideal—that is, between the European intellectual and the

Speech by Fidel Castro in Santiago de Cuba on July 26, 1967, Havana Domestic Radio Broadcast, July 26, 1967.

peasant of the Sierra Maestra or the canecutter—there exists in common something which we revolutionaries can well understand, and that is the desire for the dignity of man.

And what do the men and the people who struggle on all continents have in common with our revolution? What does the heroic Vietnamese struggle have in common with the struggle of our people and the people of Latin America, and what does the struggle of the oppressed people of the United States—that is, the sectors deprived of the most basic rights in that country—have in common with the struggle of the Latin American, Vietnamese, or Cuban peoples? What makes this date a symbol of this struggle, a symbol of this same aspiration, a symbol of that same ideal, is what brings us together here on an afternoon such as this.

We have not reached the end of that path or anything like that, but we have already advanced a long way. That essential characteristic of the revolutionary movement which began that day is today also the essential characteristic of our revolution: the confidence of the people in themselves, the faith of the people in their cause, the conviction of the people that there will be no difficulty, regardless of how great it may be, that we cannot overcome, that there will be no path, no matter how difficult it may be, that we will not be able to follow to the end.

In what state are our people and our revolution today after 14 years? Certainly the conquest of power was not the most difficult task, regardless of how difficult that phase may have seemed. Regardless of how difficult it was, how costly it was to us, viewed from the perspective of elapsed time, it appears to us—and this of course did not surprise us—that the most difficult task was not the overthrow of the tyranny and the conquest of revolutionary power. The most difficult task was the one that came later. The most difficult was the task in which we are engaged today: the task of building a new country on the foundation of an underdeveloped economy, the task of creating a new consciousness, a new man on the ideas which had prevailed practically for centuries in our society.

We are successfully accomplishing this task. And I ask our youth and our people if we are successfully accomplishing this task? [Crowd roars: "Yes!"] The attack on one of the many fortresses that had to be taken later. Many Moncadas remained to be taken.

Among other things there remained the Moncada of illiteracy and our people did not hesitate in attacking that fortress. They attacked it and took it. There was the Moncada of ignorance, the Moncada of inexperience, the Moncada of underdevelopment, the Moncada of the lack of technicians, resources of every type, and our people have not hesitated in undertaking the attack on those fortresses either.

However, there remained the most difficult Moncada to take and that was the Moncada of the old ideas. And that Moncada of the old ideas, of old selfish sentiments, of old habits of thinking and ways of viewing everything, and of resolving problems has not yet been completely taken. There is a vanguard which is breaking through victoriously, which is taking the first redoubts and which is advancing unceasingly along that path, and that vanguard consists, without any doubts of any kind, of our youth.

There is no doubt that our youth, workers, our students, those who make up that ever-growing troop of agricultural youth columns, those who in ever-increasing numbers participate in production for part of the year, the young people of our worker-technological institutes who, like many combatants of our glorious Rebel Army participated in the sugar harvest for 90 days, that this ever-growing legion is in the forefront of the struggle against the old ideas. There is no doubt—and we can proclaim this on this 26th of July—that our young generation is a worthy follower of the Moncada fighters, of the Sierra Maestra fighters, and of the Girón combatants. Because they are demonstrating this with their outlook on life, with their attitude toward work, and with their attitude toward the revolution.

We must say that at the side of the impressive movement of our people and particularly of our youth, with their entering into productive work, there survive those whose ideas and actions isolate themselves completely from that collective interest, that collective aspiration.

We have seen many examples of this type, but also with these examples we see in many towns the loafers who produce nothing. In many towns we see strong men who devote themselves to making candy [*piruli*], and obviously anyone who makes candy here when the people have money can make as much money as he wants making and selling candy. The result is that while there are sources of youths working under the hot noonday sun in the canefields, or working in the mountains, or working in the mud, or working under the most difficult conditions and who receive a modest pay for their work, we have those who do not aspire to this, to work for society, but to live on the work of society. They aspire to live on the work of these, the ones who are in the canefield at noon, the ones who are in the bogs where watercress is grown. Why? Because by selling candy, or by selling soft drinks, or by selling fritters they are going to make 10 times what the one who is working under the burning sun is going to make.

But it is the one under the sun, the one who works under the burning sun who creates the wealth, the goods of which the other one receives more than his share. These are things that our people must consider, must consider. Let it not happen that while a large part of the people make ever-increasing efforts, even more heroic and titanic efforts to increase the wealth of this country, there is a sector which does not think about that at all but rather of living parasitically from the wealth others are creating.

This is no longer exploitation by capitalists but exploitation of the working people by parasites, by those who do not aspire to create wealth but to see in what manner they can receive the largest possible share of that wealth with a minimum of effort. . . .

If you ask us now what is the fundamental thing in our revolution, we would answer without hesitation that it is work. At this point work is what characterizes the revolution. . . .

Our people have striven during these years. Our people have worked during these years. But we think it is still too little. We think we should strive still more. We think we must work more.

Our country is presently ruled by the spirit of work, and the virtues of the citizens of this country, their revolutionary spirit, are measured by their spirit of work.

What does this tell us? What does this indicate? That we have to work, and we have to work hard because we want to have the things we need to live. We always like to have an abundance of fresh things, but this is not acquired simply by good intentions. We must work, and we must work on an accurate course. . . .

This country's policy will be—and let this be known and remembered well—that if under any circumstances we find we need to urge a patriotic war against an aggressor, we will resort to a conventional war and to an unconventional war. We will confront masses of troops with masses of tanks, masses of artillery, and masses of soldiers. In the face of any combination of forces, each soldier and each citizen of this country capable of wielding a weapon will be as an army by himself. He will be his own commander. His weapon will be his gun, and his enemy will be a common one.

In other words—and this is no secret—we will defend ourselves with the technology of regular war and we will defend ourselves with the tactics of guerrilla warfare anywhere. There is a word which is absolutely banned from our revolutionary terminology. The word is "defeat." A synonym of defeat is surrender. There is a phrase that, because of a matter of profound principle, will always be abolished from the terminology of this revolution—the phrase is "ceasefire!"

"Ceasefire!" will never be uttered in this country as long as one single inch of our territory is occupied by any invader. Bear this in mind well, and remember it always. Anyone who utters this command can only be classified as a traitor, whoever he might be! An order like this can never be obeyed, whoever might give it. This order will never be carried out in this country.

READING 4 More on the New National Social Ethic

Introductory Note

Marxism-Leninism is used in Cuba as the ideological means to inculcate positive attitudes toward individual work and struggle in the building of a national Communist society, as Castro's speech of July 26, 1968 indicated (Selection 4.1). The conclusions reached by the National Committee of the Unión de la Juventud Comunista *(Union of Communist Youth or UJC) at its first meeting in 1967 provides a good example of the impact of Marxism-Leninism on young Cubans (Selection 4.2).*

The attempt to build a national Communist society is not restricted to members of the Communist Party or the Communist Youth Union. It is the task of all Cubans, as Major Juan Almeida, Acting Armed Forces Minister, indicated at Havana's Plaza de la Revolución, in his May Day speech of 1967 (Selection 4.3).

Selection 4.1: Speech by Fidel Castro in Santa Clara, Las Villas province, on July 26, 1968, published in *Granma,* Weekly Review in English, Year 3, No. 30 (July 28, 1968), pp. 3–5.

Selection 4.2: *Unión de la Juventud Comunista* report, Havana Domestic Radio Broadcast, June 29, 1967.

Selection 4.3: Speech by Major Juan Almeida in Havana on May 1, 1967, Havana Domestic Radio Broadcast, May 1, 1967. The word *machetero* which Major Almeida uses frequently means (sugar) cane cutter.

Selection 4.4: Speech by Fidel Castro at the University of Havana on March 13, 1968, published in *Granma,* Weekly Review in English, Year 3, No. 12 (March 24, 1968), pp. 2–8.

Selection 4.5: Speech by Fidel Castro in Santa Clara, Las Villas province, on July 26, 1968, published in *Granma,* Weekly Review in English, Year 3, No. 30 (July 28, 1968), pp. 3–5.

In building national unity, Castro wants to remove "selfish" interests identified with old capitalist habits. In order to eradicate these attitudes, he has spoken of eliminating money and material incentives for overtime work, to be replaced by the idea of the ultimate morality of working for the revolution (Selection 4.4). In short, Castro advocates creation of a "new man" with a fundamentally revolutionary, socialist, and Communist conscience, who will build the new Cuba (Selection 4.5).

SELECTION 4.1: BUILDING A NATIONAL COMMUNIST SOCIETY

No human society has yet reached communism. The ways along which a superior form of society is reached are very difficult. A communist society means that man will have reached the highest degree of social awareness ever achieved; a communist society means that the human being will have been able to achieve the degree of understanding and brotherhood which man has sometimes achieved within the close circle of his family. To live in a communist society is to live in a real society of brothers; to live in a communist society is to live without selfishness, to live among the people and with the people, as if every one of our fellow citizens were really our brother.

Man comes from capitalism full of selfishness; man is educated under capitalism amidst the most vicious selfishness, as an enemy of other men, as a wolf of other men.

The students here expressed the idea that communism and socialism will be built simultaneously, and that idea and the expression of that idea have led to the situation where Cuban revolutionaries have been described as wishful thinkers; have led some people to say that these are petty bourgeois ideas; have led some people to say that this is an erroneous interpretation of Marxist-Leninist ideas, that it is not possible to build communism if socialism is not achieved first and that in order to build socialism it is necessary to develop the material base of socialism. We do not deny this last point.

In the very essence of Marxist thought, socialist society and communist society must be based on a thorough mastery of technology, on the complete development of the productive forces, so that man may be able to create material goods in such quantities that everyone may be able to satisfy his needs.

It is unquestionable that the Middle Ages society, with its minimal development of the productive forces could not have aspired to live under communism; it is very clear that the old society, with even more backward and poor productive forces, could have aspired even less to live under communism; and communism arises as a possibility of man's control: a full command of nature, a full command of the processes of material goods production. . . .

And of course a people aspiring to live under communism must do what we are doing. It must emerge from underdevelopment. It must develop its productive forces. It must have a command of technology in order to be able to turn man's efforts and man's sweat into the miracle of producing practically unlimited quantities of material goods.

If we do not acquire a complete command of technology, if we do not develop our productive forces, we will deserve to be called dreamers for aspiring to live in a communist society.

The question, from our point of view, is that communist awareness must be developed at the same rate as the productive forces; an advance in the conscientiousness of revolutionaries, in the conscientiousness of the people, must accompany every step forward in the development of the productive forces.

Communism is often defined by the simple formula: from each according to his ability, and to each according to his needs.

A good part of our people, an ever-growing part. . . . For example, our students. It was said here that there are already over 200,000 young people with full and partial scholarships. These 200,000 young people receive—free of charge—room, board, clothing, medical care, recreation and books—that is, each person receives what he or she needs. And, if they do not receive more, it is because there is no more to give; if they receive two shirts a year, it is because there are only two shirts to give; if they get two pairs of shoes, it's because there are only two pairs; if there is only one, they get only one, which is what we have. Today they get one, but tomorrow they will get three, and in the future they will get four or five, as many as they need.

We deeply regret that the amount of dry goods available to our country is not sufficient to give the students, for example and all of our people, the number of square meters of cloth which we know they need, that the materials available to our country are not sufficient to distribute the number of pairs of shoes that we know they need. The Revolution cannot give what it doesn't have, but what it does have, it distributes in the fairest way. For example, we give our students what we are able to give. We cannot give the students more shirts, because we would have to take them away from other people. But the fact of the matter is that, whatever we have, our students receive it in an egalitarian manner.

Some of our students are in very modern schools, while others live in very poor student lodgings. Why? Because we do not have enough dormitories. But there is no doubt that some day there won't be a single student in this country who is not housed in a dormitory and who does not attend a school with the best possible hygienic conditions and, in general, with the very best facilities for carrying out all his activities.

Be that as it may, the fact remains that hundreds of thousands of young people for all intents and purposes live in a communist way in our society. . . .

However, the Revolution feels that every child has the right to study—not only the right but also the duty. And the right and duty to study not only two or three years, but six years. And now we are already thinking of the right and the duty to study up to thirteen years in school, with military training included in our study programs. These young people don't have to be rich or the sons of rich people. It doesn't matter how much their parents earn. All of society offers them that precious opportunity, that extraordinary possibility. And that is communism! Communism exists when society, considered as a whole, with all its resources, makes itself responsible for the education of each citizen, makes itself responsible for the health of each citizen, for the well-being of each citizen, and all of society—classes having disappeared, inequality having disappeared—works for each and all of its citizens. . . .

Unfortunately, all this cannot be done in a day; this cannot be done with everything at once. This is a long road. We can advance along that road to the extent that we develop our productive forces, to the extent that we develop our productivity, to the extent that we develop our productive processes. . . .

And we should not use money or wealth to create political awareness. We must use political awareness to create wealth. To offer a man more to do more than his duty is to buy his conscience with money. To give a man participation in more collective wealth because he does his duty and produces more and creates more for society is to turn political awareness into wealth.

As we said before, communism, certainly, cannot be established if we do not create abundant wealth. But the way to do this, in our opinion, is not by creating political awareness with money or with wealth, but by creating wealth with political awareness and more and more collective wealth with more collective political awareness. . . .

Selection 4.2: "Work" and Marxism-Leninism

We are still not satisfied with the work being done in the *Unión de la Juventud Comunista* [Union of Communist Youth or UJC] since its third national plenum this January. We have progressed greatly in our work of mobilizing masses of young people for farm work; more than 23,000 are already in camps and more than 120,000 enrolled. The pioneer movement is developing tremendously; at present we have the large number of more than 800,000 children organized. We are reinforcing our political work in schools. . . .

We have embarked on a course that has completely revolutionized our style of work. We must continue on that course and strive to improve it constantly. The drive to curb meetings must be a continuing activity admitting to no relaxation. We must work with a guerrilla method, linked as much as possible to the rank and file, seeking to have every cadre given the authority to execute and make executive decisions, shouldering individual responsibility to the proper extent, and living the revolution intensely.

This new work method that we have been introducing throughout our organization requires constant checking and supervision so that shortcomings and mistakes can be corrected while work progresses, without waiting for the long periods of analysis to which we were accustomed and which were preceded by tedious reports that completely bureaucratized our work of supervision. . . .

We are absolutely convinced that the system of constant criticism, emulation among ourselves, eradication of compromises, and revolutionary intransigence guarantee maximum authority to everybody—although one must not fall into a philosophy of criticism and an abuse of criticism. Along with this problem it is necessary to develop confidence in the cadre and the functions he performs, develop criticism among ourselves to the utmost, and encourage any revolutionary to criticize us and teach us. . . .

Instead of lamenting our shortcomings and mistakes or shedding crocodile tears over them, the thing to do is set about correcting their effects immediately in each case through concrete action that will solve the problems. It is necessary to check carefully and keep after problems until we have succeeded in solving them. . . .

Advancing in the maximum development of the parallel building of socialism and communism has a special significance in childhood and youth. Where we must make communist forms take root first is in the child and the youth. All vestiges of the old society that still persist in our youth must be destroyed, particularly through stress on educational matters, social relationships, economic interest, the question of stimuli in the case of the young, and so on.

Selection 4.3: Cubans and Communism

Those who want to learn what a man under communism is, what a man of the new society we are building is, let them talk to the workers who are building the harrows for agriculture, let them discuss it with the *macheteros* [canecutters] throughout the nation, let them ask the Banao women, let them ask the young women in Güane and the Isle of Pines, let them ask the tens of thousands of technological students who have been cutting cane for three months during the sugar harvest, let them ask the workers who are building the industrial city of Nuevitas, the small farmers who are working on the coffee growing plans, the soldiers who are cutting cane anywhere in the nation. Those who would know what man under communism is, who want to know what his ideas are, his yearnings and preoccupation, let them go to our fields, let them talk there to the comrades working on the Banao, La Caoba, Pinares de Mayarí, Isle of Pines, San Andrés de Caiguanabo, and Cunagua plans anywhere in the nation. . . .

This formidable movement is only possible because of an ideological factor and high revolutionary consciousness in our people. These 4,000 men who are here with us today from various parts of the country, representing millions of workers from throughout the country, are inspired by an ideal of work and effort. They feel moved by that ideal, encouraged by a revolutionary consciousness. These thousands and thousands of workers, peasants, youths, and women are not made of any different material than the rest of the people. Millions of men like them are making heroic efforts to advance. They advance the production plans, agricultural-livestock plans in various regions of the country. It is revolutionary consciousness, the duty to work, communist enthusiasm, the conviction that it is work being done for the future, that it is work for all the people, which inspires these men.

If we trust in these ideas, we believe in communism. If we believe in the strength of these feelings and the sureness of these ideas, we believe in the people. We believe in this immense mass of workers, peasants, students, women, and youth, in all our people. If these people have been capable of facing the greatest dangers, if they are not afraid of imperialism, if they have shown their willingness to fight and to die if necessary—if this is so, we have more than enough reasons to declare that our people and the coming generations will create a society that improves daily through their work, and ever better future. And they will do it happily, with enthusiasm inspired not only by the benefits each will receive individually but by the benefits which all the people will gain collectively, because our people today have the conviction that what is wanted for each of us is also wanted for all the people. . . .

In communism you build so that man may live better and have his basic spiritual and material needs satisfied. However, it will be impossible to build communism unless we also create the communist man, unless we educate ourselves in these ideas, unless we train ourselves in these ideas, and unless we carry out the great technical and educational plans that we are promoting. The increase in this revolutionary consciousness and this life of work have been accompanied by greater precision in our plans of agricultural and economic development in general. Years ago we were not clear as to what steps we should take for the building of communism. There were many ideas, but we were not aware of the basic lines, the essential lines on which we should work to build our future. . . .

Selection 4.4: Removing Material Incentives

Capitalism was a pyramid of exploitation, a pyramid where those on top exploited those below them, who in turn exploited those below them, etc. . . . . And often it spread even among the workers, for there were workers who had salaries five times as great as the ones who cut sugar cane. There were workers who could buy used cars from the United States, who had salaries of 300 to 400 pesos a month, perhaps working in a U.S.-run bank or for one of the monopolies. And the one who cut sugarcane and sustained the economy was the one who really paid for that car, the gas and everything, and he didn't have enough to eat. Capitalism, by principle, establishes this ladder of exploitation and it is clear that capitalism has to be pulled out by the roots. We cannot encourage or even permit selfish attitudes among men if we don't want man to be guided by the instinct of selfishness, of individuality; by the wolf, the beast instinct; man as the enemy of man, the exploiter of man, the setter of snares for other men.

The concept of socialism and communism, the concept of a higher society, implies a man devoid of these feelings; a man who has overcome such instincts at any cost; placing above everything his sense of solidarity and brotherhood among men. And this brings to mind the famous topic of incentives. For a long time they were theoretically discussed, and it appeared to be a question of method, but, in our opinion, it is a much more profound question. And we don't feel that the communist man can be developed by encouraging man's ambition, man's individualism, man's individual desires. If we are going to fall because we believe in man's ability, in his ability to improve, then we will fall, but we will never renounce our faith in mankind! . . .

And, furthermore, material incentives here? Who can offer more material incentives than imperialism? With its developed economy, with its technically equipped industry, it can offer more than any other, and, indeed, does. And many of those who pack their bags and leave with I don't know what excuse are simply fleeing from the realities of their country, are fleeing from today's work to go there as parasites in a way, to earn more and have more things that a country with a standard of living, as we said, with income standards 20 times as great on the average as those of an underdeveloped country can offer. . . .

We are beginning to narrow that gap with the efforts we are making. But, really, many use the pretext of the Revolution, people who have no ideals, who have no spirit of struggle, who are incapable of having intense feelings about anything, in behalf of anything. And they emigrate. . . .

Selection 4.5: The "New Man"

. . . The great task of the Revolution is basically the task of forming the new man of whom we spoke here, the new man of whom Che spoke, the man of a truly revolutionary conscience, the man of a truly socialist conscience, the man of a truly communist conscience. And when we reach the point where our young people are capable of such deep thought, when our young people are capable of expressing themselves correctly on all these questions, when our young people are capable of such profound meditation and analysis, and when they reach these conclusions and in these conclusions categorically express their conscience of young people who really want to live in a communist society, it is then that we can be completely sure of the fact that the effort in favor of liberation which began one hundred years ago and which marked a milestone 15 years ago, on that morning of July 26, 1953, when many young men like them gave their lives for the future of their country, gave their lives for the Revolution. . . .

READING 5 *Anti-Imperialism and Cuban Sovereignty*

Introductory Note

The language of anti-imperialism permeates Cuba's attacks on past dominance by the United States and lends itself to the defense of contemporary Cuban sovereignty in the face of real or imagined military threats from Washington. One interpretation of United States policy in Latin America is given below.

Without any doubt, the Cuban revolutionary phenomenon has become the determinant factor of the conditioning of North American policy to more intelligent tactics with respect to the so-called Western Hemisphere. Cuba brought with it in Latin America not only the possibility and reality of the triumph of an armed movement without the imperialists and against them, but also this example made the Latin American capitals vibrate with anti-imperialist manifestations of a magnitude and combativity never seen before. The question of support to our country provoked schisms within many traditional parties and we cite as examples the cases of Democratic Action in Venezuela, the Liberal Party in Colombia, the Colored Party [Partido Colorado] in Uruguay, etc.

In parallel fashion, large masses of intellectuals and students are joining with the popular forces in their cries of support to

Eduardo H. Gispert, "The Concepts, One Continent," in *El Caimán Barbudo,* Havana, March 1967, pp. 3–5, JPRS 40,819 (May 1, 1967).

the Cuban Revolution. And it is that Cuba serves as a very clear expression of the disintegration of the colonial system of imperialism, and is solving in practice the same problems which oppress countries of Latin America and shatters the famous myth of "geographic fatalism." . . .

Then the interesting stunt of imperialism appeared: the Alliance for Progress, and with it a hybrid of demagogic theory and anti-popular "revolution": the so-called Reformism.

. . . In these words there was a hidden objective: the neutralization, at all costs, of the growing influence of the Cuban Revolution. Paradoxically, once the central organization of the Alliance was created in Washington, the message of its president [sic], Teodoro Moscoso, was decorated with signs which could have a double interpretation: "Be Brief, We Are 25 Years Behind.". . .

With regard to the so-called "Peace Corps," this organization was also created by President Kennedy as a complement to the Alliance and the selection, training and care of its members is in the hands of the Central Intelligence Agency. For the most part, the members are young North American professionals and technicians, recently graduated from United States universities, duly trained by them, among other things, to exercise works of co-operation in peasant education, to construct roads, to make topographical maps, to plan water works, to do sanitary labors, etc., besides the valuable co-operation in the ideological struggle they give to their Government. With them, the case of the Alliance is repeated. Many of the groups of the left and progressive parties daily accuse them of being "CIA agents," "bears of hunger and accusation," but this Yankee activist works in far-off places, difficult to reach, with the great mass of the peasants, where perhaps no revolutionary militant of any party of the left has ever gone. Thus, ideological recruitment is made easy for the enemy.

The active role of the Alliance and the Peace Corps offers us an interesting experience and the new imperialist ideological forms of struggle require new forms of revolutionary struggle, new tactical and strategic concepts. This means that only the revolutionary popular war, supported and directed from the peasant scene, destroys the very able work of the enemy and obligates him to a frontal struggle with an entire people.

It should be said that we do not say that the ideological penetration is an absolute, the only form of struggle on the Latin American scene, but this form is becoming the most subtle, important and difficult one of North American imperialism at the present time. The accession to this form has a clear trajectory. The militarization of the economy has been and is one of the fundamental characteristics of contemporary imperialism. This is why, during the democratic government of General Eisenhower (1953-61) the "hard handed" Pentagon line appeared as the fundamental one, flaring up again and surpassing all the previous stages. During this period, dozens of military coups took place in Latin America, Yankee aggression in Guatemala took place and the preparations for Playa Girón took place, after many aggressions and provocations on Cuba.

With the accession of the republicans to the Presidency an internal struggle began between the defenders of such methods and those which, like Kennedy, were in favor of the preferential utilization of the "State Department" instrument, although during his government an entire series of interventionist actions, coups, etc. were also permitted.

With the assassination of Kennedy, the Pentagon line is imposed again and the most war-like circles support Johnson and even compromise and recruit him (if he was not so before). As of this moment, military coups are increasing, with their highest exponent being in the case of Brazil, where the most perfect and organized "putsch" in the history of America took place.

Recently, Johnson seems to struggle desperately to combine his policy of "hard hand" (Santo Domingo) with that of "showcase revolution" (Chile), trying to direct not only Chile along the reformist path, but also Ecuador, Colombia, Peru, Venezuela, and even Uruguay. . . .

Constructing showcase revolutions, in miniature and as free samples, should not lull the people, although lamentably it often does so with some of the revolutionary parties. When revolutionary action does not put a stop to this contemporary stunt, the masses will be detoured from truly revolutionary objectives, the leaders of the left will turn to the center and Marxism will be tied hand and foot by those who say they are its supporters.

To combat Reformism with "reformism" is to make a counter revolution and lose the support of the masses. Reformism is not combatted by attracting it with substantial loans, because this would be the equivalent of the erroneous application of the policy of *zanahoria* [carrot]; Reformism cannot be compromised with money, because other money has already compromised it since its birth. The War of the People is the only effective instrument, and this is where we must give our support, our loans, and our decorations. . . .

READING 6 *Political Independence—The Soviet Dimension*

Introductory Note

Cuban radical nationalism and concern for political independence is not restricted to Havana-Washington affairs. Cuba is tied closely to Moscow by virtue of its economic dependence, a potential Soviet threat to Cuban independence. It is not surprising that Havana has expressed its determination to keep Cuban policy in its own hands. The first selection, a 1967 speech by Raúl Castro, shows strong independence from Soviet advice on Cuba's export of revolution in Latin America. The second selection, the court martial of Aníbal Escalante in 1967, indicates Havana's feelings about old-line pro-Soviet Cuban Communists who fraternize too closely with Moscow.

SELECTION 6.1: NO "DADDY" FOR CUBA

The increasing revolutionary wave in Latin America, the exemplary and heroic showing of Vietnam, the slogan to create two,

Selection 6.1: Speech by Raúl Castro, Havana Domestic Radio Broadcast, July 24, 1967.

Selection 6.2: Summation of court martial of Aníbal Escalante, accused of "microfactionist" activities against the Revolutionary Government. Escalante, a member of the old pro-Soviet group in the Cuban Communist Party, was accused of distributing clandestine propaganda against the party line and supplying false information to officials of foreign countries (the USSR). Havana Domestic Radio Broadcast, February 2, 1968.

three, or many Vietnams, and the courageous guerrillas that are fighting in the mountains of America fills them with panic. Aware of just what the situation is, imperialism is trying with its enormous power to stifle in blood the Latin American revolution. For this reason, it invaded Santo Domingo with thousands of soldiers. It is lending every kind of aid to its puppets. It is training the "gorillas" in its schools and is hastily dispatching its "Green Berets" to Bolivia.

To give you an account of all the threats, statements, conferences, committees, comings and goings, and so forth, is practically impossible. It would take several volumes to cover them all. Choosing at random from the tons of paper invested in these tasks, it suffices to stress some facts. The immense majority of this continent's puppet governments accuse us of all their problems. If there is a labor strike, the Castro-communist agitators are to blame. If there is a student strike, the hand of Castro-communism is in it. If there is a demonstration in the streets, the same is true.

The bulk, the largest part, comes from the U.S. imperialist press and especially from its most important military and civilian leaders. Thus we see in the press reports of February and March that the leaders of the U.S. Armed Forces make statements in the Yankee Senate. Statements are made by Admiral David McDonald, the chief of Naval Operations; General Harold Johnson, Chief of the Army General Staff; General John McConnell, Chief of the Air General Staff; and General Wallace Greene, the Commander in Chief of the Marines. . . .

Meanwhile, the investigation committee which studied the Venezuelan guerrilla problem continues to work on the report it will present to the aforementioned OAS [Organization of American States] consultative meeting. Concerning these investigations which said committees are carrying out to satisfy and to promote hysteria in the enemies of our revolution—the imperialist masters as well as their Latin American puppets—we can give them very important—and a great variety of—details, which we will refer to later on. But before this, in connection with this campaign, which is increasing and which has been repeated by high-ranking United States imperialist leaders, let me read a cable dated early July from Alaska:

" 'Aleksey Kosygin' "—This is an AFP [Agence France Press] cable—" 'tried to discourage Fidel Castro from exporting the Cuban revolution to Latin America,' United States Vice President Hubert Humphrey said yesterday at a press conference. Humphrey, who stopped in Alaska on his way back from South Korea, where he attended the farce to keep in power the imperialist puppet Pak Chong-hui, said at the press conference that at the Glassboro meetings Johnson told Kosygin that the United States frowns on the activities of the Cuban Government and Cuban agents in Latin America and the export of weapons to the continent's revolutionaries.

"Humphrey continued: 'It seems that President Johnson asked the Chairman of the Soviet Council of Ministers to speak about this to the Cuban Prime Minister. We have firm knowledge that he did so,' said Humphrey in conclusion."

As far as we know, the United States vice president is in charge of very unimportant matters. Other than some short junkets of a formal and protocol nature, his great mission is to wait for the death of the President to take over his office. It does not matter whether the President's death be from natural causes or as a result of the murders which we are used to learning about in the history of that nation. It seems that the present vice president of the United States, in addition to his other unimportant functions, has lately dedicated himself to hatching international intrigues. It can be seen that despite the constant efforts which CIA agents carry out to take advantage of the problems of our relations with our sister nations, Humphrey, the United States vice president, and his government ignore the fact that relations between Cuba and the USSR can only exist on the basis of the strictest mutual respect and absolute independence, and it is on this basis that they were born, are maintained today, and will always be maintained.

In addition, in answer to Mr. Humphrey, the United States vice president, we do not have a daddy. . . . Our nation was under the Spanish regime until the end of the last century. Spain was defeated in the half-century war by our Mambises, and when the right time came, proclaimed by President Jefferson years before, and when we had the Spanish monarchy beaten with our war of independence, the imperialist army came and without fighting took over the island. Since that time the second "daddy" was United States imperialism until 1 January 1959. *This is why, imperialist sirs, we do not have a daddy* [editors' italics]. I do not know what was told Mr. Humphrey or who told it to him, but it is evident that he is having childish daydreams. . . .

Selection 6.2: Cuban Independence

They [the microfaction] say that a strong anti-Soviet current existed and emphasized, moreover, that the USSR is the country that must be in control. As for the USSR, no one can fail to respect Lenin's party and that heroic country that bravely withstood the shock of the terrible wars that afflicted it. However, when our revolution demands the right to think with its own head, we are not failing to pay that respect; we are merely requesting the right to think and act for ourselves.

If there is anything that irritates us, it is the servility of these gentlemen who want to deny our fatherland the right to think about and decide its own problems and those of the world. Our revolution was born among our own people and developed by them, by their own effort. It is encouraging to see that a small country like ours is in a position to think for itself in today's convulsed and agitated world and that it is in a position to speak to the world with the authority it does. What these midgets cannot forgive is our ability to think and act independently, the fact that we shun the cliches and the texts, and the ability of our people to pursue their path and their determination to contribute to the revolutionary cause. No one can call us a satellite state and that is the reason we are respected in the world. Our revolutionary activity conforms to the principles of Marxism-Leninism and the essence of Marxism-Leninism. . . .

If we are to be loyal to Marxism, we must engage in the creative development of its principles; we must apply it correctly so as to find formulas that fit the new situations that spring up in the world today.

Other arguments advanced by the microfaction attack the revolution because it uses moral inducements to encourage the construction of communism. Our revolution has stated that the dented arms of capitalism cannot lead us along the path of socialism.

. . . It has also been proven that, on the instruction of Aníbal Escalante, the other defendants contacted foreigners—especially, members of the Soviet, German Democratic Republic, and Czechoslovak communist parties—so that the group's differences with our party could be learned abroad. In this way, and by giving false and calumnious information to some officials of these countries on the plans of the revolution, they tried to undermine the international relations between Cuba and other governments. Aníbal Escalante himself made several attempts to travel to the USSR and other countries so that he could explain his position.

It has also been proven that defendants Escalante and Octavio Fernandez drafted documents that were to be sent abroad. These documents presented the position of the microfactionalist group and pursued the same aim. Furthermore, Aníbal Escalante received secret documents of the Central Committee and the Ministry of Industries of that time. These documents were stolen from those agencies so that Escalante could be kept informed of their secret contents. . . .

READING 7 *History and the Revolution*

Introductory Note

Castro and other members of the Cuban Communist Party devote much of their energy to analyses of Cuba's past, with specific focus on early struggles for independence. Castro has indicated clearly that these early struggles for sovereign independence, dating back to 1868, form a continuous thread with the current revolution and with the national history of the homeland. A reading of his speeches on Cuban national history, at times detached from the language of Marxism-Leninism, exposes the resonant nationalist overtones in this revolution which shape the way Cubans view their history, as the two following excerpts from speeches in the late 1960s illustrate.

Selection 7.1: The Revolution in History

. . . What does October 10, 1868, signify for our people? What does this glorious date mean for the revolutionaries of our nation? It simply signifies the beginning of one hundred years of struggle, the beginning of the Revolution in Cuba because in Cuba there has been one revolution: that which was begun by Carlos Manuel de Céspedes on October 10, 1868, the revolution which our people are still carrying forward.

Selection 7.1: Speech by Fidel Castro in Manzanillo, Oriente Province, on October 10, 1968, published in *Granma*, Weekly Review in English, Year 3, No. 41 (October 13, 1968), pp. 2–5.

Selection 7.2: Speech by Fidel Castro at Playa Girón on April 19, 1968, published in *Granma*, Weekly Review in English, Year 3, No. 17 (April 28, 1968), pp. 2–6.

There is, of course, no doubt that Céspedes symbolized the spirit of the Cubans of that time. He symbolized the dignity and rebelliousness of a people—still heterogeneous in nature—which began to take shape as a nation in the course of history. It was, without doubt, Céspedes who, among the conspirators of 1868, was the firmest in his determination to rise up in arms. . . .

This commemoration today is like a meeting of the people with its own history. It is a seeking out by the people with its own history. It is a seeking out by the present generation of its own roots. Nothing could better teach us how to understand what a revolution is, nothing could better teach us to understand what the term "revolution" means, than an analysis of the history of our country, a study of the history of our people, of our people's revolutionary roots.

Perhaps there are some who have regarded the nation and the homeland as just a natural development. Perhaps many think of the Cuban nation and of awareness of nationality as things that have always existed. And perhaps many persons have seldom taken time out to think about just how the Cuban nation was born, how our awareness came into being.

One hundred years ago, this awareness did not exist. One hundred years ago, Cuban nationality did not exist. One hundred years ago, a nation, in the sense of a people with common interests and a common destiny, did not actually exist. A century ago, our people were simply a motley mass, made up in the first place of citizens of the Spanish colonial power dominating us; there was also a mass of citizens born in this country, many direct descendants of Spaniards, others more distantly related—of whom some favored colonial rule, while others were allergic to that rule; and a large mass of slaves, criminally brought to our country to be pitilessly exploited after the exploiters had already virtually annihilated the primitive Indian people here. . . .

In the first decades of the last century, when the rest of Latin America had already won its independence from Spain, Spanish power still rested on a very firm basis in our country, which they called the last and the most precious jewel in the Spanish crown.

The emancipation of Latin America had very little real influence on our nation. . . .

Selection 7.2: The Revolution in Past, Present, and Future

This evening the chorus recalled the history of the 100 years of struggle for our independence: the struggle was begun by Céspedes, Agramonte, Maceo and Máximo Gómez 100 years ago, and this generation has had the privilege of seeing it bear fruit. This generation of Cubans is privileged to unfurl its flag in complete freedom, complete sovereignty, with a degree of independence and dignity never before achieved, freedom in the fullest sense of the word, freedom won through 100 years of sacrifice, 100 years of bloodshed. This generation of Cubans is privileged to see the results of the efforts made in those years reflected in the young people who are growing up, in the young people who make up the most enthusiastic and combative sector of our people today!

It is only 7 years since Girón; almost 10 years since January 1, 1959; some 12 years since the Granma landing; some 15 years since the 26th of July; it would have been impossible for any people to have changed more in such a short time, it would have been impossible for any people to have become more different in so few years, it would have been impossible for any people to have created more than has been created in these years—above all, that spirit, that outlook, that awakening to our history, that awakening to our duty in this continent and in this world, that awareness of the importance the efforts of our people have today, of the chapter they are writing in history. And we realize that we have just begun. While things have happened rapidly in these years, while our people have advanced rapidly in these years, from now on we will go forward even more rapidly, more united, more aware and stronger. . . .

This generation can feel that it has done something, can feel that it has lived up to its duty and that it has a right to look to the future, that there is no reason to blush when looking at the past. For, we of this generation, unlike others that were hobbled for one reason or another—hobbled, basically, by imperialism, by Yankee intervention, which interrupted the revolutionary process, which imposed corruption and neocolonialism on us for fifty years—unlike generations that could not see the results of the bloody, self-sacrificing struggles of this people, unlike those less fortunate generations, we can look upon the present, the past, and the future with a spirit of tranquility, satisfaction and optimism, as could no previous generation. . . .

READING 8 *National Objectives in Cuba*

Introductory Note

The following speeches by Castro during 1968–69 highlight national objectives which, if the Marxism-Leninism were removed, date back to his "History Will Absolve Me" speech of October 1953. What is distinctly new in the later speeches, when compared to the pre-1959 period, is not the emphasis on education, agrarian reform, improved housing, health, and cultural conditions. It is rather the replacement of political democracy as a goal by the drive to forge a national Communist society out of new "solidarity" and "brotherhood" attitudes among the Cuban masses, indicated by the following selections.

Selection 8.1: Cultural, Social, and Economic Development

On this anniversary our celebration is characterized by its simplicity. There is no military parade, even though we had thought that the 10th anniversary might possibly include a military parade. However, this has been a year of arduous work, a year of great effort in every field of activity, a year of great savings in every respect and a year in which every man and woman in our country played an important role. And, since the most important

Selection 8.1: Speech by Fidel Castro in the Plaza de la Revolución on January 2, 1969, published in *Granma,* Weekly Review in English, Year 4, No. 1 (January 5, 1969), pp. 2–6.

Selection 8.2: Speech by Fidel Castro at Playa Girón on April 19, 1968, published in *Granma,* Weekly Review in English, Year 3, No. 17 (April 28, 1968), pp. 2–6.

thing for us was work and fulfillment of the goals we had set ourselves, we decided—and we did so with the absolute confidence that we were acting in accord with our people's best interests—not to use up one single gallon of fuel or to stay away from work one minute longer than necessary for a military parade on this 10th anniversary.

Today marks the beginning of another year of great effort, the beginning of an 18-month-long year! This is because this year we have to complete the 1969 harvest and carry out part of the 1970 one. Thus, we have to work in two harvests.

Next year, the traditional year—that is, next December—and quite probably, next January 2—it is quite possible that we will not be able to gather here in this Plaza, since a great many of us in this country will be out in the fields cutting sugarcane. Thus, the next New Year will probably be celebrated on July 1, while the next Christmas will be celebrated between the 1st and the 26th of July.

This doesn't mean that we intend to change traditions or to give up, once and for all, the traditional holidays to which we are accustomed. We will go back to the regular New Years, and the regular Christmases, but only the use of machines will make that possible. The machines will have to come to the rescue of our traditional holidays!

But the fact is that we are all involved in a giant task, a task we will fulfill at any cost!

Several celebrations of this type have been held during the past few years, but this one certainly seems to be the one in which the greatest number of people have gathered in this *Plaza de la Revolución.* Not only does this multitude extend over a large area, but there are no empty spaces within that area. And much more important than the size of the crowd is the fact that this is a multitude, a people, with an extraordinarily greater political awareness.

We sincerely believe that there are reasons why the conscience and the strength of the Revolution should have increased. We believe that we have sound reasons for being optimistic, and we believe that this optimism is based on actual, palpable facts.

We believe that the time is near when the material benefits we will have reaped by then will be less important to us than the moral satisfaction we will get from the way and period of time in which such gains were achieved.

Naturally, on this 10th anniversary, on which we have actually been graduated—though not as revolutionaries from the highest grade, not with a university diploma—as graduates, we might say, of the primary school of the Revolution, who are now entering junior high in that school, we should make a brief review of the effort that has been made. This should be done now as we close a ten-year period and begin a new decade, at a time that marks the close of the ten most difficult years and the beginning of the ten most fruitful years, a time that marks the point where we pass from a period of almost absolute ignorance to a certain level of accumulated experience, at a time when we have achieved a tempo of work and of progress that is incomparably more rapid than the tempo that we managed to set in the beginning. But rather than actually making a review, or even a summary, it is better that we give an idea of what this effort has meant to the Revolution and, at the same time, outline the policy to be followed. . . .

Our country has concentrated its efforts—and we think this is interesting—in the field of cultural development in general, in social development, and, at the same time, in economic development.

There is no need to speak of anything so familiar to so many people as our efforts in education, which were undertaken from the beginning and are fundamentally marked by the wiping out of illiteracy and the tremendous progress achieved thus far in the field, exemplified not only by the fact that each Cuban child has a teacher but also by the fact that after ten years of Revolution we have more than 300,000 live-in, full scholarship students. This unquestionably places our country far ahead of any other Latin-American country.

Nor is it necessary to stress the efforts made in public health, another field where we have left all other Latin-American nations far behind.

In the sphere of social development, as well, the Revolution's social institutions have brought retirement benefits and pensions to all the workers in the country. The process culminated this year with a heartening event—discussed and decided upon by the masses. The minimum pension has been raised to 60 pesos a month for all retired and pensioned people who received less, beginning practically immediately. This measure benefits approximately 180,000 people and shows all Cubans alike the way to well-being and security for all who have in one way or another contributed to create the wealth of this country. . . .

Other notable steps forward in the social and political spheres—measures which were also discussed this year by the masses—have to do with the remuneration received—when illness prevents them from going to work—by workers who maintain communist work conduct and by their families if their economic mainstay should become disabled or lose his life while at work.

Among many institutions that have been established to create conditions of human dignity for all the citizens of this country, these are some which constitute just sources of satisfaction for all.

In the ideological sphere the distance covered has been unimaginable. Today's people, with their political culture, experience, organization, discipline, awareness and sense of responsibility, can hardly be compared with the people of ten years ago.

However, a revolution must base itself upon an economic structure. And it has been precisely in the field of economic structure that our people have faced the most difficult challenge, the most extraordinary task: confronting underdevelopment in the conditions of today's world, and confronting it, as our people did, with nothing more than the enthusiasm of the masses. Because the few trained people belonged, almost exclusively, to the privileged minority that was not, nor could be, in agreement with the changes made in the economic structure of this country.

And, as we commented last night to some guests, it was as if overnight all of us, with a vast ignorance of everything had taken charge of everything and of doing everything with an utter lack of experience.

Then, there was in addition, that great mirage produced by capitalist society, by class society: the mirage of the full store shelves. That mirage is the boast of privileged societies and makes the masses believe in the illusion of a sky's-the-limit abundance and that all you have to do is break down a barrier to obtain access to those endless riches, as if they came from inexhaustibly rich mines.

But what such masses do not know is that those supposed riches are none other than the by-product of misery, the by-product of misery that is allowed and which must exist to incite and oblige a country's citizens to work in the middle of un- and under-employment. They are, of course, illusory riches which quickly disappear as soon as the masses have some access to them. . . .

Cuba's agricultural production will increase in the next 12 years—and we give this figure with complete assurance and will assume full responsibility for it—at an average rate for the 12-year period of no less than 15 percent per year.

We can point out that this rate of growth for the period will be several times higher than that reached by any other country in a similar period of time.

We are not trying to say that the Cubans are the best workers or that anyone knows more than anyone else, but we have had the good fortune of certain factors coinciding at this time: the concept of our agrarian reform, the concept of our agricultural plans, the mass application of technology, and, above all, a people carrying out this program in a tropical climate.

At the beginning, it is more difficult to overcome natural factors in a tropical climate, but, once these have been overcome, there is the sun, and thus sunlight, for agriculture the year round. Once droughts have been overcome; once hurricanes have been coped with through the proper protection of crops against this type of natural phenomenon; once floods have been prevented; once plagues are eliminated, underbrush cleared—that is, land cleared which is covered with dense vegetation; and once technology and mechanization are at our command, then it is possible to achieve results that cannot be achieved in a country without adequate conditions of sunlight and temperature all year round.

But the comparison we are making is with countries that also have favorable conditions of sunlight and temperature the year round—not Canada or Finland. We are making a comparison with countries that have the same natural conditions as ours. . . .

Selection 8.2: Workers and Soldiers

At present a great part of the machines I mentioned are working day and night. They are in operation for twenty hours, leaving four hours for upkeep. So that the great drive to develop the country which is now under way requires tens of thousands of operators.

Therefore the Army reserve, the motorized and armored units of the reserve, which have 8000 vehicles, will be deeply involved in the country's development. Twenty-five thousand men with eight thousand machines! They will be under the orders of their own cadres, their own officer; these brigades will require the participation of the same military command cadres, who, at a given moment, will pass with all their personnel, or a part, over to the manning of tanks or artillery. And the rest of their personnel, as I have explained, will back up the military units with the same motorized equipment.

So that the greater part of the campaign to develop the country in the years to come will be entrusted to the Army reserve, consisting of 25,000 men with 8000 machines, more or less. This will be our Army; an organization of cadres who are highly skilled technically and share a profound revolutionary awareness.

The main shock troops, composed of soldier-workers, or worker-soldiers, constitute the dialectics of this process, along with the planes manned by pilots who are in service in either civil aviation or military aviation, and the regular units composed of technological or senior high school students. And behind them will be the rest of the people, the whole people, every man or woman capable of shouldering a weapon. Because this country must be determined never to lower its guard—never—and to arm itself increasingly, prepare itself increasingly. The day that we are so foolish as to feel secure we will have committed an enormous error. The stronger we are, the better prepared we are in all respects, the more we can count on a united, conscientious, hard-working people; the more arms we possess, the more secure we will be able to feel.

This will have to be an underlying principle for a long time, for we do not think imperialism will come to an end tomorrow, nor do we think the imperialists will turn into tame lambs. And an essential principle of the revolutionary philosophy of this country will be to make itself increasingly stronger, to be progressively better armed, better prepared.

When a country such as ours makes a revolution 90 miles away from the United States, when a powerful enemy such as Yankee imperialism declares that its aim is to crush it, when a country such as ours has already received so many lessons as to the criminal and aggressive nature of that imperialism, that country must become truly a nation wholly composed of workers, of soldiers, of students—both its men and its women.

At present our Institute of Military Technology has a contingent of almost 300 women comrades. They are the first 300 women in our country to take up military studies. And both men and women will receive military training. Young people will have it in the schools, the high schools. So that imperialism will see how the strength of this people is on the rise and how this people—which they thought they would be able to take by surprise one day, would be able to crush one day—is daily a better organized, more conscientious, stronger people.

It is necessary for everybody, and especially for our officers, to understand the line, the course, we are going to follow in the coming years relative to our Armed Forces.

And when we have achieved this we may be sure that we have achieved something which no other army in the world has been able to do. We will have achieved what no other country has been able to achieve. Since the real fact of being so near such a powerful and such a criminal neighbor has obliged us all to become soldiers, we must all be soldiers just as we must all be workers and students.

These ideas will be our guidelines, our norms, in the military training of our people in the years to come.

READING 9 *Nationalism and Internationalism*

Introductory Note

The following selections indicate Castro's commitment to proletarian internationalism and Cuban identification with revolutionary struggles elsewhere in the world. It should be noted, however, that not until late 1967 did Castro begin to admit direct aid to revolutionary activities in Latin America (see Part VII, Reading 6).

SELECTION 9.1: CUBAN INTERNATIONALISM

Another of the calumnies used to accuse our revolution is that of chauvinism and lack of proletarian internationalism. The Cuban revolution cannot be called chauvinist or nationalist because these terms imply that we favor national interests over international. The Cuban revolution gives good proofs of its revolutionary internationalist spirit—internationalism in the full sense of word and not satellitism. The Cuban revolution has given proofs of its militant solidarity with all the peoples who struggle for their liberation. . . .

. . . And when we say the Cuban revolution, we are speaking of the Latin American revolution. When we speak of the Latin

Selection 9.1: Excerpt from court martial of Aníbal Escalante and thirty-six others accused of "microfactionist" activities, Havana Domestic Radio Broadcast, February 2, 1968.

Selection 9.2: Speech by Major Juan Almeida in Havana on May 1, 1967, Havana Domestic Radio Broadcast, May 1, 1967.

American revolution, we are talking about revolution on a universal scale—the revolution of the peoples of Asia, Africa and Europe. The internationalist principles of the Cuban revolution are contained in the first and second Havana declarations—documents that were approved at public meetings attended by more than 1 million of our citizens in the capital alone. Our people have backed up these documents day in and day out, always with greater integrity and revolutionary determination.

In an interview granted to a Yankee journalist who wanted to know about the question of aid to the revolutionary movement in Latin America, our prime minister said: "Look here, the aid given to the revolutionary movements cannot be negotiated." He added further on: "That would not be proper for revolutionaries. If we give any aid at any time, or were to give any aid, we do not do so to negotiate on the basis of it."

This is an open lesson in revolutionary solidarity. Our internationalism is expressed in concrete facts and not in formal declarations. It is expressed in an attitude of inviolable principles that materialize daily and that show our unconditional determination to go as far as to shed our blood for Vietnam. Our internationalist position was expressed—not in a chauvinistic spirit—by Major Fidel Castro in his July 26, 1962, speech when he said: "We are always more Marxist and we shall always fight with greater fervor for a world composed of generous men and for a people that will be like a big family, where every man and woman will not have just a single brother but millions of brothers and sisters, millions of children, and millions of fathers and mothers."

The idea of compulsory unity of all the revolutionary movements came from Marx and was developed by Lenin because only a world-wide revolution of the proletariat would be in a position to rout international capital. Lenin's idea of internationalism meant the close alliance of the revolutionary elements of all countries. He also believed that to renounce insurrection and to refuse help to the rebels was to "deny the idea of the revolution." Lenin upheld the thesis that the international proletariat must actively support the exploited peoples' revolt against their oppressors. As a corollary to this, in June 1920 he summed up proletarian internationalism in the following points:

1. Subordination of the interests of a proletarian struggle in a country to the interests of this struggle on a world-wide basis;
2. A nation that has won over the bourgeoisie must be capable of and ready to make the greatest national sacrifice with a view to defeat international capital. . . .

Selection 9.2: Cuba and the World Revolutionary Struggle

The Cuban workers have embraced the ideology of Marxism-Leninism, and this ideology teaches us to comply with sacred international duties. We are passionately and with determination constructing the country's future. At the same time we are part of a continent in revolution and this continent is part of a world fighting Yankee imperialism, foremost enemy of the peoples, with fire and blood. Our armies, our great victories, will never make us forget our duties.

When the people of South Vietnam achieve a victory, it is also our victory. When a patriot falls in the fight for the freedom of his people, he is dying for the freedom of our people and all the peoples of the world. When the workers of the Democratic Republic of Vietnam [North Vietnam] heroically resist the criminal bombing by Yankee planes, or down an imperialist plane, they are resisting and fighting on behalf of the revolutionary cause of all the peoples of the world. And whoever fights in America for the cause of the freedom of our peoples will be fighting for the cause of the deliverance of all the exploited peoples of the world.

This is why the Cuban workers have adopted an irrevocable decision: to struggle and fight. We Cuban workers have adopted an irrevocable decision: to struggle and fight for the triumph of the revolution in America and to help, with all our strength, the advance of the revolution in the world.

We are fighting and struggling on behalf of the exploited

classes and the oppressed peoples of the world. The Cuban workers feel that the cause of the revolution in America—in Asia, in Africa, and in Latin America—is their own. The movement for the liberation of the peoples subjected to imperialist and colonialist exploitation in these three continents constitutes a single and great revolutionary current. This revolutionary torrent will destroy imperialist exploitation throughout the world, and the peoples of the continents who have been exploited and oppressed for centuries will develop a revolutionary force and action which will exert a decisive influence for mankind.

This tricontinental force is playing a leading role in the world struggle against imperialism and against all the systems and governments that exploit the peoples. Our country, our revolution, is an inseparable part of this great revolutionary wave. The Cuban revolution is not an isolated event in the world. The Cuban revolution is only the beginning, the starting point of the Latin American revolution. Cuba is part of a continent in revolution.

To understand our party's policy, to understand the views of our people, it is necessary to understand what this event signifies. Otherwise, with other standards, from another point of view, it is not possible to understand Cuba and the revolution. We Cuban workers and peasants have clearly understood the international ideas of Marxism-Leninism. We have embraced those ideas.

Moreover, our fatherland shares a common history with the Latin American peoples. We shall never renounce this common history. We shall never renounce the internationalist duties taught us by Marxism-Leninism.

Each of us loves the fatherland. Each of us loves its traditions of struggle, and each of us also knows that Cuba is part of a larger fatherland of the world, the fatherland of the workers of the world. We shall never betray these principles. We shall never betray these ideas. If we were to overlook these truths, we would not be worthy of the history of our fatherland, nor would we be worthy of the glorious tradition of struggle of our continent.

That is why the Cuban people have affirmed their profession of Latin American and communist faith. That is why the Cuban people have sworn to triumph or die in defense of the ideals of all the workers of the world. These are the ideals of the proletariat. These are the ideals of the workers. These are our revolutionary and communist ideals.

During recent years, great changes have taken place in our continent. Before the revolution, imperialism had never spoken of any kind of reform or social structure changes in the continent. When the Cuban revolution triumphed and when it was consolidated, some imperialist leaders and spokesmen began to speak, brazenly and hypocritically, of the need to make changes in the social structures of the continent. The leftist forces and the progressive sectors had been struggling for social changes for many years. However, the imperialists never mentioned the need for such changes. . . .

READING 10 *Political Integration in Cuba*

Introductory Note

Of the many organizations involved in Castro's process of political integration the Comites de Defensa de la Revolución *(Committees for the Defense of the Revolution or CDR) developed steadily in importance after September 1960. It is fundamental organization created to involve all citizens in work for the revolution at the grass roots level (Selections 10.1 and 10.2). The degree of political control in Cuba by Castro through his new organizational structure is suggested by the outpouring of praise from the different organizations for Castro's position in backing Moscow in its August 1968 invasion of Czechoslovakia (Selections 10.3, 10.4, and 10.5).*

Selection 10.1: History and the CDRs

The *Comites de Defensa de la Revolución* (Committees for the Defense of the Revolution or CDR) ordered to be constituted by

Selection 10.1: "The CDR on Farms and Rural Areas," a pamphlet published by the *Comité de Defensa de la Revolución* (Havana: CDR, 1965), pp. 9–13, JPRS 38,549 (November 8, 1966).

Selection 10.2: "The Defense Committees of the Revolution," *Granma* (September 28, 1966), p. 2, JPRS 38,911 (December 1, 1966).

Selection 10.3: *Unión de la Juventud Comunista* statement, *Granma,* Weekly Review in English, Year 3, No. 35 (September 1, 1968), p. 3.

Selection 10.4: Declaration by the national leadership of the *Asociación Nacional de Agricultores Pequeños, Granma,* Weekly Review in English, Year 3, No. 35 (September 1, 1968), p. 2.

Selection 10.5: Cuban Trade Unions statement, *Granma,* Weekly Review in English, Year 3, No. 35 (September 1, 1968), p. 2.

Major Fidel Castro as a citizen's response to the aggressions committed by imperialism against the people, especially in the urban centers, started to grow and become stronger in the fields when the counterrevolution and US imperialism diverted their maneuvers toward the field, trying to evade the vigilance of the organization.

In 1963, more than 1,300 sectional committees of the CDRs in rural zones and 487 CDRs on people's farms already were powerful organizations of the Revolution led by the *Partido Unido de la Revolución Socialista de Cuba* (United Party of the Socialist Revolution of Cuba or PURSC), which developed by exercising revolutionary vigilance and rich creative initiatives on the various work fronts and its own makeup, adjusted to the physical and social circumstances of the environment.

During the previous year the CDRs vastly expanded in the fields and grew deep roots among their peasant memberships through the daily fulfillment of such difficult and transcendental tasks as the supervision—and in many cases even the distribution in remote zones—of supplies.

The peasants, made cohesive in the Committees, began to experience their collective work force in the common interest; through the Voluntary Work Front, roads and schools were built; on top of an isolated mountain the "miracle" of a school made of cemented rubble work appeared such as that built by the CDR of Manacal. Water arrived through "aqueducts" built by the townspeople themselves in the smallest and most forgotten sugar plants and the example became widespread in entire zones such as that of Alquizar in Havana. Our peasant leaders developed and were themselves learning while they gave sanitation lectures, advocated the use of latrines, combated gastroenteritis by teaching hygiene and organizing anti-poliomyelitis vaccination in the most difficult places.

In 1963 many sectional farm and rural boards attained higher registration figures than those of the cities and towns, some of them reaching 100% of the population over 15 years of age signing up and working through the Committees. The political study circles of Marxism-Leninism came to the Indian hut and so did basic reading and primary education which followed on the successful literacy campaign. All this together with a similar victory to that obtained in the cities, paralyzing with popular revolutionary vigilance the activities of the enemy. . . .

In 1963 our organization had 104,425 base committees. Of these, 47,793 were located in urban zones, in town wards and in cities; 17,793 in work centers and 38,718, the ones described here, in rural zones. Of these, 25,943 were located on peasant land, providing orientation to nearby family cells; 8,949 on People's Farms and 3,826 in the mountain zones.

Each CDR is subordinate to the directives of a Sectional Administration which controls a maximum of 30 base committees; in the rural zones with more dispersed populations, a sectional committee generally supervises only some 7, 10 or 12 committees. Throughout the country there were a total of 4,064 sectional administrations during the year in reference; 1,305 of these were located on peasant property, 487 on People's Farms and 223 in mountain zones. The districts supervise the sectional administrations and in turn are responsible to the directives of the various provincial administrations which number six. In 1963 there were 171 districts throughout the country.

Since then, as a result of the advance of the Revolution and the strengthening of the Party, changes have occurred. Following the second law of Agrarian Reform, many of those that were then peasant wards were converted into farm departments as 70% of the land of the country became state-owned. On the other hand, our organization has continued growing incessantly while at the same time it has made organizational adjustments, more rational divisions of districts and sectional administrations, thus facilitating the supervision of base organizations. It is therefore possible that some of the sectional administrations whose work will be outlined here were subdivided, giving rise to new organizations, or are today being supervised by other districts.

It should be pointed out also that the work in the sectional administrations is performed on an exclusively voluntary basis, without remuneration, during the hours left free by the hard agricultural toil or by the care of home and children since there are no professional leaders in this organization. The tasks on the various fronts are carried out in coordination with the Ministries and state organizations such as Public Health, Education, National Administration of the *Escuela de Instrucción Revolucionaria* (Revolutionary Training School or EIR, a school phased out by 1968), Culture, etc. . . .

The study of revolutionary theory has acquired a well-adjusted format within the CDR as well as its characteristics and work methods. Hundreds of thousands of our members have been familiarized with this material, basically through the Study Circles and the CIR. The former are established in each committee and each leadership organization from the sectional to the provincial level. Here they study from a theoretical-political angle the immediate practical revolutionary problems as well as the theory itself of the Revolution through the work of its creators and the speeches of our leaders.

The CIR operates on a sectional level and performs a more systematic and assiduous study. While the Study Circle meets only once a week, the CIR meets daily for a time period preestablished for the course which extends over a three-month period. The course is given by an instructor—a graduate of political schools or a short course in the orientation schools—who in turn is a member of the Committee on Sectional Revolutionary Instruction. Each CIR course must be attended by sectional leaders and by a member selected within each committee.

Health meetings have become a very positive way of disseminating the most urgent measures of hygiene. They are held at the CDR and sectional level, all the townspeople are invited, and in their course, orientation material of the Public Health Ministry is explained. Special lectures are given by a physician of the Ministry of Public Health. They have been particularly effective in the battle against gastroenteritis and in the preparatory work of the vaccination campaigns.

The Education teams consist of those responsible on this front in all the CDRs and of the Sectional Committee. They work on all matters covering the radius of action of the Sectional Committee, dividing up tasks such as visits to parents of absentee children from school, attendance control at worker-peasant classes and others.

The Family Circle, on the committee level, brought to the home primary and follow-up study; the Education Thursday, in coordination with the Worker-Peasant Education, dedicated this day of the week to educational qualification within the CIR. . . .

Selection 10.2: The Defense Committees and the Revolution

The history of the Defense Committees is a piece of the history of our Revolution. Their advancement as a mass organization reflects the advancement of the Revolution. The CDR, as a genuine product of the Revolution, form an inseparable and indestructible part of it. The militants in the Party and the masses of the people in general consider them in this light.

The Revolution has advanced extraordinarily in the most diverse fields. Each one of its accomplishments, independent of the moment or place in which it may have been produced, has taken into account that it will not affect—but, rather, on the contrary—it will aid in the fundamental task which is the formation of the new man, the man profoundly conscious of his role in society, of his duties and social responsibilities. It will aid in the formation of the man capable of building Communism and living in it.

The building of Communism demands, as an essential criterion, fighting for the formation of the new man and not finishing until this job has been finished. All political, economic and social tasks which move our mass organizations have to be inspired by this principle.

The struggle to make the spirit and social meaning predominate over what is limited, narrow and individual ought to be our main effort in shaping the new man. This battle is becoming more and more important in our country.

We see the new man rising in the educational institutions developed by the Revolution, in the border guards who protect our country from imperialistic enemy threats and aggression, in the heroic people fighting against counter-revolutionary bandits, in the permanent volunteer workers, in women helping in agriculture, and in the labors undertaken today by the labor union movement and the *Unión de la Juventud Comunista* (Union of Communist Youth or UJC) in order to bring together thousands of workers for farm work. The new man is the one who is rightly indignant at the imperialistic aggressions in Vietnam and who is ready to increase the front-line soldiers fighting in the jungles of that heroic country to assure full and total liberation.

We see the new man producing in the factories, working in our fields, studying in the class rooms, and showing an interest in technical ability, in science and in production. We see him in the trenches of our Revolutionary Armed Forces.

This concept obliges the Revolution to develop all of its plans, achieving a growing participation of the masses in the performing of diverse jobs. On the road to Communism, the masses will have to show greater participation in social tasks, and they will have to be more attentive to these tasks and to the management and orientation of them. This concept was very clearly expounded by comrade Fidel in the closing of the Congress of the *Confederación de Trabajadores de Cuba* (Cuban Workers Confederation or CTC).

Without this concept, the Party could not even be understood. The Party's reason for existing is its tie with the masses. Its role as vanguard springs from its indispensable relationship with the people, with the masses; a vanguard exists only when there is a more extensive and numerous military post. In order for the Party to fulfill its role as vanguard, it needs to organize the masses and give them greater participation in the diverse social tasks. Neither would it be possible for the mass organizations to be able to fulfill their role in the construction of the new life, if they were not oriented and directed by the vanguard of the people, i.e., by the Party.

The tasks of the CDR have to be analyzed with this projection.

The CDR, as organizations of the mass of the people, are a fundamental instrument serving to assure, develop and explore the participation of the masses in the great tasks of the Revolution.

The Party needs the CDR as an organization of the masses of the people, and the CDR needs the Party as a vanguard of the workers. . . .

Today, on the sixth anniversary of the Defense Committees, there is more clarity and conscientiousness than ever before with regard to the role that they have played in the past and that they will perform in the future as a mass organization of the people.

The CDR, which surged forth to fight against the internal enemy, has—besides revolutionary vigilance—a grandiose task to fulfill in the development of our social life and in the shaping of the new man.

In 1960, the Committees were born as the country's answer to counter-revolutionary criminal activity guided and inspired by the imperialists. Dismayed at the development of the Revolution, the bourgeoisie and the imperialists unleashed a ferocious campaign of sabotage, of attempts at dynamiting, and assassinations of workers and farmers; they created the bands of uprisers, at the same time they imposed an economic bloc against us and were getting ready to launch the mercenary invasion which afterward was crushed in Girón.

At Fidel's return from his historical appearance before the UN, when the large popular reception was prepared for him—held in front of the former Presidential Palace—the impassioned counter-revolutionaries exploded several bombs just at the moment our Prime Minister was speaking to the people. And the answer to the criminal aggression surged forth in the words of the Chief of the Revolution and, in his speech to the people, the Committees for the Defense of the Revolution were born. Therefore, their birth was characterized by the deep revolutionary spirit of the people and by their fighting attitude toward the imperialistic enemy and the lackeys and traitors. The CDR were born in the midst of a complex and difficult stage of class struggle in our country, when the bourgeoisie still had not lost faith in the possibility of defeating the Revolution; when it attempted—supported by its imperialistic master—to stop the Revolution and to cause it to fall back.

These were the months when the Revolution had just struck a decisive blow against monopolizing United States enterprises, when banking, sugar refining, telephones, electricity, and the large United States factories and stores had been nationalized. These were the months when the Embassy was still serving as a focal point and nucleus for the counter-revolution, in the midst of the most insolent of speeches and manners.

Thus, the CDR were born in the middle of the clamor of the revolutionary struggle, as an instrument serving to neutralize and strike at the class enemy and to impede internal counter-revolutionary action.

And the CDR, created in the bosom of the people—with the men and women who had the awareness to realize the necessity of drowning the counter-revolution and of defending the conquests of the Revolution—grew rapidly and contributed outstandingly in breaking the backbone of counter-revolutionary organizations and groups.

The organization, which had been born for the purpose of fighting against the counter-revolutionary class enemy and had given great service in the battle against imperialism, soon found new sources of activity and new tasks to be completed. The CDR were present in the tasks of the coin exchange, in the organization and control of supplies, in the great national literacy campaign, in the nation's sugar harvests, in the vaccination campaigns and in many other jobs undertaken by the Revolution. In many instances, the CDR were the ones who carried the main weight of drudgery over their shoulders. In others, they contributed outstandingly, but they were always present.

In some of these tasks the function of the CDR had a transitory nature. However, practice has shown that in the majority of the jobs in which the CDR have participated their function ought to have a permanent nature. The role of the CDR, regarding execution of their great mass jobs, is clear.

Upon reaching their sixth anniversary, the CDR have become the most extensive mass organization of the revolutionaries and of the fighters of the country. Their strength comes from the fact that the Defense Committees are made up of hundreds of thousands of men and women organized into groups, upon whom the only condition made is that they be sincere, honest and decisive revolutionaries. More than two million men and women are in the Defense Committees, closing up the ranks in the nation in defense of their Revolution.

The CDR continue having as their principal job the defense of the Revolution, vigilance over enemies who still dream of putting our country back in the period of discrimination, of exploitation, of unhealthfulness, of abuse, of robbery and of crime.

The CDR are and always will be a firm battle trench of the Revolution. But from that trench they are fighting not only the unmasked, open—and therefore, less dangerous–enemy, but they are also engaging—under Party orientation—in the battle against the past, against that which is old, against the worn out and decrepit which dies slowly.

Therefore, the CDR, under Party orientation–which is the maximum representation and the vanguard of the working people –will in the immediate future play a role even more important than the one they have already performed. The Defense Committees, which have efficiently executed numerous social tasks, reach their sixth anniversary consolidated as a mass organization and with new and more extensive tasks to perform.

Today more than ever the Revolution depends upon the CDR for its formidable trench. The Party, at all levels of leadership, ought to aid this mass organization in fortifying itself, in growing larger and in multiplying itself in its base organisms, and in multiplying its membership and those taking part in it. The ruling organisms of the Party must arrange for the tasks of the CDR to be properly united with those of local authorities and they must likewise take steps for the CDR to perform their work every day with great efficiency, enthusiasm and happiness.

One of the fundamental characteristics of the CDR has been their dynamism, their activism, their revolutionary enthusiasm and their great ability to mobilize extensive masses of the people.

In the Committees for the Defense of the Revolution's groups the profound revolutionary feeling of our people has been felt. The enthusiasm for their work and passion for completing it quickly and efficiently have always been present in the members of the Defense Committees. This is due to the deep popular roots of the organization and to the fact that they were structured, in agreement with Fidel's orientations, in squares and blocks.

This enormous power, oriented and led toward the performance of tasks: of local power, of recreation and social services, of mass education and of the nation's health, undoubtedly constitutes a form of organization that will not only be useful for the execution of the great immediate tasks, but also will decisively aid in the formation of the new collective conscience regarding the fulfillment of social obligations.

All mass organizations in the country, the *Confederación de Trabajadores de Cuba* (Cuban Workers' Confederation or CTC), the *Federación de Mujeres Cubanas* (Cuban Women's Federation or FMC), the *Asociación Nacional de Agricultores Pequeños* (National Association of Small Farmers or ANAP), and—especially—the *Unión de la Juventud Comunista* (Union of Communist Youth or UJC), have paid sincere and fervent homage to the CDR. *Granma,* joining in the spirit of all the Party militants and of all its base-ruling organisms, extends a fraternal, revolutionary and strong hand to the CDR on their sixth anniversary. . . .

Selection 10.3: Cuba's Youth Support Castro

The National Committee of the Young Communist League (UJC) makes public its unconditional support for the brilliant analysis made by our Commander in Chief, Comrade Fidel Castro, on the situation in Czechoslovakia.

Due to its far-reaching significance, its profound analysis of a most complex international situation, these statements must be carefully studied by all UJC members and by the young people of Cuba.

The events in Czechoslovakia prove that the lack of a firm, revolutionary and principled policy led to the stagnation and ideological decomposition of a revolution. This confirms the correctness of the policy followed by the Cuban Revolution regarding relations with the masses, the development of a communist outlook as an essential factor in building a new society, the firm resolution not to make concessions to the enemy and in general the application of Marxism-Leninism to our specific conditions.

In his speech on the events in Czechoslovakia Comrade Fidel Castro called for a deep analysis of the problems of communism very especially those which deal with moral formation, communist ideology and their bearer: the new man.

This means we must study in depth the speeches, writings and lives of Che, Fidel, Raúl and other top leaders so that we can daily improve the conditions for action and thought concerning problems faced by our Revolution and concerning the disturbing problems of today's world.

While listening to and reading Fidel's speeches, we feel the presence of Che, the outstanding revolutionary strategist who bequeathed his great ideas on the formation of the new man to the Cuban youth and whose foresight was confirmed by the events in Czechoslovakia. Once more we feel the presence of the immortal guerrilla.

Our youth—heirs to the one hundred years of struggle of the Cuban people, the anniversary of which we will celebrate next October 10; inspired by the examples of the Mambises, who, in '68 and '95, proved their unlimited willingness to sacrifice and give their all for the sacred cause of the independence of our country; followers of the men who throughout the years of Yankee imperialist oppression held high the Mambí banner, without once bending before their exploiters; admirers of the combatants of the revolutionary war against the Batista tyranny and in many cases participants in it—are willing to participate even more enthusiastically, with greater fervor and more conscientiously in all the tasks of the Revolution.

It is within the framework of these ten years of the Cuban Revolution that our youth have accepted in an ever ascending and more resolute manner all the challenges that history has placed before them; the literacy campaign, the cleanup of counterrevolutionaries in the Escambray Mountains and the struggle against bandits, Playa Girón and the October Crisis have all been schools for the transformation to and the creation of a communist attitude toward life that we observe in more and more of our youth by the day.

In the past two years the incorporation of 40,000 young people into the tasks of agriculture and construction in the hardest areas, and the incorporation of 40,000 young people this year into the Centennial Youth Column dedicated to winning the battle of agriculture, a figure that must reach 100,000 by the end of 1969, are also an eloquent indication of the direction in which our young people are moving.

Our educational plans—based on the principle of combining study and work, the fundamental pillars of the communist education of our future generations—are of the utmost importance. All our students participate directly in agriculture and cattle raising, creating material goods while at the same time increasing their revolutionary awareness.

We believe that it is of the utmost importance that these movements have taken place as a result of our young people's understanding of the importance of their task and its political and social significance. It would have been absolutely meaningless if this great mass of people had been moved by factors other than conscientiousness, factors which would have been only an added stimulus for selfishness.

Another essential aspect of our activity is the progressive stepping up of our military training which is also another instrument of ideological formation and a guarantee of the defense of our country against the threats of aggression by the Yankee imperialists.

We, the young people of Cuba, are proud to be a part of this Revolution in which the enthusiasm of the masses is ever greater, a communist attitude toward work is ever greater among the workers and the spirit of solidarity with the peoples struggling for their liberation is something which identifies every revolutionary.

The National Committee of the Young Communist League, voicing the sentiments of the youth of Cuba, fully aware and proud of being a part of this people that in its revolutionary offensive is carrying on a firm, relentless struggle against underdevelopment and is bearing aloft the banner of internationalist and revolutionary principles of an open, frontal attack against Yankee imperialism, makes it clear that our young people are ready to go wherever the leadership of our Revolution may send us and to maintain to the very end the three fundamental principles of our anti-imperialist policy: the order to fight will never need to be given to us, because it has already been given; we will never let anybody set foot in our country against the will of our Party and our people, because we will meet the invader with a frontal, merciless attack; we will never accept any order to cease fire or to surrender, because our leaders would never issue such an order.

Commander in Chief: we await your orders!

Patria o Muerte, Venceremos (Fatherland or Death, We will Triumph).

National Committee of the Young Communist League
Havana, August 26, 1968

Year of the Heroic Guerrilla

Selection 10.4: Small Farmers Support Castro

The National Association of Small Farmers [*Asociación Nacional de Agricultores Pequeños* or ANAP] resolutely supports Cuba's analysis of and position on—as presented by our Prime Minister and First Secretary of the Party, Major Fidel Castro, over national radio and television—the events that have taken place in Czechoslovakia.

The imperialists wanted to take over Czechoslovakia in order to drag that country back to capitalist exploitation and misery and use it as a springboard for aggression against and penetration of the socialist countries.

Faced with these events and confident that this will never happen in Cuba—because we are always alert to all imperialist maneuvers—we are aware that as long as the imperialists attack the heroic people of Vietnam and keep up their acts of intervention throughout the world, repressing the revolutionary movements of Latin America, Africa and Asia, there is only one possible response: to look to our defenses, to work with more fervor to attain the objectives of the ten million tons of sugar in 1970 and agricultural plans, to deepen the ideological struggle, to eliminate the hangovers of individualism and to struggle against the concept of material incentives.

We Cuban farmers participating in the various pro-independence and other revolutionary processes, in celebrating the centenary of our struggles along with the rest of our people, following this historic tradition, enter ever more enthusiastically into the tasks of the construction of socialism and communism and set ourselves the following goals:

1. To read and discuss the analysis made by Comrade Fidel in all the grass-roots organizations, with mass participation by the farmers and their families;
2. To carry out an extensive plan to explain the harmful effects of material incentives to the masses of the farmers, and especially to the young people of the countryside, as a part of ideological work; and
3. To work, in the face of the danger posed by imperialist aggression to our homeland and the difficulties that may result from the international situation, for the growth of awareness in the great mass of the farmers, not only to prepare for defense but also to put forth the greatest efforts in productive work, in the fulfilling of our great agricultural plans, using the resources available and developing the activities and initiatives which may arise and which lead not only to greater production but also to preparing the rural population to advance in the construction of the new society, in spite of the worst conditions which may present themselves.

Long live proletarian internationalism! Long live the heroic guerrilla! Long live the hundred years of struggle! Long live Vietnam and the peoples that struggle for their liberation! Long live Cuba! Long live the Communist Party of Cuba! Long live Fidel!

Selection 10.5: Cuban Trade Unions

Last Friday evening [August 23, 1968] Major Fidel Castro addressed the people, analyzing the events in Czechoslovakia which led to the sending in of troops from five of the Warsaw Pact nations.

Fidel pointed out the reasons behind this situation, such as bureaucratic policy, dogmatism, separation from the masses, the losing sight of communist ideals, the mercantile mentality and a whole series of vices and erroneous concepts present in Czechoslovakia and other European socialist countries—things that lead to a dissipation and weakening of the revolutionary spirit, thus permitting the penetration of imperialism and its agents.

Fidel explained how the actions of Yankee imperialism with the cooperation of its European agents—primarily the West German revanchists and the traitors of the so-called League of Yugoslav Communists—had caused the Czechoslovak regime to retrogress inexorably toward counter-revolution, capitalism and imperialism. He pointed out that the socialist camp had the right to prevent, one way or another, the tearing away of a socialist country and its falling into the hands of imperialism.

In the text of his address, Fidel reaffirmed our anti-imperialist position and stressed that never, under any circumstances, even under the most difficult circumstances, would this country approach the imperialist Government of the United States, not even should it one day place us in the situation of having to choose between the continued existence of the Revolution or such a step.

Once, again, in the midst of the complex situation in which we live today, our people assume a stalwart position, without cowardly hesitations or vacillations, and are ready to face whatever risks that position may entail, placing the principles of the international revolutionary movement above any personal interest.

The Central Organization of Cuban Trade Unions, voicing the sentiments of our working class and all our people, asserts its absolute support for the statements made by Fidel last Friday. Once more our working class militantly supports the firm position outlined by our Party, support that has been reflected, and will continue to be reflected, not only in statements, but in truly revolutionary deeds and attitudes.

As an example of this and as eloquent proof of the correct line adopted by our Revolution for developing revolutionary man, communist man, the new man of whom he spoke and who was epitomized by him, we can cite some of the most important ideological successes of our working class.

Every year we organize volunteer canecutting brigades that remain in the countryside from the beginning of the harvest to the end. These men, who number in the tens of thousands, increase their productivity each year but continue receiving the same salaries that they earn in their respective work centers. They have been and will continue to be one of the fundamental pillars in the implementation of our nation's sugar plans.

Today hundreds of thousands of workers leave their jobs in the cities, leave their jobs in factories and services, to participate in hard tasks in agricultural work for one month, one year or for whatever length of time they are needed.

Periodically the advance movement workers are selected in each work center. As of this moment there are 155,365 workers who have earned this honor. To be an advance movement worker means to be in the vanguard in productive effort and in revolutionary attitudes. Being an advance movement worker means more work, more effort; it means that more demands are made on them.

Therefore advance movement workers are a good source of revolutionary militants—which nearly all our working people aspire to become. This source will grow in both quality and quantity, and ever greater numbers of workers will receive this honor.

As of today, 28,093 working men have given up their jobs to women in order to take up new posts in harder and more complex tasks in sectors where there is an insufficient labor force—such as agriculture, construction and industry.

The concept of volunteer work, done after regular working hours and without any remuneration whatsoever, has reached incredible proportions. During June and July—amid the enthusiasm of the 26th of July (National Day of Rebellion)—more than 8 million hours of volunteer work were chalked up. Thousands of productive marathons, friendly competitions among workers in the same fields and competitions in quality were organized, and hundreds of work centers were declared "guerrilla" work centers. In such places the workers remained at their centers of work from one week to 15 days, working in round-the-clock shifts to fulfill their high work goals. All this meant that great quantities of products were turned out that did not have to include wages in their production cost. For some time now there has been a trend toward the renunciation of overtime pay on the part of the workers. First overtime pay was renounced by small groups of workers, later by entire work centers and today more than 290,000 comrades have announced their decision to work whatever time is needed for their normal wages.

As a result of the revolutionary offensive in work centers in the struggle to improve work discipline the following motto arose: "Our workday—what our conscience dictates."

This entails arriving early on the job, doing the best possible job during the workday and doing extra work whenever necessary to guarantee production, without any monetary renumeration whatsoever. This motto is being enthusiastically accepted everyday by ever growing numbers of workers.

The Heroes of the Moncada banner constitutes the top award for collective efforts in production and a significant advancement in the political awareness of our workers. Recently 1348 work centers—employing 170,000 workers—were honored with this banner, giving rise to great happiness and revolutionary pride among the workers. Workers throughout the country are continuing the struggle to earn this award next July 26.

What are the fundamental motivations behind these successes?

These achievements have been inspired by the example of

the nation's martyrs who have nurtured the growth of the Revolution with their own blood.

These achievements have been inspired by the example of Fidel and the rest of our leaders, who, closely linked to our people, are the first in work, in sacrifice and in willingness to give their lives for a socialist and communist homeland.

These achievements have been inspired by the awareness that we are working for our people, that through our efforts today we are creating the wealth and the well-being on which the new homeland will be established. And we are prepared to risk that wealth and well-being at any moment for the subjugated peoples who are struggling against imperialism.

These are the moral motives that inspire our workers and our people, a people forged in the lofty ideals of communism, and in which the "soft" ideology of the imperialists can never penetrate.

Today, more than ever, and as a concrete demonstration of our support for the firm position adopted by our Party, we will redouble our efforts in carrying out our revolutionary tasks and work hard to honor the date of October 10th by increasing our productive and ideological work and by showing our willingness to struggle and our military preparedness, ready to face whatever risks our implacable revolutionary principles may entail—and triumph.

OUR WORKING CLASS IS FIRM IN ITS REVOLUTIONARY POSITION!
WE DO NOT VACILLATE!
WITHIN THE REALM OF REVOLUTIONARY PRINCIPLES AND COMMUNIST IDEALS,
EVERYTHING! OUTSIDE OF IT, NOTHING!

Executive Bureau of the Central Organization of Cuban Trade Unions
Havana, August 26, 1968
Year of the Heroic Guerrilla

READING 11 *Political Socialization in Cuba*

Introductory Note

Formal education is a key means of political socialization in any country and Cuba is no exception. Castro has invested much time and energy in all levels of education, including teacher-training programs, new textbook publication, and building construction, hoping to raise the Cuban level of "political awareness" and technical competence (Selections 11.1, 11.2, and 11.3). Political socialization also occurs in the Cuban cinema, equally under governmental control as Selection 11.4 illustrates. There is official criticism, however, that contemporary Cuban literature (novels, essays, etc.) is excessively apolitical (Selection 11.5).

SELECTION 11.1: TRAINING OF A PRIMARY SCHOOL TEACHER

One of the achievements of the Revolution that without a doubt most impresses our visitors from all over the world, consists of

Selection 11.1: Abel Prieto Morales, *Granma* (July 29, 1966), p. 2, JPRS 37,777 (September 23, 1966).
Selection 11.2: Mirta Rodríguez Calderón, *Granma* (March 6, 1967), p. 2, JPRS 40,744 (April 24, 1967).
Selection 11.3: *Granma*, Weekly Review in English, Year 3, No. 48 (December 1, 1968), p. 6.
Selection 11.4: *Granma*, Weekly Review in English, Year 4, No. 3 (January 19, 1969), pp. 9–11.
Selection 11.5: *Granma*, Weekly Review in English, Year 3, No. 47 (November 24, 1968), p. 11, originally published in *Verde Olivo* for November 24, 1968 under the signature of Leopoldo Ávila.

the three centers where the primary teachers of the future Cuban schools are trained.

Within the field of comparative education there is nothing like it. And this is because the Cuban Revolution has decided to solve the problem of the rural school through the formation of a new teacher, capable of living close to the farmer and educating children with a Communist conception, while at the same time serving the rural community as a revolutionary leader. . . .

Today we shall write of the "Sierra Maestra" Vocational Center, which all the people of Cuba refer to simply as "Minas del Frío," because it is located in the historic spot where Major Ernesto Guevara had his command post during the insurrectional period.

Minas de Frío is a great school city with the capacity to accommodate 8,000 students. Although the environment is that of a camp, today the main concern of the young student is for his studies. His classrooms are rustic, but they have as much dignity as the most reputable academic hall. And this is because the professors and the students give to their humble classrooms the respect due to a center for studies. The Center is composed of 40 buildings divided into zones and groups designed to facilitate organization. Although it is a coeducation Center, there are separate zones for male and female students. Both zones are in turn divided into units attended by professors who teach in the classrooms during the day, and live by night with their students in the lodging-houses.

All activities are on a self-service basis. The students hang up their hammocks and take them down, take care of their personal hygiene, wash their own clothes and the kitchen utensils. The cleaning of the lodges is organized by brigades, as well as the maintenance of the lodges and the entire Center. In short, the students learn to overcome difficulties similar to those they will encounter as teachers of workers and peasants; but above all, they are taught and formed by means of their daily work, thus acquiring the workers' awareness without the slightest vestige or residue of bourgeois attitudes. Not a single new teacher will desert because of the contrast between the countryside and the city.

Very early each morning all the students line up outside of their lodges for the morning ceremony. It is really a beautiful spectacle: as the sun begins to peep from behind the mountains, 6,000 youths observe the raising of the Cuban flag and sing the national anthem with revolutionary fervor. Immediately afterward, the professors comment on the previous day's activities and explain some national or international event to their students. A Minas student should know what is happening in Cuba and the world, and must learn to analyze events with a critical sense.

From the morning ceremony they march to breakfast, and from there they go to the classrooms. From the little building known as "Fidel's house," because the Prime Minister once stayed there, many of us have many times enjoyed the morning sun that shines on thousands of youths when, like ants, they march toward their rustic classrooms in the mountains of Minas de Frío.

The most significant thing about Minas is the transformation it produces in the young student. A few months after his arrival at Minas, he or she acquires a conscious discipline, becomes aware of his future responsibility, gets rid of all individualism and fundamentally begins to concern himself about the group.

The course of studies at Minas del Frío is divided into two semesters, during which four basic subjects are taught: Spanish, Mathematics, Plant Biology and the History of Cuba. . . .

The teaching staff has the obligation to study. If the word "training" is an element that pervades all revolutionary activity, the teaching staff at Minas is aware of the role they must individually play as professors, and of the need to continue improving themselves in order to more efficiently perform their teaching duties. The Center's professors study in collective groups and at the same time attend classes by professors from the University of Santiago de Cuba.

One of the most entertaining activities at Minas are the field trips or excursions to historic sites near the Center. On these trips, physical education activities acquire a special importance. During the month of August or the beginning of September, there will be a symbolic graduation ceremony for the students of Minas del Frío. The student may not pass the courses included in the Study Plan and transfer to the Topes de Collantes School as a first year repeat student, but it is mandatory to graduate from the nonacademic requirements, which consist of climbing Pico Turquino, which is the maximum field trip and the culmination of the course at Minas.

After a stay of 9 months and his graduation on Pico Turquino, the student and future teacher feels more sure of himself: he has lived in the land that has been filled with heroism by the rebel soldiers; he has overcome the rigors of swamp and cold; he has risen above greater and minor difficulties; has lived an intense community life; he has learned to love the countryside: he is morally prepared to return some day to the countryside as a teacher of peasants.

The formation of a new teacher is of capital importance to the Cuban Revolution. For in this new type of teacher, the Revolution has placed its hopes for the Communist education of Cuban children, which is to create the solid foundations for a man who will later be capable of living a full life in the future society. . . .

Selection 11.2: New Books in Worker-Peasant Education Program

A second level reader for the Worker-Peasant Education Campaign, dealing basically with various aspects of our agricultural economy, a dictionary including terms in the vocabulary of our revolution pertaining to various regions of the country, and an arithmetic book entitled *The Arithmetic Tables in the Worker-Peasant Education Campaign* are among the works the Worker-Peasant Education Office is engaged in preparing. They will soon go to press, according to an announcement made to *Granma* by officials of that department of the Ministry of Education.

The three works are being prepared with the peasant reader in mind, and they will also be printed in letters larger than normal size in order to facilitate reading by the peasant. A number of color pictures will supplement the beauty of these books, in which are included narrative prose, theatrical works, tales and poetry which contribute to the didactive and literary value of the books.

In the work on the three books, which has been done by the comrades in the Worker-Peasant Education Campaign Office of the Ministry of Education, they have had the collaboration of Cuban political and administrative organs, which, for example, have contributed definitions and explanations of the main functions of these bodies and organs for the dictionary.

In order to adapt these books to the real situation in our country, the practical problems encountered in the agricultural production process, concepts having to do with technical knowledge of the soil, harvest, rural life, etc., were chosen as the subject matter.

Moreover, the dictionary sets forth the terminology which has come into general use since the triumph of the revolution, with such words as emulation, overfulfillment, activist, bureaucracy, etc., clearly defined. It also includes phrases which have become popular, such as "*voy abajo*" (I am going down), "*eso es negativo*" (this is the negative), and words in common regional usage, such as "*guarandinga,*" which is what the peasants call the means of mountain transport in use in some sectors of our ranges. Also included in the vocabulary are the names of the weapons, countries and nations of the world, and their flags, and the places where the liberation war is currently being waged on the three continents.

When it comes to soils and their usages, the book of readings explains and describes the factors on which soil fertility depends, "how to maintain soil fertility, with organic materials, and the use of fertilizers," and details in connection with the importance of agriculture and the advances which are being achieved in this sector of our economy. This section of the book ends with quotations from *El Cultivador* (The Farmer), by José Martí.

Also, the book will include some native takes and accounts of the liberation war, the letter written by Che Guevara to our Prime Minister, parts of the Second Havana Declaration and the Agrarian Reform Law, popular peasant jokes, production figures and goals for the future, account of historical and geographical facts, comparative readings from the past and present, etc., etc.

Each one of these books will be put out in 100,000 copies, and it is hoped that the Book Institute will have completed printing work by the end of the month of May. The convenient size of the books, their apt illustration and the care with which they have been prepared from the literary point of view (for example, in their editing figurative images and language were avoided) are such that not only the usefulness of these books will be assured but we can also be certain of a warm welcome on the part of the users. However, these books will be subjected to collective criticism. . . .

Selection 11.3: Technical and Political Awareness in Education

Thanks to the work and effort of all the people, within the next few days the University of Oriente will graduate the largest number of students in its entire history: 69 engineers, 119 doctors and dentists, 6 chemists, 46 economists and accountants, together with 106 high school teachers and some 170 workers from all over the province who have completed their studies at the Worker-Farmer School and are now qualified to enroll at the University's School.

This graduating class is not only larger than any of the other classes which have been graduated since this university was founded on October 10, 1947, but also the graduating students from this University are better qualified from a political and professional point of view.

The fact that the graduating students from the University of Oriente are better qualified than the graduates of previous years stems from the comprehensive system for university students which coordinates education activities with agricultural work and military training. This system teaches the students to face life not just as professionals but also as citizens of a developing nation, a nation in Revolution and facing the constant threat of aggression.

The organization of the students' activities is what is responsible for this coordination and for the graduation of professionals with a higher level of technical and political integration every year.

This organization is partially a result of the policy of not including in the schedule of educational activities—which accounts for some thirty weeks out of the school term—a series of nonscheduled activities, which formerly interrupted the program of study with considerable frequency.

Now the students actually devote more time in studying than in any previous year although the curriculum includes spending some 30 days a year and a weekend every month doing productive work. Also included in the curriculum are 30 days of intensive military training every year and a weekend every month going over what they learned in the military courses. Moreover, on the third weekend of every month they engage in recreational activities sponsored by the University.

All this is what the students at the University of Oriente call the "three for one" program, and it alone supports our thesis.

A better qualified faculty, the preparation and application of new study programs and the evaluation system—all of which make teaching more effective and efficient—support our judgment that the new university graduates are better qualified than the graduates of previous years.

The evaluation of the students is no longer based, as it was in the past, on the results of exams and tests which were graded, we might say mechanically. Under the old system, with a knowledge of three fourths of the subject matter covered, the student generally passed. This was known as "averaging."

With the new evaluation system, the professors in the different departments grade the student not just on the basis of exams at the end of the semester, but also taking into consideration the student's attitude regarding his professional studies throughout the whole term. This attitude is what determines whether or not the student will qualify for the final exams. This professional study is no longer based on theory and work in the lab alone, but rather on direct study and productive work, for future technicians on research and different kinds of jobs, for the future economists and the students in other fields.

Of course, to be truly effective this method demands a lot more from the professors who are obliged to stay in closer contact with the students so as to be able to correctly determine whether a student has qualified for the final exams or not. For the same reason, the student not only finds himself obliged to fulfill his daily obligations but he is also obliged to clear up any doubt on the spot, bringing it to the professor's attention. This, in turn, obliges him to increase and broaden his knowledge through research work and study.

This is possible because the faculty is now contracted on a full-time basis. The organization of the departments along the lines of the different specialties further encourages the faculty to keep up to date on the progress made in the various subjects and to do research work in the different fields together with the students.

Thus we maintain that this year's graduates from the University of Oriente and those who will graduate in the future are politically and professionally better qualified than those of previous years—without of course, slighting the skill of those who have already graduated and whose weaknesses undoubtedly have been overcome through their work in the various fields.

As to quantity there is no room for doubt—the two charts included with this article are quite eloquent.

But we must add that the fact that the University of Oriente is graduating 69 engineers, 119 doctors and dentists and 108 high school teachers, while at the same time 170 workers have quaified to enroll in the School of Technology is eloquent proof of the drive and development of the nation at all levels. It is also eloquent proof of how the efforts of the working people—who make this development possible—are applied. Nor have we mentioned the scores of young people who have already enrolled in the recently inaugurated School of Agriculture or the 50 young people who are already studying to become engineering technicians.

Since 1960, 285 students have graduated as technical experts from the School of Technology of this University. In the year 1970, more than 200 students will graduate as engineers.

Although these achievements—together with what undoubtedly has been accomplished in the last 20 years—are quite impressive, the University of Oriente still has a long and complex road to follow in order to serve the country in its daily work. The fact that this graduating class is the best qualified in the University's 21 years of existence should serve as a stimulus for continuing to work and study so as to accelerate this upward trend.

Selection 11.4: The Cinema

Our movie-makers—directors, cameramen, writers, editors, composers, etc.—have had the privilege of working with some of the most renowned movie-makers of other countries. In some cases this contact was simply through meetings, lectures or courses, but in others it has involved working directly together in the creative process. This policy of providing a direct contact between our movie-makers and the representatives of other important cinema movements and industries reflects not only the desire to become familiar with these trends in cinema—available to the public in general through our Cinematheque, Cinema Clubs, movie theatres, etc.—but also the rejection of conditions that lead to the intellectual impoverishment that comes from being under the influence or domination of a single style, school or form.

If we were to make an analysis, it would have to be pointed out that the accelerated development which in the Revolution has overcome a legacy of centuries of colonialism and neo-colonialism has today in Cuban cinema a source of experience which provides those solutions which have solved the concrete problems. Without going into detail, we can state that this situation has created the tensions in discipline needed for the ideological and artistic training of artistic, technical and directing cadres. Thus, our movie industry has—within its capacity and significance—become an integral part of the Cuban Revolution in fulfillment of its revolutionary duties. And in this case, as one of the artistic manifestations of culture, it has become an outstanding medium for information and ideological and cultural formation.

The result of ten years of movie production makes it clear that Cuban cinema, born with the Revolution, has served not only as a narrator of the Revolution but also as a protagonist, a participant that enriches the Revolution and that enriches our reality through its vision of the Revolution. Cuban cinema is a part of these ten years of struggle by our people, constituting an inseparable part of our people's battle for the construction of socialism and communism and of their struggle to the death against imperialism. . . .

Our participation in international festivals has two objectives: to measure the results of each year's work with the most outstanding films and cinema movements in the rest of the world and to break the imperialist blockade. It cannot be forgotten that every shot, every sequence, every short subject, every documentary, every newsreel, has but a single theme: the Cuban Revolution. But this does not mean that only one theme is dealt with, even though we may seem to be contradicting ourselves. A true revolution—and the Cuban Revolution is that—encompasses so many and such highly complex situations, it enriches life in such a way and widens man and society's sphere of action to such a degree, opening up so many questions and presenting so many possible solutions, that no situation can have as many facets as a revolution has. Included in a few rolls of film is the living image of the Cuban Revolution, and this cinematic image has been projected in the most surprising places and for varied audiences. . . .

Selection 11.5: Cuban Literature

One of the most interesting and surprising characteristics of Cuban literary criticism and Cuban literature in general is its apparent depoliticization. Except for producing an occasional essay—of a more or less successful nature, essays very often dealing with the past—those who must consistently contribute to our cultural publications very seldom make their evaluations or write their works with a revolutionary approach uppermost in their mind. The reasons for this phenomenon are not completely known to us, even though some of the reasons are quite obvious. Some time ago the bogey of pamphleteering took root here; fear of this bogey hovered over our literary circles. It is very true that this fear seemed at times justified. But behind, there was also the unjustified fear that the Revolution might encourage it. Anyone who understands the depth of this Revolution, who grasps its dynamic nature, its constant vigor, cannot continue to harbor any fear whatsoever that the official patronage would try to obstruct the work of creative persons by reducing it to slogans. Moreover, the scorn for the pamphlet has made some go beyond the limits; it has become "scorn" for the political point of view in favor of an ideological vacuum that is truly unfortunate. Hastily avoiding supposedly dogmatic points of view, critics and writers have become bogged down in positions in which "political" is a dirty word. . . .

In most of the literary works published in Cuba the possibility of a critical approach has been replaced by elegant wordiness that is scarcely able to veil the absolute vacuum or the disgraceful evasions. A militant point of view in judging a specific work of art is still something of a novelty. And in certain circles it is considered scandalous. However, what should really scandalize us is the exhibition of this unfortunate cliquishness, this falsification of criticism that fills so many printed pages in this country, a nation in which we must also learn to economize on paper. If a novel or a poem is analyzed in the light of the Revolution, those who vacillate, and the troublemakers become disturbed. But if an atmosphere of sacrosanctity is created, where six or seven initiates reserve the applause for themselves, covering up their errors and elevating themselves to the illusionary status of sacred cows, without producing work that justifies such vanity, no one seems to be the least disturbed. And this is precisely what does disturb us.

When we are surprised that the great and moving drama of the Revolution has so little impact on our writers, it is not a question of setting up the themes to write on, nor of restricting the possibilities of developing forms, research and experimentation. Quite the contrary, we believe that such things as research and experimentation have been allowed to degenerate because of problems of another kind.

What worries us about criticism—with certain exceptions which are truly admirable—is not just the depoliticization (which seems to be a kind of nonrevolutionary political trick) but a complete lack of sincerity. It is inadmissible that here, where so much serious and arduous work is being done in the field of science and technology, a situation characterized by a facile and superficial shuffling of names that have been falsely exalted for reasons of a not exactly artistic nature, should be allowed to continue.

The jockeying for prestige through favoritism, personal friendships or identification among certain writers because they have the same personal defects has been such a common practice that when one of these persons is removed from his usurped position there is a real commotion, even though the one expelled from the temple is a known counterrevolutionary. And we hear ridiculously contradictory opinions which are quite logical since some damage must already have been done by so much nonsense poisoning our literary world.

In judging a literary work we start from a certain, very definite, point of view. And that is:

> This means that within the Revolution, everything; against the Revolution, nothing. Against the Revolution, nothing, because the Revolution also has its rights and the first right of the Revolution is that of existence and against the Revolution's right to be and to exist, nothing. Since the Revolution encompasses the interests of the people, since the Revolution signifies the interest of the entire nation, no one can justly claim a right that is against the Revolution. . . .

Regardless of our many tasks, however wide our combat front may be, we cannot abandon our ideological struggle or relax our vigilance in the ideological field. An oversight in this would be a risk we are not going to take. The writers here who attack the Revolution or attempt to sow defeatism, weakness and doubt, are launching an artillery barrage in the field of ideology so as to soften up the positions we hold in preparation against future enemy attacks. That is why we unmask their attitudes and provocations.

We are not propounding the forced appearance of a generation of revolutionary writers. That will come in time. It will be created by the Revolution itself. It will emerge from its ranks, gradually, and as a logical product of a new society. What must be avoided is this emergence—which we desire but do not force—being frustrated by the obstacles placed in its path by a group of vacillating, smug, arrogant and nonrevolutionary people. We hold the opinion that the new generations must be protected against negative influences.

Renewing the concepts expressed in Fidel's words to the intellectuals, proceeding from those political positions, we can save from disaster those works that deserve something more worthwhile than becoming the subject of liberal intrigue in certain ivory towers and thus cleanse our culture of extravagant, weak-kneed counterrevolutionaries. Let us look at things from the point of view of the Revolution, from the point of view of a nation at war, that is, from a realistic point of view. New creators would be aided and guided by the sort of criticism that includes political analysis, that goes to the heart of the literary work. These new creators are the same ones who thus far have only received, from some false eminent figures, either an absolute "freeze" or a wary acceptance or, at worst, the accolade that contaminates. A style of politically alert criticism would not constitute a danger to our culture but rather an opportunity to rescue it from the murky world of mutual praise and mutual complicity to which several gentlemen have devoted their efforts for quite some time. . . .

READING 12 *The Agricultural Revolution*

Introductory Note

Rural Cuba underwent radical transformation as Castro expanded state control over land ownership after 1959 and departed from the individual ownership that his early supporters had expected of land reform. Ernesto Che Guevara (1928–67) explains this transition in Selection 12.1. The Agrarian Reform Law of May 17, 1959 declared that all large estates were to be abolished (those over 30 caballerías *or approximately 995 acres) and that sugar-cane "cooperatives" and peoples' farms were to be established and administered through the* Instituto Nacional de Reforma Agraria *(National Agrarian Reform Institute or INRA). The law's significance is suggested by the amount of farm area then consisting of estates over 1200 acres. It was over one-half the total farm area of Cuba.*

The agricultural revolution is related closely to the process of political integration and socialization insofar as it incorporated large numbers of peasants into national institutions, thus expanding the politically relevant sector of the population. Contemporary Cuban nationalism is in large measure campesino*–based.*

Selection 12.1: Ernesto Che Guevara, "The Cuban Economy: Its Past and Its Present Importance," *International Affairs*, Vol. 40, No. 4 (October, 1964), pp. 589–99.

Selection 12.2: Speech by Fidel Castro in Havana on January 2, 1969, published in *Granma*, Weekly Review in English, Year 4, No. 1 (January 5, 1969), pp. 2–6.

Selection 12.3: Interview with Fidel Castro, *Granma*, Weekly Review in English, Year 4, No. 6 (February 9, 1969), pp. 2–6.

Selections 12.2 and 12.3 suggest the significance of agriculture in Castro's strategy of national change.

Selection 12.1: Economic Decision Making

The Paris Peace Treaty of 1898 and the Platt Amendment of 1901 were the signs under which our new Republic was born. In the first, the settlement of accounts after the war between two Powers led to the withdrawal of Spain and the intervention of the United States. On the island, which had suffered years of cruel struggle, the Cubans were only observers; they had no part in the negotiations. The second, the Platt Amendment, established the right of the United States to intervene in Cuba whenever her interests demanded it.

In May 1902 the political-military oppression of the United States was formally ended, but her monopolistic power remained. Cuba became an economic colony of the United States and this remained its main characteristic for half a century.

In a country generally laid waste the imperialists found an interesting phenomenon: a sugar industry in full capitalistic expansion.

The sugar cane has been part of the Cuban picture since the 16th century. It was brought to the island only a few years after the discovery of America; however, the slave system of exploitation kept the cultivation on a subsistence level. Only with the technological innovations which converted the sugar mill into a factory, with the introduction of the railway and the abolition of slavery, did the production of sugar begin to show a considerable growth, and one which assumed extraordinary proportions under Yankee auspices.

The natural advantages of the cultivation of sugar in Cuba are obvious; but the predominant fact is that Cuba was developed as a sugar factory of the United States.

The American banks and capitalists soon controlled the commercial exploitation of sugar and, furthermore, a good share of the industrial output and of the land. In this way, a monopolistic control was established by U.S. interests in all aspects of a sugar production which soon became the predominant factor in our foreign trade, due to the rapidly developing monoproductive characteristics of the country.

Cuba became the sugar producing and exporting country par excellence, and if she did not develop even further in this respect, the reason is to be found in the capitalist contradictions which put a limit to a continuous expansion of the Cuban sugar industry, which depended almost entirely on American capital.

The American Government used the quota system on imports of Cuban sugar, not only to protect her own sugar industry, as demanded by her own producers, but also to make possible the unrestricted introduction into our country of American manufactured goods. The preferential treaties of the beginning of the century gave American products imported into Cuba a tariff advantage of 20 per cent over the most favoured of the nations with whom Cuba might sign trade agreements. Under these conditions of competition, and in view of the proximity of the United States, it became almost impossible for any foreign country to compete with American manufactured goods.

The U.S. quota system meant stagnation for our sugar production; during the last years the full Cuban productive capacity was rarely utilised to the full; but the preferential treatment given to Cuban sugar by the quota also meant that no other export crops could compete with it on an economic basis.

Consequently, the only two activities of our agriculture were cultivation of sugar cane and the breeding of low-quality cattle on pastures which at the same time served as reserve areas for the sugar plantation owners.

Unemployment became a constant feature of life in rural areas, resulting in the migration of agricultural workers to the cities. But industry did not develop either; only some public service undertakings under Yankee auspices (transportation, communications, electrical energy).

The lack of industry and the great part played by sugar in the economy resulted in the development of a very considerable foreign trade which bore all the characteristic marks of colonialism: primary products to the metropolis, manufactured goods to the colony. The Spanish empire had followed the same pattern, but with less ability.

Other exports were also primary products, but their proportion only reached 20 per cent of Cuba's total exports. They were: tobacco, principally in leaves; coffee—only occasionally, due to the small production; raw copper and manganese; and, during later years, semi-processed nickel.

Such was the picture of the Cuban economy: in effect, a mono-productive country (sugar) with one particular export and import market (the United States), and vitally dependent on its foreign trade. . . .

The two main economic problems of the Cuban Revolution during its first months were unemployment and a shortage of foreign currencies. The first was an acute political problem, but the second was more dangerous, given the enormous dependence of Cuba on foreign trade.

The Revolutionary Government's economic policy was directed primarily towards solving these two problems. It is therefore appropriate to make a short analysis of the actions taken and the errors made during the first months.

The Agrarian Reform implied such a profound institutional change that it became immediately possible to make an effort towards the elimination of the obstacles that had prevented the utilisation of human and natural resources in the past.

Because of the predominant part which had been played by the *latifundia* in agricultural production, and the enormous size of the sugar cane plantations organised along capitalistic lines, it was relatively easy to convert this type of rural property into state farms and co-operatives of considerable size. Cuba thus avoided the slow-moving development characteristic of other agrarian revolutions: the division of land into a fantastic number of small farms, followed by the grouping of such small units to enable more modern techniques, feasible only on certain levels of production, to be applied.

What was the economic policy followed in agriculture after the transfer of the large estates? As a natural part of this rural unemployment disappeared and the main efforts were directed towards self-sufficiency as regards the greater part of foodstuffs and raw materials of vegetable or animal origin. The trend in the development of agriculture can be defined in one word: diversification. In its agricultural policy the Revolution represented the antithesis of what had existed during the years of dependence on imperialism and of exploitation by the landowning class. Diversification versus monoculture; full employment versus idle hands; these were the major transformations in the rural areas during those years.

It is well known that, nevertheless, serious agricultural problems immediately arose, and these have only begun to be solved during recent months. How can we explain the relative scarcity of some agricultural products, and particularly the decline in sugar production, when the Revolution began by incorporating all the idle rural productive factors in the agricultural process, thus greatly increasing its potentialities? We believe we committed two principal errors.

Our first error was the way in which we carried out diversification. Instead of embarking on diversification by degrees we attempted too much at once. The sugar cane areas were reduced and the land thus made available was used for cultivation of new crops. But this meant a general decline in agricultural production. The entire economic history of Cuba had demonstrated that no other agricultural activity would give such returns as those yielded by the cultivation of the sugar cane. At the outset of the Revolution many of us were not aware of this basic economic fact, because a fetishistic idea connected sugar with our dependence on imperialism and with the misery in the rural areas, without analysing the real causes: the relation to the uneven trade balance.

Unfortunately, whatever measures are taken in agriculture, the results do not become apparent until months, sometimes years, afterwards. This is particularly true as regards sugar cane production. That is why the reduction of the sugar cane areas made between the middle of 1960 and the end of 1961—and, let us not forget the two years of drought—has resulted in lower sugar cane harvests during 1962 and 1963.

Diversification on a smaller scale could have been achieved by utilising the reserves of productivity existing in the resources assigned to the various traditional types of cultivation. This would have permitted the partial use of idle resources for a small number of new products. At the same time, we could have taken measures to introduce more modern and complex techniques requiring a longer period of assimilation. After these new technical methods had begun to bear fruit in the traditional fields, particularly in those related to exports, it would have been practicable to transfer resources from these fields to the areas of diversification without prejudice to the former.

The second mistake made was, in our opinion, that of dispersing our resources over a great number of agricultural products, all in the name of diversification. The dispersal was made, not only on a national scale but also within each of the agricultural productive units.

The change made from monoculture to the development of a great number of agricultural products implied a drastic transformation within relatively few months. Only a very solid productive organisation could have resisted such rapid change. In an underdeveloped country, in particular, the structure of agriculture remains very inflexible and its organisation rests on extremely weak and subjective foundations. Consequently, the change in the agricultural structure and diversification, coming simultaneously, produced a greater weakness in the agricultural productive organisation.

Now that the years have passed, conditions have changed and the pressure of the class struggle has lessened, and so it is fairly easy to make a critical assessment of the analysis made during those months and years. It is for history to judge how much was our fault and how much was caused by circumstances.

At any rate, hard facts have shown us both the errors and the road towards their correction, which is the road the Cuban Revolution is at present following in the agricultural sector. Sugar now has first priority in the distribution of resources, and in the assessment of those factors which contribute to the most efficient use of those resources. The other sectors of agricultural development have not been abandoned, but adequate methods have been sought to prevent a dispersal of resources of which the effect would be to hinder the obtaining of maximum yields.

In the industrial sector our policy is directed towards the same two objectives: the solution of the two problems of unemployment and scarcity of foreign exchange. The Agrarian Reform, the revolutionary measures as regards redistribution of income, and the increase in employment observed in other sectors of the economy and in industry itself, extended the national market considerably. This market was further strengthened by the establishment of a government monopoly of foreign trade, and by the introduction of a protectionist policy as regards the importation of goods which, without any disadvantage to the national consumer, can be manufactured in Cuba.

What industry there was in Cuba only worked to a fraction of its capacity, due to the competition of American goods, many of which entered the country practically duty free, and also to the fact that national demand was limited by the concentration among the parasitic classes of a large part of the national income.

Immediately after the Revolution the explosive increase of demand permitted a higher degree of utilisation of our industrial capacity, and nationally-produced articles accounted for a greater share of total consumption. This industrial growth, however, aggravated the problem of the balance of payments, for an extraordinarily high percentage of the costs of our industry—which was nationally integrated only to a small degree—was represented by the importation of fuel, raw materials, spare parts and equipment for replacement.

The problem of the balance of payments, and that of urban unemployment, made us follow a policy aimed at an industrial development which would eliminate these defects. Here, too, we both achieved successes and committed errors. Already during the first years of the Revolution we ensured the country's supply of electric power, acquiring from the socialist countries new plant-capacities which will meet our needs until 1970. New industries have been created, and many small and medium-sized production units in the mechanical field have been re-equipped.

One result of these measures was that our industry could be kept running when the American embargo on spare parts hit us hardest. Some textile factories, some extractive and chemical installations and a new and vigorous search for fresh mineral resources have all contributed to successes in the more efficient use of native natural resources and raw materials.

I have spoken of certain achievements in the industrial field during the first years, but it is only just that I should also mention the errors made. Fundamentally, these were caused by a lack of precise understanding of the technological and economic elements necessary in the new industries installed during those years. Influenced by existing unemployment and by the pressure exerted by the problems in our foreign trade, we acquired a great number of factories with the dual purpose of substituting imports and providing employment for an appreciable number of urban workers. Later we found that in many of these plants the technical efficiency was insufficient when measured by international standards, and that the net result of the substitution of imports was very limited, because the necessary raw materials were not nationally produced.

We have rectified this type of error in the industrial sector. In planning new industries we are evaluating the maximum advantages which they may bring to our foreign trade through use of the most modern technical equipment at present obtainable, taking into consideration the particular conditions of our country.

So far the industrial development achieved can be described as satisfactory, if we take into account the problems caused by the American blockade and the radical changes which have occurred in only three years as regards our foreign sources of supply. Last year our sugar production fell from 4.8 million metric tons to 3.8 million but this was offset by an increase, in general terms, of 6 per cent in the rest of industry. This year, 1964, given the greater strength of our internal productive organisation and our greater experience in commercial relations with our new sources of supply, the industrial advance should be still greater.

The transformations so far made in the Cuban economy have produced great changes in the structure of our foreign trade. As regards exports the changes have been limited chiefly to the opening up of new markets, with sugar continuing to be the main export article. On the other hand, the composition of our imports has changed completely during these five years. Imports of consumer goods, particularly durables, have decreased substantially in favour of capital equipment, while a small decrease can be noted in the import of intermediate goods. The policy of substitution of imports is showing slow but tangible results.

The economic policy of the Revolution having attained a certain integral strength, it is clear that imports of durable consumer goods will once more increase, to satisfy the growing needs of modern life. The plans being made for the future provide for both an absolute and a relative increase in the importation of these articles, taking into account the social changes which have occurred. It will be unnecessary, for example, to import Cadillacs and other luxury cars, which in former years were paid for to a great extent with the profits derived from the labour of the Cuban sugar worker.

This is only one aspect of the problems connected with the future development of Cuba which are at present being studied. The policy we shall follow in years to come will largely depend on the flexibility of our foreign trade, and on the extent to which it will permit us to take full advantage of opportunities which may present themselves. We expect the Cuban economy to develop along three principal lines between now and 1970.

Sugar will continue to be our main earner of foreign exchange. Future development implies an increase of 50 per cent in present productive capacity. Simultaneously a qualitative advance will take place in the sugar sector, consisting of a substantial increase in the yield per unit of land under cultivation, and an improvement in technology and equipment. That improvement will tend to make up for the ground lost through inefficiency during the last 10–15 years. During that period the complete lack of expansion of our market led to technological stagnation. With the new possibilities which have opened up in the socialist countries, the panorama is changing rapidly.

One of the main bases for the development of our sugar industry, as well as for the development of the country as a whole, is the agreement recently signed between the U.S.S.R. and Cuba. This guarantees to us future sales of enormous quantities of sugar at prices much above the average of those paid in the American and world markets during the last 20 years. Apart from this and other favourable economic implications, the Agreement signed with the U.S.S.R. is of political importance inasmuch as it provides an example of the relationship that can exist between an underdeveloped and a developed country when both belong to the socialist camp, in contrast to the commercial relations between the underdeveloped countries exporting raw materials and the industrialised capitalist countries—in which the permanent tendency is to make the balance of trade unfavourable to the poor nations.

The second line of industrial development will be nickel. The deposits in north-eastern Cuba offer great possibilities for making this part of the island the future centre of the metallurgical industry. The capacity of the nickel smelting works will be increased, making Cuba the second or third largest producer in the world of this strategic metal.

The third line of this future development will be the cattle industry. The large number of cattle, great indeed in proportion to the size of the population, offers rich possibilities for the future. We estimate that within about 10 years our cattle industry will be equalled in importance only by the sugar industry.

As I have indicated, the role played by foreign trade in the Cuban economy will continue to be of basic importance, but there will be a qualitative change in its future development. None of the three principal lines of development will imply an effort to substitute imports, with the exception of the cattle industry, during the first years. After these first years the character of our new economic development will be fully reflected in our exports, and although the policy of substitution of imports will not be abandoned, it will be balanced by exports. For the decade following 1970 we are planning a more accelerated process of substitution of imports. This can only be achieved on the basis of an industrialisation programme of great scope. We shall create the necessary conditions for such a programme, making full use of the opportunities offered to an underdeveloped economy by our external trade.

Selection 12.2: Increased Agricultural Productivity

. . . Here is an amazing fact: we are at the beginning of 1969 and by 1970 Cuba's agricultural production will be approximately double—twice as much!—what it was before January 1, 1959. This is truly amazing, perhaps even incredible. Something we can examine in the light of all the studies of the increases in agricultural production in every country and under all circumstances without finding another case that even remotely resembles this achievement. Because doubling agricultural production in ten years is something that cannot be done even by the so-called developed countries.

And actually this doubling of production has not been achieved in ten years; it has been achieved through an effort of less than five years. It has been achieved through efforts, organization, experience and concepts that were arrived at after five years of Revolution had passed.

Thus, this nation will have doubled its agricultural production in a period of not actually more than four years—at the most. It is quite enough to point out that during 1968 most of the cane for the famous 10-million-ton sugar harvest has been planted. . . .

Increases in agricultural production are achieved by means of the application of modern techniques and the extension of land area. We are going to move full speed ahead on both fronts. Fertilization plays an important role in the application of modern techniques to increase the yield per land area.

This program proposes two million tons, net content, of fertilizer for all of South America. What is meant by "net content"? The formulas that can be produced chemically in a ton to be applied to the soil. Many persons know this, but perhaps some who are not involved in agriculture need this explanation. It is not 100 percent nitrogen; it may have, for example, 20 percent of this element in a compound fertilizer—15 percent phosphorous, let's assume; 15 percent potassium. This is already a relatively high formula. It's not 100 percent net content, but 50 percent net content. The formulas are variable. To apply two million tons net content, one has to calculate four to eight million tons of fertilizer to be applied in the fields, according to their level of concentration.

Very well. This year Cuba is applying more than one and a half million tons of fertilizer in the fields—more than a half million tons net content.

But, as we said, two million tons net content is proposed for South America; let us say six million in actual volume. In 1975 Cuba will apply not less than a million tons in net content, approximately three to four million in volume. So that in 1975 Cuba will be applying more than 50 percent more than the amount of fertilizer proposed for all of South America.

In the third place: irrigation. In that program a yearly increase between now and 1975 of 200,000 irrigated hectares (almost 500,000 acres) of land is proposed.

Irrigation plays a decisive role, but its major importance lies less in its facilitating growth, counteracting the effects of lack of rainfall, than in the fact that the ready availability of water permits planting at the most favorable time, the application of fertilizers in the most favorable form and herbicides at the most favorable time, the preparation of the land at the most favorable time, maximum use of machinery and labor by its distribution over the entire year and optimum conditions for cultivation. More is obtained through these factors than through the mere application of water to the plant. In other words, irrigation makes possible the maximum employment of agricultural techniques, a factor often overlooked when the problem of irrigation is discussed. Irrigation not only insures against drought but permits the optimum application of modern techniques.

For a country such as ours, its importance is extraordinary. It is much more important for a country which has sunshine all year than for a country such as Finland, I repeat, which is frozen over a good part of the year. Even if it had water, it couldn't accomplish anything during the winter. In those months we are not frozen over, but neither do we have water. Ah! But if we have water in these so-called dry months—which they indeed are—then unquestionably our advantage is extraordinary. It is for that reason that irrigation is extraordinarily important for us, more important than for any temperate or cold country. Any cold country can build dams and assure its water supply in August or any other hot month, but that does not help it in December, January of February. With water, we can insure our Augusts against drought and also cultivate in January, February and March or any other dry month. In other words, we are able to benefit from sunshine and the soil all year, from our machinery all year, our technology all year, and our work force all year. Otherwise, we would have to wait for rain with folded arms and then plant everything in a matter of 15 days. Of course, that is impossible. The result would be a wild growth of weeds long before we had finished planting everything. We know this very well from the hectares of cane that we have had to plant in the rain in these years—and, above all, this year. . . .

Selection 12.3: Agricultural Manpower Training

. . . Many people are being trained in these fields. We have had to develop agriculture without technicians, but there are now close to 40,000 people specializing in agriculture. Of course, many of them had only a third-, fourth- or fifth-grade education. Where could you have found high school level people in the early days? Then there was the need to send some to become doctors, to become engineers and so forth. Therefore, agriculture had to depend on young people many of whom had only a second-, third- or fourth-grade education. Then they have had to cut cane, they have had to mobilize for defense. This has taken time.

Of course, in the case of the inseminators it was different, because it takes very little time to train them: from six months to a year. That is why it has taken longer to train other technicians: veterinary assistants, agricultural specialists in different fields.

Agriculture is being developed without technicians. But an army of technicians is now studying and will go to work.

Of course, all this is on a general-information level: how much fertilizer must be applied to surgarcane, how much cane in a row, how much iron is to be applied to the soil. That is how it is being done. Centralized genetics, so many insemination centers, centralized selection of bulls: so many bulls have to be shipped to Pinar del Río, to this, that or another place. . . . Thus the work has been done massively without the cooperation of an army of technicians, but this army of technicians is on its way!

I think the greatest accomplishment of these years has been our doing all this without technology. . . .

READING 13 *Technological Modernization*

Introductory Note

Castro knows that if he is to achieve total independence, and this means from Moscow and its technical expertise as well as from the United States, he must develop sophisticated labor skills in Cuba. These skills will be required for the agriculture-livestock sector and its supportive industries, that is, in fertilizer and farm machinery production, all of which means a radical shift in education from training lawyers and doctors to stress on engineers, technicians, and agronomists. Moreover, Cuba will require more technical training to expand in textiles, clothing, wood and paper products, and petroleum, as well as in nickel and cobalt mining.

This drive for technological modernization is co-ordinated by Castro, through the party's control over education and the com-

Selection 13.1: Oscar F. Rego, article on education in Cuba, *Siglo Veinte,* No. 63 (Mexico City: February 1966), pp. 13 and 40, JPRS 36,612 (July 21, 1966).

Selection 13.2: Interview by M. Marín with José Ramón López, director of *Brigadas Técnica Juvenil* of the national committee of the *Unión de la Juventud Comunista,* in *Juventud Rebelde* (Havana: June 23, 1966), p. 2, JPRS 37,643 (September 15, 1966).

Selection 13.3: G. R. Morejón, *El Mundo* (Havana: September 25, 1966), supplement pp. 6–7, JPRS 38,823 (November 28, 1966).

Selection 13.4: Marcelino Ortiz, *Juventud Rebelde* (Havana: June 23, 1966), p. 2, JPRS 37,643 (September 15, 1966).

Selection 13.5: José Gabriel Guma, *Granma* (Havana: July 24, 1966), p. 8, JPRS 37,442 (September 6, 1966).

Selection 13.6: Speech by Fidel Castro in Jaruco (Havana Province) on November 15, 1968, published in *Granma,* Weekly Review in English, Year 3, No. 47 (November 24, 1968), pp. 3–5.

munications media, as the following selections indicate. It should be stressed that the trend toward technological modernization is in part a product of the serious deficiencies in technical manpower faced by Castro, since many individuals with those skills left Cuba after the revolution took its turn towards the Marxist-Leninist path.

Selection 13.1: Education in Cuba

When commander Fidel Castro addressed, in September 1960, the General Assembly of the United Nations, concerning the literacy campaign which the Revolutionary Government would begin in 1961—the Year of Education—many persons outside Cuba did not believe that the astonishing results would be produced culminating in the eradication of illiteracy.

The blemish from the past was reduced from 23.6 percent to 3.9 percent, one of the lowest figures of the whole world. Within this figure, one must discount the 25,000 Haitians resident in Cuba who, not being able to control the Spanish language, are therefore illiterate in it, as well as those having physical and mental defects and persons of advanced age or who are deficient in health.

But that was only the beginning of what the Revolution was to accomplish on the education front. The Revolution came to the assumption of power and was faced with a lamentable and incredible state of instructional disorganization and abandonment. The assigning of teaching posts was in the hands of politicians that sold them or distributed them among their cronies and followers. At the triumph of the Revolution there were only 15,000 classrooms for primary instruction in Cuba. At the present time at this level—the statistics as of June 1965—there are 38,683 classrooms. More than 500,000 children, before January 1959, under the Batista tyranny, were lacking in any school attendance; 182,192 children were enrolled in the public schools, and around 120,000 in what are called private schools for the children of the well-off class of exclusively white people. The Revolution nationalized all schools, sweeping away that kind of discrimination. The final enrollment figure for the 1965–66 school year was 1,267,707 pupils.

The Revolution, in creating the thousands of classrooms, guaranteed the teaching of all children of school age, an achievement without precedent in Latin America. Not a single child in the mountains or in the plains areas was left without his studies, and all have classrooms and teachers, and the Revolutionary Government is preparing, at the Schools of Teacher formation, via the plan of Minas del Frío, Topes de Collantes, Tarara, the new teachers that will forge ahead in the mountain areas. They are the ones charged with serving the classrooms in the mountains and in the more inaccessible rural areas of the island.

With the formidable quantitative effort of the Revolution in the creation of thousands of classrooms, the formation of hundreds of revolutionary teachers, the erection of school houses, etc., one must also add the permanent advance of the teaching personnel and the work for improvement of the quality of teaching. This effort is being realized to an equivalent degree of responsibility at the levels of secondary and pre-university instruction. The pupils, in order to graduate, must pass the Level Examination, which is a final examination taken after having fulfilled all of the course requirements of the last grade.

The methods of instruction have also undergone radical transformations and now the effort is directed at integrated education, an education that closely ties the school to the productive work and life; and there is also being formed in teachers and pupils alike a solid agriculture-livestock awareness, in accordance with the economic reality of Cuba.

The training and advance of workers and farmers, including the women, is not at all deterred. The 707,212 adults made literate are continuing with their studies. To appreciate the extension obtained by the teaching services, one can say that the 7,600,000 inhabitants—more or less the total population of Cuba—2,415,638 were enrolled in the past courses of instruction at the centers of teaching assigned to the Ministry of Education. In the education of adults, in the 1964–65 school year program, some 243,934 workers passed through their grades, of which number 23,512 are from the schools of the mountain areas. At the close of that school year, there were 18,835 urban classrooms for workers, 6,891 in the rural areas and hundreds of youths classrooms attended by youths between the ages of 15 and 25.

More than 10,000 farm girls are undertaking primary instruction, in the Ana Betancourt School of the Plan for Training Women. Hundreds of classrooms for adult women are functioning under the plan throughout the Republic; in these classrooms attend principally the older workers in the domestic services that formerly were exploited in their work by the mistresses of wealthy homes.

At the secondary or middle level, 114,595 students attend the basic secondary schools, both urban and rural, and also attend the Pre-University Institutes (statistics as of June 1965). The most outstanding activity in the 1964–65 course in these classes of instruction was the promotion of 81%, which reflects an enormous quantitative and qualitative leap forward. Technological instruction, to which no attention was given during the years of capitalist government that we all suffered under, now has the major attention of the Revolutionary Government.

Thirty-six technological schools and institutes are providing preparation to 16,535 students that soon will incorporate themselves in the Scientific-Technical Revolution of the country. There are six agriculture-livestock technological centers; six language schools, five centers for the preparation of primary teachers; ten centers with 62 groupings in the provinces of schools for Pedagogical Training. The Union of Secondary Students and the Union of Communist Youth of the various schools are concerned with the quality of teaching and are directing their student companions as to their obligations in study, productive work, revolutionary philosophy, and student confraternity.

The higher education charged to Havana University—two hundred years old—Las Villas, and Oriente, has undergone a profound transformation after the triumph of the Revolution. Its life has been linked up intimately with the political history of our homeland. It has always been locked in combat against the tyrants and against imperialism; today, it is the brave bulwark that defends the socialist revolution of Cuba and the revolutionary movement of the whole world.

The university today has an enrollment never before reached. More than 29,000 students are taking courses in Humanities, Sciences, Technology, Medical Science, and Agriculture-Livestock Sciences. Of that number, 7,565 are scholarship students. The teaching at all levels—primary, secondary, and university—is free of charge for them.

In Cuba no student pays in order to study. It is the state that provides all means to the students, thus functioning, at all the levels, in the most gigantic plan of scholarship of all Latin America.

Selection 13.2: Youth Technical Brigades

Question. Comrade López, would you explain for us what a *Brigada Técnica Juvenil* is?

Answer. The *Brigada Técnica Juvenil* (Youth Technical Brigades or BTJ) are a mass movement; they are young people with specialized knowledge who have rallied around a basic objective: the carrying forward of the Technical Revolution as proposed by Fidel.

Q. How are the Brigades formed? Who are their members? What role is played by the *Unión de la Juventud Comunista* [Union of Communist Youth or UJC] in connection with them?

A. The Brigades are composed of comrades who are graduates of the technological schools and institutes, and of University faculties, but others can belong who carry out equivalent functions in practice. The latter are accepted as candidates until such time as they acquire the corresponding technical level.

The requirements for membership are: to be under 30 years of age, and naturally, to be a good worker. Each Brigade has a chairman and four comrades who constitute the executive committee; when the Brigades are large and perform their work in different departments or on different schedules, sub-Brigades may be formed.

The Technical Brigades are an organization that on all levels is directed by the Communist Youth Union.

Q. When and how did the idea of creating them originate?

A. The idea of the Brigades originated in July 1964. Fidel suggested it to [Education Minister Armando] Hart as a solution to the problem which confronted over 4,000 graduates of the technological schools after completing their studies. There was concern lest these comrades, when starting to work, would be scattered, cease studying, receive no political attention, and run the real risk of being absorbed by the technically-backward environment and not following the correct line of development.

Q. What relationship should a good Brigade maintain with the management at its center of work?

A. A great part of the work that the Brigades can do depends on the management. So that they can function, the management should assign them technical tasks of training, experimentation, and publication, since the management alone is familiar with the problems at the work center and has the material means to this end.

In a unit where there is not close coordination between the Brigade and the management, it is very difficult for the former to function. And it is up to the Party and the UJC to secure the development of such coordination.

Q. What positive role has been played by the Brigades up to the present moment? What contribution have they made to the country's economy?

A. These Brigades, consisting of youthful personnel, have injected enthusiasm into the work centers. Organizing them into Brigades has helped to solve many human problems caused when this generation—with its great enthusiasm and some theory but with little practice—comes up against a mass of technical experts and skilled workers who have spent years on the job, men who generally have succumbed to the routine, men with much experience and practice but with little theoretical knowledge.

The Brigades have served to train the young people who belong to them. By living a collective existence they learn to help each other, to discuss the problems that confront them, and moreover become accustomed to supervision and the collective criticism of errors. And during the most recent sugar-cane harvest they organized themselves into groups and helped to maintain the hoists and combines, working extra hours. This was easily accomplished, because the young people were already organized.

They have increased the knowledge of the most recent scientific and technical advances among the working masses, which opens new perspectives and creates greater enthusiasm among the workers.

In many places they have set up courses of technical self-improvement for the workers in which they themselves are the instructors. And although they have had little experience, many of them have already solved serious technical problems. At the Asbestos and Cement factory, the Technical Brigade built a machine which automates the process of grooving and cutting the tiles, and is valued at between 20,000 and 30,000 pesos; this means a 40 percent saving of labor force and over a 50 percent increase on the production line.

The voluntary technical labor of the Brigades contributes a total of more than 150,000 pesos per month.

We are certain that since October 1964, when they began their work, to the present time these young technical experts have made a contribution to our economy of more than [two] and a half million pesos from their after-hours activities.

Q. What can you tell us regarding the size of the organization and its future prospects?

A. As of 25 April, there were in the country a total of 638 Brigades with a membership of 8,154 young people. Our goal for 26 July is 800 Brigades with more than 10,000 young people as members.

As of the end of this year, we shall have 1,000 Brigades with some 10,000 [sic] members. Our growth after that will depend on the new graduating classes of technical experts. . . .

Q. How can the Brigade members help the workers assimilate the new scientific and technical advances?

A. The principal element that the Brigade members can contribute to the workers is confidence and a desire to apply the new techniques in production, and the use of their influence so that every worker will want to be a specialist. To achieve this, the members of the Brigades must set the example by striving to apply everywhere the most modern techniques.

It is the duty of the young technical expert to aid the worker in raising his own technical and cultural level.

Q. What should be the constant attitude of the young technical expert?

A. Labor and self-improvement should become a habit in the young technical expert. Studying must be a necessity, like sleeping.

Experimentation, seeking the causes of things so as to master them, must become an attitude. A Technical Brigade member must be eternally restless, one who is never satisfied with what has been done.

Q. What is required of the rural dweller in order to join the Agricultural Technical Brigades?

A. In agriculture, because of the low cultural level, inseminators and other skilled agricultural workers are admitted who do not have a technical level equivalent to that of the graduates of Technical Schools. We do demand, however, that they have at least a level above that of the sixth grade and a minimum of one year of technological studies, and that they pledge to the UJC that they will become genuine technical experts.

Q. How do the young technical experts raise their cultural level?

A. We are fighting to develop suitable ways for the young people not to abandon their home study; and for this reason we have sent to the Agricultural Brigades collections of books and technical pamphlets, the majority of which were published by the *Instituto Nacional de la Reforma Agraria* [National Institute for Agrarian Reform or INRA].

Q. Can the Youth Technical Brigades eventually become a great mass organization?

A. Within two or three years; and indeed today, in practice, they are already beginning to be a mass organization of young technical experts, guided, of course, by the UJC.

Q. Is it possible that this future mass organization will be made up of technical experts in general and not just young technical experts?

A. In the future, in our country, it will be necessary to have a great mass organization of all technical experts.

This organization will be the great army of the Technical Revolution, in which there will be different divisions. One of these will be that of the young technical experts. In others will be the innovators and inventors, and there will be a high-level corps of university professionals with several years of experience as well as a corps of amateur scientists.

This movement, which has already begun to be organized, will at a future date have to be placed under Party guidance.

Competition has taken place in honor of 21 October and 26 July. Last year we were able to verify that the Provinces of Camagüey and Havana, which made greater use of the competition principle and established incentives for the workers, made much greater progress in their work.

Q. What importance does this movement have in the development of our Revolution?

A. The Technical Brigades movement is, at the present moment, the embryo of the great army of the Technical Revolution, which within a few years will have tens of thousands of members. Many of those who are today skilled workers and middle-grade technical experts will by then be engineers and scientists.

Q. Has the importance of this movement been completely understood in all the Regional Districts of the country?

A. No. The work of the Technical Brigades throughout the country is very unequal.

There are Regional Districts and Provinces where the importance of this movement has been understood from the very first moment.

Others have gained this understanding more slowly, after a major struggle with the UJC leaders, and are now steadily improving their work. But there are still only a few middle-grade cadres of the UJC who control and serve with enthusiasm and constancy the activity of the Technical Brigades.

A part of the efforts of the National Commission of the Technical Brigades is directed toward bringing to the cadres the problems of science and modern technology.

Q. Have the technical Brigade members received good political support?

A. The work has been good, but we are not satisfied. It seems to us that this political work is not of the best, inasmuch as many Technical Brigades are not functioning as well as they should.

We do not conceive of political work as an abstract thing. If a UJC rank-and-file committee does not support its Technical Brigade as it should, there can be no talk of political work. Although there are cases where Brigades function on their own account, because there are young enthusiasts and even UJC and Party militants in their ranks. . . .

Q. Do all the cadres who work in the movement have sufficient technical qualifications?

A. No. In many cases they are skilled workers. This, in a Sectional District, is not serious, but in work at the provincial level there is an undoubted need for a cadre of high cultural level. To achieve this, a struggle is being waged against the belief of many comrades who think that a "small cadre" of a low level can orient technical experts and engineers.

In general, the organizations and the middle-grade cadres of the Technical Brigades movement will have to put much effort into their own development, because in many instances they are below the technical level of the masses whom they direct.

Selection 13.3: Education in Science and Technology

We are now facing another aspect of the impressive educational plan of our Fatherland, the Technical Revolution.

This phase which impels with increasing force our advance toward industrialization, agricultural mechanization and the extraction of natural riches, has various stages and numerous fronts. One of the stages stems from primary education itself, and one of its fronts is found in the Plan To Sponsor The Fundamental Work Camps for the development of our country. In this plan are found the Circles of Scientific and Technical Interest.

What Are the Circles of Interest

They are small groups of students (from 8 to 15 students), who meet periodically with a technical guide (who in many instances is a professor from an educational institution and in others is a technician from a State owned company). At these meetings they make experiments and carry out theoretical-practical exercises in some field of science or technology.

The department which gives them orientation at the national level is that of Psychological Education of the Ministry of Education. Its technicians explain that the objective of the Circles of Scientific and Technical Interest "is to awaken interest and develop aptitudes in our children and young people toward the branches of knowledge and work which play a basic role in the Technical Revolution."

They function from the fourth grade of Primary School (including in rural schools) to the Secondary Superior, which is to say at the Basic and Preuniversity levels.

How Are They Organized

The answer is simple: "The Circles may be composed of students from three grades or years, or of students from one grade or year only. In considering the selection of the students participating in a Circle, consideration must be given fundamentally to their interest and conduct. Those of low scholastic standing must not be included, since they need time to overcome their difficulties.

"At the beginning of the activities, the technical guide will plan their program, including interesting and understandable projects, in accordance with the age of the students. Maximum effort is made to bring theory to the practical level, keeping in mind that the Circle is not a class. The meetings are held during hours when school is not in session and although in many cases the Circles meet in schools, it is preferred that they meet in industries, on farms, in laboratories, etc."

They interchange experiences and ideas, and in addition meet other people, personally as well as by correspondence, etc.

What Is Required For Their Operation

A technical guide as we have said can be a person from the zone who voluntarily offers his time for this activity. He may also be and in many cases is a teacher from the institution.

Collaboration of the Council of the School or sponsors of the Circle who give materials or resources to help in the work.

A group of no more than 20 students.

A program of activities. . . .

This year stimulus is being given to three fundamental areas: agriculture and animal science, fishing and nautical, and teaching. Within agriculture and animal science there are Circles in insemination, cane cultivation, cattle genetics, biological control of the borer, soil analysis, strawberry cultivation, apiculture, aviculture, citrus cultivation, etc.

Other Circles include: Laboratory work, Biological Physics, Chemistry, Meteorology, Taxidermy, Telecommunications, Teaching Methods, Electricity, Carpentry, Mechanics, Mineralogy, etc.

Selection 13.4: Magazine Juventud Técnica

Have you read the magazine *Juventud Técnica* (Technical Youth)? No? Well, the magazine *Juventud Técnica* is a monthly publication which writes on technical problems for all levels but basically for middle-grade technical experts.

At the same time, however, the magazine is written with the clarity necessary so as to cooperate in [general] technical development, as in a sense Mecánica Popular (Popular Mechanics) did with its practical and constructive content.

In July of last year, the first issue was published, of 5,000 copies. Very few comrades on that issue, and by working in their spare time they succeeded in producing a feuilleton of only 24 pages, which was then offered as a magazine. But the title page on chromo paper and in four colors raised the question: what country is it from?

Between then and now the magazine has grown: the number of pages has doubled, the number of copies printed per issue has tripled, and the quality of the contents has also improved.

Juventud Técnica today has more than 118 technical editors (*redactores técnicos*) throughout Cuba and 18 collaborators abroad, principally in Japan, the Soviet Union, the German Democratic Republic, Poland, and Czechoslovakia.

Fifteen thousand copies were printed of the latest issue, which has 50 pages; but these were not enough to supply the members of the *Brigadas Técnicas Juveniles* (Youth Technical Brigades or BTJ), students of the technical sciences, students of the Technological Institutes and University Faculties, and scholarship-holders abroad. Price per copy is 20 centavos, and the magazine is on sale the 15th of each month.

To satisfy present needs, the magazine plans to expand its printing to 25,000 copies per issue, whereby it will emerge from the state of "semi-clandestinity" in which it now finds itself, and will attain general circulation by means of yearly subscriptions costing $2.40 [pesos] for 12 issues, or $3.00 if the magazine is enlarged to 64 pages. This will mark another step forward for the magazine toward the goal of reaching all those who have technical interests or who desire to broaden their technical knowledge. . . .

Selection 13.5: Cuban Industrialization Progress

Important initial steps in the industrialization policy of the Party and the government can now be detected at the end of 7½ years of revolution and less than 3 years during which we have been able to watch the concrete expression of the determination to earmark and channel most of the investments toward the intensive development and modernization of the agricultural and animal husbandry sector and related industries; this, in turn, should enable us to establish new branches of industry in a correct fashion and to expand and improve the old manufacturing centers.

The result of this tremendous effort, which was pushed under difficult circumstances and which was accompanied by a radical change in the ownership of the means of production as well as the seizure of political power by the working class, are expressed in frequent and substantial growth in various branches of industry in Cuba including among others the steel industry, the cement industry, soft fibers, textiles, shoes, nickel, petroleum refinery, mixed fertilizers, soap and detergents, paper, electric power, beverages, and tobacco.

In spite of the mistakes made during the first phase, we are now accomplishing another of the basic objectives of the heroes who attacked the Moncada Barracks.

Agriculture and animal husbandry are the basic points on which rest the plans for our industrialization, now that the fundamental means of production have been nationalized; in other words, 95% of the industrial output is now located in the state-owned sector.

The general industrialization program, both on a short-range and a long-range basis, is developing and progressing in accordance with the specific conditions in Cuba which, among other factors, feature the economic blockade, the dependence of foreign trade on a supply of fuel from abroad and a whole series of raw materials, semifinished products and machinery; in addition there is a shortage of skilled workers and we are subject to inflationary pressures which of course are due to the discrepancy between availability of money and supply of consumer goods.

Contrary to the announcements in the imperialist press, the emphasis on agriculture and especially cane sugar and animal husbandry, will not lead to the abandonment of other industrial projects; on the contrary, we are going to strengthen industry on the basis of the strongest possible support we can provide and we will do this against the background of the situation prevailing in Cuba; Cuba was an underdeveloped country which has just started out on the road to complete national independence; we have broken with the United States which exploited us for more than half a century and which dominated our basic economic activities.

Early during the revolution, when the system of capitalist production still prevailed and when all of the resources of the nation were not yet in the hands of the revolutionaries, our economic policy was determined by the traditional idea of combining the development process with an ever increasing degree of diversified industrialization.

But in a relatively short period of time, no more than 3 years, we abandoned the attempts of industrialization and we decided to develop domestic industry and achieve domestic growth by simply replacing imports and by planning a very intensive domestic factory development program on the basis of the traditional concept.

At the same time, the need for exportable merchandise and new relations with the socialist camp caused us to reconsider the position of the main source of national income: the sugar industry.

The decisive period came during 1964 and 1965. During these 24 months we achieved appreciable increases in the per-capita output and we emerged from the stagnation which we had during the immediate preceding 3 years.

A quick look at the basic production items here will give us an idea of the qualitative and quantitative change that has occurred.

The sugar industry is now in a position to accomplish the long-range plan aimed at turning out new historical record crops. The outlook for the next [sugar] harvest is highly promising especially now that we are overcoming the mostly natural difficulties which we encountered during the rather poor 1966 harvest.

In basic industries, such as nickel, foreign publications who are certainly not in favor of the revolution admit we have had "notable success." We can point to two outstanding victories with the commissioning of the sulfur-nickel and cobalt plant in Moa and the continued maintenance of production at Nicaro.

Although there are some items which are still rationed and

which we do not have enough of to meet the national demand, we have made rather important progress, for instance, in the textile and shoe industries.

The modernization and expansion of the metallurgical industry, which was pushed through at a cost of 60 million pesos, constitutes another extraordinary effort resulting in undeniable advances. The steel output during the 4-year period prior to the revolution totalled 120,000 tons whereas it went up to 285,000 tons in 1962–1965. During the coming years, the figure will go up to about 300,000 tons of steel per year, in terms of ingots.

As far as our petroleum refining industry is concerned, we were able to keep up production without interruption and we were even able to exceed the maximum estimates for the capacity of some of our refineries. These achievements are even more significant if we keep in mind the changes in the specifications and in the sources of supply of black gold, when we had to replace the United States sources with USSR sources as a result of the imperialist blockade. Now we have one petroleum tanker arriving in Cuban ports every 72 hours just about from the other end of the world. . . .

Parallel to this we have been able to establish major production complexes at a cost of tens of millions of pesos. Here are some of them: the glass combine, the Alquitex textile plant, the fishing port of Havana, the diesel engine plant in Cienfuegos, the machine-building plant in Santa Clara, the *Industria Nacional de Productos de Utensilios Domésticos* [National Industries for Domestic Products and Utensils or INPUD], the Kovo shoe factory. Plans for the coming years call for considerable increases in the processing of meat, milk, fish, fruit and canned foods, not only to meet our domestic needs but also to enable us to export these items.

Plans call for emphasis to be placed on the production of farm tools; the chemical industry is supposed to turn out technical products for agriculture and we also want to build some more cement factories.

In his remarks to the court which judged him in 1953, Fidel

stated that, as of that time, "industrialization can wait until doomsday." The revolution changed all that.

Selection 13.6: Development and Technology

. . . A country cannot develop if it does not apply technology. Everyone understands that we want to produce 10 million tons of sugar, besides a half million tons of rice, in addition to all the things we need so that the people can satisfy their needs completely in all areas, in order to achieve the rapid development to which our country aspires. This cannot be achieved with primitive techniques. With picks and hoes and teams of oxen it is absolutely impossible; everybody understands this.

There are more and more institutions, schools, and technological centers; there is a growing population. Today it is not a question of some eating and others not eating, but rather we must work for everyone, we must satisfy all the needs for clothing, shoes, housing and food in quality and quantity. Later, we will not only satisfy all needs for food but we will achieve the industrial development of the country. This must be paid for today and we need resources to pay for all this.

If our country doesn't master technology and apply it, it can't develop. Everyone knows this and knows that our present problem is a problem of labor force everywhere . . . people are needed here, people are needed there. We have to carry out all these activities now as best we can. That is why we are forced to make the giant effort we are making now, but in the future it will be a giant effort of a different type. It will be a much more intellectual task than a physical one. At present the work is basically physical; in the future the work will be much more intellectual than physical.

Our country cannot develop, nor can our people fulfill all their aspirations if they do not master technology. But the mastery of technology is not a job for illiterates, nor is it a job for semi-illiterates, nor in the future will it be something for people with a fifth- or sixth-grade education. Suffice it to say that within ten years a young man with a sixth-grade education will be a semi-illiterate: in twenty years in this country even a person with a junior high school education will be practically an illiterate. An illiterate with a junior high school education! Because when he finishes junior high school he will have the minimum general knowledge that every citizen should have, the minimum liberal education, the minimum general information. It will be at this point that his training for production will begin. Within 10, 15 or 20 years the person who has a junior high school education and has not studied any further will be an illiterate from the point of view of production.

Today all the industrial machines are very complex. All of them require specialized knowledge . . . in all fields. A teacher doesn't become a teacher merely by finishing junior high school, but by studying to be a teacher; a nurse does not become a nurse by merely finishing junior high school education; the same could be said of a mechanic. In the future it will be impossible to carry out any activity without specialized knowledge. We have to work toward that goal. The present generation has to make much greater efforts today and to fight a tremendous battle for development because we lack the equipment, the means and even the training. . . .

VI Chile: The "Revolution in Liberty" of 1964

CHILEAN MODERATE NATIONALISM

Eduardo Frei Montalva's inaugural address in November 1964 defined moderate nationalism (Reading One). Based upon Christian Democratic philosophy—with its core values of human dignity and welfare which Frei called *Humanismo Integral* (Integral Humanism)—his "Revolution in Liberty" was designed to encourage maximum spiritual, personal, and community development.[1] Unlike Castro's approach in Cuba, the Chilean "Revolution" was not an attempt to create a highly politicized and militant "new man" who scorns material incentives and private property.

Nor did Frei urge struggle against "enemies" both inside and outside the nation-state. With a conspicuous absence of "enemies" and a militant drive to imbue all citizens of the state with revolutionary values, Christian Democratic nationalism appears more secure, and less frustrated, than Cuban nationalism. Chile's national history, of course, *was* more stable than Cuba's to begin with—Chile having gained sovereign independence early in the nineteenth century, having waged successful war against Peru and Bolivia in the War of the Pacific (1879–83) to win access to valuable nitrate areas to the north, and having evolved a highly

1. See Gerardo Mello Mourão, *Frei y la revolución en América Latina,* translated from the Portuguese by Jorge Mellado (Santiago, Chile: Editorial del Pacífico, 1966), pp. 81–83.

developed "democratic" political system early in the game. Small wonder that its nationalism would exude moderacy, law, and democracy. Thus, unlike revolutions in Mexico and Cuba, the Chilean "Revolution" centered upon social and economic change within the *de facto* political system, rather than through armed struggle and destruction of the old structures.

Frei had specific goals in mind when he spoke of social and economic reforms (Reading Two). He sought to increase government investments in education and housing, while insuring better working conditions for what he called the "popular masses"—the workers, miners, peasants, and city people. To deal with labor problems, he enacted minimum wage and social welfare laws. In economic policy, he concentrated on accelerated economic growth based upon increased agricultural and industrial production. In addition, he sought higher revenues from expanded state ownership of the copper industry. A crucial question behind his policies was: how to provide social welfare while raising enough capital for industrial development.

Frei's programs would move the people of Chile, he believed, toward the style of national life envisioned by Christian Democracy. In this first book, *Chile desconocido* (Unknown Chile), he argued that education would establish a national consciousness and serve also as the base for building the technical competence required for sustained economic growth. He also thought that better housing, full employment, and improved working conditions were necessary to develop the standard of living which he regarded as essential to free human energy for the pursuit of humanist ideals.

The "Revolution in Liberty" was intended to unify Chile by means of interaction between the government and the people and through participation by the people in such groups as unions and co-operatives (Reading Three). Thus, Chilean citizens would become linked to national life through new channels of political power. Chilean integration assumed a pluralist nationalist community, like Mexico after 1945, where diverse schools of thought and belief might flourish.

FREI'S STRATEGY FOR CHANGE

A similarity between Eduardo Frei's peaceful reforms in Chile and violent revolutions in Mexico, Bolivia, and Cuba lies in the primary role played by the state in the strategy of change (Reading Four). This similarity stems from traditional Latin American culture in which state, church, and family are suffused with paternalism. Yet state power could not assume the large proportions in Chile that it acquired in Cuba. Chile's multiparty system contributed to a break-up of government power. Even so, Frei never wanted total state control of the political system. He encouraged private industry to contribute to economic development and promoted interest groups as a bulwark against the threat of a centralized state and totalitarian society. No doubt he had the Cuban centralized model very much in mind after he came to power in 1964.

Once in power Frei turned toward traditional instruments of raising governmental revenue—taxes, loans, credits, and trade—to augument his agrarian reforms, anti-inflation, and copper nationalization projects (Reading Five). Two major differences between his use of these policies and that of former administrations can be cited. First, the new government put teeth into enforcing income tax collection, thereby enabling it to raise tax revenues substantially. Secondly, rather than aligning Chile principally with one country as did Cuba with the Soviet Union, Frei expanded his diplomatic ties with socialist and nonsocialist countries, thus paving the way for improved trade relations and increased co-operation in the industrial, economic, and cultural spheres. Frei also toured Western Europe in 1965 and obtained several credit offers to finance equipment and machinery purchases and to establish new technical assistance agreements. Finally, he made strong attempts to improve Chile's diplomatic relations with other Latin American countries with the aim of establishing trade ties.

Frei's theme of expanded diplomatic ties with the world community as a basis for sound economic and political relations led him to support the concept of Latin American integration. Through numerous speeches and publications, Frei became the leading Latin American spokesman for integration, which was eventually discussed by the hemisphere presidents at Punta del Este, Uruguay, in April 1967.

Thus Frei developed a strategy of change with broad internationalist implications—as did Fidel Castro in Cuba—but with sharply contrasting ideological imperatives. Where Castro attacked the regimes clinging to the status quo, which included most governments in Latin America, Frei would encourage those same countries to expand the markets available to private and public producers through co-ordinated regional management programs and customs agreements. Regional integration would become the catalyst for economic development.

OBSTACLES TO REFORM

The "Revolution in Liberty" was plagued from the outset by serious difficulties. Chile's multiparty system, while admittedly democratic, bred legislative obstruction and fragmented party strength.[2] Whereas Mexico, Bolivia, and Cuba developed dominant single-party systems to strengthen ruling *caudillo* (political leader) power during their revolutions, the Chilean president resembled the executive of the French Third and Fourth Republics. He was weakened by a dominating legislature and caught in a web of competing interests and strong party opposition to his program. The Chilean Socialists and Communists had a Marxist model but disagreed over how to build a Marxist society. The Chilean Radicals were less ideological than the Socialists or Communists but also promised improved living conditions for Chile's lower classes. The Chilean Conservatives and Liberals wanted as little change as possible. Moreover, ideological splits

2. For more detailed description of Chilean politics, see Frederick M. Nunn, "Chile's Government in Perspective: Political Change or More of the Same," *Inter-American Economic Affairs,* Vol. 20, No. 4 (Spring 1967), pp. 73–89; Federico G. Gil, *The Political System of Chile* (Boston: Houghton Mifflin Company, 1966); and Ernst Halperin, *Nationalism and Communism in Chile* (Cambridge: M.I.T. Press, 1965).

within the Christian Democratic Party itself, examined more in detail in Part VII, compounded Frei's problems. These political difficulties account for the slow pace of policy implementation.[3]

Another basic problem is inflation and its impact on the politics of reform.[4] Continued inflation in Chile, while substantially reduced during the Christian Democratic years in office, was fed by leftist strikes and trade union demands for increased wages at a time of relatively low productivity. The inflation issue was a political wedge for leftist parties which could maintain that rising prices were the responsibility of the Christian Democrats. And extreme leftists within the Christian Democratic Party itself began to follow the path of traditional leftist parties by supporting strikes and trade union demands which only increased inflationary pressures. Labor strikes embarrassed the government. Although Frei was committed to wider worker participation in national life, he was also attempting to hold down the wage-pulled inflationary forces for the sake of long-term economic growth.

The decline in copper prices in early 1967 undermined Frei's plans to invest in reform. He had expected to use the funds received from increased copper production under favorable price conditions. This problem was added to increasing general discontent with his taxation drive. It was difficult to fulfill the promises of "Revolution in Liberty" (housing, health, education,

3. Frei was elected president in September 1964. The copper project was not approved until late 1966; agrarian reform did not become law until July 1967. In contrast, Castro came to power in January 1959 and established the Agrarian Reform Law in June 1969; the MNR of Bolivia decreed Agrarian Reform in August 1953 after taking power in April 1952. The latter two programs have been considerably more extensive than Chile's, as might be expected.

4. The rates of inflation for Chile were:
1964–38 per cent
1965–25 per cent
1966–17 per cent
1967–21.9 per cent
1968–26.9 per cent
1969–29.1 per cent

higher living standards) in the long run—which depended upon sustained industrialization through government investments from revenues generated by higher taxes and moderate wage policies —while at the same time meeting the short run demands for increased wages, lower taxes, social security, and housing. Thus Frei's reform theories contained, as the facts bore out, a central paradox.

Short run demands underminend the available financial resources for government-sponsored industrialization projects. But if the government cannot meet those demands—generated by the election campaign promises—it runs the risk of losing popular support and, eventually, presidential power. The failure of Frei's forced savings plan in January 1968 is a case in point. He was unable to withhold approximately one-fourth of mandatory annual wage increases for investment in bonds with an equal mandatory contribution from employers. The forced savings would have created a capital investment fund for new housing and industry, but he withdrew the bill from Congress once it appeared that the Senate would defeat it.

Other difficulties can be added to the list. Like all Latin American countries, Chile faces a high birth rate of approximately 2.5 per cent per year. Although this figure is lower than that in other countries—3.8 per cent in Costa Rica, 3.4 per cent in Venezuela, 3.3 per cent in Guatemala, and 3.0 per cent in Brazil —it exacerbates the government's difficulties, particularly when it reduces Chile's expansion of gross national product per capita to 1.4 per cent.[5] Another population problem is suggested by a mere 2 per cent growth in agricultural production annually be-

5. These figures suggest that the gross national product must be far beyond what might be considered satisfactory, that is, 5 per cent annually, if it is to raise expansion of the gross national product per capita to an acceptable level, where the increased national product is not canceled out by the burgeoning population pressures. It should be said, however, that Chile has embarked upon a healthy family planning program under the Christian Democratic government. See Thomas G. Sanders, "Family Planning in Chile," Parts I and II, *American University Field Staff Reports,* West Coast South America Series, Vol. XIV, Nos. 4 and 5 (December 1967) for further discussion of these points.

tween 1939 and 1965. That is, the increase in agricultural production is less than population growth, which creates a deficit to be met through food imports.

It is possible that the most telling blow to Frei and the Christian Democrat fortunes, although its full impact is not clear, was the massive drought which hit virtually every part of Chile in late 1967 and continued through 1968. Frei tried to boost agricultural production, and thus cut back on food imports caused by the drought, regarded by some as the worst in Chilean history. Acres upon acres of parched fields lay idle even in generally fertile regions and Chileans were still hoping for an end to drought conditions in 1969. Not only were farm production totals down sharply in estimates for 1968, but copper production fell off because hydroelectric power to fuel the copper mines and refineries was in short supply of dried-up rivers.[6]

Voter support for the Christian Democratic Party began to decline once it was in power. The Christian Democrats received 36.5 per cent of the popular vote in the April 1967 Municipal elections, compared to their earlier 42.3 per cent in the 1965 Congressional elections. Then, in the March 1969 Congressional elections, they declined even more to 30 per cent, while a high 29.5 per cent of Chile's three million voters either abstained or cast blank votes—an indication of middle-class discontent with inflation and high taxes during the Christian Democratic tenure of office. Equally significant in the March 1969 Congressional elections were the slight increases in support for the *Partido Comunista Chileno* (Chilean Communist Party or PCC) from 15 per cent in April 1967 to 15.7 per cent in March 1969, and a strong increase for the National Party. A relatively new amalgam of liberals and conservatives (right wing), the National Party emerged as the second strongest party in the election with 20 per cent of the vote. This result gave a sharp boost to the 1970

6. Chile's plight is not dissimilar to that faced by other nations—including Fidel Castro's Cuba which saw its hopes in sugar production cut back in 1968 as a result of the drought. The full impact of such natural disasters on reform efforts and revolutions in process is not clear. It opens up another field for investigation.

presidential candidacy of former President Jorge Allesandri, who is seventy-two years old.[7]

The Chilean "Revolution in Liberty" is not alone in its problems. Latin America's "Revolutions" also face difficulties. Cuba is plagued with such obstacles as continued illiteracy, cutbacks in Soviet oil shipments, sugar underproduction, low technical competence, juvenile delinquency, and periodic counter-revolutionary activities. Mexico faces the task of balancing between government and private sector initiative for continued economic development. It is running out of land to redistribute as part of the agrarian reform and faces student discontent with the government. Bolivia had enormous difficulty resolving its intra-party conflict during the 1952–64 MNR years. Víctor Paz Estenssoro (1908–) and the MNR fell from power in November 1964.

7. Comparative percentages of the popular vote from April 1967 and March 1969 are as follows:

April 1967	*Per cent*	*March 1969*	*Per cent*
PDC	36.5	PDC	30.0
Nat'l Party	14.6	Nat'l Party	20.0
PCC	15.0	PCC	15.7
Radicals	16.5	Radicals	12.9
Socialists	14.2	Socialists (two factions)	14.4

READING 1 *Moderate Nationalism Outlined*

Introductory Note

As the Bolivian Revolution under the government of the Movimiento Nacional Revolucionario *ended in November 1964, the Chilean experiment in moderate nationalism began. Eduardo Frei's inaugural (Selection 1.1) spelled out several dimensions of Christian Democratic approaches to change in foreign and domestic policy, emphasizing expanded diplomatic relations, legalism, and change within the existing political system. It was conspicuously devoid of militancy, appeals to xenophobic supernationalist sentiments, or a rigid ideological stance—so characteristic of Fidel Castro's speeches during the 1960s. Frei has long expressed a firm belief in democracy, illustrated by Selection 1.2.*

SELECTION 1.1: FREI'S INAUGURAL ADDRESS

People of Chile: On this solemn day on which I assume office, freely elected in an exemplary manner, I greet all the men and women of our nation and also the honorable representatives of many nations, whose presence earns our gratitude and emphasizes the magnitude of the commitment we have contracted with Chile and America.

I greet the brother peoples of Latin America, with whom we do not want to live in the old way, which has not really expressed the demands for integration, for real cooperation and unity, which

Selection 1.1: Inaugural address by Eduardo Frei, Santiago Domestic Radio Broadcast, November 4, 1964.

Selection 1.2: Translated from Eduardo Frei, *Pensamiento y Acción* (Santiago, Chile: 1958), pp. 70–71.

are the inescapable condition for reaching the advanced frontiers of creative thought, scientific effort, and technical demands we need to attain in order to expand our economy, provide justice, and have a respected and vigorous voice in the world community.

I greet our friends, the people of the United States, part of our great America, with whom we have a real association based on a worthy equality which does not originate in an imbalance of power and wealth but in a real alliance that permits our progress in freedom, as a man [John F. Kennedy] who has died, but whose message is still alive and present, pointed out.

I greet the peoples of old Europe, whose presence, image, and ideas have nourished our spirit and have educated us in their long and glorious history, and who now have taught us the miracle of their prodigious recovery and of their growing integration through overcoming age-old antagonisms. Today they are beginning to discover Latin America and to realize what a grave and outright error it would be for them and for the world not to have an attitude of solidarity with and an open door to peoples so closely linked with the very essence of their civilization.

I greet the peoples of the Afro-Asian world, who are undergoing a great revolution for the conquest of political and economic independence and who are struggling for just international relations, without which peace and freedom would only have a precarious existence.

I also greet the so-called socialist world, whose dramatic human adventure we cannot disregard. Other peoples of the Western world may disregard it, but it would be blindness on our part to do so despite the deep ideological differences separating us, since the fact of their existence in the world community cannot be erased and peace cannot be attained in the world without coexistence with them. . . .

. . . The people of Chile faced a historical crossroads, and after a long process of free discussion, of conscious reflection, they have chosen a path which calls for carrying out profound changes and for swift advances in the social and economic fields with a government which respects the freedom and dignity of human beings. You, the people of Chile, did not vote for a man alone. You gave wide, vigorous, and unquestionable support for a direction and a program, for a philosophy which inspires the Christian Democratic Movement for a national and popular position which received the generous backing of other political forces and of large independent sectors.

This election has heralded a new era in national life. This is what I represent. None of the words I said during the election will be forgotten. No one has the right to demand of me more than what I said but no one has the right to ask me to go back a single stop on what I said and what the people voted for. I represent a generation with a new orientation. I am here to bring education to all Chilean children and give them every opportunity, in the certainty that a nation that conquers ignorance will inevitably conquer misery and servitude.

I am here so that in an ever-increasing manner, the peasants will be owners of the land and property will not be concentrated in a few hands, so that those who work in the fields will have a just wage and income so that the laws of the nation will be strictly obeyed. I am here so that all Chilean families will live in their own house in a decent community, where their children can live in dignity and happiness. I am here to promote economic development and free initiative so we may increase the production of foodstuffs, expand our industries, and exploit our mineral resources for the benefit of Chile.

I am here to stop inflation, to protect the value of the currency, to provide steady employment and give youth an opportunity. I am here to break the rigidity of a social order which no longer responds to the demands of the times, and thereby open progressive access for the people to culture, to responsibility to the nation, and to a real participation in the wealth and the advantages which mark contemporary affluent societies. Without such participation by the people, basic principles of justice are violated and it becomes impossible to have an authentic democracy where the initiative and intelligence of thousands of men and women can be put to effective use.

I am here to awaken the old spirit of Chileans; to see that Chile does not close itself off behind a wall of customs privileges;

to see that Chile competes in the world; to see that the ships under our flag play the oceans as before; to see that our work and our technology are presented in world markets and thereby continue to give employment and foster general prosperity.

I am here to defeat the red tape and centralism which are burying us.

I represent those who want to carry out this profound revolution with freedom and within the law . . . where we will never permit any type of discrimination or persecution, whether ideological, religious, racial, or political.

I am here to exercise, within the law, the authority of the state, and I make it clear that I will not permit anyone to force it to yield or weaken it.

There is no easy road to building anything. The nation has overwhelming financial commitments abroad. The internal resources available to us do not cover our own expenses. There is misery and unemployment. I have never concealed the hard and heavy burden I was going to receive, but I am not here to cry over spilled milk.

The greatest weakness of the peoples of this hemisphere has been the pressure of long-suffered injustice and misery, of postponed ambitions and resentment; and a great deal of impatience, which sterilized and often made the work of rulers who represent the desires for renovation and justice impossible. It has often occurred that those who bowed their heads either to a dictator or the powerful have become insolent and intolerant enemies of governments which, freely elected by the people, carry forward the most profound and sincere reforms. . . .

I know that I cannot in a day or a month or a year stop a train going at a speed built up through decades. The problem has very deep roots. I cannot in a year change . . . our economy. But I also know that if, from the very first day, the people see their path open and see the unbreakable will of their president, no one can break this common bond established between my government and the people who elected me. This is why I have the right and the duty to ask the real popular masses—the workers, the miners, the peasants, the city people—to join me now.

I have unyielding faith in Chile's future. The nation has greater resources than money; it has the goodwill of all the people, many technicians and professions; businessmen who once shut themselves off in silence but are now willing to cooperate loyally. Above all, we have a generous people with a wonderful sense of balance. What matter the errors we may commit, the crises we may face? They are inevitable in human affairs. What is important is the will to serve justice and better the living conditions of the Chilean poor.

Today we embark on a great crusade which no one has the right to stop and which no one will be able to stop. Everything is working for us—our resources and the caliber of our citizens. What is taking place in the world opens marvelous opportunities. With great faith in my fatherland, I want on this day to greet every man, every woman, every family at home, because, as I said, I am the president of all Chileans without exception. I humbly ask God to protect Chile and help me fulfill my duties and keep me firm and resolute in the path set by the people and by me.

Selection 1.2: On Democracy and Independence

Maritain said in one of his most profound observations: "Democracy is the only way to achieve a moral rationalization of political life. Democracy is a national organization of fundamental liberties under the law. Democracies carry terrestrial hopes in a fragile boat, carrying also the biological hope of humanity."

A weak boat, but in it goes the only human experiment in founding society in the free consent and in the accord of men always free.

The road is difficult. Across it fall unjust economic patterns; miseries that cause fear; and also hate, egoism, ambition, because we all know that the human fraternity requires a dose of Christianity that does not exist. But are we going to renounce it all and flee in desperation because nothing surrenders to the yoke of the master?

Democracy will not be saved by those who praising it seek to stratify it, but much less by those who see in it only its defects and not its infinite possibilities.

Our job is to complete it, to enrich it, in order to defend it. We will serve it in the measure that we infuse it with dynamism; we perfect the representation of the people and we make it for the people so that the resources, the riches, the goods of the nation are not only the patrimony but also the real and concrete possession of each one of those who inhabit Chile. Then the Chilean will not have to be a man fearing the night, but a citizen capable of feeling for his neighbor and understanding that he is part of a great family. . . .

READING 2 *Social and Economic Development in Chile*

Introductory Note

Eduardo Frei, like Lázaro Cárdenas in Mexico and Fidel Castro in Cuba before him, emphasized work, discipline, and austerity as cardinal virtues in the total development process—thus moving toward modern attitudes distinct from traditional Hispano-Catholicism. His approach was far less militant than his predecessors'. He did not, for example, emphasize an "external enemy" as did Castro.[1]

1. On the external enemy theme, see Richard R. Fagen, "The Cuban Revolution: Enemies and Friends," in *Enemies in Politics,* by David J. Finlay, Ole R. Holsti, and Fagen (Chicago: Rand McNally & Company, 1967), pp. 184–231. Although the Chilean government has solid ties with the United States, it did oppose a number of Washington's hemisphere policies in 1965, including military intervention in the Dominican Republic without prior consultation with the Organization of American States, proposals to set up an Inter-American Police Force, Pentagon involvement in Project Camelot, and the United States House of Representatives' approval of the concept that it was right for Washington to carry out unilateral intervention in any Latin American nation subverted by Communism. Frei always made clear that his opposition was due to his desire for national independence, not to a desire for friction with Washington.

Selection 2.1: Speech by Eduardo Frei, report to the nation on the opening of Congress, Santiago Domestic Radio Broadcast, May 21, 1966.

Selection 2.2: Speech by Eduardo Frei, report to the nation on the opening of Congress, Santiago Domestic Radio Broadcast, May 21, 1965.

Selection 2.1: Development Goals

First I will speak of social development, beginning with education. The extraordinary elementary school program has resulted in an increase of 174,168 student registrations during 1965, of which 155,000 were in public education. The increased school registration made necessary the appointment of 5,000 new elementary school teachers, and an additional 2,000 will be appointed this year.

This growth also affected secondary education, which increased by 30 percent, and professional education, which increased by 12 percent. The national scholarship program granted 17,500 scholarships during the year. A total of 800,000 breakfasts and 400,000 lunches have been served daily to public school students during the last few months. Some 3,500 new schoolrooms were built in the country, giving us a total of 6,038 today.

As a result of the education reform program during 1965 and 1966, one out of every four Chileans is now registered in some educational activity, since statistics indicate that total school enrollment exceeds 2 million students in 1966.

The second part of the social development program is the housing plan. In my message last year, I expressed the desire that the construction of 46,000 new housing units be started during the year. In 1965, a total of 52,500 new housing units were under construction between the public and private sector. The government started building 36,846 new housing units, while the private sector started 15,600, a considerable increase over the previous year. The associations controlled by the Central Savings and Loan Fund granted 6,181 loans amounting to 145 million escudos for financing 8,288 housing units.

Congress enacted several social welfare laws, among them the agriculture, mining, and industrial minimum wage laws and those on labor union freedom, which permitted the signing of important labor bargaining contracts. The bill providing for compulsory social security for workers, which will replace an article of the labor code, is currently before Congress.

The government also took action to adjust wages in line with the cost of living. Social security pensions were also raised 51 percent. We are absolutely certain that the wage policy has helped the workers, as wages were raised realistically, with the aim of countering inflation and raising the national income.

The Social Welfare and Labor Ministry has drafted a general social security bill, whose main object is to relieve the situation of those not obtaining sufficient benefits and to provide adequate social welfare. Our main task is to do away with poverty, and this calls for tremendous sacrifices. I am aware that there may be much opposition to the bill, but I am confident that the majority will support it, because the reforms envisioned by it are necessary.

The administration has given much attention to developing farming and agriculture, and through arduous efforts, the production pace of the past two years was maintained. Demographic growth has increased the demand for foodstuffs, however, and this will compel the government to increase imports, entailing an outlay of foreign exchange paralleling the funds spent last year.

We have adopted an agrarian policy, whose salient features I will point out. Agriculture and livestock prices had dropped to such a level that it was necessary to raise wholesale prices. The increase in the consumption of milk in Chile went hand in hand with a drop in production. Last year we imported 100 million dollars worth of dairy products. Our price control policy is working to obtain a better price for the producer.

In many cases, the peasants of Chile live in infinitely worse conditions than urban dwellers of low-income groups. The greatest problem in this respect is that of land distribution. That is why I sent the agrarian reform bill to Congress. The purpose of agrarian reform is not to deny the right to property, but exactly the opposite. The agrarian reform is aimed at a more rigorous recognition of the right to own land by means of a fairer distribution of that land.

That is why my government has embarked on this reform, and the least it can ask is support for its program. Costly as the reform may be, it cannot be deferred. Those who do not want to carry out agrarian reform by democratic means may see it imposed tomorrow by violence and disorder. I ask for the cooperation of farmers and peasants. They must understand that no one is trying to trick them.

Without waiting for the agrarian reform bill to be passed, my government, supported by existing legislation, has appropriated 642,000 hectares of land, which are being cultivated by 3,850 families. It should be noted that between 1929 and the beginning of my administration, only 5,454 families had been given land, and most of them were not peasants.

One of my administration's tasks has been to provide the peasants with the benefits of education and social welfare enjoyed by the rest of the population.

In regard to the situation in the copper mines, the successive increase in the price of copper has led to the highest producers' price known in the country's history. This means an extraordinary source of revenue for the country. It is to be expected that today's prices will reduce tomorrow's costs.

Our iron ore production, which in 1963 totaled 7 million tons signifying a revenue of 55 million dollars, rose to 9 million tons that sold for 71 million dollars in 1964, and to 11 million tons worth 75 million dollars in 1965.

Everyone knows the conditions under which I took over the government. In the preceding 15 months, inflation had risen by 47 percent; the growth index had fallen off 2.4 percent annually; and with the 2.7 percent population increase, per capita income had dropped. Naturally, the lowest income groups were the hardest hit.

During the first seven months of my term, an opposition majority in Congress held up our efforts. And to this was added the serious, costly catastrophes of the earthquake and the nationwide storms. Then came the copper strike, which caused a loss of 24 million dollars' revenue to the country, and a treasury loss of 37 million dollars, or 147 million *escudos* [the Chilean unit of currency] in round figures.

Things improved thereafter, however, and if nothing extraordinary occurs, we will reach this year the targets that I had outlined. Thus we will have won the second stage in the battle for effecting the changes needed to fulfill our program.

In regard to economic development, it had been estimated that the national growth index for 1966 would be from 2.2 to 2.4 percent. However, the government's program envisaged a national product increase of five percent, and the National Industrial Development Association reports that industrial growth has increased by nine percent . . .

In regard to employment, many workers have been laid off in various points of the country for various reasons. Nonetheless, these problems are being duly studied.

Even before taking office I advocated a redistribution of income—a policy of social justice. But I realistically served notice that it would be undertaken in stages. I was aware that this would cause a reaction from those whose income would drop and those who would be affected one way or another by the measures . . .

Selection 2.2: The Need for Discipline and Work

I am firmly convinced that the Christian Democratic movement is a positive factor in the country's progress. I speak not so much as a Christian Democrat but as President. The results of September 4 were not an accident. The people voted for a program of action. I reiterate that I will carry this program forward. The people voted for an acceleration of economic growth, employment, the checking of inflation, agrarian reform, and our housing projects. The people voted for better education and reform of the administrative system.

The people voted for the strengthening of our sovereignty and for trade with the rest of the countries in the world. In short, the people voted for a program to solve the Chilean crisis. This program will be carried out in liberty. This program is evidence of the fact that we live in a society in which freedom of expression must be respected. Such is not the case under single-party government systems.

Many demagogues promote the myth that social changes can be made overnight. They promote the idea of social changes in order to destroy freedom. However, no country has developed economically without sacrifice. I do not offer immediate prosperity. I ask for sacrifice for a future prosperity. As an example, I ask my fellow citizens to think about the steps we must take to solve the economic crisis. All the capitalist countries developed by restricting consumption. All the socialist countries are developing by sacrificing consumption. Chile will not develop without savings, and the only way to obtain savings is to restrict the consumption of those who enjoy a higher standard of living.

The capitalist countries in the nineteenth century developed by decreasing the people's consumption. This is against our moral principles. . . . We believe that everyone should save, but without a lowering of the lowest level of consumption. We cannot develop economically without discipline and hard work. The people must understand the seriousness of the economic situation. . . .

READING 3 *National Integration*

Introductory Note

The following selections illustrate the importance of national integration in Chilean Christian Democracy. This goal meant common effort between the government and the people, closer contacts between local communities and state organizations, and expanded interest articulation into the decision-making process.

National integration is a natural goal of Christian Democracy. This ideology is based upon the papal encyclicals of Leo XIII (Rerum Novarum, 1891) and Pius XI (Quadragesimo Anno, 1931) and the writings of Jacques Maritain. These works stress individual dignity, social welfare, and worker participation in national life. Christian Democrats urge attainment of these goals through enlightened state intervention in the private sector to break up disproportionate concentrations of economic wealth and to redistribute national income on a "socially just" basis.

SELECTION 3.1: CHRISTIAN DEMOCRACY AND INTEGRATION

The second national convention of the *Partido Demócrata Cristiano* (Christian Democratic Party or PDC), at the close of its deliberations resolves:

Selection 3.1: Declaration of the second national convention of the *Partido Demócrata Cristiano,* Santiago Domestic Radio Broadcast, August 29, 1966.

Selection 3.2: Speech by Eduardo Frei at Quinta Vergara, Viña del Mar, Santiago Domestic Radio Broadcast, September 4, 1966.

1. To call upon all Chileans to rally behind the historic endeavor of a revolution amid liberty, which is aimed at effecting the political, social, and economic transformations that the Chileans chose on electing the President of the Republic;

2. To reiterate its firm party unity and its responsibility for the administration's success insofar as it expresses the people's will and the party's program;

3. To proclaim as its immediate objective the acceleration of economic development and social changes, fully realizing its responsibility for giving the Chileans stable employment, education, housing, health, and land by means of the agrarian reform;

4. To reiterate its determination to promote popular organization as a way of giving the people full training and responsible participation in the country's life;

5. To reiterate its stand of working toward the integration of Latin America as a basic goal for our people's liberation.

6. To place the party at the service of the Chilean people, as the ideal instrument for political, economic, and cultural liberation, while the party will be zealously vigilant to preserve freedom in our national life.

7. To extend fraternal greetings to the Christian Democratic parties throughout the world, particularly those in Latin America, with which it feels united in the struggle for liberty, justice, and peace. . . .

Selection 3.2: The State and National Integration

Dear friends: We are gathered here today to commemorate the anniversary of Operation Emergency in Valparaíso. Today we are giving a resume of what has been accomplished up to now and what we shall do to continue this task.

I would like to review this work. In Valparaíso and Viña del Mar 1,882 meters of sewer lines, 275 kilometers of roads and 17 kilometers of streets have been built. Drinking water has been power. Some 37,500 persons have worked as volunteers, and this effort has helped 160,000 persons.

To continue this task begun in Valparaíso, the government requested additional funds in the budget. When the Senate refused to grant those funds, it was your effort—the effort of the people of that city—that made the majority in Congress change its mind, making it possible for the government to insist on obtaining such funds.

In other provinces of the country, 200 kilometers of roads were completed, 27 kilometers of streets were made usable; 250 kilometers of street curbing were built, and over 9 kilometers of cattle roads were constructed. Sewers have been installed in 27 towns, drinking water plants in 61 cities, and electric power stations in 52. New drainage canals were built which have spared the people from flood disasters for the first time in history. This was possible not because of the government's action, but because of the voluntary work of almost half a million people. This effort by an organized community was mentioned in my message to Congress.

However, the figures do not always show the many human problems faced in implementing the projects. For instance, they do not show how a group of workers, seeing the determination of the people to accomplish a task, called off a strike and joined in the work.

This is the result of a common effort. Many projects that were impossible to execute through channels were realized through the effort of an organized community, free of political or religious discrimination, because nobody asked about these things; they only went to work to improve their own living conditions.

There is a third experience envisaged in this operation: the coordination of the state's responsibilities through obviating bureaucratic barriers and by bringing about—with goodwill and common sense—closer contacts through representatives between the community and the state and its organizations so that the people may participate in all the decisions of the government.

The meeting between the people and its leaders is not held

every six years anymore; now, those meetings are held more regularly. Today, for instance, the people have met with their government.

I have repeatedly said that it is impossible for the government to solve all the problems of the people in a short time. With us today is the intendant of Santiago, one of my useful aides. Also with us is Juan Francisco Rivera, governor of Pedro Aguirre Cerda Department, which has almost one million inhabitants and is faced with very serious problems. Yesterday [September 3, 1966], however, we toured almost 50 kilometers and saw the people, the 2,200 new houses, the 800 multi-story buildings; and all this surrounded by health centers, roads, and other facilities.

There are persons who still think the people are fools and who still try to exploit them. I repeat again and again: I am head of a family and have a salary. I cannot give my family more than I earn. My children constantly want more. If the family works more, it will be able to have more. If the children help their father, they will then increase the family's earnings and the family will have more. That is what we need, the cooperation of all of you. That is what a country needs in order to give more than what it alone can offer: the cooperation of her children.

You have given the country a lesson in this respect. You have shown that offering your potential to the government is the only way it can solve the problems that are otherwise impossible to overcome. We must find new ways aside from regular channels.

Public works have continued along with the work of the ministries, but you have contributed to this with your effort. Because of this, I am confident that we are organizing the people, and because of this I have introduced in Congress a bill calling for setting up the official instruments to create what is known as popular promotion. I am sure that with the people's help we shall make this law work well.

Almost two years ago, on November 4, 1964, the glorious and historic unity of the people opened the way to the government—not just to me—for this great revolution in liberty. I wish to report to you at this time that today, after two years of experience and after having seen the problems at close range, I feel better qualified to make good my promise as a candidate to solve the problems of Chile, to help the needy, and to bring about the great progress to which this country is entitled.

Nothing of what we said has lost its effect. More so, I would say that in the face of the inevitable critics, I did not think we would be able to work so effectively in solving the basic problems of Chile. Surely, dear friends, many of the hundreds of kilometers of roads we have built will not be seen by those who make a habit of criticizing, because they do not care to visit them.

In this country, 4 million people are living well while the other 4 million live in proletarian sub-standard circumstances. . . .

Perhaps some people do not see the revolution because no spectacular acts are performed, but I have seen here the widespread benefits provided for men, women, and children, with hundreds of new schools and teachers. And this means changing Chile without an execution wall. . . .

. . . We have seen how a rightist paper one day complains that the government does not set prices, and later, when the government establishes them, they score the government for its actions. Naturally, liberty has a price. We must pay the price of seeing things criticized when they are done, but we need laws in order to act.

We must also pay the price of being silent when the self-same ones who seek to bind the government's hands for enacting regulatory laws deny it special legislative powers in Congress. They seek to tie the government's hands and then ask why something cannot be done. The people should be aware of this fact: a price must be paid for liberty. . . .

READING 4 *The Expanded Role of the State*

Introductory Note

The expanded role of the Chilean state after 1964, so natural a phenomenon in Latin American political cultures and to be expected in violent and nonviolent forms of change, is clear in the following speech of Eduardo Frei. Within this expanded role of the state, Frei still believes in the importance of trade unions.

SELECTION 4.1: EXPANDED STATE ROLE

. . . The government is making great economic efforts to improve social life. The effort is so great that 75 percent of all investments in the country are now made by the government. This is a limit that cannot be exceeded and can hardly be maintained. The situation that we face is very clear: to decrease current expenditures would amount to reducing salaries, appropriations to universities, public health, and others. Is there anyone who believes that this is possible? A reduction of investments would result in unemployment and protests. Therefore, we cannot reduce either current .expenditures or investments. However, at the same time we must spend the whole day resisting all kinds

Selection 4.1: Speech by Eduardo Frei, report to the nation on the opening of Congress, Santiago Domestic Radio Broadcast, May 21, 1966.
Selection 4.2: Translated from Eduardo Frei, *Pensamiento y Acción* (Santiago, Chile: 1958), p. 82.

of pressure to increase them. And pressures have one serious aspect: they always have a clear basis of reasoning.

Increasing expenditures under these conditions would cause the crumbling of our program and uncontrolled inflation. We have arrived at the limit of the possibilities as far as government expenditures are concerned. These cannot be increased and no pressure can change this. This is the hardest task of a ruler, but he cannot launch the country into an inflationary race which would give an appearance of prosperity that would end in ruin and failure.

Many sectors and groups are daily demanding that the government spend more money, but these are the same who would object to increases in taxes. The problem of obtaining new income is practically insoluble. I believe that it would be very difficult to raise taxes, and it is also impossible to obtain new loans.

Close to 25 percent of the country's investments or over 30 percent of foreign currency available for imports originate in foreign loans. That is a limit which cannot be surpassed, and which it is our obligation to reduce if we want to be a truly sovereign country. We have only one road left: to speed up our economic development by increasing savings. We have to have the high income groups place a large portion of their income in savings. But all sectors must contribute in whatever small proportion or the country cannot have true economic development.

In Chile the state controls the basic resources and possesses the mechanisms permitting it to watch over the common good of the people, preventing any economic group from controlling national life. . . . The state directs and guides the people's economic life. . . .

Private industry must be encouraged and given security for its legitimate action—action which creates new sources of employment. That sector does not represent a danger, but rather something good, since no group can threaten the state's high-level control. Thus the private sector should act and assume its proper role. On our part, we know the factors which small, medium-size, and large private sectors worry about, and when their grievances are just, they should be examined and settled.

In the final instance, the only way to better the Chileans' life is by increasing production and productivity, and I am aware of my responsibility in this respect. Perhaps some measures might dismay those who seek to launch new enterprises, build new factories, expand production, or bring in capital and technicians. But such persons should rest assured that they can count on firm support from the government, as the country needs men who can augment employment opportunities and develop new wealth for the nation's benefit. The whole world is following such a course, and we could not act differently.

We are guided by an economic humanism which brings the community's interests into line with free, cooperative efforts. Classic economic individualism is now a historical study for us. We are not going to establish a totalitarian . . . economy. The nations of the world are seeking a way of expressing themselves in the new society in accordance with their own historical and geographical characteristics and the technological revolution.

At this moment, Chile faces the historic, and I would say international, imperative of setting the foundations for a new society in which the state is the directing factor. And, in the key sector of the economy, property is the one where the vigorous assertion of personal initiative will be fundamental. A society in which the community's interests are held predominant does not rule out the rights of the individual or his creative capacity.

But we must cite basic factors to comprehend the image of this new society for which we are struggling: work and the participation of the people. In Chile, as in the rest of Latin America, we have the problem of all underdeveloped countries—insufficient participation by the people. . . . Most Chileans are disorganized and therefore unprotected. Those who lack economic power also lack political power, as is evident in the unions, cooperatives, and other groups. . . .

I must refer to two of the country's social powers. One power is the Chilean women. Women now participate in all national activities, including the government, and they are performing admirably. Chilean youth is the other power. We have created a youth advisory office at the presidential level to attend to their problems. Youths are being given due importance over and above education and sports. We are proud of their school buildings and other endeavors. Only by using such forces can we create a society in which the state works for the common good and controls the basic elements of economic power.

Vigorous private enterprise and an organized people fully sharing in the country's cultural, economic, social, and political life will create a genuine system of counterweights over and against a centralizing state or the monopoly of a private group. We are not moving toward a totalitarian society, but toward a humanism free from sectarianism.

The people support me because they know I am attentive to their needs. This is so true that, despite resistance from certain strongly-formed, albeit minority groups, we have been confronted by the broad support of the majority, which thus far has been disorganized in the face of organized interests. . . .

Selection 4.2: On Work and the Condition of Man in Political and Economic Life

. . . It is evident that work through its organizations is acquiring an increasingly greater importance in the conduct of the life of nations [a reference to the key role of trade unions]. The greatest consciousness and learning in the masses makes impossible that which deals with forced work as a commodity. Work is known as the fundamental element in the production of all goods. Its power is well-known and no one could rationally admit to being a passive and inert subject in the economic process in which he participates.

The common man knows that as a citizen he is equal to all other men, and that through suffrage he helps create the Public Power and helps to supervise the direction and orientation of the State; but he finds himself in the curious contradiction of one who, accepting political and theoretical equality, does not experience it in the social-economic sphere and in the company where he works for eight hours of each day, and to which he gives his capabilities and his time and his future; although he and his family live from this, he is only an instrument without a voice, without responsibility, without any say in his own fate. He is responsible to the extent that on his success or failure depends not only the value of a share on the stock market, but also his security, his food, his home; yet he has no voice in his conduct, while he sees that others who do not live with, nor depend upon, nor know him, direct and arrange his destiny. . . . [*After this, Frei argues strongly for unions to play a key role in national political and economic life, due to the powerlessness of single individuals.*]

READING 5 Taxes, Loans, Credit, and Trade

Introductory Note

Eduardo Frei set out immediately after 1964 to strengthen the tax collection system internally and to solidify Chile's diplomatic and trade ties externally.[1] *The following selection, an excerpt from Frei's May 21, 1966 report to the nation, outlines these approaches to development.*

I should mention the tax policy. While in 1965 there was a general 24-percent-tax increase over the previous year, Chileans in the highest income brackets are paying 40 percent more direct taxes, while indirect taxes have been raised by 19 percent. To complete the tax picture, it should be noted that 48,000 of the 86,000 persons who paid income taxes had not paid them before. What is more important is the fact that 12,000 of the 166,000 persons subject to pay the complementary tax paid 62 percent of the tax revenue, which indicates the gains made and the net tax yields that are obtained. Moreover, of the 86,000 persons

1. Frei opened diplomatic channels with Moscow after a nineteen-year lapse. On March 12, 1967, Máximo Pacheco, Chilean ambassador to the Soviet Union, said that the Soviet government considered Frei's administration forthright, progressive, and independent. Santiago Domestic Radio Broadcast, March 15, 1967.

Speech by Eduardo Frei, report to the nation on the opening of Congress, Santiago Domestic Radio Broadcast, May 21, 1966.

subject to the minimum income tax law, only 14,000 were white-collar employees, while only 396 were workers.

But for the government to fulfill its objectives, we need the cooperation of the people and the Congress. The results of the new tax measures, the upturn of the copper market, and the regular flow of foreign credits has made it possible to raise fiscal expenditures from 3.7 billion *escudos* [the Chilean unit of currency] in 1964 to 4,697,000,000 in 1965, and to 5,562,000,000 in 1966. Fiscal investments were considerable: while they totaled 1 billion *escudos* in 1964, they rose to 1.7 billion in 1966.

It is interesting to compare government allocations of 1963 with those of 1966 for the various ministries. Agriculture: In 1963, 103 million *escudos;* in 1966, 423 million *escudos.* Education: In 1963, 519 million *escudos;* in 1966, 1.18 billion. Public Health: In 1963, 398 million *escudos;* in 1966, 564 million. Public Works: In 1963, 436 million *escudos;* in 1966, 619 million.

The highly expanded education budget is attributed to the tremendous increase in the number of new schools and teachers and the raise of teachers' pay. Allocations for housing are also much higher this year, and should be included in the Public Works allotment. Furthermore, we must continue to set aside funds for various important projects, as demanded by the people.

At this point I should recall that the financial losses of the copper strike are only now being felt by the government.

Our foreign trade policy has definitely led to a recovery of the exchange balance. Some points must be stressed. First, we have a 72-million-dollar surplus in our foreign trade balance after an uninterrupted history of deficits. This is the highest surplus our country has ever had. Licenses for imports, given at 90-day terms before, nowadays are issued for 30 days. Payments of debts abroad, which had a decisive effect upon the country's industrial and economic budget, had reached a 270-day delay, but this was reduced to only 90 days after we renegotiated debts on this kind.

We have started trade relations with several socialist countries, and our foreign debt has been renegotiated.

Gentlemen, I could not say here that I am interpreting the feeling of all Chileans today if I would refrain from alluding to the armed forces. I am proud to note their exemplary conduct in fulfilling their constitutional and legal duties, and their selfless work in helping with the disasters caused by the storms throughout Chile last year. For this, they have my sincere gratitude. The Chilean *Carabineros,* following their brilliant tradition, have continued their task of preserving public order, contributing their efforts to cope with all national emergencies.[2]

My trip to Europe last year was effected because I believe that personal contact between leaders of nations is increasingly needed. My visit to Queen Elizabeth, President de Gaulle, President Saragat, and President Luebke led to an increase in prestige and understanding in the European continent for the Chilean nation. Our history and democratic tradition was highlighted, and our government's program aroused great interest. Once more we express gratitude for the affection with which we were received and for the interest shown by those governments in their financial, technical, and cultural cooperation with Chile. Proving Europe's interest were the visits here by [Italian] President Saragat, the King of Belgium, and Britain's foreign minister.

As a result of my European tour, we have had credit offers from several European countries. France, Germany, England and even Spain have granted us most important credit for the financing of specific projects and the purchase of equipment and machinery. Moreover, there are several similar agreements pending with other countries. We have signed technical assistance agreements with Belgium, Denmark, and Israel, and complementary agreements with West Germany, Great Britain, and the Technical Food Cooperation Program of the Organization of American States.

The talks I held with Latin American chiefs of state were very profitable. Not only did we discuss bilateral problems, but I was permitted to directly express opinions on the great problems involving our hemisphere policy: the OAS and Latin American integration.

The first has been suffering from a series of failings which led

2. Chile's *Carabineros* are an elite corps of national policemen.

to the deplorable events in the Dominican Republic. We consider the reasons underlying the establishment of our regional organization to be still valid and necessary for the coexistence of our nations and the aims expressed in the charter. There are geographical and ideological imperatives that demand our coexistence and this causes us to set up a system founded upon unquestioned principles of economic and social solidarity, of mutual duties and advantages, and of active cooperation within a respect for individual national personalities.

The Alliance for Progress was a transcendental step in this direction, but there is no doubt that existing institutions are not adequate for the size of the task or the visionary spirit that conceived it. With our critical but sincerely constructive view of the subject, we outlined a series of reforms at the Rio de Janeiro extraordinary conference which would lead to a new foundation for hemispheric solidarity. These reforms would call forth demands for the effective protection of human rights and would give the organization a new . . . structure.

For these reforms to be effective, recognition, not mere lip service, must be given to the strength and depth of the popular movement which is rising in demand for speedy sharing in the advantages of modern civilization. They must be founded on justice, take account of the risks that liberty entails, and appraise our true progress.

Our relations with socialist states, particularly with the Soviet Union, proceed in a regular way, increasing the possibilities of cooperation in the industrial, economic, and cultural fields. Since these relations are founded upon the principle of respect . . . and interdependence of nations, we are convinced that they will be beneficial for our development and for peace.

We have established embassies in Morocco, Sudan, and Ethiopia, and have agreed to establish relations wth Zambia, Mauretania, and Indonesia. Naturally, our closest relations are with the countries of our own continent. I would like to dwell at length upon those closest to us, and in the first place, the Republic of Argentina.

From the very beginning, my government tried to strengthen

relations with neighboring countries. The Argentine and Chilean foreign ministers have exchanged several visits, and I, myself, was received by President [Arturo U.] Illia, in whom I found the same fervent desire for a real and fruitful Chilean-Argentine friendship. Unfortunately, when we seemed close to the achievement of this purpose, a serious incident occurred which resulted in the death of a *Carabinero* officer. However, both governments were able to overcome the subsequent tension. Now, the Mendoza agreements have led to the permanent work of joint commissions, which I hope will not only prevent further incidents, but will accurately demarcate the border within five years. The Chilean-Argentine commission has considered the problem of transportation and has prepared agreements and studies for complementation in many industries.

Diplomatic relations with Bolivia remain interrupted, but not because this is our desire. This has not interfered with our continuing desire to cooperate with that country. We are completing the Arica port project, which will notably improve the possibilities for Bolivian traffic to move through there.

We have just approved the new contract on the Tica-Tica-Arica pipeline that was drafted by the Bolivian state petroleum monopoly. We hope that this pipeline will be placed in service very soon and will greatly benefit Bolivia.

A special Chilean mission visited Venezuela last October to draft trade agreements. Several weeks ago we received a Venezuelan mission, with which we signed important agreements for the benefit of both countries. Colombia has entrusted its destiny to a statesman whom we wish every success. I am sure that he will do his part for the unity of Latin America. Today we have the satisfaction of having with us the Uruguayan foreign minister, whose country has always been a friend of Chile and with which we maintain very close relations.

I could not end these references to several friendly nations without mentioning the United States. The government as well as public opinion of that country have understood that the pro-place in our government are the only way for the complete es-found political, social, and economic changes that are taking tablishment of democracy and the basis of our progress. Therefore, we have received permanent and decisive financial aid with broad understanding and respect for our domestic decisions. I can affirm that our relations with the United States have never been better than now. . . .

VII The Great Debate: Revolution vs. Reform

Most Latin American leaders, including members of the Church, the military, and the landed aristocracy—in other words, even members of the established order—recognize the necessity for reform in Latin America. But there is a great deal of conflict within parties, interest groups, and elites over methods of reform. Political parties can rarely translate conflicting reform programs into government policy. And interest groups often serve as stepping stones for political careers rather than as organized pressure from below. Nor do elections always guarantee effective representation: rigged (*imposición*) or single-candidate (*candidato único*) elections are a traditional occurrence. Constitutions are often amended to allow incumbent presidents to remain in power (*continuismo*).

Traditional Hispano-Catholic attitudes lie behind this picture of Latin American political life. They are basically personalistic (focusing upon unique inner differences between people), paternalistic (the expectation of "protection" by individuals in higher stations of life of others in lower positions), fatalistic, hierarchical, and emotional in terms of self-fulfillment.[1] They

1. For excellent attitude studies, see John F. Gillin, "Some Signposts for Policy," in Richard N. Adams, et al., eds., *Social Change in Latin America Today* (New York: Harper and Row, 1960), pp. 14–62; Gillin, "Ethos Components in Modern Latin American Culture," in Dwight B. Heath and Richard N. Adams, eds., *Contemporary Cultures and Societies of Latin America* (New York: Random House, 1965), pp. 503–17; Seymour Martin Lipset, "Values, Education, and Entrepreneur-

include *machismo,* expressions of manliness and action-orientation. These attitudes establish authoritarian relationships between leaders and the led within political groups, stimulating a highly personalistic and many times autocratic leadership by *caudillos* (political leaders) and *caciques* (local leaders). Thus one finds a deep respect for personalities, individualism, and traditional authority within the very groups, elites, and political parties advocating new national reforms. The political consequence of these traditional attitudes is twofold: first, limited sharing of decision-making power and second, restricted co-operation, dialogue, and bargaining between or within political parties.

As we have seen, talk of reform and revolution abound in Latin America. Will reform remain as pure ideology without corresponding concrete policy? How will future charismatic leaders respond to national problems? Will they unite support behind policy innovations or merely divide consensus on policy options? How will rising urbanization and population growth

---

ship," in Seymour Martin Lipset and Aldo Solari, eds., *Elites in Latin America* (New York: Oxford University Press, 1967), pp. 3–60. See also Ann Ruth Willner, "The Underdeveloped Study of Political Development," *World Politics,* Vol. XVI, No. 3 (April 1964), pp. 481–82, where she stresses continuity of traditionalism in modern politics; see Vernon Fluharty, *Dance of the Millions* (Pittsburgh: University of Pittsburgh Press, 1957), pp. 165–67; and Ernst Halperin, *Castro and Latin American Communism* (Cambridge: M.I.T. Press, 1963), where they discuss the absence of the *homo burocraticus* mentality in Latin America. Interpersonal relations within political parties, based upon traditional attitudes and values, are examined by Robert E. Scott, "Political Parties and Policy Making in Latin America," in Joseph LaPalombara and Myron Weiner, eds., *Political Parties and Political Development* (Princeton: Princeton University Press, 1966), pp. 331–67, see particularly pp. 338–40. The development of increased participation in political structures without corresponding development of effective organizations and institutions is in part the subject of Samuel P. Huntington's "Political Development and Political Decay," *World Politicos,* Vol. XVII, No. 3 (April 1965), pp. 386–430; also David E. Apter, *The Politics of Modernization* (Chicago: University of Chicago Press, 1965), pp. 81–122; and Tomas Roberto Fillol, *Social Factors in Economic Development: The Argentine Case* (Cambridge: M.I.T. Press, 1961), pp. 16–17, 60–61.

rates affect governmental capacity for organized problem solving? How will governments feed, clothe, house, educate, and find jobs for its population which is estimated to grow from 290 million in 1970 to 750 million in the year 2000?

PEACEFUL VS. VIOLENT CHANGE: MARXIST-LENINIST POLEMICS

Fidel Castro's revolution, framed as it was in Marxist-Leninist terms, directly challenged the traditional practice and ideology of the older Latin American Communist Parties. Whereas Castro demanded immediate violent guerrilla warfare as the principal means to change, the legacy of traditional Communist Parties was far more opportunistic and tied to Soviet policy, which in the 1960s was one of peaceful parliamentary change and anti-imperialistic popular united fronts.[2] This conflict between the Fidelista approach—voluntarism, militancy, guerrilla warfare—and the traditional Communist Party tactics—opportunism, adherence to the prevailing Soviet line, struggle for limited goals within the national political system—became increasingly clear after 1959. Although muted during the years 1964–65, it reached a new intensity after the Tricontinental Conference in Havana, January 1966, when Castro began to emphasize the violent rather than the peaceful road to socialism in his communications with Latin American leaders.[3]

Havana's shift toward full support of the "armed struggle" thesis after January 1966, with its direct challenge to orthodox Communism in Latin America, took several forms. In early February 1966, in response to a letter sent to the United Nations Security Council by representatives of eighteen Latin American governments protesting the militant and "interventionist" line of the Tricontinental Conference, Castro declared that "The

2. On the legacy of traditional Latin American Communism in Latin America, see Ernst Halperin, *Nationalism and Communism in Chile* (Cambridge: M.I.T. Press, 1965); Rollie Poppino, *International Communism in Latin America* (Chicago: Free Press of Glencoe, 1966); D. Bruce Jackson, *Castro, The Kremlin, and Communism in Latin America* (Baltimore: Johns Hopkins University Press, 1969), pp. 8–10.
3. For analysis of the 1964–65 period, see D. Bruce Jackson, op. cit.

people of these Governments have the right to sweep . . . and sooner or later will sweep them [the governments] away by means of the most violent revolutionary action."[4] Also during 1966 Havana broadcasted a series of interviews with Latin American guerrilla leaders from Guatemala, Colombia, Venezuela, and the Dominican Republic, stressing in each interview that the predominant struggle for national liberation must be an armed struggle. Throughout 1966 the Cuban government continued its drive for recognition of the militant Venezuelan *Fuerzas Armadas de Liberación Nacional* (Armed Forces of National Liberation or FALN) rather than the *Partido Comunista Venezolano* (Venezuelan Communist Party or PCV, advocate in that year of more conventional "broad front" tactics) as the only legitimate representative of the Venezuelan liberation movement. This policy brought Castro and the PCV into open conflict (Reading One) which increased after 1966. Moreover, Havana called repeatedly upon the peoples of Haiti and the Dominican Republic to revolt. In May 1967 Havana sharply criticized the Marxist-Leninist "pseudo-revolutionaries," that is, the traditional Communist Parties, for their lack of revolutionary élan (Reading Two). This militant line was reaffirmed in Havana during the *Organización Latino Americana de Solidaridad* (Organization of Latin American Solidarity or OLAS) meetings of Communist Parties during late July and early August 1967.

Following the Soviet line of peaceful parliamentary change and united front tactics, Latin American Communists resent Castro's attempt to force his "single solution" on the rest of Latin America. In this sense the Communist Parties are as imbued with noninterventionist sentiments as are the established governments of Latin America! While discreet in their disagreements with Castro, the traditional Communists also firmly maintain the necessity of united action in the hemisphere—which Castro fragmented by his attacks on traditional Communists like those of the PCV—and the critical importance of each party's

4. See *New York Times,* March 12, 1966; also Havana Domestic Radio Broadcast, February 10, 1966.

assessing its *sui generis* internal conditions as a basis for adopting correct policy. Only separate parties, they argue, can really know what is appropriate policy for separate countries. These points of disagreement with Castro were highlighted by Luis Corvalán, secretary general of the Central Committee of the large Chilean Communist Party, in a key article which appeared in *World Marxist Review* (July 1967) and in nothing less than *Pravda* on July 30, 1967, just before the opening Conference of OLAS in August 1967 (Reading Three). It indicated not only the feelings of many traditional Communists in Latin America, but of the Soviets as well who were opposed to Castroite militancy. The debate over revolution and reform involved other Communist Parties. The Mexican Communists praised Fidel and his revolution, even as Havana launched its renewed "armed warfare" offensive in January 1966 (Reading Four).

CASTRO VS. THE LATIN AMERICAN "REFORMISTS"

Castro's pronounced stress on violent over peaceful methods stimulated a corresponding unwillingness to compromise in any way on the question of "reformism" as he had done modestly before the Tricontinental Conference.[5] Among leaders classified by Havana as reformist—Carlos Lleras Restrepo of Colombia, Julio César Méndez Montenegro of Guatemala, Eduardo Frei Montalva of Chile, and Raúl Leoni of Venezuela (Rómulo Betancourt before Leoni)—Frei (Reading Five) and Leoni (Reading Six) have been subjected to particular criticism.

The major thrust of Castro's attack is upon "compromises" made by "reformists" with Yankee imperialism and with local oligarchies, which means for Castro that "reformist" governmental policies are essentially "timid," "unprogressive," "temporizing,"

5. For example, in May 1965, shortly after Frei's democratic government came to power in Chile, Castro said that if Latin American nations "want to make Christian Democratic reforms, let them make their Christian Democratic reforms," and that every people "may make the revolution it deems most convenient." *New York Times,* May 2, 1965.

and designed to maintain the status quo.[6] He insists that "reformists" lack the will and determination to act radically and resolutely, and that behind all reformist activities one finds the shadow of United States imperialism, now cast by the Alliance for Progress and the Peace Corps. As a radical nationalist, Castro has little time for moderate nationalists in Latin America. His appeal is to other radical nationalists like himself—Marxist-Leninist or not—who are willing and committed to armed struggle against the status quo, as events since the January 1966 Tricontinental Conference and the August 1967 OLAS Conference so vividly suggest.

Interestingly enough, Castro's unmitigated scorn for "reformist" parties in Latin America parallels traditional Soviet hostility toward moderate leftists, who Soviets fear will gain long-range control of liberalizing trends in developing areas.[7] Moscow has made it quite clear that certain national reformist parties—Peru's *Alianza Popular Revolucionaria Americana* (American Popular Revolutionary Alliance), Venezuela's *Acción Democrática* (Democratic Action), Costa Rica's *Liberación Nacional* (National Liberation), Paraguay's *Febrerista* Party, Guatemala's *Partido Revolucionario* (Revolutionary Party), and the *Partido Revolucionario Dominicano* (Dominican Revolutionary Party)—"have never been really revolutionary and anti-imperialists," are very much "akin to the West European Social Democrats," are often anti-Communist and aligned with private property and North American monopoly capital.[8] Since they are not, in Moscow's perspective, in the forefront of progressive revolutionary change, they are in essence conservative and to be castigated accordingly. This position is clearly in tune with Castro's polemics against reformism and reformist leaders like Leoni.

A striking exception to this general compatibility of views, how-

6. Havana Radio Broadcast, beamed to Latin America, April 15, 1966.
7. See Thomas Perry Thornton, *The Third World in Soviet Perspective* (Princeton: Princeton University Press, 1964), for additional commentary on this point.
8. A. Shulgovsky, "Political Trends in Latin America," *International Affairs* (Moscow), No. 11 (November 1965), pp. 42–49.

ever, is Moscow's recognition of Christian Democratic parties, notably that of Frei's, which are not included among the run-of-the-mill reformers. The Christian Democrats are favored by the Soviet Union, given their increasing affinity with noncapitalistic paths of development. On this point, Moscow parted company with Castro after the Tricontinental Conference as it also did on the question of trading and lending money to certain "reformist" governments.[9]

PARTY AND GUERRILLA FRAGMENTATION OVER REVOLUTION VS. REFORM

The revolution vs. reform debate splinters the parties and guerrilla movements of different Latin American countries. The peculiar characteristics of this disunity depend upon the degree of governmental commitment to change, the political structure of the country itself, and the strength of the guerrilla movement. Much of Latin America (that is, Uruguay, Mexico, Ecuador, Paraguay, Costa Rica, Argentina, and Brazil) may be involved not at all or very little in this particular debate; yet it is a real and divisive issue in other countries (that is, in Cuba, Chile, and Venezuela).

Cuba is a case in point. The dominant single-party system of Castro's Cuba, from whence the debate radiates, might not appear susceptible to fragmentation upon first observation, given Castro's personal dominance over the party hierarchy. A closer study suggests that several signs of *intra*-party conflict have emerged since Castro consolidated his control. During March 1966, for example, about the time Castro began to attack the Frei government, there was unrest at Havana University, reports of deep-seated corruption in the Cuban government, and a highly publicized trial of Majors Rolando Cubela Secades and Román Guin Díaz, arrested February 26th and accused of plotting to assassinate Premier Castro.[10] Moreover, governmental corruption, which involved Major Efigenio Amijeiras, a deputy minister for

9. Ibid., p. 45.
10. *New York Times,* March 6, 1966.

the armed forces in the Cuban regime and a former hero in Fidel's revolutionary movement, combined with governmental arrests of several dozen persons termed "pseudo-revolutionaries" living a "disorderly" life or "the sweet life" and the plot to assassinate Castro suggest the demise of that revolutionary fervor, austerity, and militancy judged so vital at the January 1966 Tricontinental Conference.[11] This evidence of intra-party conflict—which may help to account for Castro's focus upon "pseudo-revolutionaries" elsewhere in Latin America—was particularly visible in February 1968, when he uncovered what was termed a "microfaction" in the very heart of the Cuban Communist Party (Reading Seven).

Chile also has its difficulties in reaching party consensus on the method of change issues. Operating in the multiparty system, the Christian Democrats face severe criticism and obstructionism from the socialists and other opposition parties who refuse to support much of their reform legislation and policies (Reading Eight). Another indication of inter-party conflict over revolution vs. reform is the Socialist-Communist split within the *Frente de Acción Popular* (Popular Action Front or FRAP) (Reading Nine). Splits are also present *within* the parties themselves, including the Chilean Socialist Party, the Radical Party, and—most important for the years 1964–70—within the Christian Democratic Party (Reading Ten). The Christian Democratic disagreements began to undermine the party's publicized unity when it assumed political power behind the president in November 1964.

The situation is different in Venezuela, where guerrilla warfare has a longer history and where the Communist Party split in 1966 over the question of armed struggle vs. peaceful "united front" tactics. Although neither the Venezuelan Communist Party nor the guerrillas agreed with the "bourgeoisie reformism" of the Acción Democrática (Democratic Action) government of Raúl Leoni or Rómulo Betancourt, they by no means were in accord on policy options (Reading Eleven). This split appears

11. *New York Times,* March 18, 1966; *London Times,* March 18, 22, 1966.

wider and more irreconcilable than that between the socialists and Communists in Chile, but the difference in the positions in the "great debate" are similar.

HEMISPHERIC UNITY

Within four years of its launching, the Alliance for Progress was facing difficulties. President John F. Kennedy, whose vision had sparked the Alliance in the first place, was dead, and his successor, Lyndon B. Johnson, evoked none of the enthusiasm in Latin America that had greeted President Kennedy. But there were other problems for the Alliance. Cuba's abstention from it, together with Castro's support of revolutionary change rather than evolutionary reform, provided a sharp counterweight to the Alliance. Equally disturbing was the continuing problem of how to actually achieve the reform goals spelled out in the Charter of Punta del Este of 1961. Tax reforms, for example, proved difficult to work out in most countries where established interests had seldom paid taxes, or, at least, had paid very low taxes. If it was hard to work out tax reform, so were reforms in a host of other spheres difficult to implement.

The Alliance planners could, of course, look with satisfaction on numerous infrastructure projects—dams, highways, big buildings, and the like. Moreover, the speed of development projects of this sort quickened, but the overall assessment of the Alliance at the end of its first five years was one of considerable lag. To some, it looked as if the Alliance goals had been set too high. To others, it seemed that the Alliance framework just did not have the strength and overall vision to carry out the 1961 goals.

One of the sharpest critics of the Alliance, yet one of its most sincere exponents was Chile's reformist President Frei. In an article in 1967, he held that the Alliance had lost its way and he outlined some of the changes he wanted to incorporate into a revitalized Alliance (Reading Twelve). Some of these changes were made official in the meeting of hemisphere presidents in Punta del Este, Uruguay, in the spring of the same year (Reading

Thirteen). The presidents' accord spelled out the establishment of a hemisphere-wide common market to bring about improved trade conditions for the Latin nations. The accord was signed amidst a good deal of heady einthusiasm on the part of hemisphere chief executives like Frei, Fernando Belaúnde Terry of Peru, Raúl Leoni of Venezuela, and Gustavo Díaz Ordaz of Mexico.[12] But the enthusiasm dissipated rather quickly, and for the most part the Alliance seemed to slip back into some of its old ruts as the 1970s dawned.

Cuba also worked to set up its own organization aimed at bringing revolution and violent change to Latin America. The organization, known as the *Organización Latino Americana de Solidaridad* (Latin American Solidarity Organization or OLAS), held its first general meeting in Havana in August 1967, attended by delegates from twenty-six hemisphere nations and territories (Reading Fourteen). The OLAS structure was an outgrowth of the Tricontinental organization which Havana set up in January of 1966 to draw delegates from Asia, Africa, and Latin America in its quest for revolution to overthrow the established order in developing countries. The Tricontinental organization frequently attacked United States imperialism, particularly in Latin America, and took numerous swipes at the Alliance for Progress as well.

Cuban Premier Castro, despite the difficulties encountered in the OLAS meeting in August 1967, was optimistic about the organization and its opportunities in Latin America. His widely quoted speech closing the session was a careful enunciation of his philosophy of revolution and change (Reading Fifteen).

In late 1969, a new United States policy toward Latin America began to evolve under President Richard M. Nixon. A basic factor was the concept of partnership between the United States and its Latin American neighbors. To some, however, President Nixon's tone and his words amounted to a significant lessening of United States interest in the Latin nations. Whether this assessment would be borne out by future developments remained uncertain. But it seemed likely that a lowered United States

12. See, for example, articles by James Nelson Goodsell in *The Christian Science Monitor,* April 28, May 7, May 11, 1967.

presence in Latin America would be a part of Mr. Nixon's program (Reading Sixteen).

Mr. Nixon had sent New York Governor Nelson A. Rockefeller on a listen-and-learn mission to Latin America earlier in 1969—and to some extent Mr. Nixon's program was based on the Rockefeller report delivered to the President in September and then released in an edited version in November (Reading Seventeen).

READING 1 *Havana and the Venezuelan Communist Party*

Introductory Note

Of all the polemics among Marxist-Leninists in Latin America over peaceful vs. violent change, the most famous is that between Havana and the Venezuelan Communist Party.[1] *The chief criticism of the* Partido Comunista Venezolano *(PCV) is foreign interference in its affairs by Havana, through its attack of the PCV leadership (for its abandonment of the armed struggle road after 1966) and its recognition of those dissidents who broke with the PCV over the issue of peaceful vs. violent change instead of recognizing the PCV itself. Increasingly, Havana's* Granma *editorials after 1966 began to praise the PCV dissidents, including men like Douglas Bravo who had been expelled from the PCV for "fractionalist" activities.*

The following documents capture the major features of the Havana–PCV conflict. The first document is an unsigned article,

1. For coverage of this debate, see D. Bruce Jackson, *Castro, The Kremlin, and Communism in Latin America,* op. cit., pp. 40–59; Jackson, "Report on Latin America," *Problems of Communism,* Vol. XV, No. 3 (May–June 1966), p. 10; Martin D. Gensler, "Los Aliados Incompatibles," *Problemas del Comunismo,* Vol. XIV, No. 4 (July–August), pp. 49–63.

Selection 1.1: "Tacit Split Between the PCV and Castro," translated from *La República,* Caracas, September 3, 1966, p. 20, JPRS 38,070, September 3, 1966.

Selection 1.2: Havana Radio Broadcast beamed to Latin America, June 8, 1967.

entitled, "Tacit Split Between the PCV and Castro" that appeared in the Caracas daily, La República, *in early September 1966. It indicates the heated communication that went on between the PCV and the Communist Party of Cuba. The second document represents Castro's view of the PCV in June 1967.*

SELECTION 1.1: SPLIT BETWEEN CASTRO AND THE VENEZUELAN COMMUNISTS

The Central Committee of the *Partido Comunista Venezolano* (Venezuelan Communist Party or PCV) sent a letter of protest to the Communist Party of Cuba (PCC) because of its assistance to Venezuelan "Fractionalists" and "Guerreristas" (War Mongers).

An energetic letter of protest to the Central Committee of the Cuban Communist Party was sent by the Political Bureau of the PCV "because of the open support given by leaders of the Cuban Revolution to fractionalist elements" sanctioned by the organization of Venezuelan communists.

In the above-mentioned communication, the high leadership of the PCV accuses the Cuban Party of collaborating closely with the Venezuelan fractional group thus violating—among other things—express resolutions approved at the conference of Latin American Communist Parties held in November 1964.

The PCV, in its protest letter, says that in Cuba "the legitimate representatives of the Venezuelan Communist Party have been displaced" in order to put in their places persons who have betrayed their condition as militants with the goal of usurping positions which they were unqualified to hold.

The communication of the Venezuelan Communists translates the serious discrepancies existing between the PCV and the *Partido Comunista Cubano* (Cuban Communist Party or PCC) in the tactical and strategic order. The Political Bureau of the PCV affirms, in a clear-cut manner, "that the policy of Venezuelan communism is elaborated here," and that it will never tolerate foreign interferences, which would mean the mortgaging of an independence which the PCV says it defends above any contingency. . . .

These are some paragraphs of the letter sent by the PCV to the Cuban leaders:

> For us, the Venezuelan communists, who for more than three decades have been at the vanguard of the struggle against imperialism and the native oligarchy, who have not vacillated to face the enemies of our people with weapons in hand—and particularly the Yankee petroleum monopolies—who will continue to clutch these weapons as we utilize other forms of struggle, who keep in high esteem the fraternal relations maintained for many years with the leaders of the Cuban people and particularly with their maximum leader, Fidel Castro, we consider it a duty to preserve them and stimulate them, and it is certainly painful for us to be approaching a confrontation of methods and criteria which for the first time establishes areas of difference between the pioneers of socialism in America and who have been waging, under the hardest conditions of secrecy and repression, the battle for liberation in a region of such vital importance to the Pentagon.
>
> Comrades, this is a matter of a situation, [expressed the PCV,] created because of the open support given by leaders of the PCC to fractionalist elements already sanctioned by our organization, as well as to other anti-party groups which, internally divided, abandoned in large measure from the opinion and support of the masses because of their sectarian attitude, almost completely foreign to the guerrilla action taking place on our soil, have concentrated their efforts on confusing you by means of the distortion of the facts, the use of slander, the employment of ultra-leftist phraseology which is just on the verbal plane, and the vile utilization, finally, of the instruments and channels which our Party trustingly put in their hands. . . .
>
> Relations between revolutionaries in different countries must be maintained, fundamentally, between the Communist Parties and never to the detriment of the priorities corresponding to them. This is how the Political Bureau of our Party judges the problem. And this is how we will judge it when we have the

opportunity to discuss exhaustively at the highest level the conflict taking place. . . .

. . . We have solicited and will continue to solicit the solidarity of the international communist movement. Also, our Party, according to its possibilities, has given support to the revolutionary movement of other peoples. Furthermore, along with all of this, we wish to establish clearly that we are jealous defenders of our independence, that the policy of our Party is elaborated by our Congresses and Conferences and applied by our Central Committee, and that we will never consent to pledge away this independence.

Selection 1.2: "Rightwing" Leaders of Venezuela Communist Party Scored

. . . Fresh proof of the policy of surrender that inspires the rightwing leadership of the Venezuelan Communist Party was furnished today when the Ecuadorean Embassy in Caracas was asked for asylum by Stalin Gamarra Durán, who headed a small armed group in the state of Portuguesa under the direction of Pedro Medina Silva and Germán Lairet. That group of fighters, which has been inactive for some time on orders from the party's Political Bureau, is the one the bureau referred to in its documents as the Armed Forces of National Liberation (FALN).

Obedient to instructions from the rightwing leadership of the party, those *Fuerzas Armadas de Liberación Nacional* (Armed Forces of National Liberation or FALN), which were nothing more than the remainder of the big guerrilla movement of the early days in the hands of the Communist Party, ordered the armed groups to fall back in a move to favor the electoral process in which this political organization plans to take part.

The Venezuelan Communist Party's rightwing leadership announced this publicly, and for a long time it has been gradually dismantling the armed forces under its control in an attempt to regain legal status. Stalin Gamarra Durán's request for asylum is further evidence of the results of this policy pursued by the party's rightwing leadership.

On one side are the guerrillas and the urban and suburban fighters of the front and the Armed Forces of National Liberation, the only, true perpetrators of the first guerrillas who took to the mountains in 1962; on the other, [President] Leoni, imperialism, and those who play his pseudodemocratic political game.

For the fighter who loves his country and is ready to win freedom at any cost, the ranks of the patriotic army are open to him, in the Armed Forces of National Liberation, the revolutionary leftwing movement's front. For those who prefer politicking there will always be a place in the slates of the traditional parties or an office job ready for men who will kneel.

The choice is plain. The Venezuelan people will have no trouble making their selection. They know where duty lies, and heroism, and patriotism. In a word, they know where to look for the true revolution that carries the flag of victory forward in the ranks of the country's finest sons.

READING 2 *Havana's Criticism of "Pseudo-revolutionaries"*

Introductory Note

After the Tricontinental Solidarity Conference of January 3–15, 1966, which signaled renewed emphasis by Havana on the "armed struggle" thesis, Castro increasingly vocalized his discontent with traditional Latin American Communism. In speeches of July 26 and August 29 (1966), he singled out those who proposed the peaceful road to change as "pseudo-revolutionaries" and "defeatist" and implied that Cuba would support leftist groups advocating armed struggle even if they were not Marxist-Leninists. In the August speech, he chastized Latin American Communists who "cannot even fire a pea-shooter" and those "Latin American specimens who wage revolutions from Europe and Asia." In the earlier July speech, he suggested that failure of guerrilla movements could be attributed to the absence of revolutionary commitment by those Communists who "preach the path of electioneering and charlatanism" and those who describe Cubans as "armed struggle maniacs." [1]

Moreover, Castro scorned the traditional Communist position that "subjective conditions" might not be ripe for revolution even

1. Havana Domestic Radio Broadcast, July 26, 1966.

May Day speech by acting Armed Forces Minister Major Juan Almeida at Havana's Plaza de la Revolución. Havana Domestic Radio Broadcast, May 1, 1967.

though "objective conditions" for revolution were more suitable; he emphasized that the Cuban Revolution "would never have taken place" had this concept been applied and that "subjective conditions" mature as a consequence of armed struggle.[2] *This militant position of Castro's vis-á-vis the traditional Communist Parties was echoed again in Latin America in March 1967 when, in a polemic with the Venezuelan Communist Party (PCV), Castro announced a kind of ideological war with the traditional Communists.*[3] *It is this ideological sentiment that formed the setting for Major Juan Almeida's 1967 May Day speech which follows:*

. . . Those who condemn the fighting guerrillas in fact support imperialism and the reactionary government whose mercenary troops wage attack after attack in unsuccessful attempts to liquidate the guerrillas. The setbacks with which they try to justify this infamous action were not the results of a wrong tactical policy but rather the results of the inability of these imposters and pseudo-revolutionaries to lead the struggle of the Venezuelan people.

The Cuban example also was not completely understood by some leaders of the Latin American revolutionary movement. There had to be a painful and bitter lesson so that men capable of leading the revolution in Latin America could come forward. During the last few months we have seen these men come forward. The leadership of the struggle will fall upon the shoulders of the best and most capable fighters. The victory of the revolution in recent months is basically due to the accumulation of experiences over several years and to the fact that the leadership of the struggle is gradually falling into the hands of new men, capable and ready to win or die. . . .

2. *Ibid.*

3. Supplement to *Granma* (weekly English edition), March 19, 1967. The Venezuelan Communists responded to this position by snapping at Castro's "unmitigated gall" in presuming the right to decide who was and who was not a true "Communist." See *Ultimas Noticias* (Caracas), March 17, 1967; also Kevin Devlin, "The Permanent Revolutionism of Fidel Castro," *Problems of Communism,* Vol. XVII, No. 1 (January-February 1968), pp. 4–5.

The leftist organizations and parties for many years maintained theoretical positions in favor of Marxist, socialist, and Communist ideas. The leaders of the so-called Latin American leftists for many years fought in different ways for these ideals. Now it is not a matter of defending an idea or a program with respect to principles. Now it is a matter of fighting and struggling actively for those revolutionary ideas. It is revolutionary action, revolutionary deeds, which characterize revolutionaries.

The era of theory for Latin America is a thing of the past. The time for the peoples' actions has come. . . . The peoples of Latin America have entered into revolution. Each man, each organization, and each party in America will make its own decision. That decision will characterize them before the international revolutionary movement and history. Today it is not enough to say: I am a revolutionary. I am a Communist. I am a Marxist-Leninist. The time for deeds has arrived. The decision which each party or organization makes will characterize it before history. It will place it before its people, and the peoples will follow the fighters and join the fighting sectors of the revolutionaries—the men of action. The masses will be moved by the guerrillas and by the revolutionary action.

In Guatemala, Colombia, Venezuela, and Bolivia, action is needed. In other countries, such as Chile and Uruguay, the need is for aid and support to these deeds because all revolutionary organizations should aid the fighters. They should cooperate with the fighters. They should give all kinds of aid to the fighters. These are the internationalist principles of Marxism. These are the internationalist principles of the proletariat. The time for words has ended. . . .

The Cuban people made their decision a long time ago. The revolutionary struggle of the peoples of Latin America will develop the revolutionary awareness of the fighters and workers. The struggle—and only the struggle—will be the great teacher of the revolutionaries. The struggle will sharpen awareness. The struggle will strengthen the revolutionaries. . . .

The pseudorevolutionaries accuse our country of wanting to lead the revolution from Cuba. We know well that revolutions are made by the people. It is well known that revolutions are made by revolutionaries. Neither the peoples nor the revolutionaries will permit themselves to be led from abroad. The revolution is waged by millions and millions of men and at the head of the revolution are the most determined—those who are ready. It will be these active, determined men—revolutionaries from each country—who will lead the revolution in each region of the continent.

It would be absurd and ridiculous to suggest anything else. The revolution is led in keeping with the ability and competence of the revolutionary leaders in each country. This is evident to us. What we want for America is not to impose the example of our revolution. What we want for America is a greater revolution than the Cuban revolution. Our people have the honor only of being the first to set the example and have the experience, but the glory of the revolution will belong to the peoples of America. Today's world needs that revolution. It demands that revolution. A group of peoples with a common history and with a common experience of exploitation will wage an identical revolution.

READING 3 *Havana and the Chilean Communist Party*

Introductory Note

While Havana's dispute with the Venezuelan Communist Party has received most attention, there exists also a Havana-Chilean Communist Party (PCC) rift in Latin America. As Castro increasingly castigated Frei's "bourgeois reformism" (examined in the next section) and expanded on the relevance of armed struggle as the only way to change, the Chilean Communist Party was challenged directly by Castro's ideological and organizational invective. If this point were not clear by implication, Castro's July 26, 1966 speech against "pseudo-revolutionaries" included the Chilean Communists by name. This accusation occurred in the very presence of Chilean Communist Party Deputy, Orlando Millas, who departed Cuba in protest! [1]

1. Buenos Aires Radio Broadcast, July 30, 1966. These accusations were aired publicly by Havana later in broadcasts to the hemisphere, though not by Fidel himself. For example, Havana radio was not reluctant to broadcast "letters" from Chileans, viz., "There are some so-called leftwingers here who are not really revolutionaries. Time has made them middle class, particularly the leaders. It appears that they only exist for elections, and once the elections are held they return to their hibernation." Havana Domestic Radio Broadcast, February 14, 1967.

Article by Luis Corvalán, secretary general of the Central Committee of the Chilean Communist Party, "The Alliance of Revolutionary and Anti-Imperialist Forces in Latin America," *Pravda*, 30 July 1967, p. 4; also in *World Marxist Review*, Vol. 10, No. 7 (July 1967), pp. 44–51.

Castro's militant position on revolution complicates political tactics for the PCC. One difficulty is the PCC's relationship with the Christian Democratic Party. Traditionally oriented to the Moscow-line "united front" thesis, legally operative within the Chilean democratic political system, and by far the strongest Communist Party in Latin America (Cuba excepted), the Chilean Communists could not but give partial support to Frei whose domestic and foreign policies blended a unique mixture of reform, anti-imperialism and close ties with the Soviet Union and East Europe.[2] *Havana's "armed struggle" thesis after 1966 could cause only problems for the Chilean Communist Party in adjusting its "united front" tactics with Frei's policies, on the one hand, and with the importance of the Cuban "Marxist-Leninist" Revolution—now militantly advocating revolution throughout the hemisphere—on the other.*

This central difficulty of internal adjustment was exacerbated by a second dimension of PCC problems, its precarious alliance with the socialists in the Frente de Acción Popular (*Popular Action Front or FRAP*). *After 1966 the socialists began to identify increasingly with Havana's militant thesis, while the PCC stuck to its "broad national front" position; thus, Havana enlarged an ideological fissure between Chile's two Marxist parties which had existed before Castro came to power. Havana's militancy strengthened socialist long-standing criticism of the peaceful road, sharpened socialist inflexibility toward Frei's reform government, and worked against PCC efforts for partial support of Frei and for compromise within the FRAP. Given the PCC's peaceful "united front" policy, it is natural that it would take the lead in stressing conciliation where possible, especially since it is organizationally superior to the Socialist Party and since the socialists have been by far the more militant of the two parties and more loyal to the cause of revolution.*

2. In January 1967, the Soviet Union signed a $15 million loan and technical aid agreement with Chile, which Havana chastised as "making cause with one of the Cuban revolution's bitterest enemies"—thus a criticism of the Moscow-PCC relationship. Havana Radio Broadcast, beamed to Latin America, January 22, 1967.

This background places the following document in perspective. The PCC is decidedly against "armed struggle" and has publicly —although discreetly—opposed Havana's "single road" approach to change. It has called for struggle against "opportunist deviation and sectarianism" and condemned "leftist extremism" in Latin American revolutionary parties just as it has condemned the dogmatism of the Chinese Communist Party leadership.[3]

. . . Many trends—men, women and youth of varying political views and social backgrounds—have joined the liberation struggle. The important thing is to extend the anti-imperialist front and engage against the common enemy all sections of the public, including those who may not be admirers of the Cuban revolution and revolution in general, but who have taken a stand in behalf of Cuba's right to build socialism and the right of all Latin American peoples to opt for the system of their choice.

Any attempt to impose the communist view on the other anti-imperialist forces, and similarly any attempt by the latter to impose their views on others, can but hamper unity of action and narrow the struggle against the common enemy. . . .

Experience has shown that open polemics results in senseless name-calling and in arbitrary judgments. It serves no useful purpose and only aggravates the difficulties. Sometimes, it is true, a party has no choice but to express its opinion publicly. We have nothing against this. But we are sure that direct contacts, bilateral and multilateral meetings, a tactful fraternal dialogue and, most important of all, steadfast unity of action, are the best way to further mutual understanding.

The driving force of the revolution in Latin America comprises the working class, peasants (the majority of whom in many countries are Indians), students, middle strata and some sections of the national bourgeoisie. There are contradictions between them, but common interests in the fight against U.S. imperialism and the oligarchies predominate. This offers a serviceable basis for unity and calls for closer bonds. Our policy of united action by all anti-imperialist and anti-oligarchic forces builds on the

3. Belgrade Radio Broadcast, August 22, 1966.

belief that an alliance of workers and peasants, of the proletariat and the non-proletarian elements is the best possible basis for an enduring and militant united front. To make headway, mutual understanding between proletarian and petty-bourgeois revolutionaries is absolutely essential.

The proletariat, the most powerful social class on our continent, is still growing. As many as 40 million people (of whom one out of every three is a factory or farm laborer), or more than half the gainfully employed population between the Rio Grande and Cape Horn, earn a livelihood by selling their labor power. In five countries, that is, Mexico, Brazil, Argentina, Uruguay and Chile, with nearly two-thirds of the total population of Latin America, the proletariat is relatively strong, and not in numbers only.

Communist parties exist in all Latin American countries. Like the fraternal parties elsewhere in the world, irrespective of their degree of development, they expound ideas that strike terror into imperialism, of which they are the most relentless enemies. . . .

Communists organize the workers in trade unions, fight for the economic and social demands of the people and safeguard working class unity by inspiring a new, anti-imperialist patriotism.

The most advanced section of the working class and the best of the Latin-American intelligentsia have joined the Communist parties. These parties have their sources in the proletariat of their respective countries, in the October Revolution, in the victory of Leninism, of revolutionism over reformism. . . .

The Latin-American Communist parties are aware of the need for understanding with the other Left forces, above all those espousing socialism. However, this does not apply to anti-Party groups and splinter parties, who represent no one and who live off fractional activity and dissent. . . .

What Communists do want is a progressive alignment of all champions of democracy and socialism, recognizing the right of every ally to participate in all stages of the revolutionary process and in all governments that the people's struggle may bring into being. . . .

As for the other Latin-American countries, it appears that the need for united action by Communist parties and other revolutionary forces fits in with the need for cooperation at the level of joint leadership by those revolutionary forces which, in a definite sense, share the function of vanguard.

A vanguard cannot conceivably be built by arbitrary or synthetic means around a leader or a few men, who individually, at least in their own opinion, adopt radical standpoints and prepare for revolutionary action. The exceptions to this rule only bear this out.

A vanguard is the result of the fusions of Marxism with the working-class movement, the moulding of revolutionary thought (above all among proletarians) and the application of Marxism-Leninism to the concrete conditions of a country, that is, the result of purposeful activity and of a natural, rather than spontaneous, process. . . .

READING 4 *The Mexican and Cuban Revolutions Compared*

Introductory Note

The Mexican Communist Party, nowhere near as large as the Chilean Communist Party, views Cuba from the perspective of its country's own revolutionary past. In comparing the Cuban and Mexican Revolutions, Arnoldo Martínez Verdugo, first secretary of the Mexican Communist Party, finds Mexico coming off second best in terms of accomplishments. His position is, unlike that of Luis Corvalán, one of high praise rather than warning for Castro. Yet it ends by adhering to the "united front" position of other traditional Communists—combined with waiting and working for the "favorable conditions among the masses" before the triumph of revolution is possible—which Havana so harshly debunks. Mexico is the only member of the Organization of American States (OAS) that maintains diplomatic relations with Cuba.

. . . The great merit, the historic merit of the Cuban Revolution and of its leader, comrade Fidel Castro, lies in having opened the first breach of the revolution in Latin America. This was the first revolution that was able to defeat, really defeat, imperialism on our continent, and it was the first to place the glorious banner of socialism on American soil. . . .

Translated article by Arnoldo Martínez Verdugo, first secretary of the Mexican Communist Party, in *Política,* Vol. VII, No. 151 (August 1, 1966), JPRS 38,070, August 1, 1966 (article is from a tape recording of a speech made in Mexico City's Teatro Lírico on July 31, 1966).

The Cuban Revolution, more than any other phenomenon, has demonstrated very clearly that the worker movement, the Latin American anti-imperialist movement, has entered and is already in a new period, in the period of triumphant democratic, anti-imperialist revolutions that are rapidly becoming socialist revolutions, which are not stagnating, which are not stopping, which are not establishing or improving capitalist exploitation.

Let us recall the process that existed in the period preceding the Cuban Revolution and the Second World War. Some democratic-bourgeois revolutions, like the Mexican and the Bolivian revolutions, had triumphed in Latin America, but these revolutions went only half-way; they did not progress; they only set up some new features of exploitation of the workers and farmers, precisely because of the bourgeois nature of their leadership, but also because of the correlation of forces in the world.

The international situation at the time of these revolutions was radically different from the situation that we have at the present time and from the one that the Cuban Revolution had. Therefore, the Cuban Revolution, like all the revolutions that are maturing and progressing on the Latin American continent, is developing as an inseparable part of one single world-wide revolutionary process, in which the working class in the capitalist countries, the peoples in the countries oppressed by imperialism and the countries that make up the world-wide socialist system are uniting. . . .

The Cuban Revolution came along, with all the powerful force of its example, to destroy a series of myths, a series of sophisms worked out for the sole purpose of justifying the oppression of imperialism and of the bourgeoisie on the peoples of Latin America. As is known, it put an end to the myth of the invincibility of imperialism in Latin America, giving, thereby, new strength to the Latin American patriots. It also overthrew the cowardly and discredited theory of geographic fatalism that condemned our peoples to imperialist domination until the triumph of socialism in the United States. It also defeated the trap of the conciliators, those who were attempting to lead the Latin American masses to the illusion of a mythical "third world," which supposedly would separate them both from socialism and from imperialism, but which, actually, would make new revolutions fall again into the orbit of imperialism. . . .

Another great lesson of the Cuban Revolution also is very important to us, to the Mexicans. Its course came to confirm the effectiveness of the revolutionary methods for solving the acute problems created by under-development, by imperialism's exploitation and by the rule of the reactionary oligarchies. It raised the problem of the need and inevitability of a revolution in our countries. And in this sense it revealed the failure of the ideology of the Mexican Revolution, the bankruptcy of the reformism with which the Mexican bourgeoisie has been operating in recent years, the falseness of the course of snail's-pace reforms.

It is not offensive for us, as some believe, it is not offensive for us Mexicans who love our nation and who therefore want to see it free from foreign and domestic oppressors, it is not offensive for us to make a comparison between the concrete economic and social results of the Mexican Revolution and all that which the Cuban Revolution has given its people and all the peoples of Latin America. The only ones who may feel offended by this comparison are those who make use of the name of the Mexican Revolution merely as a demagogic shield, as a banner behind which they can perpetuate the deceit of a "revolution that became a government" and the myth of the revolutionary spirit of the Mexican bourgeoisie.

But this parallel is mandatory; it is mandatory and timely also, because there are those who are attempting to show that the way the Latin American peoples should follow is precisely the way of the Mexican Revolution and not the way of the Cuban Revolution. They want to sell their false merchandise to the other peoples of Latin America under the label of the last word for solving the problems of underdevelopment. Therefore, we Mexicans are the ones who are obliged to make this comparison.

Many numbers or any effort whatsoever are not needed to make that comparison or to establish the difference. Sixty years after having triumphed, fifty years after having placed the bourgeoisie in power, over three million Mexican farmers lack land, while a little over 9,000 large landowners have over 75,000,000 hectares of land in their possession. On the other hand, the Cuban Revolution did not need more than a few months to turn over all the land to the farmers.

It took only a few months for Cuban and foreign landlords to cease to exist on the island as a class. Fifty years after the Revolution, almost one-third of the Mexicans continue to be illiterate. But the Cuban Revolution did not need more than a year to put an end completely and forever to illiteracy. Fifty years after the Revolution, Mexico not only has not achieved one of the main objectives of the armed 1910–1917 movement, the one for complete economic independence, but rather in the last twenty-five years our nation's economic dependence has increased with regard to imperialism. What happened in Cuba? Barely two years of revolutionary period were sufficient for the Cuban revolutionaries to put an end definitively to the exploitation of United States monopolies.

In fifty years of revolution, the Mexican bourgeoisie not only has not granted the democratic freedoms for which the Mexicans shed so much blood, but rather it has set up one of the most anti-democratic regimes on the continent. It not only deprives a considerable number of Mexicans, like the ones represented by the People's Electoral Front and the Communist Party in the last election campaign, of voting rights, but it also imprisons, tries and sentences to long prison terms those who bravely exercise the right to strike and those who make common cause in worker activities. Our comrades who were imprisoned under this regime have been in prison for seven years now.

What did the Cuban Revolution do in this matter? It brought the workers and the farmers into power and gave the people the weapons so that these people would have a simple and practical way of defending their sovereignty and of exercising democracy.

It must be said, because this must be pointed out very clearly, that those problems I have indicated, only a few of them, could not be completely solved even by those national bourgeoisie governments of a more democratic and progressive nature. I am referring, in particular, to the period of government under President Cardenas. Although a blow was struck at that time at large landowning and imperialism, they were not eliminated. Not even those governments were capable of solving the problems that the Cuban Revolution solved in a very short period of time.

And I have deliberately eliminated from this comparison the main, fundamental measure, the greatest achievement of the Cuban Revolution, which was the elimination of private ownership of the instruments and means of production, and I have eliminated it from this brief comparison, in order to emphasize only those changes that a democratic-bourgeois revolution, like the Mexican Revolution, could solve, if it had not stopped halfway. . . .

After all this, the ideologists of the bourgeoisie and imperialism want the peoples of Latin America to take as their model of a revolution the Mexican Revolution and to draw away from Cuba's example! We can draw from the foregoing another of the lessons that have been emphasized by the triumph of the Cuban Revolution: in our times the bourgeoisie is no longer capable of heading any revolution that is truly of the people, truly democratic and truly anti-imperialist. Under present conditions, this can only be done by forces that are not interested in the development of capitalism, of which the principal force is the working class, which unites around it the farmers, the petty bourgeoisie in the cities, and the progressive intellectuals. The basic nucleus around which these classes are uniting is the alliance of the workers and the farmers. . . .

. . . The Cuban Revolution has shown that the solution to the serious problems brought upon our peoples by the oppression of imperialism, feudal vestiges and the rule of the reactionary oligarchies, can only be found by the revolutionary course, by means of a revolution, and not by means of reforms, regardless of whether they are of the Alliance for Progress type or of some other. . . .

The present solutions, the urgent solutions demanded by the Mexican people can no longer be found in a simple reform of the present economic and political systems, but rather in a radical and revolutionary transformation. That is the main content of the new program of the Communist Party. . . .

What is our Party doing at the present time to fulfill those objectives in the best way possible? First of all, our Party is striving to remove the worker, farmer and student masses from the ideological influence of the bourgeoisie, which for many years has kept them under a control that we cannot overlook. . . .

For that reason, the Communists, together with many young people without party affiliation and from other parties, have contributed to building up an independent national organization of the Mexican students, which will group, under an anti-imperialist, revolutionary program, the great masses of the students outside the control of the bourgeoisie, outside the control of its ideologists, and which will put them in a position of deciding themselves the method of struggle.

For that reason, the Party is also striving, together with many other forces and trends in the labor union movement, to group independently, at the base now (because conditions for a federation do not exist), active, aware, revolutionary workers, who will be the base, the seed, that will encourage our worker movement to regain its traditions and its activities of the years 1957–1960.

The Party is also striving to unite all the democratic, anti-imperialist forces in a broad front, because it is necessary to unite all those who are ready to fight for the first stage in the revolution. . . .

The experience of every revolution, and we also include in this the experience of the Cuban Revolution, proves very clearly that without the existence of a specific degree of favorable conditions among the masses, without a specific degree of organization of the revolutionary forces and without the attainment of a specific level by the crisis of the ruling classes, the triumph of the revolution is practically impossible. . . .

READING 5 *Castro Challenges Frei Reforms*

Introductory Note

The substantive and ideological features of Castro's attacks on "reformism" in Chile and President Eduardo Frei Montalva's response are suggested by the following documents. Castro clearly disagreed with Frei's argument that Christian Democratic reforms provide a "third way" of development in Latin America, being neither Marxist nor capitalist. This disagreement is captured in Selection 5.1. Selection 5.2 illustrates the kind of radio broadcast on Chile which emanated weekly from Havana during the late 1960s.

SELECTION 5.1: CASTRO SPEECH SCORES CHILEAN GOVERNMENT

Eduardo Frei, the president of Chile by the grace of his great demagogy and abundant help from Yankee and German financial capital–and according to his own belief, by the grace of God–speaking during an event held in front of the presidential palace, stated that he would not answer the statements I made on 13 March because he has too much respect for his country, too much respect for the post he holds, and too much self-respect to enter

Selection 5.1: Speech by Fidel Castro made in reply to statements of President Eduardo Frei Montalva, Havana Domestic Radio Broadcast, March 20, 1966.

Selection 5.2: Havana Domestic Radio Broadcast, "The People's Revolution vs. Bourgeois Reformism," February 2, 1967.

into a contest of insults which once was aimed against President Kennedy, today is aimed against China, and tomorrow is aimed against Chile.

Then he added: We will not allow anyone to stick his hand into the country or we will break his hand. He said this even though a few hours before the event to which I am referring he had personally announced to reporters that the government would issue a declaration, and it did so a few hours later through the Department of Government.

From news agencies' dispatches I have taken a text of the statements made by Frei during the event held in front of the presidential palace and of the paragraphs of the declaration released a little before by the Department of Government which were filed by these news agencies and which say:

> From time to time and since he has been in the government, Fidel Castro has systematically insulted nation after nation. President Kennedy heard his diatribes and so did many other rulers. Nations of the socialist world, such as Yugoslavia and the People's Republic of China, to which he referred with extraordinary violence during the same speech in which he attacks Chile, have not escaped. That is his way of covering up his internal difficulties. The Chilean Government has never attacked him.
>
> The attitude of Fidel Castro confirms the conditions under which revolution is intended to be carried out in Latin America —either through his system based on the capricious dictatorship of one man, without elections, without congress, with a single party, with an official press, without freedom, with thousands of executions, and with the dependence of a political and economic satellite of a foreign power, or through the revolution in freedom which Chile selected in 1964 and which is being carried out with the voluntary participation of the people, with free elections, an open congress where all currents of opinion are represented, with free radio and press, with labor freedoms, and with active political opposition.
>
> The Chileans who desired the Castro system were overwhelmingly crushed in 1964, 1965, and 1966 by the secret vote of the people. The Chilean people are not willing to see our

> nation turned into the toy of a temperamental man or a battlefield of the cold war. We are building a nation to free ourselves from all sorts of imperialism, not to be slaves to anyone. There are groups in Chile which do not accept their defeat, which want to destroy the country's economy, to disregard the authority of law and are now inciting violence in an attempt to gain advantage from the misfortunes which they caused.
>
> The nation now knows where these groups obtain their inspiration and the respect in which they are held by Chile. Castroism lost its opportunity to turn the tide to the left in Chile and in Latin America. Its lack of freedom and its economic failure carried it to extreme rationing and its subjection to foreign interests took away its meaning. The Chilean Government will not move an inch from its revolutionary course or from its vocation to serve the people who express their support freely and not through fear.
>
> For this reason, Castro's insults only serve to confirm his desperation. Castro does not know Chile, nor its history, nor the dignity of its people. Chile has never nor will it ever accept foreign interference in its internal problems. His insults only provoke the unity of the nation.

Amen.

For my part, I am not going to create a scandal and shout that I am insulted. However, will Your Immaculate Excellency permit me, will the gentlemen of the Christian Democratic parliamentary majority, which also is in solidarity with his offended excellency, permit me to answer these beautiful statements addressed to us without saying pharisaically later on that this is an insult to Chile?

The poor bourgeois that exists in Frei is enmeshed in his own contradictions. His role is to prevent a revolution in Chile, but he has become fond of calling himself a revolutionary. He swears up and down that he is effecting a revolution, and yet at the same time nothing frightens him as much as revolution. Ah, if only what he is doing in Chile could be revolutionary; but it is not revolution. . . .

Our cause is ennobled, not dishonored, by the comparisons Frei makes between the Cuban revolution and his laughable political pantomime, which can be called revolutionary only by the enemies of revolutions. Between the two processes there is the difference that exists between the true and the false, the heroic and the ridiculous, the fact that will go down in history and the farce that will be tossed into the historians' wastebasket.

Frei got into office with the help of imperialist money and the almost complete support of press, radio, television, and other media which are the weapons used in legal political fighting and which, in Chile as in any other capitalist oligarchical society, belong to the rich.

Bourgeois freedom of the press, which is the one to which Frei refers, is the freedom of the rich to own the greatest part of the media for disseminating ideas, they use them to defend their class interests against the exploited. It also means a lack of freedom for the poor and dispossessed to have available such media —which entail increasingly more fantastic expenditures—unless it be within very tight limits, in small number, allowing no comparison with the means at the disposal of their rich exploiters.

Every means at the disposal of imperialism, the oligarchy, and the bourgeois—their political, social, cultural, and religious institutions, their lies, prejudices, and fears—were mobilized to make Frei's victory possible. A section of the people was while being offered a beatific "revolution" that could be carried out by the bourgeoisie aided by the imperialists.

If the case of Chile has really served for anything it is not to point a new way for the revolutionary masses, but to put before all revolutionaries in the hemisphere still more forcefully the question of whether the peaceful triumph of the revolution is possible in the face of the exploiting classes which, led by imperialism, possess all the society's gold and a monopoly on the weapons that are used in this kind of battle, even though they may be willing inside their bourgeois institutions to grant a few crumbs of legality to the revolutionary forces. Cuba's course has not served to justify Chile's experiment. Just the reverse is true; Chile's experiment will serve to justify Cuba's course still further to the revolutionaries of the hemisphere. . . .

In any mass event held in the large provinces of Cuba we can gather more citizens ready to give their lives for the revolution than the votes that Frei obtained with the help of the imperialists, the oligarchs, and the bourgeoisie together in the elections that took him to power. And this can be verified by Frei himself, if he desires to do so.

Those who proclaim political and social forms which today act as a brake on the development of man and his livelihood cannot call themselves revolutionaries. For this reason, we cannot believe that Frei and his group understand the Cuban process, nor can they judge it with their prejudices, with their limited viewpoints, and with their myopic bourgeois political eyes. How could Frei's mentality be reconciled with the communist idea of a classless society in which even the state does not exist as a coercive power nor do any of the institutions that distinguish it as a state? . . .

The reactionaries have never been concerned over shedding the people's blood in defense of their own class interests, and nothing is more common than for a reactionary to accuse revolutions of being cruel. . . .

Frei, who likes to call himself a revolutionary, in the field of economics, social affairs, and politics will never be more than a reformist bourgeois whose program tends to consolidate in Chile the capitalist system of production, and this without clashing with the interests of imperialism.

Frei dreams the impossible dream of reconciling the antagonistic classes. He thinks that the interests of the workers can be reconciled with those of imperialism and the bourgeoisie, those of the bourgeoisie with those of imperialism, those of the petty bourgeoisie with those of the big bourgeoisie, and those of the peasants with those of the oligarchy. . . .

Selection 5.2: Chileans Consider Revolution and Reformism

. . . The large masses of Chileans have no access to independent sources of information. Their political points of view are shaped by the newspapers, the dailies, magazines, and radio broadcasting stations owned by various kinds of reactionaries. Under these circumstances which hinder development toward the political maturity of the masses, the Chilean voters, nevertheless, voted in 1964 for the revolution. What thoughts motivated the Chileans? What did the Chilean man on the street think about when he cast his vote for Allende or for Frei? Did he think that his sentiments, reflected in his vote, would shake the bases of the corrupt society in which he lived?

These voters firmly believed that Chile deserved a future better than the one traditional politicians could give it. They thought Allende or Frei would melt the foundations of exploitation and bring justice to Chile. They thought the time had come to put an end to the political life of the domestic oligarchy.

However, once in the presidential seat, Eduardo Frei exchanged the revolution for the most repugnant kind of charity among the fringes of the population. Frei, the chief executive, decided that our people should not be free, but a slave to the United States. Eduardo Frei, the Christian Democrat, drafted his policies from the high olympus of government without consulting the Chilean peasants and workers. To put it bluntly, Frei mocked his voters and trod over the ideals and dreams of his political opposers who spoke sincerely of a revolution. . . .

If Frei had been loyal to the ideas for which his supporters voted, the revolution in Chile would have become a reality already. Agrarian reform would now be a dynamic reality, as would urban reform, plans for the protection of our basic wealth, the limitless expansion of our country's international relations. . . .

However, Frei has forgotten these election plans and promises. Instead of interpreting the people's desires, President Frei has sought to satisfy the voracious appetites of the domestic oligarchy and of the Chilean nouveaux riches who carry the membership card of the Christian Democratic Party.

READING 6 *Castro Opposes Venezuelan Reforms*

Introductory Note

The Venezuelan government received much criticism from Havana after 1966, in part due to its own public accusations against Castro and his militant line (Selection 6.1). The circumstances of this polemic are different, however, from Cuban criticism of Chile. First, the guerrilla movement, led by those militants who split with the Venezuelan Communist Party in 1966 over the peaceful vs. the violent road debate, is far stronger in Venezuela than in Chile. Whereas Castro lauds the militant but legal Socialist Party in Chile, he praises the illegal guerrillas in Venezuela (Selection 6.2).

Secondly, unlike Chile, Venezuela took the lead in 1967 in pressing for hemispheric denunciations of Havana for its "subversive" activities in Venezuela (Selection 6.3). This Venezuelan action only raised to a new level Castro's verbal bombast of

Selection 6.1: Speech by Fidel Castro attacking the Venezuelan government, March 13, 1967; Havana Domestic Radio Broadcast, March 14, 1967.

Selection 6.2: Havana Radio Broadcast beamed to Latin America, entitled "Venezuelan Events," July 15, 1967.

Selection 6.3: Venezuelan Chamber of Deputies Resolution Adopted May 16, 1967; Caracas, Venezuela, Radio Continente Broadcast, May 17, 1967.

Selection 6.4: Statement by the Central Committee of the Cuban Communist Party, Havana Radio Broadcast, beamed to Latin America, May 18, 1967.

Venezuela and the "imperialist" activities of the United States (Selection 6.4).

Selection 6.1: Fidel Castro's 13 March [1967] Anniversary Speech

. . . Again today circumstances demand that we attack a subject of this type: the problems of Venezuela, the problems of the Venezuelan revolutionary movement, the imputations that the puppet Government of Venezuela has made against our revolution and the accusations of the official rightist leadership of the Communist Party of Venezuela.

For several days a big campaign against our country has been unleashed by the government of that country and the Yankee news services because of the death of a former official of the Venezuelan Government. Also, for the past several months, in the clandestine and semiclandestine press, including the legal press of that nation, and at various international events, the rightist leadership of the Venezuelan Communist Party has been levying similar imputations against our party. . . .

There is not a single event of all that takes place in this uneasy continent that does not lead to an immediate and trite accusation blaming Cuba. A few weeks ago, because of the elections in Nicaragua, Somoza's forces perpetrated a massacre of the opposition party. Immediately, as is logical, even though it was a party named "the Conservative Party," Cuba was blamed for having fomented that clash, that bloodshed.

Anything that happens anywhere: If it takes place in Colombia, Cuba is immediately blamed; if it is in Guatemala, Cuba is immediately blamed; if a military uprising occurs in Santo Domingo which leads to intervention by Yankee troops—an intervention that still continues—the inevitable reason for it is Cuba. Practically nothing can happen in this continent that Cuba is not blamed for. And Cuba only has one responsibility—carry out a revolution and be ready to carry it to its ultimate consequences! . . .

We Cubans are accused of promoting subversion; we Cubans

are accused of directing the revolutionary armed movement in Venezuela. If the Cubans had had anything to do with directing that revolutionary movement we would never have fallen, and that revolutionary movement would have never fallen, into those two great errors in concept. Why? Because revolutionaries and only revolutionaries are the ones who determine, the only ones who can determine, their general strategy and their tactics. And the revolutionaries must do this always, always. In Venezuela and in all the other countries the concepts may be wrong many times but they can only be corrected through the revolutionary process itself, by the experiences of the process, from the blows they receive during the process.

We Cuban revolutionaries are not leaders who tell them what they should do. It is their own experience that tells them. The best teachers of the revolutionaries in each Latin American country, as it was in Cuba, the best teachers, the great teachers, were reverses. Naturally the Venezuelan revolutionary movement suffered reverses. The revolutionary movement in all parts of the world has suffered reverses also. The Latin American movement, as is logical, had to go through a long apprenticeship. Today it can be declared that this movement has learned much, not from Cuba but from its own experience from the blows it received. This is why this revolutionary movement with more experience grows and consolidates itself and the rulers are powerless to crush it; powerless to crush it in Guatemala, powerless to crush it in Colombia, powerless to crush it in Venezuela. . . .

Selection 6.2: Venezuelan Guerrillas Gaining Strength

The Raúl Leoni regime has ordered the dispatch of fresh military contingents to the states of Trujillo and Portuguesa. Caracas reports reveal that the border area between the two states has been declared a military zone and that peasants living in that area must have a safe-conduct pass issued by the army in order to move about.

Several clashes have occurred in this border area between the forces of tyranny and the "Rafael Urdaneta" guerrilla columns led by Major Freddy Carques. The guerrillas led by the former Caracas youth leader seized the towns of Tostos and Niquitao and later fought army soldiers in the neighborhood of these two towns.

They say that lies have short legs. It would be opportune to ask the Venezuelan dictatorship if its repeated statements about the weakness of the patriotic forces and these armed deployments in the western part of the country are not entirely contradictory.

Since the reorganization of the leadership of the National Liberation Front and of the Armed Forces of National Liberation, we have noted an evident development and strengthening of the guerrillas. The Leoni [President Raúl Leoni] tyranny, with its lavish announcements of alleged guerrillas captured in the mountains and of losses inflicted on the guerrillas–announcements that are never confirmed—has lately been discreetly silent about the guerrilla activity in the western states of Venezuela.

The recent dispatch of forces, which the Leoni regime has been unable to conceal, proves that the Venezuelan regime is facing an increasingly difficult situation on that front. We must not forget that the forces of tyranny have maintained several antiguerrilla camps in this area for a long time. The repeated euphoric statements released by the Leoni officials were recently questioned by Paz Galarraga, secretary general of the official government party, when he said that it would be illogical to say that the guerrillas do not exist. . . .

The Leoni regime no longer has to deal with the static fronts on which it dropped its forces provided with Yankee supplies. Now it has to deal with agile columns that are capable of incessant hammering away because of great mobility. This conception of the struggle, although it does not seem too far removed from the traditional style, represents a more advanced stage in the development of the Venezuelan guerrilla struggle.

There is no doubt that the Venezuelan regime is facing today a much more experienced guerrilla body, which has been operating in the mountains for five years now. It is better supplied and has a better range of action. The revolutionary fighters commanded by Douglas Bravo have in him a man forged in that five-year-old school of guerrilla warfare. Most of the commanders of the patriotic forces are men of the same stature. The Venezuelan tyranny must fight against this growing force that is being forged in the very heart of the nation and that has the undoubted support of the peasantry. The results of wars between peoples and tyrannies, history tells us, unfailingly favor the large dispossessed majorities. Imprecations, charges, and maneuvers against Cuba will not avail Leoni and his imperialist masters. The fire is burning in the very heart of Venezuela and of the people, who in the long run will be victorious in a war that can only be settled by revolutionary arms.

Selection 6.3: Venezuelan Chamber of Deputies Resolution

Whereas on 12 May the national government disclosed the presence in Venezuela of regular Cuban army and Cuban militia elements who had entered the country for the purpose of taking part in subversive activities against Venezuela's democratic system, whereas said fact constitutes an act of aggression against national sovereignty and violates the principles and provisos of non-intervention sustained in the OAS Charter and the U.N. organization; whereas this new act of aggression against Venezuela by the Cuban Government—a reassertion of its interventionist policy against our country—has evoked the unanimous repudiation of our people.

Therefore, the Chamber of Deputies of the Republic Venezuela resolves

1. to categorically condemn the brazen aggressive policy of the Fidel Castro regime against our country;
2. to once again denounce the subversive, antinational conduct of those Venezuelans who, acting as accomplices of Castroite aggression, have committed treason against Venezuela;

3. to support the steps being taken by the government to denounce the Cuban regime before international organizations and to demand the sanctions which it deserves; and
4. to request that all the congresses in America express their solidarity with the Venezuelan Government and people in its rejection of the aggression of which it has been the victim at the hands of the Cuban dictatorial government, whose actions jeopardize the continent's peace and security, and to seek continental solidarity now being put to the test by the outrageous facts that have been denounced.

Selection 6.4: Central Committee Answers Venezuelan Charge

As our people have been able to learn from cables released by all the international press agencies—cables that have been published in textual form by our newspapers—the lackey government in Venezuela, following the evident instructions of its masters in Washington, is trying to unleash an hysterical, violent, aggressive, and belligerent campaign against our country. They are using such really shameful terms as naval and air blockade, ultimatum, collective armed attack, economic boycott of the countries trading with Cuba, and so forth. This means that they are threatening and are trying to intimidate our country in the crudest fashion.

Are they demanding that imperialism cease the criminal and cowardly economic blockade of a Latin American country—a blockade that is being carried out in violation of all international and human laws and with the repugnant complicity of all the Latin American governments, with the honorable exception of Mexico? No! These and many other deeds of the kind are not important. They are absolutely unworthy of being taken into consideration. What incites their fury and their hysterics is the report of the presence of three Cubans—one of whom was killed and two arrested—when, according to their statement, they were trying to help a group of eight Venezuelan revolutionaries return to their country.

These are precisely some of the Venezuelan revolutionaries who have been fighting for years to liberate their country from the tutelage and exploitation of the Yankee monopolies. For that, they are murdered—ipso facto—when they fall into the hands of the repressive policy of the regime. That, indeed, is reason to urge them to demand an immediate, fulminating, and exterminating action against Cuba. This is the philosophy, the concept of right and international law, the ethics, and the rules that the imperialists want to impose on the world.

The fact is that when these blessed boys [*santos varones*] speak of war against Cuba, they speak of a war that must be fought by the Yankee army, navy, and air force. In other words, they think in cowardly fashion about what in their opinion would be a simple and easy genocide of our people by the imperialists. After all, this is what lies behind the melodramatic boastings of Señor Leoni. Moreover, his statements contain a series of lies. None of the three Cuban youths he mentions belongs to the regular Cuban Army. . . .

It is also false that a Soviet-made rifle coming from Cuba could have been seized, because all weapons of the kind that the USSR has supplied the Republic of Cuba are perfectly registered and controlled by the army's Arms Control Center, and none of them has disappeared. Concerning all the statements contained in the official declaration, they cannot show anything but the testimony attributed to persons who are absolutely at the mercy of their jailers and whose lack of scruples and brutal methods are well known.

However, let it not be said that we are trying to elude any responsibility. It is neither necessary to invent any lie nor to prove any truth when it comes to the aims pursued by imperialism and its repressive policy against the Cuban revolutionary movement. Yankee imperialism constitutes a system that is trying to impose itself on the world, using for this purpose the most draconian and pitiless methods.

Imperialism is waging a war to the death against the revolutionary movements of the entire world. Our people have been acquiring a firsthand knowledge of the results of the imperialist design since the very day—after a long and heroic struggle—we achieved for the first time in four centuries of history, the right to direct our own fate and to forge our future. We are fighting unceasingly, and shall continue to do so, against criminal imperialism and against all its accomplices and lackeys. . . .

READING 7 *Intra-Party Friction in the Cuban Communist Party*

Introductory Note

Of the many dramatic events publicized by Castro during the course of any single year, perhaps the most dramatic was the exposé and trial of thirty-seven "old guard" Communists, identified in the past as having pro-Soviet sentiments. This trial in February 1968, coming just two years after the militant announcements of the Tricontinental Conference of January 1966, reconfirmed Castro's policy of commitment to promotion of revolutionary violence in Latin America, strengthening the new alliance of many non-Communist revolutionary groups under his control through the Cuban-led Organización Latino Americana de Solidaridad (*Organization of Latin American Solidarity or OLAS*), *challenging the vanguard role of national Communist Parties and intervening in their affairs, attacking reformist regimes and Soviet efforts to improve relations with some of those governments.*[1] *Simultaneously, it revealed a rift within the Cuban Communist Party itself over the question of revolution vs. reform, although it is difficult to know how deep was the fissure.*

The key figure in this exposé was Communist veteran Aníbal Escalante, member of the old guard which has gradually lost

1. See Kevin Devlin, "Castro Strikes at Communist 'Microfaction' in a Challenge to Moscow," *Radio Free Europe Report,* February 6, 1968.

Court Martial of Aníbal Escalante and the "Microfaction," Havana Radio Broadcast beamed to Latin America, February 2, 1968; see also *Granma,* February 2, 1968.

power since the early days of the revolution. Old Communists retained a few seats on the 100-man Central Committee when the Communist Party was formed in 1965, but real power lay in the 8-member Politburo, composed of Castroites.[2] *It should be noted that Escalante and the "microfaction" accused in this trial had no formally established organization. They were rather a loose association of malcontents who opposed Castro's policies in several ways which are enumerated in the court martial summation which follows.*

. . . 1. Microfaction: We reach the conclusion of this trial of the accused group that form part of the so-called "microfaction." This name has been used because—in view of the small number of those who composed the group and the views it maintained—it cannot really be considered a real faction. In the list of charges read at the beginning of the trial, all the activities that this group engaged in against the revolution were brought out. Therefore, we are not going to repeat them in detail. However, we can summarize these activities here as follows:

a. Attacks, by means of intrigues and calumnies, on the principal measures adopted by the revolution;
b. Distribution of clandestine propaganda against the party line;
c. Attempt to convey distorted guidelines to several party cells;
d. Supplying false and calumnious information to officials of foreign countries about the plans of the revolution with the aim of undermining Cuba's international relations with other governments;
e. Theft of secret documents from the Central Committee and the former Ministry of Industry;
f. Proselytic and ideological activity among some activists of the Popular Socialist Party (PSP) and other activity intended to destroy the unity and firmness of the revolutionary forces. . . .

These hypocrites wanted to create the impression that the

2. See Kevin Devlin, "Making the Most of a Microfaction," *Radio Free Europe Report,* February 13, 1968.

revolution persecutes those of its members who come from the ranks of the old Popular Socialist Party [old Cuban Communist Party]. Nothing could be more base, more deplorable. True communists—those who have not betrayed their principles, who are loyal to the ideology of Marxism-Leninism—are part of this revolution; they are and they will continue to be within this revolution. It is not just that many good communists are burdened with the guilt and with the disrepute of those who have betrayed communist principles, allying themselves with the reformists and the traitors of Marxism-Leninism. The fact is the old communists enjoy full respect, recognition of their merits and recognition of their militancy, which they have not betrayed. It should be stated that the traitors can never pretend to represent the old Popular Socialist Party, because this microfactional group is not even a perceptible part of those old militants. . . .

This group of resentful persons, of resentful opportunists, confounded the generosity of the revolution. It began to regroup 2 years ago: began to form this microfactional group. However, even on this occasion, the generosity of the revolution did not fail them. . . . Beginning then and on many occasions, the revolution warned them. It advised them publicly on several occasions and it advised many of them also personally and in private. . . .

We do not believe the masses of our people would have let themselves be convinced by these gentlemen. A section of history vouches for the lives of our leaders, and it cannot be destroyed by slander. The deeds of this revolution cannot be destroyed by slander. But this propaganda, this plot, this conspiracy were aimed at destroying that history and those deeds. The dissemination of that propaganda was intended to undermine certain sectors of public opinion in the country. The ideas they put forward, the theses they proposed, the arguments they upheld were intended to undermine our revolution.

Concurrence with the enemy.

And these ideas and arguments are the ones that suit our enemies best. In this the microfaction concurs with imperialism and the revolution's enemies. What do the revolution's enemies say? What did imperialism say about our revolution? That the revolution was carried out by the petty bourgeoisie, which Fidel betrayed. What a coincidence that now the men of the microfaction are accusing the revolution of being "petty bourgeois."

What does the enemy say about the guerrilla action and armed struggle by other peoples? That this is not the right way, that conditions are not right. In their anxiety to crush the revolutionary surge to maintain their exploitation, the enemies seek arguments that will prevent the seizure of power through armed struggle by the peoples. And what do the men of the microfaction say? What is said by those who diverge from Marxist theses, like certain Latin American Communist parties?

[They say] that conditions are absent, that this is not the way, that it is necessary to wait, that the revolutionary outbreak must be put off. What do dispatches of the UPI, AFP, and other imperialist agencies say? That Cuba's economy is going to pieces, that the agricultural programs cannot produce the expected results, that the sugar crop will be a failure, that Cuba is governed by one man alone. These same arguments are used by the microfaction. What a coincidence! Those theories, those theses suit imperialism and the counter-revolution perfectly; they also coincide in propaganda. . . .

Similarly, as products of Catholic training or petty bourgeois education, some counterrevolutionaries also failed to understand the process and began plotting against the revolution or came in the Girón beach invasion. The revolution has a right and the duty to defend itself from such action and from individuals that are allied to imperialism or, without seeking to ally themselves with imperialism, nevertheless play into its hands and provide it with a pretext. The revolution has a right to protect itself, to prevent the revolutionary advance from being thwarted; it has a right and the duty to destroy its enemies. . . .

They [the microfaction] say that the revolution is controlled by the one-man government of Maj. Fidel Castro. The charge that the revolutionary leadership imposes its belief on the masses and that this nation's government is a one-man government is not only the belief of the microfaction—the counterrevolutionaries also subscribe to this statement. This statement deceitfully ignores the creative ability of the masses in our revolution. It ignores that in many cases our leaders are only the receptors of our people's ideas.

For example, the Committees for the Defense of the Revolution (*Comites de Defensa de la Revolución* or CDR) were started by the people before they were legally recognized. The first CDR was founded in Pinar del Río on the initiative of the people before it was officially instituted as a social creation of the revolution. The CDR is a genuine mass organization and not the result of a satellite mentality or a mechanical copy. It is rather an authentic creation of our revolution. As a mass organization, the CDR constitutes a magnificent liaison between the masses and the institutions of the revolutionary power. . . .

The microfactionalists not only say that the Revolutionary Government is controlled by Maj. Fidel Castro alone, but also that the Central Committee does not meet and that it does not resolve anything. Now that you are seated here, you tell me whether it meets or not! That is what made it possible for you to be seated here, although this is not all that was discussed at the meeting!

Our party's Central Committee is not a parliamentary institution. We do not know what idea the microfactionalists have of our party's Central Committee, but what we do know is that it is not a deliberating organization. Moreover, the meetings do not determine and define the course of the revolution. When sectarianism prevailed at every meeting, not a single problem was ever resolved. The Central Committee is the organization where basic matters of the revolution should be presented and discussed, and in this connection, our Central Committee has always set the policy and the strategy of the revolution.

For these microfactionalist gentlemen, formal matters may be very important, but the revolution has not been exactly characterized by formalities. It has been so since the struggle against [Fulgencio] Batista. History itself refutes the charge that Maj. Fidel Castro has been a concentrator of power. During the armed struggle against the tyranny, Camilo [Cienfuegos], Che [Ernesto Guevara], and all the military leaders had full powers within the scope of the strategy to carry out their campaigns, organize their own forces, and carry out the invasion. It is well known by all that when the government was constituted in 1959, Fidel did not participate in the appointments. . . .

READING 8 *Party Opposition to Chile's President Frei*

Introductory Note

Party opposition to Eduardo Frei Montalva's reform legislation grew steadily after his inauguration in November 1964. Parties to the left of Chilean Democrats—the Communists and socialists—accused them of not implementing basic change fast enough or deep enough; the far right seemed increasingly convinced that he was delivering the country up to Marxism. This opposition reached a peak on January 17, 1967, when the Chilean Senate, where the Christian Democrats were in the minority, refused by a 23–15 vote to allow President Frei to leave the country for his planned visit to the United States.

Various specific reasons motivated the different parties to oppose this trip as they did. The socialists and Communists blocked the trip partly because of their opposition to United States policies in Vietnam, Cuba, and the Dominican Republic and partly to embarrass the president publicly. The rightist parties—conservatives and liberals—were not enamored with Frei's agrarian, tax, or social reform policies, and the more liberal radicals were threatened by Christian Democrats in future elections. Radicals felt they had to establish an independent image from the Christian Democrats since they shared a number of ideological similarities.

President Frei's vigorous protest against this Senate action, and

Speech to the nation by Chilean President Eduardo Frei Montalva, Santiago, Chile, Domestic Radio Broadcast, January 19, 1967.

his perceptions of legislative obstructionism, are contained in the following speech, in which he called for dissolution of the Congress and new national elections.

The country has been rocked by an all-important political event, by the Senate's denial of constitutional permission for the President to leave Chile. I repeat, the constitutional permission for the President to leave Chile in response to the honored and very special invitation from the President of the United States.

Those Chileans who are politically responsible fully understand the implications of this. The Senate action undoubtedly climaxes a process that began the very day the people elected me. The country has been witness to my tolerance and effort, and to the sacrifices I have made to assure that democracy could operate within a framework of liberty.

The country likewise realizes that we have been unable to enact the constitutional reform bill, the law on neighborhood improvement boards, the steel bill, and that other bills have been delayed, including the agrarian reform bill. This lack of action means that the country is losing valuable opportunities. Furthermore, as time passes, the opposition not only does not hesitate to block the enactment of necessary legislation, but it also unites to obstruct the government.

Why has it now come to pass that a great number of people have gathered here, demanding to be heard. They must indeed be heard. . . . It has now come to the point where the President is prevented from directing foreign policy, a power expressly granted him under our political constitution. I want to stress the seriousness of what has happened: the injury to me, to the government, and to the country's permanent, sacred interests.

I have considered the matter and I believe that to deny the Chilean President the right to meet personally with the U.S. chief of state is something which has never been denied any Chilean President . . . and that it is an antagonistic act against that nation, which has given to Chile financial, economic, and technical cooperation of vast proportions.

An attempt has been made to prevent the President of Chile from holding an interview with the U.S. President and that nation's congressmen, and from receiving the honors of the highest universities of that country, where some of the most prestigious figures of world thought are living.

And this has come at a moment when there are so many problems to resolve in our continent—and listen closely to what I am going to say—many problems which closely affect us.

On the eve of the meeting of the American presidents, an attempt is being made to prevent the Chilean chief of state from going forth and exchanging views with the U.S. President. . . .

Up to now, the collusion against us had been aimed at balking the enactment of legislation, at discrediting and distorting government action. But this country, with a high concept of nationalism and patriotism, had kept its quarrels apart from problems linked to international relations, inasmuch as that would injure the country's vital, permanent interests.

Cabled dispatches are bringing us the world repercussion which this action has provoked. In Europe, the reaction could not have been more severe and disheartening.

And in the United States, its leaders voice their deep dismay, amazement, and disappointment. Those who had wanted to offer to the Chilean President—not to me personally—an exceptional reception, are also at a loss.

That feeling has been so evident that—please listen—I do not even hesitate to repeat the closing words said yesterday in the U.S. Senate by the U.S. Senator leader, Senator [Mike] Mansfield. I am going to repeat his words because the Chileans can then see the great respect they have for us.

The Senate majority leader said:

> Allow me to declare that on the part of the United States, the invitation to President Frei was only an expression of friendship and respect toward the Chilean people and their institutions. But of course it would have offered the most appropriate atmosphere for both chiefs of state to hold a frank discussion. Therefore, the cancellation of President Frei's visit will mean

> losing the opportunity to hold such a discussion. That is deplorable as much for Chile as for the United States. . . .
>
> I reiterate that all of the problems that may exist between the United States and Chile can be solved, if we face them, and if we meet together with complete honesty and mutual understanding. . . .

Thus, if that has been the reaction in the United States and Europe, what will it be in our own Latin America?

What will the American democrats say? They must look up with admiration, because we always have displayed a spirit of respect and understanding which has characterized and made possible our democracy. And now they have seen it shattered in a way for which there is no justification. . . .

I ask the nation; I ask you. I have left Chile on several occasions and I believe that not even the most bitter of my adversaries can ever say that I did not act with dignity, or that I compromised anything. Instead, I served the nation's interests. . . .

Never before were conditions so auspicious for a trip by a Chilean President. For that reason I have a right to think that the refusal to grant the authorization is what jurists call an abuse of power, a misinterpretation of the spirit of the constitution, and that it tends to negate the right given to the President of the republic to direct the nation's foreign policy. Consequently, I will settle this problem definitively. . . .

I have heard those who, while ignoring the most fundamental facts, affirm that this country is isolated and blame the government for it. Relying upon false information, they do not object to voting against permitting the President to go to the United States.

It is the same old story. They do not pass legislation to construct factories, but then they go into the provinces and say that the government does not provide jobs. They say that the government is deceitful and refuse the President permission to leave Chile that he may strengthen Chile's international position. They are the ones helping to isolate Chile and to weaken its international standing. This occurs at a time when, far in advance of others, Chile has expanded its international relations, as was promised during the election campaign, to include all nations of the world, no matter what their ideology. We are respected and listened to in those countries. . . .

As a result of what has happened, the cabinet ministers, in a gesture giving them credit, submitted their resignations. I have rejected these resignations, because they are not responsible for what has happened, inasmuch as they have been complying faithfully with the policy outlined to them. It would be contradictory and show weakness on my part to sacrifice them to the opposition, or to satisfy those who are plotting or discussing changes in the cabinet. . . .

Our country is not facing a political crisis. We are experiencing an institutional crisis. This is a reality the nation cannot deny. In other countries, when a government is chosen, it has the means to act. The Chilean people, in an extremely significant election and by overwhelming majority, in an expression of their resolute will, elected me to govern them. A few months later, when choosing the Congress, the people again expressed their will. However, today the country is facing a situation which in the political field apparently has no solution.

The people elect their government and congressmen to carry out the platform that the government promised. But it happens that those who were defeated, who are the minority, are trying to upset the government in its task. They are increasing their opposition with every success of the government. . . .

READING 9 *The Socialist-Communist Rift in Chile*

Introductory Note

Another Chilean inter-party debate over revolution vs. reform centers on the tenuous alliance of the Communist and Socialist Parties—the Frente de Acción Popular (*Popular Action Front or FRAP*)*—formed in 1958 to strengthen the Marxist and proletariat vote in the presidential elections. Socialist support of Fidel Castro's position and Communist adherence to the more peaceful "united front" tactics, which included some compromises with the Christian Democrats, have split this coalition apart.*[1] *In recent elections, including the March 1969 Congressional elections, the two parties ran separately, unlike the 1958 and 1964 Presi-*

1. An interesting point in this debate is Luis Corvalán's article in the July 30, 1967, edition of *Pravda,* scoring Castro's position in the hemisphere, compared to Aniceto Rodríguez's announcement shortly before in May 1967, after an eight-day visit to Cuba, that the Chilean Socialist Party had "reached an agreement" with Havana dealing with the maintenance of permanent political contact between the Socialist Party and the Cuban Communist Party. Santiago Radio Broadcast, May 4, 1967. Rodríguez was secretary general of the Socialist Party when the announcement was made.

Selection 9.1: Translation of a letter signed by Aniceto A. Rodríguez, Secretary General of the Chilean Socialist Party, entitled "A Document on Chilean Socialism," in the weekly organ of the Uruguayan Socialist Party, *El Sol,* No. 311 (Montevideo), July 8, 1966, pp. 4–5 and 7; JPRS 37,126, July 8, 1966.

Selection 9.2: Santiago Radio News Broadcast, July 12, 1966.

dential elections. The socialist disagreements with the Communist Party over its attitudes toward the Frei government (reform orientation) and the Organization of Latin American Solidarity (OLAS) are indicated in Selection 9.1. Selection 9.2 outlines the Communist reply to the socialist letter and the general schism between these two Chilean Marxist parties.

Selection 9.1: A Letter from the Socialists to the Communists in Chile

To comrade Luis Corvalán and the members of the Central Committee of the Communist Party.

Esteemed Comrades: In connection with your Thirteenth National Congress, we addressed ourselves publicly to you, setting forth our political thinking frankly and honestly. On that occasion, we told you of the well-founded concern we felt about the obvious differences which were developing and which subsequently were reflected in difficulties on the various battlefronts. Setting forth the practical and theoretical need for a unity of action between our two parties, we outlined in that document the necessity of clarifying these differences in order to seek a common policy which would permit us to give the struggle of the working masses greater force and content.

Unfortunately, during the course of this year the difficulties have been extended because of the different approaches of the two parties to the evaluation of various aspects of Chilean political and social life. These differences have inevitably come to the public attention, a fact which we should not lament, because it shows the vigor of the left, which is capable of analyzing them with critical energy, instead of concealing them, in the manner of the ostrich which refuses to face up to what is happening. . . .

We believe that all our statements and yours about unity and the need to maintain it would be more literary figures without a common goal to sustain and dynamize them. For the maintenance of unity, it does not suffice that we both adhere to Marxism as a method of interpreting reality. Nor does it suffice that we have the same historical goal of battling for socialism, if each of us uses a different method and comes to different conclusions. If we choose different paths in order to reach socialism, how then can we advance together? If unity is to be something more than formal statements, we must have the substantive similarities mentioned above. In addition, moreover, it is essential that we agree on what to do now and how to do it.

Without wishing to reiterate the concepts set forth in our previous letter, we should like to note that in our evaluations of the new situation there are profound differences. They are of an international and national nature and are linked with very different strategies and tactics, and as a result, they mean lack of understanding on the concrete level.

During its history, the Socialist Party has on various occasions devoted concern to developing coordination among the revolutionary forces in Latin America which would culminate in a well-structured political front capable of standardizing the common struggle against imperialism. We believe that this attitude is a part of the essence of proletarian internationalism. On the other hand, we have never believed that a relation of this nature would limit the logical independence of each movement in the struggle in its own country.

In this connection, we promoted and welcomed the holding of the Tricontinental Conference with enthusiasm. With some regrettable exceptions, for example Yugoslavia and Israel, it was broadly representative of the revolutionary movement on the three backward continents and was not subject to any of the ideological centers which are seeking to control the modern workers' movement. Our initiative lay behind the establishment of the Latin American Solidarity Organization (OLAS) which, inspired by the revolutionary spirit of mutual aid which governed the work of the Tricontinental Congress, examined the strategical and tactical problems which made the establishment of this continental organ to unite and coordinate the struggle against U.S. imperialism desirable. From the analysis made by the delegations developed the decision to establish that organ as a necessity imposed by the current conditions of struggle in Latin America and the aggressive behavior of the imperialists, as well as the duty to extend active and well-structured solidarity to the liberation movements on other continents.

We believe that the Latin American Solidarity Organization should fiulfill its mission in the light of these factors. It should be an active tool of combat against the aggressive actions of the imperialists and for the development of the liberation struggle on this continent.

What do you think about this matter? In our view, it seems that the Chilean Communist Party, like those in Argentina and Uruguay, lacks any serious interest in promoting this undertaking, or at least is seeking to limit its action to a mere traditional form of solidarity. . . .

Comrades, do you feel that a continental organ such as the Latin American Solidarity Organization deflects the Chilean Communist Party from the world strategy and the concept maintained by the communist parties which are united by a common ideological center?

We do not want to suggest any dependence on your part on their resolutions and political activities, but indeed we do observe a certain rigidity in closing the door to general prospects, abandoning or setting aside to a secondary level the broad range of possibilities which exist for the revolutionary movements in Latin America to make coordinated use of all means necessary to force imperialism to retreat and in the final analysis to defeat it. . . .

Thus it is urgent that you clarify your position in this sector, because the current position seems to suggest a conflict between the agreements and objectives of the Latin American Solidarity Organization and the communist strategy. . . .

In almost two years of Christian Democratic government, the people of Chile have been able to learn from their own experience and hard sacrifice the real and fraudulent meanings of the term "revolution in liberty." The old unjust economic and social structure has been maintained intact, and there is no immediate prospect that the government of Mr. Frei will change to any great extent. Moreover, his announced successor, Mr. Tomic, has proven to be a new theoretical advocate of close political and economic links between Chile and the United States.

To summarize, then, different views on the international level on the way of meeting the aggression of the imperialists and different evaluations of the role of certain sectors of the bourgeoisie (the Christian Democrats and their government in Chile) have made it difficult to reach an understanding in practice between the two parties [Communist and Socialist Parties]. . . .

Selection 9.2: The FRAP Split

The unity of the Chilean Marxist parties has been practically destroyed, thus solidifying the disappearance of the Popular Action Front (FRAP) as a federation of the socialist and the communist parties with smaller local Marxist groups. The exchange of letters between the central committees of the two parties has revealed the secret they had been guarding for 10 months.

Last Saturday, the communists replied to a political proposal made by the socialists 20 days ago. The socialists asked the communists to express their views on three points the socialists consider fundamental to unity or disagreement in Marxist action: the position toward the Organization of Latin American Solidarity (OLAS) which was created at the Havana Tricontinental Conference; political conduct with regard to the Christian Democrat government of President Eduardo Frei; and ways to increase Marxist strength in the country.

The communists have said that they consider the Tricontinental Conference an important event, despite the absence of important international Marxist groups, such as the socialists from Israel and the Yugoslav communists. However, they classify as "vague" many of the resolutions adopted during the January meeting in Cuba. Senator Luis Corvalán, secretary general of the Communist Party, told INTERPRESS: We would like to know exactly what OLAS is, how to make solidarity effective, and what type of continental political events makes it possible to require solidarity. We are accustomed to hearing many proclamations of support, but we have not yet seen any concrete deeds or plans. However, in the document released recently, the communists declared they are in favor of solidarity.

With regard to the Christian Democrat government of Eduardo Frei, the Communist Party notes: The struggle is not proposed in terms of the popular movement and the current bourgeois government alone. To think of the social conflict in these terms reduces the scope of the great conflict in which we are protagonists. The exploiting classes are wise, and they take advantage of the opportunity we give them when we weaken the present bourgeois government, which is, nevertheless, a reformist government.

However, the socialists, in their letter to the Communist Central Committee said that not even an iota of cooperation should be granted to the government, because to do so would be suicide for the Marxist movement.

The communists, through the secretary general of the Central Committee, noted that they will support the government in the following programs: Reform of the constitutional guarantee of the right of ownership, constitutional reforms, agrarian reform, peasant labor union organization, district juntas and popular improvements, and changes of the capitalist enterprises. But they have announced that such support will not be total, for they will offer their own ideas with regard to certain specific topics, such as livestock raising and the minimum number of expropriable hectares, in the field of agrarian reform and in other government plans.

The socialists insist on noting that since the present government is bourgeois, according to them, everything it produces will benefit the grande bourgeoisie. However, the problem that most concerns the communists is that socialists and communists see Marxism in different ways. The memorandum the communists sent to their Marxist comrades notes their concern in this regard. The communists point out that both parties should have different roads, but not divergent paths, as the socialists indicated in their memorandum of three weeks ago.

Events, however, demonstrate that the socialists are correct. The FRAP, which was conceived as a federation of Marxist organizations designed to produce a common political program and to coordinate the work of its members, has ceased to exist as such ten months ago. The direct or indirect support the communists have given to populist aspects of the Christian Democrat or government initiatives have caused the socialists to resist and even abandon parliamentary work. The leadership of the FRAP had not met since October of last year, and the parties have adopted and carried out their own individual strategies against the several bills the National Congress has discussed in recent times. . . .

This split within the Marxist front and the fading of the FRAP does not signify the death of the federation or of unified Marxism in Chile. It means that, in view of the system of government instituted by the Christian Democrats and President Eduardo Frei, some have opted for intransigent opposition and others for indirect support. Luis Corvalán, secretary general of the Communist Party, told INTERPRESS: We shall go divided into the coming municipal elections of April 1967, and we shall have to prepare separately for the parliamentary elections of 1969. The FRAP only exists in the minds of those of us who formed it and, unfortunately, it has ceased to be the guiding force of the popular movement.

READING 10 *Friction Among Chile's Christian Democrats*

Introductory Note

Chile's Partido Demócrata Cristiano (*Christian Democratic Party or PDC*) *has experienced serious internal disagreement over the rate of change required for the nation's social and economic development. Party friction became particularly acute in July 1967, when the PDC held its anual national meeting to elect party officers. In anticipation of the event, forty-four PDC deputies and five party senators issued a manifesto calling for PDC unity, for closer liaison between the government and the party, and for an end to factionalist activities that tended to undermine the government's program* (*Selection 10.1*). *Another version of party priorities was the so-called "Plan Chonchol" or* Proposiciones para una acción política en el periodo 1967–70 de una vía no capitalista de desarrollo (*Propositions for Policy Action in the Period 1967–70 for a Non-Capitalist Way of Development*), *which was named after one of its key sponsors, Jacques Chonchol*

Selection 10.1: Translated excerpts from *Proposiciones para los delegados ante la junta nacional,* prepared and subscribed to by forty-four deputies and five senators of the PDC, Santiago, Chile, July 1967. Translation from p. 5.

Selection 10.2: Translated excerpts from *Proposiciones para una acción política en el periodo 1967–70 de una vía no capitalista de desarrollo* from the review, *P.E.C.* (*Política, Economía, Cultura*), Year 5, No. 239 (Santiago, Chile) July 28, 1967, special supplement, pp. 1–22. Translations from pages III and IV.

(1927–). This "Plan" stressed the need for a rapid step-up of PDC reforms. Excerpts of this "Plan" appear in Selection 10.2. Both selections indicate internal Party disunity.

The "Plan Chonchol," adopted at the July 1967 PDC meeting, represented leftist opinion within the party. It charged that President Frei's reforms were too moderate and too slow; it called for a speeding up and expanding of the reform process.

In January 1968, Frei regained control of the PDC by winning a critical vote of confidence at a special party convention. The leftist directorate, elected in July 1967, immediately resigned.

Selection 10.1: Propositions of PDC Deputies and Senators—1967

. . . (a) Unity—The revolutionary task of transforming the socio-economic order that we have today has to mobilize all the strength and energies of the militant bases with the objective of winning mass participation of the people in the program for national liberation. Without this participation, the Revolution will lack the democratic support and the necessary dynamic element for its development. From there comes the need to renounce internally, without waste of time, any subordinate personal interest, division, and attitudes of negative criticism that divert or distract the militants and public opinion in the fulfillment of the revolutionary tasks.

Whoever is in the PDC should share this spiritual and active position at the service of our cause. It is a serious transgression against the internal unity and against the efficacy of the Revolutionary action to form factions or groups marginal to the statutory organism and that will pretend to indicate the ends of the Party or to have the function of judging its comrades, excluding those who do not share their position from the possibility of being there and from fraternal dialogue.

Let us recognize the fact that in these last months our internal unity has deteriorated. Our objective and presence in this National Junta is to recover it completely.

SELECTION 10.2: THE "PLAN CHONCHOL"

. . . Starting from the fact that Chile is today a subdeveloped country, characterized besides, as all the countries in this condition, by a high degree of external dependency, and that it has a political system of representative democracy, which does not mean that the Chilean society is fully democratic in all the sense of the word, since the equality of opportunity is not today as yet a reality to broad sections of our population, the Non-Capitalist Way of development seeks simultaneously the following compatible objectives:

a. to accelerate the rhythm of Chilean economic growth;
b. to diminish the foreign dependency of the country;
c. to make the benefits of development affect the whole national community, but with the first priority to those more in need, which means encouraging a policy of national income redistribution;
d. whatever the plan of development to be adopted should imply a widening degree of popular participation at all levels; and
e. the economic and social system and the structure of power should become democratic as soon as possible. This means the redistribution of property, of economic power and of social action and the amplification of equal basic opportunities that society should grant to all its members. . . .

Out of each one of these [proposals] comes a number of concrete propositions, the detail and foundation of which can be found in the various chapters of this report.

First, the state should act as the fundamental dynamic element of Chilean economic development and it must control effectively and use with all its power the instruments and mechanisms of the economic system. . . .

Third, it must delimit the area of the work, and the "rules of the game" of the public sector and of the capitalist private sector in respect to the State. This means it must distinguish between the areas which should belong to the absolute public domain and those in which the State participates with the mixed society, whether as the owner of most of the social capital or as minority associate with the right to veto in the important decisions.

Fourth, it must introduce a definite program for the development and expansion of the social economy of the people, in which stands out the fast acceleration of the progress of agrarian reform, giving it first priority in the assignment of financial resources.

Fifth, it must encourage the tasks of organization of the people and to obtain its effective participation in the different plans of the government as the only possible method of work compatible with a revolutionary process. . . .

The Party—on its part—should resolve simultaneously two important problems:

a. The first concerns the relations between the Party and the Government. In this regard it is fundamental that both have the same strategy. It is not possible for the government to act with one determined strategy and the Party with another, which they could be. If this happened, it will mean permanent misunderstandings and difficulties, weakening the action of the Party as well as that of the Government.

This strategy should be elaborated by common agreement and should be institutionalized in the most explicit possible way; it should be a concerted action. It could not be defined by the Party without knowledge of the concrete problems encountered by the Government, neither alone by the Government, since it will be compromising the future of the Party. . . .

b. It is indispensable to make an internal readjustment of the Christian Democratic Party in order to make it an instrument capable of becoming the vanguard of the Chilean Revolution. . . .

It is necessary to transform the Christian Democratic Party into . . . a modern and efficient Party, capable of performing an adequate political education for all its militants; with an active and ideological debate; with a preparation of its middle and popular leaders; finally, a Party that is in condition to undertake national campaigns in all the sectors in order to win adhesion to the chosen strategy. . . .

READING 11 *Guerrilla–Communist Party Debate in Venezuela*

Introductory Note

In April 1966 the Central Committee of the Partido Comunista Venezolano (*Venezuelan Communist Party or PCV*) *determined to "abandon the armed struggle in order to incorporate the party in the movement for integration of the national Left."*[1] *Shortly thereafter, Douglas Bravo—leader of the hard-line faction within the PCV—and four other guerrilla leaders notified the PCV that they were going to reorganize the guerrillas (FALN and FLN) under a separate leadership. In May 1966 the PCV condemned Bravo for having "arbitrarily proceeded to establish a parallel and objectively divisive center," and expelled him from the Central Committee.*[2] *Later, the PCV ousted him totally from the*

1. See "Il P.C. venezolano cessera la guerriglia?" in *Avanti* (Rome), April 8, 1966. Also Kevin Devlin, "The Permanent Revolutionism of Fidel Castro," *Problems of Communism,* Vol. XVII, No. 1 (January-February 1968), p. 4.
2. This announcement was published in *Confidencial* (Caracas), No. 32 (TICD, No. 895, pp. 13–16). Also Devlin, *op. cit.,* p. 4.

Selection 11.1: Interview with Venezuelan guerrilla leader, Douglas Bravo, conducted by Mario Menéndez Rodríguez of the Mexican magazine *Sucesos.* The interview took place "somewhere in the Iracara mountains," Havana Radio Broadcast beamed to Latin America, December 31, 1966.

Selection 11.2: Interview with Teodoro Petkov, leading member of the Venezuelan Communist Party, from *World Marxist Review,* Vol. 11, No. 4 (April 1968), pp. 59–65.

party. An interview with Bravo in December 1966 follows in Selection 11.1, which highlights the diverse views on strategies of change in Venezuela and Latin America. Selection 11.2 is an interview with Teodoro Petkov, a leading member of the PCV, denigrating Bravo's "armed struggle" argument.

Selection 11.1: An Interview with Douglas Bravo

Question: There is a trend within the Venezuelan revolutionary political opposition which is opposed to armed struggle. What are your views on this, what is behind this trend, and how does it affect the National Liberation Armed Forces?

Bravo: Different trends exist in all revolutionary movements throughout the world. We can even go further and say that within these trends, there are degrees of discrepancies. It is normal for this to happen. Venezuela cannot be the exception to this general rule among revolutionary movements the world over. Hence, people who follow certain trends think differently. They broach problems differently. These different trends, these different ways of attacking problems in the various countries do not necessarily contradict—or rather, discrepancies do not become acute whenever revolutionary upheavals have occurred free of violence. However, it is normal for differences of opinion to become more pronounced among some revolutionaries whenever a revolutionary event occurs in a country. This is nothing new in Venezuela, or in America, or in other countries. . . .

Your question stems from the idea that if there is a trend today opposing the armed struggle in Venezuela, would it be possible for us to utilize all of these elements. For some years, polemics have broken out in the open throoughout the world, particularly among the Marxist-Leninist revolutionaries, over the problem of armed struggle. We are experiencing this polemic here in Venezuela. It stems from the problem of the armed struggle. Venezuelan revolutionaries are discussing the matter of the armed struggle. They are primarily weighing the merits of the armed struggle as a means of liberating the country. Some differences of opinion exist—even among those who advocate the use of arms as a general policy, as a way of achieving liberation.

In other words, revolutionaries are discussing whether or not the armed policy to be used in Venezuela toward liberation will be that of the guerrilla warfare kind—the classic way—or the insurrectional kind. However, the difference between those who advocate the armed policy—that is, those who believe that the armed approach is the best way to liberate the country—this difference is not as critical as discrepancies over whether or not the armed way is valid at all. Among the latter—those who advocate armed struggle to the exclusion of everything else—important common factors exist that can serve as the basis for important agreement. There is a radical difference, though, between those who believe that conditions for the development of an armed struggle in Venezuela are nonexistent and those who advocate armed struggle. . . .

Selection 11.2: An Interview with Teodoro Petkov

The name of Teodoro Petkov, a leading member of the Venezuelan Communist Party, flashed across the front pages of the world press early last year when he and his Party colleagues, Pompeyo Marquez and Guillermo García Ponce, made a daring escape from the San Carlos fortress-prison in Caracas, where they had been held without trial for nearly three years.

This was not the first time Petkov had made a prison break. On a previous occasion he simulated sickness and, transferred from his prison cell to a military hospital, lowered himself by a rope from a fifth story window after sawing through the window-bars of his isolation ward.

Petkov is known as a man of indomitable courage and keen political vision, who made a name for himself first as a student leader in Caracas University, and later as a member of the Miranda State Legislative Assembly and Member of the National Congress.

At the beginning of 1968, a *World Marxist Review* correspondent interviewed Petkov on the current political situation in Venezuela.

Question: What can you say about the armed struggle presently being waged in Venezuela?

Petkov: The revolutionary movement has hit on difficult times. The success of an armed struggle depends on the general revolutionary situation; and not until we cope with our political difficulties can we hope to overcome the difficulties in our armed movement. . . .

What we have today is not armed struggle in the proper sense of the word, but merely armed units: two under Communist leadership which, by a decision of the Party, are not engaged in military action at the moment; then there is one headed by Douglas Bravo, which engages only in sporadic actions, and there are two of the Left Revolutionary Movement which are in much the same position. But that applies to the countryside. The situation in the towns is worse. That part of the urban apparatus which joined Douglas Bravo has been almost entirely wiped out in government reprisals. . . .

Question: What in your opinion is the military and political weight of the Bravo group?

Petkov: At present, the Bravo group exists chiefly in foreign propaganda reports, though it started as a fairly large force. When Bravo broke with the Party, he took over the bulk of our urban military apparatus and the José Leonardo Chirinos guerrilla front in the state of Falcón, also 19 men of the Simón Bolívar front in Lara, Portuguesa and Trujillo. That made a considerable force, the largest in numbers and the best armed, with a strong urban military apparatus.

Bravo's tactic was to mount what he called an armed offensive. Predictably, however, his offensive ended in disaster. If the army and police succeeded in crippling a military apparatus like ours, this applied doubly to Douglas Bravo's, for it had no political shield since Bravo had no party to back him, no political links and no influence among the people. His unit buckled in face of the police reprisals, and his urban force was, in effect, almost entirely wiped out in three large police actions in the first six months of 1967. Not only the original members of Bravo's urban apparatus, but also guerrillas sent from the mountains "to reinforce the town" were arrested, with the result that the strength of his guerrilla column was considerably reduced.

This was when differences broke out among his colleagues. A split developed, and some of them are now abroad. So there are grounds to think that the Bravo group is breaking up. I am trying to be as impartial as I can, because when factional differences arise, each side usually tends to say the worst about the other. But I may be more objective, because my brother is on the other side and I am deeply attached to him and feel badly about his defeat. Besides, some splendid people are on the other side, too, with whom our spiritual bonds are still alive because only recently they had been our comrades and we know that they are not counter-revolutionaries despite their unfortunate choice. They are men frustrated by years of armed struggle with no tangible results, men somewhat like the old anarchists who thought a declining movement could be revolved by plots or acts of terror. But they are good people all the same, fired with revolutionary ardor, and their defeat is not just their own, being to some extent also a setback for our entire revolutionary movement, affecting the movement as a whole because it is difficult for the people to distinguish between the various groups. What the people see is an armed movement suffering setbacks—the sad picture of a movement with no real victories, while the newspapers report the number killed and the number captured, and that there are informers in their ranks. This naturally reflects adversely on the armed struggle and the revolutionary movement. . . .

READING 12 *"The Alliance That Lost Its Way"*

Introductory Note

Chile's reformist President Eduardo Frei Montalva (1911–   ), leader of his nation's Christian Democrats, was a leading spokesman for the Alliance both before and after he became chief executive of Chile. In articles and speeches, Frei held that the Alliance was the only way for Latin America to bring about a reform unless it was willing to undergo violent revolution–something which he eschewed.

In a major article in the United States quarterly, Foreign Affairs, *Frei outlined his view of the Alliance, a view which won wide respect and praise in some quarters, but also sharp criticism in others.*

. . . The Alliance for Progress is committed to the achievement of a revolution which, as a political instrument, should be placed in the service of democratic ideas and the interests of the majority so that it will bring forth a substantial change in the political, social and economic structures of the region. This change must be swift, and the responsibility for bringing it about belongs not just to a group of leaders or to a technocratic elite but to the whole of society. The Latin American origins of the Alliance for Progress were specially evident in the non-Marxist political

Eduardo Frei Montalva, "The Alliance That Lost Its Way," *Foreign Affairs,* Vol. 45, No. 3 (April 1967), pp. 437–39, 441–45, 447–48, passim.

parties which had no links with the national oligarchies and were strongly opposed to the traditional Latin American Right.

The Latin American revolution, as a force for rapid and substantial change, has been germinating for the last decade; it is now a permanent and dynamic torrent which is weakening the political and social institutions of the continent. The form taken by this drastic change will depend on the time which elapses before the forces of revolution are finally released. The greater the delay, the greater will be the accumulated pressure and the greater the violence of the eventual explosion.

The Latin American revolution has clearly defined objectives: the participation of the people in the government and the destruction of the oligarchies; the redistribution of land and the ending of the feudal or semi-feudal regimes in the countryside; the security of equal access to cultural and educational facilities and wealth, thus putting an end to inherited privilege and artificial class divisions. Finally, a main objective of the revolution is to secure economic development, coupled with a fair distribution of its products and the utilization of international capital for the benefit of the national economy.

These are precisely the same objectives as those of the Alliance. Obviously a revolution thus defined is not the only means whereby rapid change can be achieved in Latin America, but it is the one with which the Alliance has been identified from its very beginnings.

The immediate goal of those who support the Alliance should not be the achievement of perfect inter-American coöperation and solidarity; their task is rather to accelerate the liberation of the forces of freedom, justice and solidarity among peoples who are hindered in their advance by the intellectual limitations of those unwilling to adapt to anything new, and by the material limitations retarding development. The task is to construct a dynamic image of the Alliance on the basis of facts and not to permit it to become a mere formula. The responsibility for the success of the Alliance is that of the whole hemisphere, because, as John F. Kennedy said, "Those who make peaceful revolution impossible will make violent revolution inevitable."

International coöperation is essential to secure these objectives. However important the internal effort of the developing countries may be, it will inevitably be insufficient in view of the enormous requirements of economic development and structural change. It would not be difficult, under a totalitarian regime, to arrange for the rapid accumulation of resources and thus advance economic development by sacrificing democracy; but neither the permanent values of the people of Latin America nor the international community as a whole would really benefit from such a solution. This is why international coöperation as established by the Alliance for Progress is absolutely necessary.

There are two basic positive aspects of the Alliance as it was originally proposed: first, it established principles for hemispheric coöperation with a clear ideological orientation expressed by its forthright support for a democratic revolution in Latin America; second, it represented a change in the hitherto prevalent concept of financial and economic assistance given by the United States. In future, this assistance would cease to be given haphazardly or lent to this or that country to face emergencies, and it would not longer be designed to solve problems solely in a form determined by the donor. According to the terms of the Alliance, donor and recipient nations coöperate. Foreign aid is only part of a program of common achievement previously agreed on by countries which subscribed to the Charter of Punta del Este. Such arrangements for multilateral mutual coöperation were certainly new in the history of economic relations within the hemisphere. If we concentrate on these two basic characteristics and ascertain whether they have led to the achievement of concrete results during the last few years, we shall have a clear understanding of the evolution of the Alliance and the reaction it has elicited in Latin America. . . .

Latin American public opinion received the Alliance with enthusiasm; it was regarded as the beginning of a period which would open enormous possibilities for the economic and social development of Latin America. At the same time it marked the end of an unhappy period in which, as President Kennedy said, North Americans had not always grasped the significance of the

Western Hemisphere's common mission. In fact, the Alliance was essentially a Latin American conception which became reality because it was accepted by the United States and specially by President Kennedy, who understood it and injected new life into it.

In spite of its limitations, the Charter of Punta del Este had an immediate and significant impact. In the first place, from a political point of view it was clearly seen that the United States supported basic change. As a result, economic and political interests became active in opposition. An unholy alliance of the extreme Right and Left took form to prevent the Charter's implementation. The reactionaries, mindful of their vested interests, maintained that the Alliance was a utopian and unrealistic program; the Marxist groups described it as an instrument of imperialism, useless for bringing about the needed change. Though using different reasons and channels, both were in accord—neither for the first time nor for the last. The victims have been the Latin American people, because this collusion prevented the reforms necessary for instituting a rapid and authentic democratic process in the hemisphere.

Thus started a long controversy on the nature of the Alliance. Its ideas have been interpreted and reinterpreted; its objectives, principles and achievements have been openly and covertly distorted. Moreover, governments which had accepted and wanted to put the Punta del Este program into operation were either overthrown or found themselves threatened by the reactionary forces of the continent or by violence of the extreme left.

This has resulted in many divergent opinions being formed about the Alliance. Some regard it as a scheme to finance corrupt governments uninterested in reforming anything; others think of it as a program to make the rich richer. To the landed, industrial and financial oligarchies, the Alliance represents a danger because, by placing an exaggerated emphasis on social revolution, it deters foreign investment. To others, emergency aid is only a way of propping up a false stability which in turn prevents the working class from truly understanding its situation and opportunities, thus retarding the real revolution. Many others, especially those representing governments, complained that the work of the Alliance was being slowed up by the requirement that planning and reform precede the granting of aid. . . .

Has the Alliance achieved these objectives? Has it preserved democracy and helped to implement substantial changes? Unfortunately the answer is negative; the Alliance has not achieved the expected success. It cannot be said that since 1961 there has been a consolidation of democratic regimes in Latin America. On the contrary, various forces have threatened democratic governments, seeking either to overthrow them or to prevent the implementation of their programs. Nor have structural reforms taken place at the expected rate. . . .

Many Latin American governments have used the Alliance as a bargaining lever to obtain increases in U.S. aid precisely so as to avoid changing their domestic situation. These governments have committed themselves to international reforms which later they knowingly allowed either to become a dead letter, or worse, to be completely controlled or used for the benefit of those in power. . . .

This is one of the most serious criticisms made of the Alliance: that the people have not been able to participate in it. Could it have been otherwise? The people are grateful for the assistance received, but they have no sense of belonging to the scheme. The revolutionary awareness of the Latin American people has evolved in such a way that it can now be considered as a norm —giving direction to their principal activities. The Alliance has failed to channel this awareness, and it has not provided the needed leadership; in fact, it does not belong in this revolutionary mainstream. . . .

Another grave problem of the Alliance is its inability to promote the integration of Latin America. The process of integration lacks speed and direction; it is hard to avoid the conclusion that it has stagnated. This is certainly the case with the Latin American Free Trade Area. The number of approved concessions declines annually; even now there is not a single product enjoying preferential treatment in all the LAFTA countries. Although the Treaty of Montevideo has been in operation for only five years, the rate of increase of the intra-zonal trade has actually started to decline.

Faced with this frustrating experience, one is inclined to look at the success of the Central American Common Market. Yet the objective of the Alliance is a *Latin American* common market which means that integration must be successful in both groupings. Again, we come up against the absence of a political decision on the part of each individual country and a lack of leadership in the Alliance as a whole. The forces of nationalism, and of those committed to the status quo, have been stronger than those representing the real interests of these countries. Noisy voices are raised to decry the more advanced schemes of integration as utopian. But what is really utopian and illusory is to pretend that the countries of Latin America will be able to develop and achieve their destiny in the world of the future if each is locked up in its own isolated compartment.

The alternatives are clear: either the Alliance achieves one of its most important objectives by giving integration the needed vital impulse, or in a few years it will become evident to all that in the 1960s a great opportunity was lost because of petty nationalism. . . .

The salvation of the Alliance depends on the implementation of all these measures: the support of integration, the discouragement of the armaments race and the finding of a coöperative solution for the problems of external trade. The problem is not one of financial resources only, though at certain times these have been scant when compared with the legitimate needs of the region. It is essentially a political problem requiring the expression of the will to change, together with the acceptance of measures needed to bring about this change. People do not support governments because they have dutifully complied with directives from this or that international organization; they support them when they offer a promising political and economic alternative to present frustrations, and the hope of moving into a better future.

The necessary measures can be secured only by overcoming age-old resistance and destroying privileges which have remained unassailed over the years. To achieve this will also return to the

American continent its true revolutionary mission. This is both possible and necessary because, as Toynbee said, "If America can bring herself to go this far, she will, I believe, have worked her passage back to a point at which it will become possible for her to rejoin her own revolution. The American Revolution was a truly glorious revolution. It was glorious for two reasons. The basic issues that it raised were spiritual, not material; and, even if this may not have been the intention of some of the Founding Fathers, it was, in effect, as Jefferson perceived and Emerson proclaimed, a revolution for the whole human race, not just for the people of the Thirteen Colonies."

READING 13 *Declaration of the Presidents of America*

Introductory Note

Eduardo Frei Montalva's call, and that of others, for significant restructuring of the Alliance for Progress led the nations of the Western Hemisphere, which were members of the Organization of American States in early 1967, to adopt major reforms in the Charter of the OAS and to arrange for a meeting of hemisphere chief executives at the same site where the Alliance had been originally set up, Punta del Este, the Atlantic coast resort in Uruguay.

The presidents of the American States, with the exception of Cuba which had been barred from taking part in OAS activities, met in Punta del Este in mid-April 1967. Along with the prime minister of Trinidad and Tobago, Dr. Eric Williams, whose island nation had just been admitted to OAS membership, the chief executives resolved to work all the more closely to bring about economic and social reform in their lands through establishment of a common market for the Western Hemisphere, through broad multinational projects, and through efforts to boost hemisphere trade.

THE PRESIDENTS OF THE AMERICAN STATES AND THE PRIME MINISTER OF TRINIDAD AND TOBAGO MEETING IN PUNTA DEL ESTE, URUGUAY.

Declaration of the Presidents of America: Meeting of American Chiefs of State, Punta del Este, Uruguay, April 12–14, 1967, published by the Organization of American States, pp. 1–5, passim.

RESOLVED to give more dynamic and concrete expression to the ideals of Latin American unity and of the solidarity among the peoples of America, which inspired the founders of their countries;

DETERMINED to make this goal a reality within their own generation, in keeping with the economic, social and cultural aspirations of their peoples;

INSPIRED by the principles underlying the inter-American system, especially those contained in the Charter of Punta del Este, the Economic and Social Act of Rio de Janeiro, and the Protocol of Buenos Aires amending the Charter of the Organization of American States;

CONSCIOUS that the attainment of national and regional development objectives in Latin America is based essentially on self-help;

CONVINCED, however, that the achievement of those objectives requires determined collaboration by all their countries, complementary support through mutual aid, and expansion of external cooperation;

PLEDGED to give vigorous impetus to the Alliance for Progress and to emphasize its multilateral character, with a view to encouraging balanced development of the region at a pace substantially faster than attained thus far;

UNITED in the intent to strengthen democratic institutions, to raise the living standard of their peoples and to assure their increased participation in the development process, creating for these purposes suitable conditions in the political, economic and social as well as labor fields;

RESOLVED to maintain a harmony of fraternal relations in the Americas, in which racial equality must be effective;

PROCLAIM

The solidarity of the countries they represent and their decision to achieve to the fullest measure the free, just, and democratic social order demanded by the peoples of the Hemisphere.

Latin America will create a common market.

THE PRESIDENTS OF THE LATIN AMERICAN REPUBLICS resolve to create progressively, beginning in 1970, the

Latin American Common Market, which shall be substantially in operation in a period of no more than fifteen years. The Latin American Common Market will be based on the complete development and progressive convergence of the Latin American Free Trade Association and of the Central American Common Market, taking into account the interests of the Latin American countries not yet affiliated with these systems. This great task will reinforce historic bonds, will promote industrial development and the strengthening of Latin American industrial enterprises, as well as more efficient production and new opportunities of employment, and will permit the region to play its deservedly significant role in world affairs. The ties of friendship among the peoples of the Continent will thus be strengthened.

THE PRESIDENT OF THE UNITED STATES OF AMERICA, for his part, declares his firm support for this promising Latin American initiative.

THE UNDERSIGNED PRESIDENTS AFFIRM THAT:

We will lay the physical foundations for Latin American economic integration through multinational projects.

We will join in efforts to increase substantially Latin American foreign-trade earnings.

We will modernize the living conditions of our rural populations, raise agricultural productivity in general, and increase food production for the benefit of both Latin America and the rest of the world.

We will vigorously promote education for development.

We will harness science and technology for the service of our peoples.

We will expand programs for improving the health of the American peoples.

Latin America will eliminate unnecessary military expenditures.

READING 14 *Cuba and Latin American Revolution*

Introductory Note

The first meeting of the Cuba-sponsored Organización Latino Americana de Solidaridad, *held in Havana in August 1967, produced a good deal of debate and fierce disagreement over the course that Communists and other leftists should follow in carrying out change and reform in Latin America. In the end, the Cuba-sponsored resolution calling for the vigorous pursuit of revolutionary activity in the hemisphere won out.*

That resolution, reprinted here, caused ripples throughout the hemisphere—and some of the Latin American delegates from twenty-six hemisphere nations and territories subsequently disavowed the platform. But the majority of those attending were clearly in favor of the resolution.

1. That making the Revolution constitutes a right and a duty of the peoples of Latin America.

2. That the Revolution in Latin America has its deepest historical roots in the liberation movement against European colonialism of the 19th century and against imperialism of this century. The epic of the peoples of America and the great class battles that our peoples have carried out against imperialism in earlier

Proclamation of the general declaration of the conference of the *Organización Latino Americana de Solidaridad,* August 10, 1967, published in *Tricontinental* (English edition), No. 1 (July–August 1967), pp. 33–34.

decades constitute the source of historical inspiration of the Latin American revolutionary movement.

3. That the essential content of the Revolution in Latin America is to be found in its confrontation with imperialism and the bourgeois and landowner oligarchies. Consequently, the character of the Revolution is the struggle for national independence, emancipation from the oligarchies, and the socialist road for its complete economic and social development.

4. That the principles of Marxism-Leninism guide the revolutionary movement of Latin America.

5. That armed revolutionary struggle constitutes the fundamental course of the Revolution in Latin America.

6. That all other forms of struggle must serve to advance and not to retard the development of this fundamental course, which is armed struggle.

7. That, for the majority of the countries of the continent, the problems of organising, initiating, developing and crowning the armed struggle at present constitutes the immediate and fundamental task of the revolutionary movement.

8. That those countries in which this task has not yet been undertaken nevertheless will regard it as an inevitable sequence in the development of revolutionary struggle in their countries.

9. That the historic responsibility of furthering revolution in each one of these countries belongs to the people and to their revolutionary vanguards in each country.

10. That the guerrilla is the nucleus of the liberation armies, and guerrilla warfare constitutes the most effective method of initiating and developing the revolutionary struggle in most of our countries.

11. That the leadership of the Revolution demands, as an organizational principle, the existence of a unified politico-military command as a guarantee of success.

12. That the most effective solidarity that the revolutionary movements may practice among themselves, is the furthering and the culmination of their own struggle in their respective countries.

13. That the solidarity with Cuba and the collaboration and

cooperation with the armed revolutionary movement is an undeferrable international duty of every anti-imperialist organization of the continent.

14. The Cuban Revolution, as a symbol of triumph of the armed revolutionary movement, constitutes the vanguard of the Latin American anti-imperialist movement. The peoples that develop the armed struggle, as they advance along this road put themselves in the vanguard.

15. That the peoples who have been directly subjected by colonialism of the European countries, in order to achieve their liberation, must have an immediate and basic objective: that of struggling for independence, and uniting with the general struggle of the continent as the only means of avoiding being absorbed into U.S. neocolonialism.

16. That the Second Declaration of Havana that expresses the beautiful and glorious revolutionary tradition of the past 150 years of American history, constitutes a document outlining the program of the Latin American Revolution which has been confirmed, deepened, enriched and made more radical by peoples of this continent during the last five years.

17. That the peoples of Latin America have no differences with any other peoples in the world and extend their hand of friendship also to the peoples of the United States, whom they exhort to undertake the struggle against the repressive policy carried out by imperialist monopolies.

18. That the Latin American struggle strengthens its ties of solidarity with the peoples of Asia and Africa and those of the socialist countries, the workers of the capitalist nations, and especially with the black population of the United States which suffers class exploitation, poverty, unemployment, racial discrimination and the denial of their most elementary human rights, and which constitutes an important force within the revolutionary struggle.

19. That the heroic struggle waged by the people of Viet Nam gives invaluable aid to all revolutionary peoples who are fighting imperialism, and constitutes an inspiring example to the peoples of Latin America.

20. That we have approved the Statutes and created the Permanent Committee, in Havana, of the Organization of Latin American Solidarity, which constitutes the genuine representation of the Latin American peoples.

We, the revolutionaries of our America, the America south of the Rio Grande, successors of the men who gave us our first independence, armed with an undaunted will to fight, and with revolutionary and scientific guidance, and with nothing to lose but the chains which oppress us

ASSERT:

That our struggle constitutes a decisive contribution to the historic struggle of humanity to liberate itself from slavery and exploitation.

THE DUTY OF EVERY REVOLUTIONARY IS TO MAKE THE REVOLUTION.

READING 15 *Fidel Castro's Waves of the Future*

Introductory Note

Cuban Premier Fidel Castro outlined to delegates to the conference of the Organización Latino Americana de Solidaridad *his views on Latin American revolution in a speech closing the meeting. His remarks, which were widely reprinted throughout Latin America, began with a long discussion of a number of hemisphere issues including an attack on the United States for alleged imperialist designs in Latin America. Then, he turned to the OLAS meeting itself:*

We sincerely believe that we would not be fulfilling our duty if we did not express here that the OLAS Conference has been a victory of revolutionary ideas, though not a victory without struggle.

In OLAS, a latent ideological struggle has been reflected. Should we conceal it? No. What is gained by concealing it? Did OLAS intend to crush anyone, to harm anyone? No. That is not a revolutionary method, that does not agree with the conscience of revolutionaries. Let's be clear about this—*true* revolutionaries!

And we believe it is necessary that revolutionary ideas prevail. If revolutionary ideas should be defeated, the revolution in Latin

Excerpted from a speech by Fidel Castro at the closing of the conference of the *Organización Latino Americana de Solidaridad,* at the Chaplin Theater, Havana, August 10, 1967. Official Cuban Government translation.

America would be lost or would be indefinitely delayed. Ideas can hasten a process—or they can considerably delay it. And we believe that this triumph of revolutionary ideas among the masses —not all the masses, but a sufficiently vast part of them—is absolutely necessary. This does not mean that action must wait for the triumph of ideas—and this is one of the essential points of the matter. There are those who believe that it is necessary for ideas to triumph among the masses before initiating action, and there are others who understand that action is one of the most efficient instruments for bringing about the triumph of ideas among the masses.

Whoever stops to wait for ideas to triumph among the majority of the masses before initiating revolutionary action will never be a revolutionary. For, what is the difference between such a revolutionary and a latifundium owner, a wealthy bourgeois? Nothing!

Humanity will, of course, change; human society will, of course, continue to develop—in spite of human beings and the errors of human beings. But that is not a revolutionary attitude.

If that had been our way of thinking, we would never have initiated a revolutionary process. It was enough for the ideas to take root in a sufficient number of men for revolutionary action to be initiated, and through this action the masses started to acquire these ideas; the masses acquired that consciousness.

It is obvious that in Latin America there are already in many places a number of men who are convinced of such ideas, and have started revolutionary action. And what distinguishes the true revolutionary from the false revolutionary is precisely this: one acts to move the masses, the other waits for the masses to have a conscience already before starting to act.

And there is a series of principles that one should not expect to be accepted without an argument, but which are essential truths, accepted by the majority, but with reservations on the part of a few. This useless discussion about the means and ways of struggle, whether it should be peaceful or non-peaceful, armed or unarmed, the essence of this discussion—which we call useless because it is like the argument between two deaf and dumb people—because it is that which distinguishes those who want to promote the revolution and those who do not want to promote it, those who want to curb it and those who want to promote it, is useless. Let no one be fooled.

Different words have been used: the road is the only one, it is not the only one, it is exclusive, it is not. And the conference has been very clear in this respect. It does not say *only* one road, although that might be said: it says a fundamental road, and the other forms of struggle must be subordinated to it, and in the long run, it is the only road. To use the word *only,* even though the sense of the word is understood and even if it were true, might lead to errors about the imminence of the struggle.

That is why we understand that the declaration [Second Declaration of Havana], by calling it the fundamental road, the road must be taken in the long run, is the correct formulation. If we wish to express our way of thinking, and that of our party and our people, let no one harbor any illusions about seizing power by peaceful means in any country in this continent; let no one harbor any illusions. Anyone trying to tell such a thing to the masses will be completely deceiving them.

This does not mean that one has to go out and grab a rifle and start fighting tomorrow, anywhere. That is not the question. It is a question of ideological conflict between those who want to make revolution and those who do not want to make it. It is the conflict between those who want to make it and those who want to curb it. Because, essentially, anybody can realize if it is possible, or if conditions are ripe, to take up arms or not.

Not one can be so sectarian, so dogmatic, as to say that one has to go out and grab a rifle tomorrow, anywhere. And we ourselves do not doubt that there are some countries in which this task is not an immediate task, but we are convinced that it will be their task in the long run.

There are some who have put forward even more radical theses than those of Cuba: that we Cubans believe that in such and such a country there are no conditions for armed struggle, but they claim that it is not so. But the funny thing is that it has been claimed in some cases by representatives who are not quite in favor of the theses for armed struggle. We will not be angered by this. We prefer them to make mistakes trying to make revolution without the right conditions than to have them make the mistake of never making revolution. I hope no one will make a mistake! But nobody who really wants to fight will ever have differences with us, and those who do not want to fight ever, will always have differences with us. . . .

The importance of the guerrilla, the vanguard role of the guerrilla. Much could be said about the guerrilla, but it is not possible to do so in a meeting like this. But guerrilla experiences in this continent have taught us many things—among them the terrible mistake, the absurd concept that the guerrilla movement could be directed from the cities.

That is the reason for the thesis that political and military commands must be united.

This is the reason for our conviction that it is not only a stupidity but also a crime to want to direct the guerrillas from the city. And we have had the opportunity to appreciate the consequences of this absurdity many times. And it is necessary that these ideas be overcome, and this is why we consider the resolution of this conference of great importance.

The guerrilla is bound to be the nucleus of the revolutionary movement. This does not mean that the guerrilla movement can rise without any previous work; it does not mean that the guerrilla movement is something that can exist without political direction. No! We do not deny the role of the leading organizations, we do not deny the role of the political organizations. The guerrilla is organized by a political movement, by a political organization. What we believe incompatible with correct ideas of guerrilla struggle is the idea of directing the guerrilla from the cities. And in the conditions of our continent it will be very difficult to suppress the role of the guerrilla.

There are some who ask themselves if it is possible in any country of Latin America to achieve power without armed struggle. And, of course, theoretically, hypothetically, when a great part of the continent has been liberated, there is nothing surprising if under those conditions a revolution succeeds without opposition—but this would be an exception. However, this does not mean that the revolution is going to succeed in any country without a struggle. The blood of the revolutionaries of a specific country may not be shed, but their victory will only be possible thanks to the efforts, the sacrifices, and the blood of the revolutionaries of a whole continent.

It would therefore be false to say that they had a revolution there without a struggle. That will always be a lie. And I believe that it is not correct for any revolutionary to wait with arms crossed until all the other peoples struggle and create the conditions for victory for him without struggle. That will never be an attribute of revolutionaries. . . .

To those who believe that peaceful transition is possible in some countries of this continent, we say to them that we cannot understand what kind of peaceful transition they refer to, unless it is to a peaceful transition in agreement with imperialism. Because in order to achieve victory by peaceful means, if in practice such a thing were possible, considering that the mechanisms of the bourgeoisie, the oligarchies, and imperialism control all the means for peaceful struggle. . . . And then you hear a revolutionary say: They crushed us, they organized two hundred radio programs, so and so many newspapers, so and so many magazines, so and so many TV shows, so and so many of this and so and so many of the other. And one wants to ask him: What did you expect? That they would put TV, the radio, the magazines, the newspapers, the printing shops, all this at your disposal? Or are you unaware that those are precisely the instruments of the ruling class to crush the revolutions?

They complain that the bourgeoisie and the oligarchies crush them with their campaigns, as if that is a surprise to anyone. The first thing that a revolutionary has to understand is that the ruling classes have organized the state in such a way as to maintain themselves in power by all possible means. And they use not only arms, not only physical instruments, not only guns, but all possible instruments to influence, to deceive, to confuse.

And those who believe that they are going to win against the imperialists in elections are just plain naïve; and those who believe that the day will come when they will take over through elections, are supernaïve. It is necessary to have been present in a revolutionary process and to know just what the repressive apparatus is by which the ruling classes maintain the status quo, just how much one has to struggle, how difficult it is.

This does not imply the negation of forms of struggle. When someone writes a manifesto in a newspaper, attends a demonstration, holds a rally, propagates an idea, they may be using the famous so-called legal means. We must do away with that differentiation between legal or illegal means, and call them revolutionary or nonrevolutionary means.

The revolutionary, in pursuit of his ideal and revolutionary aims, uses various methods. The essence of the question is whether the masses will be led to believe that the revolutionary movement, that socialism, can take over power without a struggle, that it can take over power peacefully. And that is a lie! And those who assert anywhere in Latin America that they will take over power peacefully will be deceiving the masses. . . .

Really, the only thing that we can say is that it is an honor to our revolution that our enemies think so much about it; likewise, it must be an honor for all Latin American revolutionaries that imperialism has given so much attention to the problem of OLAS. . . .

And the OLAS Conference has been held—a true representation of a genuine revolutionary movement, whose ideas are solid because they are based on reality. OLAS is the interpreter of tomorrow's history, interpreter of the future, because OLAS is a wave of the future, symbol of the revolutionary waves sweeping a continent of 250 million. This continent is pregnant with revolution. Sooner or later, it will be born. Its birth may be more or less complicated, but it is inevitable.

We do not have the slightest doubt. There will be victories, there will be reverses, there will be advances, there will be retreats: but the arrival of a new era, the victory of the peoples in the face of injustice, in the face of exploitation, in the face of oligarchy, in the face of imperialism, whatever the mistakes that man makes, whatever the mistaken ideas that may be obstacles on the road, they are unavoidable.

We have spoken to you with complete and absolute frankness; we know that the true revolutionaries will always be in solidarity with Cuba; we know that no true revolutionary, that no true Communist on this continent, nor among our people, will ever let himself be induced to take those positions which would lead him to an alliance with imperialism, which would make him go hand in hand with the imperialist masters against the Cuban Revolution and against the Latin American revolution.

We do not condemn anyone a priori, we do not close the doors to anyone, we do not attack anyone en masse, in a block; we express our ideas, we defend our ideas, we debate these ideas. And we have absolute confidence in the revolutionaries, in the true revolutionaries, in the true Communists.

Those will not fail the revolution, the same as our revolution will never fail the revolutionary movement of Latin America.

We don't know what awaits us, what vicissitudes, what dangers, what struggles. But we are prepared, and every day we try to prepare ourselves better, and every day we will be better prepared.

But one thing we can say: we are calm, we feel safe, this little island will always be a revolutionary wall of granite, and against it all conspiracies, all intrigues, and all aggressions will be smashed. And high upon this wall there will fly forever a banner with the legend *Patria o Muerte! Venceremos!*

READING 16 *Nixon Maps a New Policy*

Introductory Note

More than most new occupants of the White House, Richard M. Nixon (1913–) began his presidency with a background of considerable experience in Latin America. He had taken two major trips (1956 and 1958) to Latin America while serving as Dwight D. Eisenhower's vice-president, the latter providing Brazilian President Juscelino Kubitschek (1902–) with some of the inspiration for his Operation Pan America, generally regarded as the forerunner of President John Kennedy's Alliance for Progress.

Nixon also visited the Latin American countries in 1967 on a personal fact-finding mission. His first foreign visitor upon assuming the presidency was Galo Plaza Lasso (1906–), secretary general of the Organization of American States, a step which suggested to some that the new president would place special emphasis on United States relations with Latin America. But as his first year in office ended, the general feeling was that he was playing down United States involvement in the hemisphere.

His speech on October 31, 1969, to the Inter American Press Association in Washington, outlined a number of his thoughts on that involvement.

. . . Often we in the United States have been charged with an overweening confidence in the rightness of our own prescriptions: occasionally we have been guilty of the charge. I intend to correct that. Therefore, my words tonight are meant as an in-

From the official White House text of Mr. Nixon's October 31, 1969, speech.

vitation by one partner for further interchange, for increased communication, and above all for new imagination in meeting our shared responsibilities.

For years, we in the United States have pursued the illusion that we could remake continents. Conscious of our wealth and technology, seized by the force of our good intentions, driven by our habitual impatience, remembering the dramatic success of the Marshall Plan in postwar Europe, we have sometimes imagined that we knew what was best for everyone else and that we could and should make it happen.

But experience has taught us better.

It has taught us that economic and social development is not an achievement of one nation's foreign policy, but something deeply rooted in each nation's own traditions.

It has taught us that each nation, and each region, must be true to its own character.

What I hope we can achieve, therefore, is a more mature partnership in which all voices are heard and none is predominant—a partnership guided by a healthy awareness that give-and-take is better than take-it-or-leave-it. . . .

I offer no grandiose promises and no panaceas.

I do offer action.

The actions I propose represent a new approach, based on five principles:

First, a firm commitment to the Inter-American system, and to the compacts which bind us in that system—as exemplified by the Organization of American States and by the principles so nobly set forth in its charter.

Second, respect for national identity in which rights and responsibilities are shared by a community of independent states.

Third, a firm commitment to continued United States assistance for hemisphere development.

Fourth, a belief that the principal future pattern of this assistance must be United States support for Latin-American initiatives, and that this can best be achieved on a multilateral basis within the Inter-American system.

Fifth, a dedication to improving the quality of life in the

Western hemisphere—to making people the center of our concerns, and to helping meet their economic, social and human needs. . . .

Our partnership should be one in which the United States lectures less and listens more, and in which clear, consistent procedures are established to insure that the shaping of Latin America's future reflects the will of the Latin American nations.

I believe this requires a number of changes.

To begin with, it requires a fundamental change in the way in which we manage development assistance in the hemisphere.

I propose that a multilateral Inter-American agency be given an increasing share of responsibility for development assistance decisions. C.I.A.P.—the Inter-American Committee for the Alliance for Progress—could be given this function. Or an entirely new agency could be created.

Whatever the form, the objective would be to evolve an effective multilateral framework for bilateral assistance, to provide the agency with an expert international staff and, over time, to give it major operational and decision-making responsibilities.

The Latin-American nations themselves would thus jointly assume a primary role in setting priorities within the hemisphere, in developing realistic programs and in keeping their own performance under critical review.

One of the areas most urgently in need of new policies is trade. In order to finance their import needs and to achieve self-sustaining growth, the Latin-American nations must expand their exports.

Most Latin-American exports now are raw materials and foodstuffs. We are attempting to help the other countries of the hemisphere to stabilize their earnings from those exports, and to increase them as time goes on.

Increasingly, however, those countries will have to turn toward manufactured and semimanufactured products for balanced development and major export growth. Thus they need to be assured of access to the expanding markets of the industrialized world. In order to help achieve this, I have determined to take the following major steps:

First, to lead a vigorous effort to reduce the nontariff barriers to trade maintained by nearly all industrialized countries against products of particular interest to Latin America and other developing countries.

Second, to support increased technical and financial assistance to promote Latin-American trade expansion.

Third, to support the establishment, within the Inter-American system, of regular procedures for advance consultation on all trade matters. United States trade policies often have a heavy impact on our neighbors. It seems only fair that in the more balanced relationship we seek, there should be full consultation within the hemisphere family before decisions affecting its members are taken, not after.

Finally, in world trade forums to press for a liberal system of generalized tariff preferences for all developing countries, including Latin America. We will seek adoption by all of the industrialized countries of a scheme with broad product coverage and with no ceilings on preferential imports. . . .

There are three other important economic issues that directly involve the new partnership concept, and which a number of our partners have raised: "tied" loans, debt service and regional economic integration.

For several years now, virtually all loans made under United States aid programs have been "tied"—that is, they have been encumbered with restrictions designed to maintain United States exports, including a requirement that the money be spent on purchases in the United States.

These restrictions have been burdensome for the borrowers, and have impaired the effectiveness of the aid. In June, I ordered the most cumbersome restrictions removed. In addition, I am now ordering that effective November 1, loan dollars sent to Latin America under aid be freed to allow purchases not only here, but anywhere in Latin America.

As a third step, I am also ordering that all other onerous conditions and restrictions on United States assistance loans be reviewed, with the objective of modifying or eliminating them. . . .

The growing burden of external debt service has increasingly become a major problem of future development. Some countries find themselves making heavy payments in debt service which reduce the positive effects of development aid. I suggest that C.I.A.P. might appropriately urge the international financial organizations to recommend possible remedies.

We have seen a number of moves in Latin America toward regional economic integration, such as the establishment of the Central American Common Market, the Latin-American and Caribbean Free Trade Areas and the Andean group. The decisions on how far and how fast this process of integrations goes, of course, are not ours to make. But I do want to stress that we stand ready to help in this effort, if our help should be wanted.

On all these matters, we look forward to consulting further with our hemisphere partners. In a major, related move, I am also directing our representatives to invite C.I.A.P., as a regular procedure; to conduct a periodic review of United States economic policies as they affect the other nations of the hemisphere, and to consult with us about them. . . .

I am also directing a major reorganization and upgrading of the United States Government structure for dealing with Western Hemisphere affairs.

As a key element of this, I have ordered preparation of a legislative request, which I shall submit to Congress, raising the rank of the Assistant Secretary of State of Inter-American Affairs to Under Secretary—thus giving the hemisphere special representation. This new Under Secretary will be given authority to coordinate all United States Government activities in the hemisphere. . . .

For three quarters of a century, many of us have been linked together in the Organization of American States and its predecessors in a joint quest for a better future. Eleven years ago, Operation Pan America was launched as a Brazilian initiative. More recently, we have joined in an Alliance for Progress, whose principles still guide us. Now our goal for the seventies should be a decade of action for progress for the Americas. . . .

READING 17 *Still Another Report*

Introductory Note

To help him formulate a new policy on Latin America, President Richard M. Nixon sent New York Governor Nelson A. Rockefeller (1908–) on a "listen and learn" mission to Latin America in mid-1969. The governor had long been associated with Latin America through business, personal, and other contacts. His family's firm, the International Basic Economy Corporation, has served as a catalyst for developing business activity which maximizes the economic and social benefit of business, providing employment and income for thousands of Latin Americans.

Still, the Rockefeller name conjures up all sorts of images to Latin American nationalists who remember the governor's ancestors and their business activities in Latin America. The "listen and learn" visit was beset with many hardships including cancellation of the visit to countries such as Peru, Chile, and Venezuela. Many of his stops were difficult ones. Rioting, protest marches, and student clashes with police and army units characterized many of the visits.

Upon his return, Rockefeller wrote a report, "Quality of Life in the Americas," which summarized his findings. He proposed improved aid and trade arrangements for Latin America, efforts to improve Latin American cities, and assistance to agriculture and rural projects. But it was the proposal to assist in bolstering Latin American armies that attracted the most attention. His

Nelson A. Rockefeller, "Quality of Life in the Americas" (Washington: Agency for International Development, 1969), pp. 17–19, 49–55.

report tells why he made the recommendation and what he specifically would have the United States do in this area.

In many South and Central American countries, the military is the single most powerful political grouping in society. Military men are symbols of power, authority and sovereignty and a focus of national pride. They have traditionally been regarded in most countries as the ultimate arbiters of the nation's welfare.

The tendency of the military to intervene when it judges that the government in office has failed to carry out its responsibilities properly has generally been accepted in Central and South America. Virtually all military governments in the hemisphere have assumed power to "rescue" the country from an incompetent government, or an intolerable economic or political situation. Historically, these regimes have varied widely in their attitudes toward civil liberties, social reform and repression.

Like the Church, the military was traditionally a conservative force resistant to change. Most officers came from the landowner class. In recent years, however, the owners of land have shifted more and more to an urban industrial life. The military service has been less attractive to their sons. As a result, opportunities have opened up for young men of ambition and ability from poor families who have neither land nor professional and business connections. These ambitious sons of the working classes have entered the military to seek an education and the opportunity for advancement.

This pattern has become almost universal throughout the American republics to the south. The ablest of these young officers have gone abroad for education and are now assuming top positions of leadership in almost all of the military groups in the hemisphere. And while their loyalties are with the armed forces, their emotional ties are often with the people. Increasingly, their concern and dedication is to the eradication of poverty and the improvement of the lot of the oppressed, both in rural and urban areas.

In short, a new type of military man is coming to the fore and often becoming a major force for constructive social change in the American republics. Motivated by increasing impatience with corruption, inefficiency, and a stagnant political order, the new military man is prepared to adapt his authoritarian tradition to the goals of social and economic progress.

This new role by the military, however, is not free from perils and dilemmas. There is always the risk that the authoritarian style will result in repression. The temptation to expand measures for security or discipline or efficiency to the point of curtailing individual liberties, beyond what is required for the restoration of order and social progress, is not easy to resist.

Above all, authoritarian governments, bent on rapid change, have an intrinsic ideological unreliability and a vulnerability to extreme nationalism. They can go in almost any doctrinal direction.

The danger for the new military is that it may become isolated from the people with authoritarianism turning into a means to suppress rather than eliminate the buildup of social and political tension.

The critical test, ultimately, is whether the new military can and will move the nation, with sensitivity and conscious design, toward a transition from military control for a social purpose to a more pluralistic form of government which will enable individual talent and dignity to flourish. Or will they become radicalized, statist and anti-U.S.?

In this connection, special mention should be made of the appeal to the new military, on a theoretical level, of Marxism: (1) It justifies, through its elitist-vanguard theories, government by a relatively small group or single institution (such as the Army) and, at the same time, (2) produces a rationale for state-enforced sacrifices to further economic development.

One important influence counteracting this simplistic Marxist approach is the exposure to the fundamental achievements of the U.S. way of life that many of the military from the other American countries have received through the military training programs which the U.S. conducts in Panama and the United States. . . .

If the quality of life for the individual in this hemisphere is to be meaningful, there must be freedom from fear and full respect for the rights and the personal dignity of individuals—not just one's own rights and dignity, but everyone's.

Unfortunately, far too many people in the hemisphere—including people in the United States—are denied such freedom and respect. Forces of anarchy, terror and subversion are loose in the Americas. Moreover, this fact has too long gone unheeded in the United States.

Doubt and cynicism have grown in the other American nations as to the purposefulness of the United States in facing this serious threat to freedom, democracy and the vital interests of the entire hemisphere.

Many of our neighbors find it incomprehensible that the United States will not sell them military equipment which they feel is required to deal with internal subversion. They have been puzzled by the reduction in U.S. military assistance grants in view of the growing intensity of the subversive activities they face.

They were concerned that their young people were being drawn to Cuba in never-diminishing numbers, for indoctrination and for instruction in the arts of propaganda, the skills of subversion and the tactics of terror.

Castro's recent restatement of his policy indicates no change in objectives. Rather, he reaffirms his revolutionary concepts and establishes a new set of priorities and conditions under which Cuban support for revolutionaries will be given.

The subversive capabilities of these Communist forces are increasing throughout the hemisphere. The inflation, urban terrorism, racial strife, overcrowding, poverty, violence and rural insurgency are all among the weapons available to the enemies of the systems of the free nations of the Western Hemisphere. These forces are quick to exploit for their own ends the freedoms afforded by democratic governments.

The seriousness of these factors when exploited by covert Communist forces is not fully recognized in the United States.

Two decades and more ago, in the presence of an overt and world-wide Soviet threat, the United States response was realistic and flexible. It included in the Western Hemisphere the training and equipping of security forces for hemisphere defense.

Fortuitously, the military capability thus achieved subsequently enabled the individual nations of the hemisphere to deal with the initial impact of a growing, covert Communist threat to their internal security. However, the threat has shifted from one based in the rural areas to one centered around urban terrorism. Realistic efforts to deal with this increasingly dangerous development are necessary, on an effective, hemisphere-wide basis.

In addition, the United States must face more forthrightly the fact that while the military in the other American nations are alert to the problems of internal security, they do not feel that this is their only role and responsibility. They are conscious of the more traditional role of a military establishment to defend the nation's territory, and they possess understandable professional pride which creates equally understandable desires for modern arms; in addition, they are subjected to the sales pressures and blandishments of suppliers from other nations—east and west—eager to sell. The result of all this is a natural resentment on the part of the military of other American nations when the United States refuses to sell modern items of equipment.

Thus, many military leaders in the other American republics see the United States acting to hold them back as second-class citizens, and they are becoming increasingly estranged from us at a time when their political role is on the rise. Our dilemma is how to be responsive to their legitimate desires for modern equipment without encouraging the diversion of scarce resources from development to armaments which, in some cases, may be unrelated to any real security requirement.

Military leaders throughout the hemisphere are frequently criticized here in the United States. However, we will have to give increasing recognition to the fact that many new military leaders are deeply motivated by the need for social and economic progress. They are searching for ways to bring education and better standards of living to their people while avoiding anarchy or violent revolution. In many cases, it will be more useful for the United States to try to work with them in these efforts, rather than to abandon or insult them because we are conditioned by arbitrary ideological stereotypes.

In addition, there is not in the United States a full appreciation of the important role played by the police. There is a tendency in the United States to equate the police in the other American republics with political action and repression, rather than with security. There have, unfortunately, been many such instances of the use of police. Yet well-motivated, well-trained police, when present in local communities, enforce the laws, protect the citizenry from terror, and discourage criminal elements. At the present time, however, police forces of many countries have not been strengthened as population and great urban growth have taken place. Consequently they have become increasingly less capable of providing either the essential psychological support or the internal security that is their major function.

Moreover, the people of the United States do not recognize that, as a whole, the other American nations spend a smaller percentage of their Gross National Product on defense than any other area except Africa south of the Sahara. Most of this expenditure, despite much talk of supersonic aircraft, is for personnel and operating costs. Relatively little has been spent on major items of equipment. For this reason, most of the military inventories of these other hemisphere nations consist of equipment acquired shortly after World War II. Such equipment is becoming obsolete and unserviceable and spare parts are becoming increasingly unavailable.

One other point not clearly understood in the United States is that no one country today can effectively protect its own internal security by itself.

The youth that go abroad for training in subversive activities, the money and directives that flow through agents, and the propaganda that comes from outside their borders are all beyond their effective control.

Only through hemisphere cooperation can these problems, which so vitally affect internal security, be adequately dealt with.

Recommendation: National Policy Objective

The United States should cooperate with other nations of the Western Hemisphere in measures to strengthen internal security.

Recommendations for Action

1. *A Western Hemisphere Security Council*

a. The United States should work with the other republics to form a civilian-directed Western Hemisphere Security Council to cope with the forces of subversion that operate throughout the Western Hemisphere. The purpose of the Council would be to help the hemisphere countries work together in creating and preserving the kind of orderly environment, free from terror and violence, in which each citizen of each country can build a better life for himself and his family. This Council would supersede the Special Consultative Committee on Security of the Organization of American States.

b. Although the United States would have membership in the Council, the Council should have its headquarters outside of our country.

2. *A Western Hemisphere Security Training Assistance Program*

a. The United States should reverse the recent downward trend in grants for assisting the training of security forces for the other hemisphere countries. (The total amount proposed for fiscal year 1970 is $21.4 million, as against $80.7 million in fiscal year

1966.) In view of the growing subversion against hemisphere government, the mounting terrorism and violence against citizens, and the rapidly expanding population, it is essential that the training program which brings military and police personnel from the other hemisphere nations to the United States and to training centers in Panama be continued and strengthened.

b. The name "Military Assistance Program" should be dropped because it no longer reflects the security emphasis we believe important. The program should be renamed the "Western Hemisphere Security Program."

3. *Internal Security Support*

a. The United States should respond to requests for assistance of the police and security forces of the hemisphere nations by providing them with the essential tools to do their job.

b. Accordingly, the United States should meet reasonable requests from other hemisphere governments for trucks, jeeps, helicopters and like equipment to provide mobility and logistical support for these forces; for radios, and other command control equipment for proper communications among the forces; and for small arms for security forces.

c. In furtherance of these objectives, the United States should provide, on request, military and technical training missions but should no longer maintain the permanent military missions in residence in other nations which too often have constituted too large and too visible a United States presence.

4. *Military Sales for Defense*

a. The Executive Branch should seek modification of the Conte and Symington amendments to permit the United States to sell aircraft, ships and other major military equipment without aid cut penalties to the more developed nations of the hemisphere when these nations believe this equipment is necessary to protect their land, patrol their seacoasts and airspace, and otherwise maintain the morale of their forces and protect their sovereignty. Realistically, if the United States doesn't sell such equipment, it will be purchased from other sources, east or west, and this would not be compatible with the United States' best interests.

b. Each country should be permitted to buy such equipment through purchase orders placed with the United States Defense Department through the Military Assistance Program, in order that each country may get full value for its military investment, more reliable delivery dates, and better maintenance.

Index